500 Air Fryer Recipes

Written by: Jamie Stewart

Copyright © 2017

Warning-Disclaimer

CONTENTS

Introduction 3

Vegetables & Side Dishes 8

Chicken 35

Turkey 64

Pork 93

Beef 122

Fish & Seafood 154

Fast Snacks & Appetizers 186

Rice, Grains & Beans 207

Vegan 226

Desserts 235

Other Favorites 269

INTRODUCTION

Let's face it, everybody loves fried food! That's a fact, what's not to love about crispy chicken nuggets, fresh French fries or banana fritters?! Whether you eat it at some fancy-schmancy restaurant, get some street food or make your own meal, fried food is truly irresistible!

Still, despite all this, fried food is considered to be unhealthy. We all know that bad eating habit leads to weight gain, serious nutritional deficiencies, and illnesses. There is an old English proverb – "Don't dig your grave with your own knife and fork."

What if you could eat fried food without guilt? What if you could enjoy fish & chips, chicken fillets, fried vegetables and the other favorite fried food that is sent right from food heaven? You can actually break the fast-food habit and enjoy fried food at the same time. In other words, you can eat healthier and more mindfully without sacrificing flavor and your enjoyment of food. The food revolution is coming. Its name is AIR FRYER!

Deep Fried Food vs. Air-Fried Food

Less oil for personal health and for the Earth.

People love fried food because of its crunchiness and full flavor. However, the oils or shortening that are used in fried foods are mostly highly processed and full of bad fats. A number of studies have shown that most vegetable oils are bad for our health and for the environment.

According to the US Environmental Protection Agency, "Petroleum oils, vegetable oils, and animal fats share common physical properties and produce similar environmental effects... Scientific research and experience with actual spills have shown that spills of animal fats and vegetable oils kill or injure wildlife and produce other undesirable effects. Wildlife that becomes coated with animal fats or vegetable oils could die of hypothermia, dehydration and diarrhea, or starvation..."

Luckily, it is a modern era and there are a lot of great and educational information available out there. Ignorance is no excuse and we all have to pool efforts to become more health conscious. When it comes to healthy eating, an air fryer will probably meet your expectations. It can cut the fat content of your food by 80%. Using an air fryer is a great start point to a better health and happier life.

Smart food choices.

As one of the key contributors to the most serious diseases, fried food is harmful to your health. It includes cancer, diabetes, heart disease, hypertension, obesity, and so on. There are a few key points:

Fried food is definitely high in harmful fats.

When it comes to nutrition concerns, fried foods are high in unnecessary calories.

Fried foods, according to most experts, increase our risk of developing high blood cholesterol that is linked to serious heart diseases.

Fortunately, we don't necessarily need to give up a favorite food. We just have to eat a balanced diet and make better food choices. If you are lucky enough to own an air fryer, you can enjoy roll-ups, French fries, snacks, desserts and other treats and fit them into your healthy dietary regimen.

How to have more meaningful homemade meals? Here are a few more tips for guilt-free eating.
Add a salad to your plate as a part of the main dish.
Eat a rainbow – make sure your protein, carbohydrate and vitamin sources are varied.

Use only 1 to 2 tablespoons of high-quality oil as well as a plenty of herbs and spices to enhance the flavor of your favorite fried food. One more reason that an air fryer may become your best kitchen companion!

Versatility is the key.

Contrary to popular opinion, healthy well-seasoned food is more delicious than deep fried one. As a matter of habit, we often reach for the same foods day after day. For instance, the eggs for breakfast, fish and chips for lunch, or a steak for dinner. Let's make a difference – explore new cooking methods, dig into a kitchen cabinet and do some spring-cleaning, check healthy food blogs, experiment with less known spices, and turn your kitchen into a magical space!

Be amazed by the versatility of air-fried recipes from around the world! You will be able to make fruit breakfast, vegetable dishes, saucy meat, golden brown fried wontons, crispy seafood, and even delectable cookies. A nearly infinite array of fried food is at your fingertips!

Instead of submerging your favorite food into a large amount of hot oil, try to make your own restaurant-style meals, and your family and friends will be delighted.

Air is the new oil!

From now onwards, you can eat anything you want but you should stick to one simple rule – Air frying instead of deep frying. As a matter of fact, air-fried food is more flavorful because it doesn't taste like fat, but, on the other hand, the texture of fried food is achieved. If you don't like a food that is soaked in unhealthy oil, you might try an air fryer. In so many recipes, air-fried food tastes even better. Just give this "little kitchen helper" a try!

Have It How You Like It:
How Does an Air Fryer Work?

An air fryer is a groundbreaking kitchen appliance that utilizes super-heated air to cook food in a specially designed chamber. In a cooking chamber, hot air circulates around your food while it cooks evenly in its natural juices.

Air fryer is a multi-cooker that can fry, bake, roast and grill foods with minimal vegetable oil. You can also use super-handy air fryer accessories such as different cooking baskets, baking pans, grill pans, double layer racks, etc. In addition to that, an air fryer allows you to cook different ingredients using a separator. By all means, always read the manual before using new accessories in your air fryer.

An air fryer offers a healthier and easier alternative to deep frying food. The whole process is super easy. Add the ingredients to the cooking basket; spritz with a cooking or pan spray; set the cooking temperature and wait for the buzzer to signal the end of cooking. That's all.

One of the greatest benefits of hot air frying is an easy press-and-go operation! An air fryer has a digital screen with automatic temperature control and timer so it will make a perfect dish without a fuss. There is no need to watch over your machine while preparing a meal. Simply set your air fryer by choosing the right buttons and let this amazing machine do the rest!

As an intelligent kitchen machine, an air fryer is safe to use. However, it sounds like a cliché, but it is worth reiterating – read carefully manufacturer's instructions.

Keep in mind that air fryers make cleaning a breeze while eliminating cooking odors.

Guide to Using This Recipe Collection

This recipe collection will help you to make the most of your air fryer creating a harmony of flavors! Here are three major points to keep in mind:

You can use culinary classics and modify them for the modern-day air fryer by simply following these recipes. It seems like a good idea, right?!?

Traditional cooking methods are great, but never be afraid to try new things in your kitchen; ultimately, you will gain a fresh perspective. The recipes in this book are created to be accessible to every home cook, a beginner or an experienced chef.

This is a guide for all air fryer owners so you should be flexible in interpreting the recipe directions. Many of these recipes are flexible. For instance, if your machine does not automatically stir the ingredients, then you should do this manually. It may seem difficult at the moment, but you'll get used to it using your common sense and reading the manual. Don't worry, this isn't rocket science, it's all just going to take practice and passion for cooking.

All recipes in this collection are grouped by food types. It is important because every food group provides essential nutrients for good health and regular everyday activities. The cookbook will share with you 350 recipes that are separated into seven main chapters: Vegetables, Pork, Beef, Chicken, Turkey, Fish & Seafood, and Desserts.

This book is chock-full of scrumptious recipes that are perfect for all occasions, whether you're hosting a dinner party or having a peaceful family Sunday lunch. From here on out, spend more time with your family, thanks to amazing "fix-it and forget-it" air-fried meals that come together in less than an hour!

Let this recipe collection inspire you to cook delicious but well-balanced meals for you and your beloved ones! Bon appétit

VEGETABLES & SIDE DISHES

1. Saucy Sweet Potatoes with Zucchini and Peppers 9

2. Herbed Potatoes with Mediterranean Dipping Sauce . 9

3. Restaurant-Style Onion Rings 10

4. Roma Tomato Bites with Halloumi Cheese 10

5. Easy Sautéed Green Beans 11

6. Ricotta and Scallion Stuffed Potatoes 11

7. Easy Cheesy Cauliflower and Broccoli 12

8. Peppery Vegetable Omelet with Cheese 12

9. Mushrooms and Peppers in Puff Pastry 13

10. Celery and Carrot Croquettes with Chive Mayo 13

11. Scrambled Eggs with Spinach and Tomato 14

12. Colby Potato Patties 14

13. Zesty Broccoli Bites with Hot Sauce 15

14. Sweet Corn and Kernel Fritters 15

15. Gorgonzola Stuffed Mushrooms with
      Horseradish Mayo 16

16. Potato Appetizer with Garlic-Mayo Sauce 16

17. The Best Sweet Potato Fries Ever 17

18. Spicy Cheesy Risotto Balls 17

19. Easy Cheesy Broccoli 18

20. Potato and Kale Croquettes 18

21. Spicy Potato Wedges 19

22. Family Favorite Stuffed Mushrooms 19

23. Mediterranean Halloumi and Garlic Omelet 20

24. Thanksgiving Mashed Ruby Yams 20

25. Mediterranean-Style Frittata with Manchego 21

26. Amazing Crispy Sweet Onion Rings 21

27. Crispy Fried Pickle Spears 22

28. Spicy Winter Squash Bites 22

29. Butter Squash Fritters 23

30. Herbed Roasted Potatoes 23

31. Indian-Style Garnet Sweet Potatoes 24

32. Easy Frizzled Leeks 24

33. Cremini Mushrooms in Zesty Tahini Sauce 25

34. Hash Brown Casserole 25

35. Pepper Jack Cauliflower Bites 26

36. Cheesy Broccoli Croquettes 26

37. Cauliflower Cakes Ole 27

38. Celery and Carrot Croquettes 27

39. Smoked Veggie Omelet 28

40. Sweet Potato and Carrot Croquettes 28

41. Manchego and Potato Patties 29

42. Mint-Butter Stuffed Mushrooms 29

43. Ricotta and Leafy Green Omelet 30

44. Basic Pepper French Fries 30

45. Oyster Mushroom and Lemongrass Omelet 31

46. Spinach and Cheese Stuffed Baked Potatoes 31

47. Pantano Romanesco with Goat Cheese Appetizer .. 32

48. Swiss Chard and Cheese Omelet 32

49. Mom's Jacket Potatoes 33

50. Skinny Asparagus and Mushroom Casserole 33

51. Winter Sausage with Root Vegetables 34

1. Saucy Sweet Potatoes with Zucchini and Peppers

Ready in about 20 minutes
Servings 4

It's time to say welcome to the vegetable season! This rich and comfort food is packed with nutrients and amazing natural flavors. Enjoy!

Per serving: 225 Calories; 12.9g Fat; 27.3g Carbs; 2.8g Protein; 8.8g Sugars

Ingredients

2 large-sized sweet potatoes, peeled and quartered
1 medium-sized zucchini, sliced
1 Serrano pepper, deveined and thinly sliced
1 bell pepper, deveined and thinly sliced
1-2 carrots, cut into matchsticks
1/4 cup olive oil
1 ½ tablespoon maple syrup
1/2 teaspoon porcini powder
1/4 teaspoon mustard powder
1/2 teaspoon fennel seeds
1 tablespoon garlic powder
1/2 teaspoon fine sea salt
1/4 teaspoon ground black pepper
Tomato ketchup, to serve

Directions

- Place the sweet potatoes, zucchini, peppers, and the carrot into the Air Fryer cooking basket.
- Drizzle with olive oil and toss to coat; cook in the preheated machine at 350 degrees F for 15 minutes.
- While the vegetables are cooking, prepare the sauce by thoroughly whisking the other ingredients, without the tomato ketchup. Lightly grease a baking dish that fits into your machine.
- Transfer cooked vegetables to the prepared baking dish; add the sauce and toss to coat well.
- Turn the machine to 390 degrees F and cook the vegetables for 5 more minutes. Serve warm with tomato ketchup on the side. Bon appétit!

2. Herbed Potatoes with Mediterranean Dipping Sauce

Ready in about 55 minutes
Servings 4

Mediterranean herbs, such as rosemary and thyme, work well with Russet potatoes. Further, mascarpone has a very smooth and rich texture that makes your dipping sauce outstanding! An excellent combo!

Per serving: 295 Calories; 12.3g Fat; 38.4g Carbs; 8.7g Protein; 4.1g Sugars

Ingredients

2 pounds Russet potatoes, peeled and cubed
1 ½ tablespoons melted butter
1 teaspoon sea salt flakes
1 sprig rosemary, leaves only, crushed
2 sprigs thyme, leaves only, crushed
1/2 teaspoon freshly cracked black peppercorns

For Mediterranean Dipping Sauce:
1/2 cup mascarpone cheese
1/3 cup yogurt
1 tablespoon fresh dill, chopped
1 tablespoon olive oil

Directions

- Firstly, set your Air Fryer to cook at 350 degrees F. Now, add the potato cubes to the bowl with cold water and soak them approximately for 35 minutes.
- After that, dry the potato cubes using a paper towel.
- In a mixing dish, thoroughly whisk the melted butter with sea salt flakes, rosemary, thyme, and freshly cracked peppercorns. Rub the potato cubes with this butter/spice mix.
- Air-fry the potato cubes in the cooking basket for 18 to 20 minutes or until cooked through; make sure to shake the potatoes to cook them evenly.
- Meanwhile, make the Mediterranean dipping sauce by mixing the remaining ingredients. Serve warm potatoes with Mediterranean sauce for dipping and enjoy!

3. Restaurant-Style Onion Rings

Ready in about 30 minutes
Servings 8

When your friends are visiting, consider preparing these great low-calorie onion rings that are sure to please. Feel free to experiment with herbs and spices.

Per serving: 231 Calories; 3.3g Fat; 41.4g Carbs; 8.7g Protein; 4.5g Sugars

Ingredients

2 medium-sized yellow onions, cut into rings
2 cups white flour
1/2 teaspoon baking soda
1 teaspoon baking powder
1 ½ teaspoons sea salt flakes
2 medium-sized eggs
1 ½ cups plain milk
1 ¼ cups seasoned breadcrumbs
1/2 teaspoon green peppercorns, freshly cracked
1/2 teaspoon dried dill weed
1/4 teaspoon paprika

Directions

- Begin by preheating your Air Fryer to 356 degrees F.
- Place the onion rings into the bowl with icy cold water; let them stay 15 to 20 minutes; drain the onion rings and dry them using a kitchen towel.
- In a shallow bowl, mix the sifted flour together with baking soda, baking powder and sea salt flakes. Then, coat each onion ring with the flour mixture;
- In another shallow bowl, beat the eggs with milk; add the mixture to the remaining flour mixture and whisk well. Dredge the coated onion rings into this batter.
- In a third bowl, mix the seasoned breadcrumbs, green peppercorns, dill, and paprika. Roll the onion rings over the breadcrumb mix, covering well.
- Air-fry them in the cooking basket for 8 to 11 minutes or until thoroughly cooked to golden.

4. Roma Tomato Bites with Halloumi Cheese

Ready in about 20 minutes
Servings 4

This is a delicious spicy side dish on its own, as well as a great addition to the main dishes such as crispy fish fingers or Mediterranean herbed chicken. Enjoy!

Per serving: 428 Calories; 38.4g Fat; 4.5g Carbs; 18.8g Protein; 2.3g Sugars

Ingredients

For the Sauce:
1/2 cup Parmigiano-Reggiano cheese, grated
4 tablespoons pecans, chopped
1 teaspoon garlic puree
1/2 teaspoon fine sea salt
1/3 cup extra-virgin olive oil

For the Tomato Bites:
2 large-sized Roma tomatoes, cut into thin slices and pat them dry
8 ounces Halloumi cheese, cut into thin slices
1/3 cup onions, sliced
1 teaspoon dried basil
1/4 teaspoon red pepper flakes, crushed
1/8 teaspoon sea salt

Directions

- Start by preheating your Air Fryer to 385 degrees F.
- Make the sauce by mixing all ingredients, except the extra-virgin olive oil, in your food processor.
- While the machine is running, slowly and gradually pour in the olive oil; puree until everything is well - blended.
- Now, spread 1 teaspoon of the sauce over the top of each tomato slice. Place a slice of Halloumi cheese on each tomato slice. Top with onion slices. Sprinkle with basil, red pepper, and sea salt.
- Transfer the assembled bites to the Air Fryer cooking basket. Drizzle with a nonstick cooking spray and cook for approximately 13 minutes.
- Arrange these bites on a nice serving platter, garnish with the remaining sauce and serve at room temperature. Bon appétit!

5. Easy Sautéed Green Beans

Ready in about 12 minutes
Servings 4

Regardless of whether you are using fresh or frozen green beans, they contain many valuable nutrients. If you prefer hotter foods, add chili pepper or hot paprika to this recipe.

Per serving: 53 Calories; 3.0g Fat; 6.1g Carbs; 1.6g Protein; 1.2g Sugars

Ingredients

3/4 pound green beans, cleaned
1 tablespoon balsamic vinegar
1/4 teaspoon kosher salt
1/2 teaspoon mixed peppercorns, freshly cracked
1 tablespoon butter
Sesame seeds, to serve

Directions

- Set your Air Fryer to cook at 390 degrees F.
- Mix the green beans with all of the above ingredients, apart from the sesame seeds. Set the timer for 10 minutes.
- Meanwhile, toast the sesame seeds in a small-sized nonstick skillet; make sure to stir continuously.
- Serve sautéed green beans on a nice serving platter sprinkled with toasted sesame seeds. Bon appétit!

6. Ricotta and Scallion Stuffed Potatoes

Ready in about 15 minutes
Servings 4

Serve these stuffed potatoes that are bursting with flavor as a light dinner or a side dish. Simply add an aromatic fresh salad and enjoy!

Per serving: 290 Calories; 14.4g Fat; 32.5g Carbs; 10.7g Protein; 1.4g Sugars

Ingredients

4 baking potatoes
2 tablespoons olive oil
1/2 cup Ricotta cheese, room temperature
2 tablespoons scallions, chopped
1 heaping tablespoon fresh parsley, roughly chopped
1 heaping tablespoon coriander, minced
2 ounces Cheddar cheese, preferably freshly grated
1 teaspoon celery seeds
1/2 teaspoon salt
1/2 teaspoon garlic pepper

Directions

- Firstly, prick your potatoes with a small paring knife. Cook them in the Air Fryer cooking basket for approximately 13 minutes at 350 degrees F. Check for doneness and cook for 2-3 minutes longer if needed.
- Meanwhile, make the stuffing by mixing the other items.
- When your potatoes are thoroughly cooked, open them up. Divide the stuffing among all potatoes and serve on individual plates.

7. Easy Cheesy Cauliflower and Broccoli

Ready in about 20 minutes
Servings 6

As hearty whole foods, cauliflower and broccoli have many health benefits. If you are looking for a quick and light vegetarian meal, try this recipe! You will make it again and again!

Per serving: 133 Calories; 9.0g Fat; 9.5g Carbs; 5.9g Protein; 3.2g Sugars

Ingredients

1 pound cauliflower florets
1 pound broccoli florets
2 ½ tablespoons sesame oil
1/2 teaspoon smoked cayenne pepper
3/4 teaspoon sea salt flakes
1 tablespoon lemon zest, grated
1/2 cup Colby cheese, shredded

Directions

- Prepare the cauliflower and broccoli using your favorite steaming method. Then, drain them well; add the sesame oil, cayenne pepper, and salt flakes.
- Air-fry at 390 degrees F for approximately 16 minutes; make sure to check the vegetables halfway through the cooking time.
- Afterwards, stir in the lemon zest and Colby cheese; toss to coat well and serve immediately!

8. Peppery Vegetable Omelet with Cheese

Ready in about 15 minutes
Servings 2

This is one of the best advantages of an Air Fryer. You can simply place your favorite ingredients into the pan and wait for the machine to do the rest.

Per serving: 317 Calories; 19.8g Fat; 16.5g Carbs; 20.1g Protein; 10.2g Sugars

Ingredients

3 tablespoons plain milk
4 eggs, whisked
1 teaspoon melted butter
Kosher salt and freshly ground black pepper, to taste
1 red bell pepper, deveined and chopped
1 green bell pepper, deveined and chopped
1 white onion, finely chopped
1/2 cup baby spinach leaves, roughly chopped
1/2 cup Halloumi cheese, shaved

Directions

- Start with spreading the canola cooking spray onto the Air Fryer baking pan.
- Add all of the above ingredients to the baking pan; give them a good stir.
- Then, set your machine to cook at 350 degrees F; cook your omelet for 13 minutes. Serve warm and enjoy!

9. Mushrooms and Peppers in Puff Pastry

Ready in about 25 minutes
Servings 4

Elegant pastries filled with vegetables and cream make a great family dinner. As a matter of fact, puff pastry rolls are only limited by your imagination!

Per serving: 533 Calories; 38.7g Fat; 39.1g Carbs; 8.4g Protein; 2.5g Sugars

Ingredients

1 ½ tablespoons sesame oil
1 cup sliced white mushrooms
2 cloves garlic, minced
1 bell pepper, seeded and chopped
1/4 teaspoon sea salt
1/4 teaspoon dried rosemary
1/2 teaspoon ground black pepper, or more to taste
11 ounces puff pastry sheets
1/2 cup crème fraiche
1 egg, well whisked
1/2 cup Parmesan cheese, preferably freshly grated

Directions

- Start by preheating your Air Fryer to 400 degrees F.
- Then, heat the sesame oil in a skillet that is placed over a moderate heat; cook the mushrooms, garlic, and pepper until tender and fragrant. Season with salt, rosemary, and pepper.
- Meanwhile, roll out the puff pastry; cut into 4-inch squares. Evenly spread the crème fraiche on them.
- Then, divide the vegetables among the puff pastry squares. Fold each square diagonally over the filling in order to form a triangle shape. Pinch the edges and coat each triangle with whisked egg. Coat them with grated Parmesan.
- Cook for 22 to 25 minutes. Bon appétit!

10. Celery and Carrot Croquettes with Chive Mayo

Ready in about 10 minutes
Servings 4

Everybody loves croquettes! This is the healthy and tasty version of this favorite comfort food. You can "perk up" these croquets with chive mayo but horseradish mayo works well too.

Per serving: 124 Calories; 2.0g Fat; 21.9g Carbs; 4.8g Protein; 3.0g Sugars

Ingredients

2 medium-sized carrots, trimmed and grated
2 medium-sized celery stalks, trimmed and grated
1/2 cup of leek, finely chopped
1 tablespoon garlic paste
1/4 teaspoon freshly cracked black pepper
1 teaspoon fine sea salt
1 tablespoon fresh dill, finely chopped
1 egg, lightly whisked
1/4 cup all-purpose flour
1/4 teaspoon baking powder
1/2 cup breadcrumbs (seasoned or regular)
Chive mayo, to serve

Directions

- Place the carrots and celery on a paper towel and squeeze them to remove excess liquid.
- Combine the vegetables with the other ingredients, except the breadcrumbs and chive mayo. Shape the balls using 1 tablespoon of the vegetable mixture.
- Then, gently flatten each ball with your palm or a wide spatula. Coat them with breadcrumbs, covering all sides. Spritz the croquettes with a non - stick cooking oil.
- Air-fry the vegetable croquettes in a single layer for 6 minutes at 360 degrees F. Serve warm with chive mayo. Bon appétit!

11. Scrambled Eggs with Spinach and Tomato

Ready in about 15 minutes
Servings 2

Scrambled eggs aren't just for breakfast. With the addition of healthy veggies, they can be served at any time in order to boost your energy and overall health!

Per serving: 274 Calories; 23.2g Fat; 5.7g Carbs; 13.7g Protein; 2.6g Sugars

Ingredients

2 tablespoons olive oil, melted
4 eggs, whisked
5 ounces fresh spinach, chopped
1 medium-sized tomato, chopped
1 teaspoon fresh lemon juice
1/2 teaspoon coarse salt
1/2 teaspoon ground black pepper
1/2 cup of fresh basil, roughly chopped

Directions

- Add the olive oil to an Air Fryer baking pan. Make sure to tilt the pan to spread the oil evenly.
- Simply combine the remaining ingredients, except for the basil leaves; whisk well until everything is well incorporated.
- Cook in the preheated Air Fryer for 8 to 12 minutes at 280 degrees F. Garnish with fresh basil leaves. Serve warm with a dollop of sour cream if desired.

12. Colby Potato Patties

Ready in about 15 minutes
Servings 8

These old-fashioned potato patties are cheap and easy to make. They are really good to serve with tabasco mayo or any other homemade flavored mayo.

Per serving: 291 Calories; 18.0g Fat; 23.7g Carbs; 9.3g Protein; 1.7g Sugars

Ingredients

2 pounds white potatoes, peeled and grated
1/2 cup scallions, finely chopped
1/2 teaspoon freshly ground black pepper, or more to taste
1 tablespoon fine sea salt
1/2 teaspoon hot paprika
2 cups Colby cheese, shredded
1/4 cup canola oil
1 cup crushed crackers

Directions

- Firstly, boil the potatoes until fork tender. Drain, peel and mash your potatoes.
- Thoroughly mix the mashed potatoes with scallions, pepper, salt, paprika, and cheese. Then, shape the balls using your hands. Now, flatten the balls to make the patties.
- In a shallow bowl, mix canola oil with crushed crackers. Roll the patties over the crumb mixture.
- Next, cook your patties at 360 degrees F approximately 10 minutes, working in batches. Serve with tabasco mayo if desired. Bon appétit!

13. Zesty Broccoli Bites with Hot Sauce

Ready in about 20 minutes
Servings 6

This recipe calls for a homemade hot sauce that is incredibly easy to make. This sauce features balsamic vinegar for a more vibrant flavor; it goes well with hearty broccoli florets.

Per serving: 80 Calories; 3.8g Fat; 10.8g Carbs; 2.5g Protein; 6.6g Sugars

Ingredients

For the Broccoli Bites:
1 medium-sized head broccoli, broken into florets
1/2 teaspoon lemon zest, freshly grated
1/3 teaspoon fine sea salt
1/2 teaspoon hot paprika
1 teaspoon shallot powder
1 teaspoon porcini powder
1/2 teaspoon granulated garlic
1/3 teaspoon celery seeds
1 ½ tablespoons olive oil

For the Hot Sauce:
1/2 cup tomato sauce
3 tablespoons brown sugar
1 tablespoon balsamic vinegar
1/2 teaspoon ground allspice

Directions

- Toss all the ingredients for the broccoli bites in a mixing bowl, covering the broccoli florets on all sides.
- Cook them in the preheated Air Fryer at 360 degrees for 13 to 15 minutes. In the meantime, mix all ingredients for the hot sauce.
- Pause your Air Fryer, mix the broccoli with the prepared sauce and cook for further 3 minutes. Bon appétit!

14. Sweet Corn and Kernel Fritters

Ready in about 20 minutes
Servings 4

To save time, you can cook some extra fritter cakes for lunch and pack the rest for dinner. It is easy to double this recipe and work in batches when you possess a magical Air Fryer!

Per serving: 275 Calories; 8.4g Fat; 40.5g Carbs; 15.7g Protein; 7.3g Sugars

Ingredients

1 medium-sized carrot, grated
1 yellow onion, finely chopped
4 ounces canned sweet corn kernels, drained
1 teaspoon sea salt flakes
1 heaping tablespoon fresh cilantro, chopped
1 medium-sized egg, whisked
2 tablespoons plain milk
1 cup of Parmesan cheese, grated
1/4 cup of self-rising flour
1/3 teaspoon baking powder
1/3 teaspoon brown sugar

Directions

- Press down the grated carrot in the colander to remove excess liquid. Then, spread the grated carrot between several sheets of kitchen towels and pat it dry.
- Then, mix the carrots with the remaining ingredients in the order listed above.
- Roll 1 tablespoon of the mixture into a ball; gently flatten it using the back of a spoon or your hand. Now, repeat with the remaining ingredients.
- Spitz the balls with a nonstick cooking oil. Cook in a single layer at 350 degrees for 8 to 11 minutes or until they're firm to touch in the center. Serve warm and enjoy!

15. Gorgonzola Stuffed Mushrooms with Horseradish Mayo

Ready in about 15 minutes
Servings 5

In this healthy mushroom recipe, Gorgonzola and garlic are added to be prepared an uncommonly rich and flavorful vegetarian dinner. A delicious horseradish mayo emphasizes the flavors.

Per serving: 210 Calories; 15.2g Fat; 13.6g Carbs; 7.6g Protein; 2.7g Sugars

Ingredients

1/2 cup of breadcrumbs
2 cloves garlic, pressed
2 tablespoons fresh coriander, chopped
1/3 teaspoon kosher salt
1/2 teaspoon crushed red pepper flakes
1 ½ tablespoons olive oil
20 medium-sized mushrooms, cut off the stems
1/2 cup Gorgonzola cheese, grated
1/4 cup low-fat mayonnaise
1 teaspoon prepared horseradish, well-drained
1 tablespoon fresh parsley, finely chopped

Directions

- Mix the breadcrumbs together with the garlic, coriander, salt, red pepper, and the olive oil; mix to combine well.
- Stuff the mushroom caps with the breadcrumb filling. Top with grated Gorgonzola.
- Place the mushrooms in the Air Fryer grill pan and slide them into the machine. Grill them at 380 degrees F for 8 to 12 minutes or until the stuffing is warmed through.
- Meanwhile, prepare the horseradish mayo by mixing the mayonnaise, horseradish and parsley. Serve with the warm fried mushrooms. Enjoy!

16. Potato Appetizer with Garlic-Mayo Sauce

Ready in about 19 minutes
Servings 4

This appetizer is definitely one of the best options to make you luncheon a delicious pleasure. In this recipe, you can substitute Greek yogurt for sour cream with the same result.

Per serving: 277 Calories; 7.2g Fat; 50g Carbs; 6g Protein; 1.7g Sugars

Ingredients

2 tablespoons vegetable oil of choice
Kosher salt and freshly ground black pepper, to taste
3 Russet potatoes, cut into wedges

For the Dipping Sauce:
2 teaspoons dried rosemary, crushed
3 garlic cloves, minced
1/3 teaspoon dried marjoram, crushed
1/4 cup sour cream
1/3 cup mayonnaise

Directions

- Lightly grease your potatoes with a thin layer of vegetable oil. Season with salt and ground black pepper.
- Arrange the seasoned potato wedges in an air fryer cooking basket. Bake at 395 degrees F for 15 minutes, shaking once or twice.
- In the meantime, prepare the dipping sauce by mixing all the sauce ingredients. Serve the potatoes with the dipping sauce and enjoy!

17. The Best Sweet Potato Fries Ever

Ready in about 20 minutes
Servings 4

Sweet potato fries are one of the favorite sides that cook perfectly in the Air fryer. Sweet potatoes and olive oil combine very good and this dish is attractive in appearance as well.

Per serving: 180 Calories; 5.4g Fat; 31.8g Carbs; 1.8g Protein; 0.7g Sugars

Ingredients

1 1/2 tablespoons olive oil
1/2 teaspoon smoked cayenne pepper
3 sweet potatoes, peeled and cut into 1/4-inch long slices
1/2 teaspoon shallot powder
1/3 teaspoon freshly ground black pepper, or more to taste
3/4 teaspoon garlic salt

Directions

- Firstly, preheat your air fryer to 360 degrees F.
- Then, add the sweet potatoes to a mixing dish; toss them with the other ingredients.
- Cook the sweet potatoes approximately 14 minutes. Serve with a dipping sauce of choice.

18. Spicy Cheesy Risotto Balls

Ready in about 26 minutes
Servings 4

Firstly, sauté the vegetables to seal the natural juices and flavors before starting air frying. Use brown rice to turn an ordinary rice dish into something spectacular!

Per serving: 176 Calories; 9.1g Fat; 16.9g Carbs; 4.7g Protein; 5.2g Sugars

Ingredients

3 ounces cooked rice
1 /2 cup roasted vegetable stock
1 egg, beaten
1 cup white mushrooms, finely chopped
1/2 cup seasoned breadcrumbs
3 garlic cloves, peeled and minced
1/2 yellow onion, finely chopped
1/3 teaspoon ground black pepper, or more to taste
1 ½ bell peppers, seeded minced
1/2 chipotle pepper, seeded and minced
1/2 tablespoon Colby cheese, grated
1 ½ tablespoons canola oil
Sea salt, to savor

Directions

- Heat a saucepan over a moderate heat; now, heat the oil and sweat the garlic, onions, bell pepper and chipotle pepper until tender. Throw in the mushrooms and fry until they are fragrant and the liquid has almost evaporated.
- Throw in the cooked rice and stock; boil for 18 minutes. Now, add the cheese and spices; mix to combine.
- Allow the mixture to cool completely. Shape the risotto mixture into balls. Dip the risotto balls in the beaten egg; then, roll them over the breadcrumbs.
- Air-fry risotto balls for 6 minutes at 400 degrees F. Serve with marinara sauce and enjoy!

19. Easy Cheesy Broccoli

Ready in about 25 minutes
Servings 4

Eating vegetables is the best way to maintain the ideal body weight, stay healthy and fuel your energy level through the day. Broccoli provides valuable antioxidants as well as vitamins and minerals.

Per serving: 103 Calories; 9.1g Fat; 4.9g Carbs; 1.9g Protein; 1.2g Sugars

Ingredients

1/3 cup grated yellow cheese
1 large-sized head broccoli, stemmed and cut small florets
2 1/2 tablespoons canola oil
2 teaspoons dried rosemary
2 teaspoons dried basil
Salt and ground black pepper, to taste

Directions

- Bring a medium pan filled with a lightly salted water to a boil. Then, boil the broccoli florets for about 3 minutes.
- Then, drain the broccoli florets well; toss them with the canola oil, rosemary, basil, salt and black pepper.
- Set your air fryer to 390 degrees F; arrange the seasoned broccoli in the cooking basket; set the timer for 17 minutes. Toss the broccoli halfway through the cooking process.
- Serve warm topped with grated cheese and enjoy!

20. Potato and Kale Croquettes

Ready in about 9 minutes
Servings 6

You can cook these croquettes after holidays in order to use leftover mashed potatoes. If you have garlic mashed potatoes, reduce the amount of garlic accordingly.

Per serving: 309 Calories; 6.9g Fat; 49.8g Carbs; 12.1g Protein; 2g Sugars

Ingredients

4 eggs, slightly beaten
1⁄3 cup flour
1⁄3 cup goat cheese, crumbled
1 ½ teaspoons fine sea salt
4 garlic cloves, minced
1 cup kale, steamed
1⁄3 cup breadcrumbs
1/3teaspoon red pepper flakes
3 potatoes, peeled and quartered
1/3 teaspoon dried dill weed

Directions

- Firstly, boil the potatoes in salted water. Once the potatoes are cooked, mash them; add the kale, goat cheese, minced garlic, sea salt, red pepper flakes, dill and one egg; stir to combine well.
- Now, roll the mixture to form small croquettes.
- Grab three shallow bowls. Place the flour in the first shallow bowl.
- Beat the remaining 3 eggs in the second bowl. After that, throw the breadcrumbs into the third shallow bowl.
- Dip each croquette in the flour; then, dip them in the eggs bowl; lastly, roll each croquette in the breadcrumbs.
- Air fry at 335 degrees F for 7 minutes or until golden. Tate, adjust for seasonings and serve warm.

21. Spicy Potato Wedges

Ready in about 23 minutes
Servings 4

If you've never had potato wedges from the Air fryer, you're missing the most flavorful potatoes ever! You can use rosemary or thyme instead of dried parsley flakes.

Per serving: 288 Calories; 4.7g Fat; 44.5g Carbs; 5.4g Protein; 3.7g Sugars

Ingredients

1 ½ tablespoons melted butter
1 teaspoon dried parsley flakes
1 teaspoon ground coriander
1 teaspoon seasoned salt
3 large-sized red potatoes, cut into wedges
1/2 teaspoon chili powder
1/3 teaspoon garlic pepper

Directions

- Dump the potato wedges into the air fryer cooking basket. Drizzle with melted butter and cook for 20 minutes at 380 degrees F. Make sure to shake them a couple of times during the cooking process.
- Add the remaining ingredients; toss to coat potato wedges on all sides. Bon appétit!

22. Family Favorite Stuffed Mushrooms

Ready in about 16 minutes
Servings 2

Mushrooms inspire every home cook in so many ways! In this recipe, they're stuffed with spices and amazing bran cereal for a quick and protein-packed dinner or side dish.

Per serving: 176 Calories; 14.7g Fat; 10.5g Carbs; 6g Protein; 4g Sugars

Ingredients

2 teaspoons cumin powder
4 garlic cloves, peeled and minced
1 small onion, peeled and chopped
2 tablespoons bran cereal, crushed
18 medium-sized white mushrooms
Fine sea salt and freshly ground black pepper, to your liking
A pinch ground allspice
2 tablespoons olive oil

Directions

- First, clean the mushrooms; remove the middle stalks from the mushrooms to prepare the "shells".
- Grab a mixing dish and thoroughly combine the remaining items. Fill the mushrooms with the prepared mixture.
- Cook the mushrooms at 345 degrees F heat for 12 minutes. Enjoy!

23. Mediterranean Halloumi and Garlic Omelet

Ready in about 17 minutes
Servings 2

Enjoy this perfectly cooked omelet with a deeply flavored Halloumi and an aromatic garlic paste. Serve with the ciabatta toasts, garnished with fresh cherry tomatoes.

Per serving: 444 Calories; 29g Fat; 11.6g Carbs; 30g Protein; 5.8g Sugars

Ingredients

1/3 cup Halloumi cheese, sliced
2 teaspoons garlic paste
2 teaspoons fresh chopped rosemary
5 well-whisked eggs
2 bell peppers, seeded and chopped
1 ½ tablespoons fresh basil, chopped
3 tablespoons onions, chopped
Fine sea salt and ground black pepper, to taste

Directions

- Spritz your baking dish with a canola cooking spray.
- Throw in all ingredients and stir until everything is well incorporated.
- Bake for about 15 minutes at 325 degrees F. Eat warm.

24. Thanksgiving Mashed Ruby Yams

Ready in about 19 minutes
Servings 4

Here is a holiday worthy side dish! Loaded with maple syrup, eggs, and heavy cream, this rich, flavorsome side dish hits the spot!

Per serving: 223 Calories; 14.7g Fat; 18.6g Carbs; 4.8g Protein; 16g Sugars

Ingredients

1/3 cup maple syrup
2 eggs, beaten
1/2 teaspoon ground black pepper
1 teaspoon cayenne pepper
1/3 cup extra-virgin olive oil
1 1/2 teaspoon pink Himalayan salt flakes
5 ruby yams, peeled
1 1/2 tablespoons heavy cream

Directions

- Boil ruby yams until they're fork tender.
- Then, combine all the remaining ingredients using an electric mixer or a wire whisk.
- Scrape the mixture into a baking dish. Transfer the baking dish to the air fryer and bake for 20 minutes at 305 degrees F. Bon appétit!

25. Mediterranean-Style Frittata with Manchego

Ready in about 40 minutes
Servings 4

Frittata is one of the most luxurious dishes you can make in your Air fryer. This recipe calls for Manchego cheese; feel free to use Pecorino Romano or Zamorano cheese.

Per serving: 153 Calories; 11.9g Fat; 3.2g Carbs; 9.3g Protein; 1.7g Sugars

Ingredients

1/3 cup grated Manchego, cheese
5 eggs
1 small onion, finely chopped
2 garlic, peeled and finely minced
1 ½ cups white mushrooms, chopped
1 teaspoon dried basil
1 ½ tablespoons olive oil
3/4 teaspoon dried oregano
1/2 teaspoon dried parsley flakes or 1 tablespoon fresh flat-leaf Italian parsley
1 teaspoon porcini powder
Table salt and freshly ground black pepper, to savor

Directions

- Start by preheating your air fryer to 350 degrees F. Add the oil, mushrooms, onion, and green garlic to the air fryer baking dish. Bake this mixture for 6 minutes or until it is tender.
- Meanwhile, crack the eggs into a mixing bowl; beat the eggs until they're well whisked. Next, add the seasonings and mix again. Pause your air fryer and take the baking dish out of the air fryer.
- Pour the whisked egg mixture into the baking dish with sautéed mixture. Top with the grated Manchego.
- Bake for about 32 minutes at 320 degrees F or until your frittata is set. Serve warm garnished with diced fresh tomatoes. Bon appétit!

26. Amazing Crispy Sweet Onion Rings

Ready in about 28 minutes
Servings 4

This is a quick and easy snack – especially when sweet onions are in season! We used cornmeal but you can use your favorite breadcrumbs too.

Per serving: 383 Calories; 5.9g Fat; 58.8g Carbs; 12.7g Protein; 10.4g Sugars

Ingredients

2 small eggs
1 ½ cups milk
1 teaspoon fine sea salt
1 ½ teaspoons cayenne pepper
1 large-sized sweet onion, cut crosswise into 1/2-inch slices
2/3 teaspoon baking powder
2/3 cup yellow cornmeal
1 1/2 cups all-purpose flour
1/2 tablespoon granulated sugar

Directions

- Begin by preheating your air fryer to about 345 degrees F.
- In a mixing dish, whisk the flour with baking powder, salt, sugar, and cayenne pepper.
- Dip the sweet onion rings into the flour/seasoning mixture; make sure to coat them on all sides. Then, fold in the egg; pour in the milk and mix again to combine thoroughly.
- Then, dip the floured onion rings into the batter. After that, roll the rings into yellow cornmeal.
- Lastly, cook the onion rings approximately 15 minutes at 345 degrees F. Bon appétit!

27. Crispy Fried Pickle Spears

Ready in about 15 minutes
Servings 6

You can boost the flavor even more with a tablespoon or two of different spices. They are ideal for a beer-tasting party!

Per serving: 58 Calories; 2g Fat; 6.8g Carbs; 3.2g Protein; 0.9g Sugars

Ingredients

1/3 cup milk
1 teaspoon garlic powder
2 medium-sized eggs
1 teaspoon fine sea salt
1/3 teaspoon chili powder
1/3 cup all-purpose flour
1/2 teaspoon shallot powder
2 jars sweet and sour pickle spears

Directions

- Pat the pickle spears dry with a kitchen towel. Then, take two mixing bowls.
- Whisk the egg and milk in a bowl. In another bowl, combine all dry ingredients.
- Firstly, dip the pickle spears into the dry mix; then coat each pickle with the egg/milk mixture; dredge them in the flour mixture again for additional coating.
- Air fry battered pickles for 15 minutes at 385 degrees. Enjoy!

28. Spicy Winter Squash Bites

Ready in about 23 minutes
Servings 8

Imagine this: spicy squash cubes are roasted to a crispy golden brown, then served with a cool and zesty dipping sauce. Yummy!

Per serving: 113 Calories; 3g Fat; 22.6g Carbs; 1.6g Protein; 4.3g Sugars

Ingredients

2 teaspoons fresh mint leaves, chopped
1/3 cup brown sugar
1 ½ teaspoons red pepper chili flakes
2 tablespoons melted butter
3 pounds winter squash, peeled, seeded, and cubed

Directions

- Toss all of the above ingredients in a large-sized mixing dish.
- Roast the squash bites for 30 minutes at 325 degrees F in your Air Fryer, turning once or twice. Serve with a homemade dipping sauce.

29. Butter Squash Fritters

Ready in about 22 minutes
Servings 4

When it comes to ease in the kitchen, an Air fryer is unbeatable! In this recipe, you should combine all ingredients and then, throw them into the chamber. It's easy, isn't it?

Per serving: 152 Calories; 10.02g Fat; 9.4g Carbs; 5.8g Protein; 0.3g Sugars

Ingredients

1/3 cup all-purpose flour
1/3 teaspoon freshly ground black pepper, or more to taste
1/3 teaspoon dried sage
4 cloves garlic, minced
1 ½ tablespoons olive oil
1/3 butternut squash, peeled and grated
2 eggs, well whisked
1 teaspoon fine sea salt
A pinch of ground allspice

Directions

- Thoroughly combine all ingredients in a mixing bowl.
- Preheat your air fryer to 345 degrees and set the timer for 17 minutes; cook until your fritters are browned; serve right away.

30. Herbed Roasted Potatoes

Ready in about 24 minutes
Servings 4

Potatoes are one of the most versatile vegetables ever! You can roast, boil, bake and mash them on their own or you can add other vegetables and spices. This time, we'll toss them with a selection of aromatics and fry them with a little bit of olive oil.

Per serving: 208 Calories; 7.1g Fat; 33.8g Carbs; 3.6g Protein; 2.5g Sugars

Ingredients

1 teaspoon crushed dried thyme
1 teaspoon ground black pepper
2 tablespoons olive oil
1/2 tablespoon crushed dried rosemary
3 potatoes, peeled, washed and cut into wedges
1/2 teaspoon seasoned salt

Directions

- Lay the potatoes in the air fryer cooking basket; drizzle olive oil over your potatoes.
- Then, cook for 17 minutes at 353 degrees F.
- Toss with the seasonings and serve warm with your favorite salad on the side.

31. Indian-Style Garnet Sweet Potatoes

Ready in about 24 minutes
Servings 4

The Garnet potato, also known as the red yam, is healthy and delicious, and it gives a sense of satiety. With a few drizzles of maple syrup, tamarind paste and fresh lime juice, they will make your taste buds really happy!

Per serving: 103 Calories; 9.1g Fat; 4.9g Carbs; 1.9g Protein; 1.2g Sugars

Ingredients

1/3 teaspoon white pepper
1 tablespoon butter, melted
1/2 teaspoon turmeric powder
5 garnet sweet potatoes, peeled and diced
1 ½ tablespoons maple syrup
2 teaspoons tamarind paste
1 1/2 tablespoons fresh lime juice
1 1/2 teaspoon ground allspice

Directions

- In a mixing bowl, toss all ingredients until sweet potatoes are well coated.
- Air-fry them at 335 degrees F for 12 minutes.
- Pause the air fryer and toss again. Increase the temperature to 390 degrees F and cook for an additional 10 minutes. Eat warm.

32. Easy Frizzled Leeks

Ready in about 52 minutes
Servings 6

Instead of tossing your leeks into the salad, use them to make these incredibly delicious bites. These little, fried strips are yummy with a brown mustard aioli, barbecue sauce or chili-sour cream sauce for dipping.

Per serving: 291 Calories; 6g Fat; 53.3g Carbs; 5.7g Protein; 4.3g Sugars

Ingredients

1/2 teaspoon porcini powder
1 1/2 cup rice flour
1 tablespoon vegetable oil
3 medium-sized leeks, slice into julienne strips
2 large-sized dishes with ice water
2 teaspoons onion powder
Fine sea salt and cayenne pepper, to taste

Directions

- Allow the leeks to soak in ice water for about 25 minutes; drain well.
- Place the rice flour, salt, cayenne pepper, onions powder, and porcini powder into a resealable bag. Add the celery and shake to coat well.
- Drizzle vegetable oil over the seasoned leeks. Air fry at 390 degrees F for about 18 minutes; turn them halfway through the cooking time. Serve with homemade mayonnaise or any other sauce for dipping. Enjoy!

33. Cremini Mushrooms in Zesty Tahini Sauce

Ready in about 22 minutes
Servings 5

When it comes to the most tender and the perfectly cooked mushrooms, the Air fryer is a must-have kitchen appliance. These mushrooms are absolutely luxurious with lemony tahini sauce!

Per serving: 372 Calories; 4g Fat; 80g Carbs; 11.2g Protein; 2.6g Sugars

Ingredients

1/2 tablespoon tahini
1/2 teaspoon turmeric powder
1/3 teaspoon cayenne pepper
2 tablespoons lemon juice, freshly squeezed
1 teaspoon kosher salt
1/3 teaspoon freshly cracked black pepper
1 1/2 tablespoons vermouth
1 ½ tablespoons olive oil
1 ½ pound Cremini mushrooms

Directions

- Grab a mixing dish and toss the mushrooms with the olive oil, turmeric powder, salt, black pepper, and cayenne pepper.
- Cook them in your air fryer for 9 minutes at 355 degrees F.
- Pause your air fryer, give it a good stir and cook for 10 minutes longer.
- Meanwhile, thoroughly combine lemon juice, vermouth, and tahini. Serve warm mushrooms with tahini sauce.

34. Hash Brown Casserole

Ready in about 23 minutes
Servings 6

This is a great recipe for the cooler seasons. The recipe calls for a cream of celery soup in order to achieve a richer flavor. A thick homemade broth works well too.

Per serving: 195 Calories; 11.1g Fat; 22g Carbs; 3.1g Protein; 3g Sugars

Ingredients

1/2 cup Cheddar cheese, shredded
1 tablespoon soft cheese, at room temperature
1/3 cup crushed bran cereal
1 ½ yellow or white medium-sized onion, chopped
5 ounces condensed cream of celery soup
1 tablespoons fresh cilantro, finely minced
1/3 cup sour cream
3 cloves garlic, peeled and finely minced
2 cups hash brown potatoes, shredded
1 1/2 tablespoons margarine or butter, melted
Sea salt and freshly ground black pepper, to your liking
Crushed red pepper flakes, to your liking

Directions

- Grab a large-sized bowl and whisk the celery soup, sour cream, soft cheese, red pepper, salt, and black pepper. Stir in the hash browns, onion, garlic, cilantro, and Cheddar cheese. Mix until everything is thoroughly combined.
- Scrape the mixture into a baking dish that is previously lightly greased.
- In another mixing bowl, combine together the bran cereal and melted margarine (or butter). Spread the mixture evenly over the top of the hash brown mixture.
- Bake for 17 minutes at 290 degrees F. Eat warm, garnished with some extra sour cream if desired.

35. Pepper Jack Cauliflower Bites

Ready in about 24 minutes
Servings 2

Here is a gluten-free and egg-free recipe that is actually lip-smacking good! If you're going vegan, simply substitute nondairy cheese for Pepper Jack!

Per serving: 271 Calories; 23g Fat; 8.9g Carbs; 9.8g Protein; 2.8g Sugars

Ingredients

1/3 teaspoon shallot powder
1 teaspoon ground black pepper
1 ½ large-sized heads of cauliflower, broken into florets
1/4 teaspoon cumin powder
½ teaspoon garlic salt
1/4 cup Pepper Jack cheese, grated
1 ½ tablespoons vegetable oil
1/3 teaspoon paprika

Directions

- Boil cauliflower in a large pan of salted water approximately 5 minutes. After that, drain the cauliflower florets; now, transfer them to a baking dish.
- Toss the cauliflower florets with the rest of the above ingredients.
- Roast at 395 degrees F for 16 minutes, turn them halfway through the process. Enjoy!

36. Cheesy Broccoli Croquettes

Ready in about 50 minutes
Servings 6

A perfect blend of vegetable and cheese in a small, light and airy ball! Parmesan cheese amplifies the crunchiness of these excellent croquettes whilst Monterey Jack gives them the perfect meltiness.

Per serving: 246 Calories; 14g Fat; 15.2g Carbs; 14.5g Protein; 1.6g Sugars

Ingredients

1 1/2 cups Monterey Jack cheese
1 teaspoon dried dill weed
1/3 teaspoon ground black pepper
3 eggs, whisked
1 teaspoon cayenne pepper
1/2 teaspoon kosher salt
1 cup Panko crumbs
2 ½ cups broccoli florets
1/3 cup Parmesan cheese

Directions

- Blitz the broccoli florets in a food processor until finely crumbed. Then, combine the broccoli with the rest of the above ingredients.
- Roll the mixture into small balls; place the balls in the fridge for approximately half an hour.
- Preheat your air fryer to 335 degrees F and set the timer to 14 minutes; cook until broccoli croquettes are browned and serve warm.

37. Cauliflower Cakes Ole

Ready in about 48 minutes
Servings 6

Serve these Mexican-inspired cauliflower cakes with a main course or enjoy them as an appetizer. Delicious, but simple, these savory bites are like eating your favorite vegetable and cheese all in one flavorful, little package.

Per serving: 190 Calories; 14.1g Fat; 4.7g Carbs; 11.5g Protein; 1.3g Sugars

Ingredients

2 teaspoons chili powder
1 1/2 teaspoon kosher salt
1 teaspoon dried marjoram, crushed
2 1/2 cups cauliflower, broken into florets
1 1/3 cups tortilla chip crumbs
1/2 teaspoon crushed red pepper flakes
3 eggs, whisked
1 ½ cups Queso cotija cheese, crumbled

Directions

- Blitz the cauliflower florets in your food processor until they're crumbled (it is the size of rice). Then, combine the cauliflower "rice" with the other items.
- Now, roll the cauliflower mixture into small balls; refrigerate for 30 minutes.
- Preheat your air fryer to 345 degrees and set the timer for 14 minutes; cook until the balls are browned and serve right away.

38. Celery and Carrot Croquettes

Ready in about 25 minutes
Servings 4

No doubt it's easy to add plenty of vegetables to every meal! Celery is a powerhouse of many valuable nutrients. Carrots improve vision, prevent cancer and cleanse your whole body.

Per serving: 142 Calories; 6g Fat; 15.8g Carbs; 7.2g Protein; 3g Sugars

Ingredients

2 small eggs, lightly beaten
1/3 teaspoon freshly cracked black pepper
1/3 cup Colby cheese, grated
1/2 tablespoon fresh dill, finely chopped
1/2 tablespoon garlic paste
1/3 cup onion, finely chopped
1/3 cup all-purpose flour
3 medium-sized carrots, trimmed and grated
2 teaspoons fine sea salt
3 medium-sized celery stalks, trimmed and grated
1/3 teaspoon baking powder

Directions

- Place the carrots and celery on a paper towel and squeeze them to remove the excess liquid.
- Combine the vegetables with the other ingredients in the order listed above. Shape the balls using 1 tablespoon of the vegetable mixture.
- Then, gently flatten each ball with your palm or a wide spatula. Spritz the croquettes with a nonstick cooking oil.
- Bake the vegetable cakes in a single layer for 17 minutes at 318 degrees F. Serve warm with sour cream.

39. Smoked Veggie Omelet

Ready in about 14 minutes
Servings 2

Here's an all-time favorite egg dish! To make this omelet more unique, serve with a high-quality sour cream and pitted olives.

Per serving: 226 Calories; 11.5g Fat; 14.2g Carbs; 16.3g Protein; 5.2g Sugars

Ingredients

1/3 cup cherry tomatoes, chopped
1 bell pepper, seeded and chopped
1/3 teaspoon freshly ground black pepper
1/2 purple onion, peeled and sliced
1 teaspoon smoked cayenne pepper
5 medium-sized eggs, well-beaten
1/3 cup smoked tofu, crumbled
1 teaspoon seasoned salt
1 1/2 tablespoons fresh chives, chopped

Directions

- Brush a baking dish with a spray coating.
- Throw all ingredients, minus fresh chives, into the baking dish; give it a good stir.
- Cook about 15 minutes at 325 degrees F. Garnish with fresh chopped chives. Bon appétit!

40. Sweet Potato and Carrot Croquettes

Ready in about 22 minutes
Servings 4

Swiss cheese, sweet potatoes and carrots are combined with eggs and flour for a quick and protein-packed dinner or appetizer.

Per serving: 206 Calories; 5g Fat; 32g Carbs; 8.3g Protein; 5.7g Sugars

Ingredients

1/3 cup Swiss cheese, grated
1/3 teaspoon fine sea salt
1/3 teaspoon baking powder
1/3 cup scallions, finely chopped
1/2 tablespoon fresh basil, finely chopped
3 carrots, trimmed and grated
1/2 teaspoon freshly cracked black pepper
3 sweet potatoes, grated
1/3 cup all-purpose flour
2 small eggs, lightly beaten

Directions

- Place grated sweet potatoes and carrots on a paper towel and pat them dry.
- Combine the potatoes and carrots with the other ingredients in the order listed above. Then, create the balls using 1½ tablespoons of the vegetable mixture.
- Then, gently flatten each ball. Spritz the croquettes with a nonstick cooking oil.
- Bake your croquettes for 13 minutes at 305 degrees F; work with batches. Serve warm with tomato ketchup and mayonnaise.

41. Manchego and Potato Patties

Ready in about 15 minutes
Servings 8

These cheesy and mellowly patties are definitely one of the best options to make you luncheon a delicious pleasure. Feel free to use your favorite combo of seasonings.

Per serving: 191 Calories; 8.7g Fat; 22g Carbs; 7g Protein; 1.4g Sugars

Ingredients

1 cup Manchego cheese, shredded
1 teaspoon paprika
1 teaspoon freshly ground black pepper
1/2 tablespoon fine sea salt
2 cups scallions, finely chopped
2 pounds Russet potatoes, peeled and grated
2 tablespoons canola oil
2 teaspoons dried basil

Directions

- Thoroughly combine all of the above ingredients. Then, shape the balls using your hands. Now, flatten the balls to make the patties.
- Next, cook your patties at 360 degrees F approximately 10 minutes. Bon appétit!

42. Mint-Butter Stuffed Mushrooms

Ready in about 19 minutes
Servings 3

Looking for a hearty, satisfying bites? These aromatic stuffed mushrooms are sure to please everyone! Adding freshly grated sharp cheese gives these mushrooms a rich and wonderful taste. Enjoy!

Per serving: 290 Calories; 14.7g Fat; 13.4g Carbs; 28g Protein; 3.3g Sugars

Ingredients

3 garlic cloves, minced
1 teaspoon ground black pepper, or more to taste
1/3 cup seasoned breadcrumbs
1½ tablespoons fresh mint, chopped
1 teaspoon salt, or more to taste
1½ tablespoons melted butter
14 medium-sized mushrooms, cleaned, stalks removed

Directions

- Mix all of the above ingredients, minus the mushrooms, in a mixing bowl to prepare the filling.
- Then, stuff the mushrooms with the prepared filling.
- Air-fry stuffed mushrooms at 375 degrees F for about 12 minutes. Taste for doneness and serve at room temperature as a vegetarian appetizer.

43. Ricotta and Leafy Green Omelet

Ready in about 17 minutes
Servings 2

Here's one of the best spring-worthy omelets that is chock full of mild cheese, amazing leafy greens and aromatic seasonings. Serve with spring onions and radishes. Sure, you don't have to wait for spring to try this recipe!

Per serving: 409 Calories; 29.5g Fat; 6.9g Carbs; 27.9g Protein; 3g Sugars

Ingredients

1/3 cup Ricotta cheese
5 eggs, beaten
1/2 red bell pepper, seeded and sliced
1 cup mixed greens, roughly chopped
1/2 green bell pepper, seeded and sliced
1/2 teaspoon dried basil
1/2 chipotle pepper, finely minced
1/2 teaspoon dried oregano

Directions

- Lightly coat the inside of a baking dish with a pan spray.
- Then, throw all ingredients into the baking dish; give it a good stir.
- Bake at 325 degrees F for 15 minutes.

44. Basic Pepper French Fries

Ready in about 33 minutes
Servings 4

If you're ready for the healthiest French fries ever, try this recipe! Serve alongside a fresh salad and tomato ketchup.

Per serving: 262 Calories; 9.1g Fat; 42g Carbs; 4.5g Protein; 3g Sugars

Ingredients

1 teaspoon fine sea salt
1/2 teaspoon freshly ground black pepper
2 ½ tablespoons canola oil
6 Russet potatoes, cut them into fries
1/2 teaspoon crushed red pepper flakes

Directions

- Start by preheating your air fryer to 340 degrees F.
- Place the fries in your air fryer and toss them with the oil. Add the seasonings and toss again.
- Cook for 30 minutes, shaking your fries several times. Taste for doneness and eat warm.

45. Oyster Mushroom and Lemongrass Omelet

Ready in about 42 minutes
Servings 2

Here's a delicious, protein packed breakfast! If you want to skip a high-calorie Swiss cheese, Cottage cheese is a perfect alternative. You will love it!

Per serving: 362 Calories; 29g Fat; 7.2g Carbs; 19g Protein; 2.8g Sugars

Ingredients

3 king oyster mushrooms, thinly sliced
1 lemongrass, chopped
1/2 teaspoon dried marjoram
5 eggs
1/3 cup Swiss cheese, grated
2 tablespoons sour cream
1 1/2 teaspoon dried rosemary
2 teaspoons red pepper flakes, crushed
2 tablespoons butter, melted
1/2 red onion, peeled and sliced into thin rounds
½ teaspoon garlic powder
1 teaspoon dried dill weed
Fine sea salt and ground black pepper, to your liking

Directions

- Melt the margarine in a skillet that is placed over a medium flame. Then, sweat the onion, mushrooms, and lemongrass until they have softened; reserve.
- Then, preheat the air fryer to 325 degrees F. Then, crack the eggs into a mixing bowl and whisk them well. Then, fold in the sour cream and give it a good stir.
- Now, stir in the salt, black pepper, red pepper, rosemary, garlic powder, marjoram, and dill.
- Next step, grease the inside of an air fryer baking dish with a thin layer of a cooking spray. Pour the egg/seasoning mixture into the baking dish; throw in the reserved mixture. Top with the Swiss cheese.
- Set the timer for 35 minutes; cook until a knife inserted in the center comes out clean and dry.

46. Spinach and Cheese Stuffed Baked Potatoes

Ready in about 18 minutes
Servings 4

This is such a comforting dish with greens, Cheddar cheese and russet potatoes. Healthy eating is easier than you think!

Per serving: 327 Calories; 7g Fat; 59g Carbs; 9.4g Protein; 2.2g Sugars

Ingredients

3 tablespoons extra-virgin olive oil
2/3 cup sour cream, at room temperature
1½ cup baby spinach leaves, torn into small pieces
3 pounds russet potatoes
2 garlic cloves, peeled and finely minced
1/4 teaspoon fine sea salt, or more to taste
1/4 teaspoon freshly cracked black pepper, or more to taste
1/3 cup Cheddar cheese, freshly grated

Directions

- Firstly, stab the potatoes with a fork. Preheat the air fryer to 345 degrees F. Now, cook the potatoes for 14 minutes.
- Meanwhile, make the filling by mixing the rest of the above items.
- Afterward that, open the potatoes up and stuff them with the prepared filling. Bon appétit!

47. Pantano Romanesco with Goat Cheese Appetizer

Ready in about 20 minutes
Servings 4

Ready in less than 20 minutes, these colorful bites would win your heart! Serve as an appetizer, but you can turn them into an entire vegetarian dinner.

Per serving: 237 Calories; 20.4g Fat; 0.9g Carbs; 13g Protein; 0.9g Sugars

Ingredients

6 ounces goat cheese, sliced
2 shallots, thinly sliced
2 Pantano Romanesco tomatoes, cut into 1/2-inch slices
1 ½ tablespoons extra-virgin olive oil
3/4 teaspoon sea salt
Fresh parsley, for garnish
Fresh basil, chopped

Directions

- Preheat your air fryer to 380 degrees F.
- Now, pat each tomato slice dry using a paper towel. Sprinkle each slice with salt and chopped basil. Top with a slice of goat cheese.
- Top with the shallot slices; drizzle with olive oil. Add the prepared tomato and feta "bites" to the air fryer food basket.
- Cook in the air fryer for about 14 minutes. Lastly, adjust seasonings to taste and serve garnished with fresh parsley leaves. Enjoy!

48. Swiss Chard and Cheese Omelet

Ready in about 25 minutes
Servings 2

If you like to experiment with egg recipes, you should try this one. This whole dish comes together in your Air fryer!

Per serving: 388 Calories; 27g Fat; 6g Carbs; 29g Protein; 2.6g Sugars

Ingredients

1 teaspoon garlic paste
1 ½ tablespoons olive oil
1/2 cup crème fraîche
1/3 teaspoon ground black pepper, to your liking
1/3 cup Swiss cheese, crumbled
1 teaspoon cayenne pepper
1/3 cup Swiss chard, torn into pieces
5 eggs
1/4 cup yellow onions, chopped
1 teaspoon fine sea salt

Directions

- Crack your eggs into a mixing dish; then, add the crème fraîche, salt, ground black pepper, and cayenne pepper.
- Next, coat the inside of a baking dish with olive oil and tilt it to spread evenly. Scrape the egg/cream mixture into the baking dish. Add the other ingredients; mix to combine well.
- Bake for 18 minutes at 292 degrees F. Serve immediately.

49. Mom's Jacket Potatoes

Ready in about 23 minutes
Servings 4

A hot air circulates around your potatoes so they get super crispy and super yummy! Also, you can add crushed or ground chili peppers to spice them up!

Per serving: 270 Calories; 10.9g Fat; 35.2g Carbs; 8.8g Protein; 2.8g Sugars

Ingredients

1/3 cup Cottage cheese, softened
1/3 cup Parmigiano-Reggiano cheese, grated
1 teaspoon black pepper
1 ½ heaping tablespoons roughly chopped cilantro leaves
1/3 cup green onions, finely chopped
5 average-sized potatoes
2 ½ tablespoons softened butter
1 teaspoon salt

Directions

- Firstly, stab your potatoes with a fork. Cook them in the air fryer basket for 20 minutes at 345 degrees F.
- While the potatoes are cooking, make the filling by mixing the rest of the above ingredients.
- Afterward, open the potatoes up and stuff them with the prepared filling. Bon appétit!

50. Skinny Asparagus and Mushroom Casserole

Ready in about 27 minutes
Servings 2

Are you struggling with your weight, needing some help? An air fryer is the perfect solution. Make this amazing casserole and see for yourself!

Per serving: 207 Calories; 19.7g Fat; 30.2g Carbs; 20.6g Protein; 3.7g Sugars

Ingredients

1/3 cup milk
1/3 cup Colby cheese, grated
5 slices of Italian bread, cut into cubes
1 1/2 cups white mushrooms, sliced
2 asparagus spears, chopped
1 teaspoon table salt, or to taste
2 well-beaten eggs
1/3 teaspoon smoked cayenne pepper
1 teaspoon ground black pepper, or to taste
1/3 teaspoon dried rosemary, crushed

Directions

- Throw the bread cubes into the baking dish.
- In a mixing dish, thoroughly combine the eggs and milk. Stir in 1/2 of cheese; add the seasonings. Pour 3/4 of egg/cheese mixture over the bread cubes in the baking dish; press gently using a wide spatula.
- Now, top with the mushrooms and chopped asparagus. Pour the remaining egg/cheese mixture over the top; make sure to spread it evenly.
- Top with the remaining Colby cheese and bake for 20 minutes at 325 degrees F.

51. Winter Sausage with Root Vegetables

Ready in about 30 minutes
Servings 4

Italian sausage, root veggies, and olive oil all in this fantastic dish! It's hard to believe that root vegetables can taste so over-the-top delicious!

Per serving: 289 Calories; 13.6g Fat; 32.5g Carbs; 13.3g Protein; 6.7g Sugars

Ingredients

1/2 pound Italian sausage
3 sprigs rosemary
1 medium-sized parsnip, sliced
1/3 pound fingerling potatoes
3 sprigs thyme
1/3 pound carrots, trimmed and cut into matchsticks
1/2 celery stalk, sliced
2 garlic cloves, smashed
2 tablespoons extra-virgin olive oil
3 small-sized leeks, cut into halves lengthwise
A pinch of grated nutmeg
Salt and black pepper, to taste

Directions

- Arrange fingerling potatoes, carrots, celery, parsnip, and leeks on the bottom of the air fryer baking dish. Tuck the garlic cloves around the vegetables.
- Sprinkle with the seasonings and top with the sausage.
- Roast approximately 33 minutes at 375 degrees F, stirring occasionally. Bon appétit!

CHICKEN

52. Chicken Wings in Piri Piri Sauce 36

53. Spring Chicken and Ricotta Wraps 36

54. Perfect Chicken Sausage with
    Mustard-Honey Sauce 37

55. Gourmet Chicken Omelet 37

56. Saucy Tarragon Chicken 38

57. Pizza-Stuffed Chicken Breast 38

58. Mustard and Turmeric Chicken Thighs 39

59. Tender Chicken in Wine Sauce 39

60. Indian-Style Chicken Legs 40

61. Buttermilk Fried Chicken Tenders 40

62. Penne with Chicken Sausage Meatballs 41

63. Cajun Chicken Wings with Cabbage-Potato Cakes ... 41

64. Majestic Maple-Glazed Chicken 42

65. Saucy Provençal Chicken with Bacon 42

66. Melt-In-Your-Mouth Marjoram Chicken 43

67. Chicken with Cremini Mushroom Sauce 43

68. Chicken and Asiago Crescent Squares 44

69. The Best Orange and Shoyu Wings 44

70. Baked Za'atar Eggs with Chicken 45

71. Chicken in Yogurt-Mustard Sauce 45

72. Brioche with Chicken and Caciocavallo 46

73. Cheese and Chive Stuffed Chicken Rolls 46

74. Chicken Drumsticks with Ketchup-Lemon Sauce... 47

75. Creamed Cajun Chicken 47

76. Chive, Feta and Chicken Frittata 48

77. Grilled Chicken Tikka Masala 48

78. Award Winning Breaded Chicken 49

79. Cheese and Garlic Stuffed Chicken Breasts 49

80. Dinner Avocado Chicken Sliders 50

81. Peanut Butter and Chicken Bites 50

82. Tangy Paprika Chicken 51

83. Super-Easy Chicken with Tomato Sauce 51

84. Mouthwatering Chicken Cheese Burgers 52

85. Herbed Passila Chicken 52

86. Indian-Style Baked Eggs with Chicken 53

87. Dad's Yummy Chicken Frittata 53

88. Skinny Chicken and Carrot Meatballs 54

89. Saucy Orange Marinated Chicken 54

90. Hot Spicy Chicken Burgers 55

91. Parsley Lime Grilled Chicken 55

92. Tangy Tomato Chicken Drumsticks 56

93. Sweet-Chili Chicken Breasts with Asiago Cheese . 56

94. Butter and Cider Chicken Drumsticks 57

95. Tortilla Chip-Crusted Chicken 57

96. Tamarind Chicken Bubble & Squeak 58

97. Melt-In-Your-Mouth Chicken Rolls 58

98. Hawaiian-Style Pineapple Chicken 59

99. Chicken Sausage with Eggs and Vegetables 59

100. Spicy Ground Chicken Omelet 60

101. Chicken Sausage and Roasted Garlic Frittata 60

102. Easy Nacho Chicken Burgers 61

103. Mozzarella and Chicken Rolls 61

104. Chicken Thighs with Mustard-Rosemary Sauce.... 62

105. Amazing Sage and Parmesan Chicken 62

106. Restaurant-Style Roasted
     Drumsticks with Potatoes 63

107. Berbere Chicken Drumsticks with Cauliflower 63

52. Chicken Wings in Piri Piri Sauce

Ready in about 1 hour 30 minutes
Servings 6

Recipes with chicken wings are endless. This recipe calls for piri piri that is also called African bird's eye chili. If you want to make this sauce less spicy and hot, just deseed and devein the peppers and simply reduce the number of those that are chili.

Per serving: 381 Calories; 17.6g Fat; 9.3g Carbs; 45.2g Protein; 5.5g Sugars

Ingredients

12 chicken wings
1 ½ ounces butter, melted
1 teaspoon onion powder
1/2 teaspoon cumin powder
1 teaspoon garlic paste

For the Sauce:
2 ounces piri piri peppers, stemmed and chopped
1 tablespoon pimiento, deveined and minced
1 garlic clove, chopped
2 tablespoons fresh lemon juice
1/3 teaspoon sea salt
1/2 teaspoon tarragon
3/4 teaspoon brown sugar

Directions

- Steam the chicken wings using a steamer basket that is placed over a saucepan with boiling water; reduce the heat.
- Now, steam the wings for 10 minutes over a moderate heat. Toss the wings with butter, onion powder, cumin powder, and garlic paste.
- Let the chicken wings cool to room temperature. Then, refrigerate them for 45 to 50 minutes.
- Roast in the preheated Air Fryer at 330 degrees F for 25 to 30 minutes; make sure to flip them halfway through.
- While the chicken wings are cooking, prepare the sauce by mixing all of the sauce ingredients in a food processor. Toss the wings with prepared Piri Piri Sauce and serve.

53. Spring Chicken and Ricotta Wraps

Ready in about 20 minutes
Servings 12

Say YES to your favorite fried food! These guilt-free wraps have a little amount of fat but they are still crispy and tasty like those that have been fried in oil.

Per serving: 468 Calories; 4.6g Fat; 80.4g Carbs; 23.4g Protein; 1.2g Sugars

Ingredients

2 large-sized chicken breasts, cooked and shredded
1/3 teaspoon sea salt
1/4 teaspoon ground black pepper, or more to taste
2 spring onions, chopped
1/4 cup soy sauce
1 tablespoon molasses
1 tablespoon rice vinegar
10 ounces Ricotta cheese
1 teaspoon grated fresh ginger
50 wonton wrappers

Directions

- Combine all of the above ingredients, except the wonton wrappers, in a mixing dish.
- Lay out the wrappers on a clean surface. Brush them with a nonstick cooking spray. Spread the wonton wrappers with the prepared filling.
- Fold the outside corners to the center over the filling and roll up every wonton wrapper tightly; you can moisten the edges with a little water.
- Set the Air Fryer to cook at 375 degrees F. Air-fry the rolls for 5 minutes, working in batches. Serve with a dipping sauce of your choice. Bon appétit!

54. Perfect Chicken Sausage with Mustard-Honey Sauce

Ready in about 20 minutes
Servings 4

Air-frying is one of the best and easiest ways to cook the perfect sausages. Meanwhile, just whip up the mustard-honey sauce in less than 5 minutes and enjoy!

Per serving: 266 Calories; 8.7g Fat; 12.6g Carbs; 33.4g Protein; 9.6g Sugars

Ingredients

4 chicken sausages
2 tablespoons honey
1/4 cup mayonnaise
2 tablespoons Dijon mustard
1 tablespoon balsamic vinegar
1/2 teaspoon dried rosemary

Directions

- Arrange the sausages on the grill pan and transfer it to the preheated Air Fryer.
- Grill the sausages at 350 degrees F for approximately 13 minutes. Turn them halfway through cooking.
- Meanwhile, prepare the sauce by mixing the remaining ingredients with a wire whisk. Serve the warm sausages with chilled mustard-honey sauce. Enjoy!

55. Gourmet Chicken Omelet

Ready in about 15 minutes
Servings 2

This recipe calls for hot sauce but you can omit this ingredient. You can add some vegetables as well – finely chopped peppers and grated zucchini are the sensible choice because the cooking time is the same as for the scallions.

Per serving: 246 Calories; 13.0g Fat; 3.5g Carbs; 28.1g Protein; 1.3g Sugars

Ingredients

4 eggs, whisked
4 ounces ground chicken
1/2 cup scallions, finely chopped
2 cloves garlic, finely minced
1/2 teaspoon salt
1/2 teaspoon ground black pepper
1/2 teaspoon paprika
1 teaspoon dried thyme
A dash of hot sauce

Directions

- Thoroughly combine all the ingredients in a mixing dish. Now, scrape the egg mixture into two oven safe ramekins that are previously greased with a thin layer of the vegetable oil.
- Set your machine to cook at 350 degrees F; air-fry for 13 minutes or until thoroughly cooked. Serve immediately.

56. Saucy Tarragon Chicken

Ready in about 40 minutes
Servings 4

You can prepare this saucy chicken for a family lunch or for an elegant supper. This is a protein-packed meal so you can serve it as a muscle-building dinner.

Per serving: 221 Calories; 6.0g Fat; 4.0g Carbs; 35.9g Protein; 2.2g Sugars

Ingredients

2 cups of roasted vegetable broth
2 chicken breasts, cut into halves
3/4 teaspoon fine sea salt
1/4 teaspoon mixed peppercorns, freshly cracked
1 teaspoon cumin powder
1 ½ teaspoons sesame oil
1 ½ tablespoons Worcester sauce
1/2 cup of spring onions, chopped
1 Serrano pepper, deveined and chopped
1 bell pepper, deveined and chopped
1 tablespoon tamari sauce
1/2 chopped fresh tarragon

Directions

- Place the vegetable broth and chicken breasts in a deep saucepan; cook for 10 minutes; reduce the temperature and let it simmer for additional 10 minutes.
- After that, allow the chicken to cool slightly; shred the chicken using a stand mixer or two forks.
- Toss the shredded chicken with the salt, cracked peppercorns, cumin, sesame oil and the Worcester sauce; air-fry them at 380 degrees F for 18 minutes; check for doneness.
- Meanwhile, in a non-stick skillet, cook the remaining ingredients over a moderate flame. Cook until the onions and peppers are tender and fragrant.
- Remove the skillet from the heat, add the shredded chicken and toss to combine. Serve right away!

57. Pizza-Stuffed Chicken Breast

Ready in about 20 minutes
Servings 4

It tastes like a pizza without the guilt of having carbs! If this sounds appealing to you, try this irresistible combination of tender chicken fillets, cheese and pepperoni!

Per serving: 561 Calories; 38.3g Fat; 2.1g Carbs; 49.3g Protein; 0.6g Sugars

Ingredients

4 small-sized chicken breasts, boneless and skinless
1/4 cup pizza sauce
1/2 cup Colby cheese, shredded
16 slices pepperoni
Salt and pepper, to savor
1 ½ tablespoons olive oil
1 ½ tablespoons dried oregano

Directions

- Carefully flatten out the chicken breast using a rolling pin.
- Divide the ingredients among four chicken fillets. Roll the chicken fillets with the stuffing and seal them using a small skewer or two toothpicks.
- Roast in the preheated Air Fryer grill pan for 13 to 15 minutes at 370 degrees F. Bon appétit!

58. Mustard and Turmeric Chicken Thighs

Ready in about 20 minutes
Servings 6

This chicken recipe is perfect for any occasion. To serve, drizzle warm fried thighs with remaining marinade for more piquant flavor. Yummy!

Per serving: 402 Calories; 16.9g Fat; 13.4g Carbs; 46.1g Protein; 1.0g Sugars

Ingredients

1 large-sized egg, well whisked
2 tablespoons whole-grain Dijon mustard
1/4 cup of mayonnaise
1/4 cup of chili sauce
1/2 teaspoon brown sugar
1 teaspoon fine sea salt
1/2 teaspoon ground black pepper, or more to taste
1/2 teaspoon turmeric powder
10 chicken thighs
2 cups crushed saltines

Directions

- Firstly, in a large-sized mixing bowl, thoroughly combine the egg, mustard, mayonnaise, chili sauce, brown sugar, salt, pepper, and turmeric.
- Add the chicken thighs to the mixing bowl; cover with foil and let them marinate for at least 5 hours or overnight in your fridge.
- After that, set your Air Fryer to cook at 360 degrees F. Remove the chicken from the marinade.
- Put the crushed saltines into a shallow dish. Roll the marinated chicken over the crumbs.
- Set the timer for 15 minutes and cook until the thighs are cooked through. Serve with remaining marinade. Bon appétit!

59. Tender Chicken in Wine Sauce

Ready in about 30 minutes
Servings 4

Inspired by white cooking wine, you can come up with this recipe that is simply scrumptious! This is a great idea for your next dinner party.

Per serving: 367 Calories; 4.0g Fat; 40.1g Carbs; 39.0g Protein; 19.1g Sugars

Ingredients

2 chicken breasts, cut into bite-sized chunks
1/3 cup cornstarch
1/3 cup flour
1 cup scallions, chopped
1 parsnip, chopped
1 carrot, thinly sliced

For the Sauce:
1/4 cup of honey
1/4 cup of dry white wine
1/4 cup of soy sauce
1/3 cup of chicken broth

Directions

- Start by preheating your Air Fryer to 365 degrees F. Toss the chicken chunks with the corn starch and flour, covering well.
- Air-fry the chicken for 20 minutes in the preheated cooker. Pause the Air Fryer and place the vegetables in; cook for a further 5 to 7 minutes.
- Meanwhile, in a sauté pan, whisk the sauce and the ingredients over a moderate flame; then, turn the heat to medium-low and simmer for 2 to 3 minutes. Serve the chicken with the warm sauce and enjoy!

60. Indian-Style Chicken Legs

Ready in about 1 hour 15 minutes
Servings 3

Make sure to get a high-quality garam masala for this recipe. This Ayurvedic spice mix does wonders for your health (e.g. it controls your cholesterol levels, protects your teeth, fights against free radicals, etc.)

Per serving: 359 Calories; 8.6g Fat; 29.7g Carbs; 40.5g Protein; 24.6g Sugars

Ingredients

1 tablespoon water
1 tablespoon cornstarch
1/4 cup soy sauce
1/4 cup honey
1/4 cup tomato puree
1 teaspoon garlic paste
1/2 teaspoon fresh ginger, grated
3 chicken legs
1 tablespoon peanut oil
1 teaspoon fresh lemon juice
1 teaspoon garam masala
Sea salt and ground black pepper, to savor

Directions

- To make the marinade, preheat a sauté pan over a low flame; then, simmer the first seven ingredients until the sauce is reduced to half.
- Transfer the marinade into a baking dish; add the chicken legs, followed by the remaining ingredients; let them marinate for at least 30 minutes. Now, set your Air Fryer to cook at 390 degrees F.
- Cook in the preheated Air Fryer for 25 minutes. Then, flip the chicken legs halfway through cooking and cook for another 20 minutes, Taste, fix the seasonings and serve immediately over naan!

61. Buttermilk Fried Chicken Tenders

Ready in about 1 hour 15 minutes
Servings 4

This is a child-friendly recipe but adults will enjoy it as well. These heavenly delicious chicken tenders go well with roasted sweet potato wedges. Lovely!

Per serving: 386 Calories; 11.7g Fat; 32.5g Carbs; 35.2g Protein; 2.5g Sugars

Ingredients

3/4 cup of buttermilk
1 pound chicken tenders
1 ½ cups all-purpose flour
Salt, to your liking
1/2 teaspoon pink peppercorns, freshly cracked
1 teaspoon shallot powder
1/2 teaspoon cumin powder
1 ½ teaspoon smoked cayenne pepper
1 tablespoon sesame oil

Directions

- Place the buttermilk and chicken tenders in the mixing dish; gently stir to coat and let it soak for 1 hour.
- Then, mix the flour with all seasonings. Coat the soaked chicken tenders with the flour mixture; now, dip them into the buttermilk. Finally, dredge them in the flour.
- Brush the prepared chicken tenders with sesame oil and lower them onto the bottom of a cooking basket.
- Air-fry for 15 minutes at 365 degrees F; make sure to shake them once or twice. Bon appétit!

62. Penne with Chicken Sausage Meatballs

Ready in about 20 minutes
Servings 4

If you probably already know, ground chicken may be healthier than ground pork or beef. However, this recipe doesn't call for any extra fat and it is a proof that you don't need it for amazing flavor!

Per serving: 384 Calories; 5.3g Fat; 60.2g Carbs; 22.5g Protein; 0.6g Sugars

Ingredients

1 cup chicken meat, ground
1 sweet red pepper, minced
1/4 cup green onions, chopped
1 green garlic, minced
4 tablespoons seasoned breadcrumbs
1/2 teaspoon cumin powder
1 tablespoon fresh coriander, minced
1/2 teaspoon sea salt
1/4 teaspoon mixed peppercorns, ground
1 package penne pasta, cooked

Directions

- Place the chicken, red pepper, green onions, and garlic into a mixing bowl; mix to combine well.
- Now, add seasoned breadcrumbs, followed by all seasonings; mix again until everything is well incorporated.
- Next, shape into small balls (e.g. the size of a golf ball); cook them in the preheated Air Fryer at 350 degrees F for 15 minutes; shaking once or twice to ensure evenness of cooking. Serve over cooked penne pasta.

63. Cajun Chicken Wings with Cabbage-Potato Cakes

Ready in about 40 minutes
Servings 4

If you like crispier skin, cook these wings for 30 minutes. You can also marinate them for a couple of hours for better flavor.

Per serving: 306 Calories; 12.8g Fat; 14.5g Carbs; 32.2g Protein; 1.3g Sugars

Ingredients

4 large-sized chicken wings
1 teaspoon Cajun seasoning
1 teaspoon maple syrup
3/4 teaspoon sea salt flakes
1/4 teaspoon red pepper flakes, crushed
1 teaspoon onion powder
1 teaspoon porcini powder
1/2 teaspoon celery seeds
1 small-seized head of cabbage, shredded
1 cup mashed potatoes
1 small-sized brown onion, coarsely grated
1 teaspoon garlic puree
1 medium-sized whole egg, well whisked
1/2 teaspoon table salt
1/2 teaspoon ground black pepper
1 ½ tablespoons all-purpose flour
3/4 teaspoon baking powder
1 heaping tablespoon cilantro
1 tablespoon sesame oil

Directions

- Start by preheating your Air Fryer to 390 degrees F. Dry the chicken wings. Now, prepare the rub by mixing Cajun seasoning, maple syrup, sea salt flakes, red pepper, onion powder, porcini powder, and celery seeds.
- Cook for 25 to 30 minutes or until the wings are no longer pink in the middle.
- Then, mix the shredded cabbage, potato, onion, garlic puree, egg, table salt, black pepper, flour, baking powder and cilantro in a mixing bowl.
- Divide the cabbage mixture into 4 portions and create four cabbage/potato cakes. Sprinkle each cake with the sesame oil.
- Bake cabbage/potato cakes for 10 minutes, flipping them once and working in batches. Finally, serve with the chicken wings and enjoy!

64. Majestic Maple-Glazed Chicken

Ready in about 20 minutes + marinating time
Servings 4

Using marinated chicken is one of the easiest ways to transform a good-enough chicken recipe into an outstanding royal meal. It would be great if you could marinate the chicken overnight.

Per serving: 189 Calories; 3.1g Fat; 9.1g Carbs; 29.5g Protein; 7.6g Sugars

Ingredients

2 ½ tablespoons maple syrup
1 tablespoon tamari soy sauce
1 tablespoon oyster sauce
1 teaspoon fresh lemon juice
1 teaspoon minced fresh ginger
1 teaspoon garlic puree
Seasoned salt and freshly ground pepper, to your liking
2 chicken breasts, boneless and skinless

Directions

- To prepare the marinade, in a mixing dish, combine maple syrup, tamari sauce, oyster sauce, lemon juice, fresh ginger and garlic puree.
- Now, season the chicken breasts with salt and pepper. Put the chicken breast into the bowl with the marinade and make sure to coat them well; cover with foil and place in the refrigerator for 3 hours or overnight.
- Discard the marinade. Air-fry marinated chicken breast for 15 minutes at 365 degrees F; turn them once or twice.
- Meanwhile, add the remaining marinade to a pan that is preheated over a moderate flame; let it simmer until reduced by half; it will take 3 to 5 minutes. Serve the chicken with the sauce. Bon appétit!

65. Saucy Provençal Chicken with Bacon

Ready in about 25 minutes
Servings 4

This chicken drumstick recipe could not be simpler - just place the ingredients into your magical Air Fryer and you will have a great protein meal! In terms of the spice mix called "Herbs de Provence", it typically contains marjoram, rosemary, thyme, savory, oregano and other herbs that grow mainly in southern France.

Per serving: 296 Calories; 13.7g Fat; 6.9g Carbs; 34.7g Protein; 2.9g Sugars

Ingredients

4 medium-sized skin-on chicken drumsticks
1 ½ teaspoons herbs de Provence
Salt and pepper, to your liking
1 tablespoon rice vinegar
2 tablespoons olive oil
2 garlic cloves, crushed
12 ounces crushed canned tomatoes
1 small-size leek, thinly sliced
2 slices smoked bacon, chopped

Directions

- Sprinkle the chicken drumsticks with herbs de Provence, salt and pepper; then, drizzle them with rice vinegar and olive oil. Cook in the baking pan at 360 degrees F for 8 to 10 minutes.
- Pause the Air Fryer; stir in the remaining ingredients and continue to cook for 15 minutes longer; make sure to check them periodically. Serve over rice garnished with lemon wedges. Bon appétit!

66. Melt-In-Your-Mouth Marjoram Chicken

Ready in about 1 hour
Servings 2

Nice and easy low-carb meal for two. Therefore, if you love chicken, this recipe will win your heart right now! Serve with a crisp Sauvignon Blanc.

Per serving: 328 Calories; 16.1g Fat; 0.0g Carbs; 43.6g Protein; 0.0 g Sugars

Ingredients

2 small-sized chicken breasts, skinless and boneless
2 tablespoons butter
1 teaspoon sea salt
1/2 teaspoon red pepper flakes, crushed
2 teaspoons marjoram
1/4 teaspoon lemon pepper

Directions

- Add all of the above ingredients to a mixing dish; let it marinate for 30 minutes to 1 hour.
- Then, set your Air Fryer to cook at 390 degrees. Cook for 20 minutes, turning halfway through cooking time.
- Check for doneness using an instant-read thermometer. Serve over jasmine rice. Bon appétit!

67. Chicken with Cremini Mushroom Sauce

Ready in about 25 minutes
Servings 6

For a delicious and saucy chicken, try this Air fryer recipe. Plus, this chicken freezes and reheats well so you can enjoy a batch cooking!

Per serving: 403 Calories; 17.2g Fat; 31g Carbs; 34.3g Protein; 1g Sugars

Ingredients

1/2 pound Cremini mushrooms, thinly sliced
1/2 cup chicken stock
1/3 cup rice wine
1/3 teaspoon Chinese 5 spice powder
3 medium-sized chicken breasts, sliced
1/2 teaspoon ground ginger
1 ½ tablespoons flour
1 teaspoon smoked paprika
1 ½ tablespoons peanut oil
1/3 teaspoon dried dill weed
3 cloves garlic, minced
1 teaspoon kosher salt
1 teaspoon red pepper flakes, crushed

Directions

- Rub the chicken with all the seasonings.
- Lower the seasoned chicken onto the baking dish. Air-fry for 18 minutes at 365 degrees F.
- Then, pause the machine; add the Cremini mushrooms, followed by the other ingredients. Air-fry an additional 8 to 10 minutes. Eat warm. Bon appétit!

68. Chicken and Asiago Crescent Squares

Ready in about 10 minutes
Servings 6

A crescent roll loaded with all the fabulous flavors of a buttery, cheesy chicken breast! It's over the top delicious!

Per serving: 311 Calories; 21.6g Fat; 3.7g Carbs; 25.9g Protein; 0.2g Sugars

Ingredients

1 pound chicken breasts, shredded
6 large-sized eggs, well beaten
6 slices Asiago cheese
1/2 can crescent roll, refrigerated
1 ½ teaspoon hot paprika
½ tablespoon fresh parsley, minced
1 teaspoon kosher salt
½ teaspoon ground black pepper, or more to taste

Directions

- Begin by unrolling the crescent rolls and split the dough into 4 rectangles. Now, fold up the edges of each rectangle.
- Lower 1 rectangle onto the bottom of the air fryer cooking basket; now, crack 1 egg into it. Sprinkle with the seasonings.
- Add 1/3 of the shredded chicken meat; top with 1 slice of Asiago cheese. Repeat with the other crescent rolls.
- Air-fry for 8 minutes at 325 degrees F, or until all sides are golden brown. Bon appétit!

69. The Best Orange and Shoyu Wings

Ready in about 50 minutes
Servings 4

Shoyu is a Japanese soy sauce. It is a great alternative for table salt. Did you know that Shoyu is high in minerals and antioxidants?

Per serving: 78 Calories; 2.6g Fat; 1.4g Carbs; 12.9g Protein; 0.8g Sugars

Ingredients

½ teaspoon smoked paprika
2 teaspoons garlic powder
1/3 teaspoon ground black pepper, preferably freshly ground
½ pound chicken wings
1 ½ tablespoons plain flour
1 teaspoon salt

For the Glaze:
1/3 cup orange juice
1/2 teaspoon Shoyu sauce
2 cloves garlic, minced
1/2 tablespoon brown sugar
1/3 cup hoisin sauce
1 ½ teaspoons olive oil
1/2 teaspoon fresh ginger root, finely grated

Directions

- Toss the chicken wings with the flour, garlic powder, paprika, salt, and ground black pepper in a baking dish.
- Air-fry the chicken wings at 365 degrees F for 24 minutes.
- In the meantime, prepare the glaze; heat the oil in a saucepan and sauté the garlic until just tender.
- Throw in the remaining ingredients; simmer for about 30 minutes or until the sauce has thickened. Pour the glaze over the prepared chicken wings; toss to coat. Bon appétit!

70. Baked Za'atar Eggs with Chicken

Ready in about 15 minutes
Servings 2

You can make Za'atar in your own kitchen. This spice blend includes sesame seeds, salt, ground black pepper, oregano, sumac, and ground cumin.

Per serving: 440 Calories; 28.5g Fat; 8.7g Carbs; 36.9g Protein; 5.2g Sugars

Ingredients

1/3 cup milk
1 1/2 Roma tomato, chopped
1/3 cup Provolone cheese, grated
1 teaspoon freshly cracked pink peppercorns
3 eggs
1 teaspoon Za'atar
½ chicken breast, cooked
1 teaspoon fine sea salt
1 teaspoon freshly cracked pink peppercorns

Directions

- Preheat your air fryer to cook at 365 degrees F. In a medium-sized mixing dish, whisk the eggs together with the milk, Za'atar, sea salt, and cracked pink peppercorns.
- Spritz the ramekins with cooking oil; divide the prepared egg mixture among the greased ramekins.
- Shred the chicken with two forks or a stand mixer. Add the shredded chicken to the ramekins, followed by the tomato and the cheese.
- To finish, air-fry for 18 minutes or until it is done. Bon appétit!

71. Chicken in Yogurt-Mustard Sauce

Ready in about 1 hours 10 minutes
Servings 6

Here's a fantastic way to get the taste of saucy chicken without grease and extra calories! The recipe calls for Greek-style yogurt; feel free to use a low-fat sour cream.

Per serving: 283 Calories; 15.8g Fat; 2.8g Carbs; 31g Protein; 0.7g Sugars

Ingredients

3 chicken breasts, skinless, boneless and cubed
1/3 cup Greek-style yogurt
3 cloves garlic, minced
1 teaspoon paprika
1/3 cup reduced-fat thickened cooking cream
1 teaspoon turmeric powder
2 ½ tablespoons yellow mustard
1 tablespoon melted butter
1/3 teaspoon freshly cracked mixed peppercorns
1 teaspoon fine sea salt

Directions

- Toss the cubes of the chicken breasts with the turmeric, paprika, sea salt, and cracked pepper.
- Add the rest of the above ingredients and let it stand for about 1 hour.
- Discard the sauce and air-fry the chicken cubes for 10 minutes at 365 degrees F. Serve with the reserved yogurt/mustard sauce and enjoy!

72. Brioche with Chicken and Caciocavallo

Ready in about 10 minutes
Servings 6

Turn a leftover chicken into an amazing dinner by using a highly enriched bread like brioche and a flavorful gourmet cheese like Caciocavallo.

Per serving: 430 Calories; 19g Fat; 22.4g Carbs; 42.9g Protein; 3g Sugars

Ingredients

6 brioche rolls
3 tablespoons sesame oil
2 teaspoons dried thyme
1/3 cup Caciocavallo, grated
1 cup leftover chicken, shredded
3 eggs
1 teaspoon kosher salt
1 teaspoon freshly cracked black pepper, or more to taste
1/3 teaspoon gremolata

Directions

- Firstly, slice off the top of each brioche; then, scoop out the insides.
- Brush each brioche with sesame oil. Add the remaining ingredients in the order listed above.
- Place the prepared brioche onto the bottom of the cooking basket. Bake for 7 minutes at 345 degrees F. Bon appétit!

73. Cheese and Chive Stuffed Chicken Rolls

Ready in about 20 minutes
Servings 6

Here's an economical but sophisticated recipe. It calls for leftover tortilla chips and chicken breasts (find family packs in your local grocery store). Additionally, you can save on cheese by buying in bulk.

Per serving: 311 Calories; 18.3g Fat; 1.3g Carbs; 33.4g Protein; 0.3 g Sugars

Ingredients

2 eggs, well-whisked
Tortilla chips, crushed
1 1/2 tablespoons extra-virgin olive oil
1 ½ tablespoons fresh chives, chopped
3 chicken breasts, halved lengthwise
1 ½ cup soft cheese
2 teaspoons sweet paprika
1/2 teaspoon whole grain mustard
1/2 teaspoon cumin powder
1/3 teaspoon fine sea salt
1/3 cup fresh cilantro, chopped
1/3 teaspoon freshly ground black pepper, or more to taste

Directions

- Flatten out each piece of the chicken breast using a rolling pin. Then, grab three mixing dishes.
- In the first one, combine the soft cheese with the cilantro, fresh chives, cumin, and mustard.
- In another mixing dish, whisk the eggs together with the sweet paprika. In the third dish, combine the salt, black pepper, and crushed tortilla chips.
- Spread the cheese mixture over each piece of chicken. Repeat with the remaining pieces of the chicken breasts; now, roll them up.
- Coat each chicken roll with the whisked egg; dredge each chicken roll into the tortilla chips mixture. Lower the rolls onto the air fryer cooking basket. Drizzle extra-virgin olive oil over all rolls.
- Air fry at 345 degrees F for 28 minutes, working in batches. Serve warm, garnished with sour cream if desired.

74. Chicken Drumsticks with Ketchup-Lemon Sauce

Ready in about 20 minutes +
marinating time
Servings 6

Ketchup-lemon sauce is the perfect sweet-tart complement to these appetizing chicken drumsticks. Serve with sautéed zucchini as a side dish!

Per serving: 274 Calories; 12g Fat; 17.3g Carbs; 23.3g Protein; 16.2g Sugars

Ingredients

3 tablespoons lemon juice
1 cup tomato ketchup
1 ½ tablespoons fresh rosemary, chopped
6 skin-on chicken drumsticks, boneless
1/2 teaspoon ground black pepper
2 teaspoons lemon zest, grated
1/3 cup honey
3 cloves garlic, minced

Directions

- Dump the chicken drumsticks into a mixing dish. Now, add the other items and give it a good stir; let it marinate overnight in your refrigerator.
- Discard the marinade; roast the chicken legs in your air fryer at 375 degrees F for 22 minutes, turning once.
- Now, add the marinade and cook an additional 6 minutes or until everything is warmed through.

75. Creamed Cajun Chicken

Ready in about 10 minutes
Servings 6

Boneless chicken pairs perfectly with a buttermilk. It gets an upgrade when breaded with a crispy Cajun seasoning and cornmeal crust.

Per serving: 400 Calories; 10.2g Fat; 48.2g Carbs; 27.3g Protein; 3.5g Sugars

Ingredients

3 green onions, thinly sliced
½ tablespoon Cajun seasoning
1 ½ cup buttermilk
2 large-sized chicken breasts, cut into strips
1/2 teaspoon garlic powder
1 teaspoon salt
1 cup cornmeal mix
1 teaspoon shallot powder
1 ½ cup flour
1 teaspoon ground black pepper, or to taste

Directions

- Prepare three mixing bowls. Combine 1/2 cup of the plain flour together with the cornmeal and Cajun seasoning in your bowl. In another bowl, place the buttermilk.
- Pour the remaining 1 cup of flour into the third bowl.
- Sprinkle the chicken strips with all the seasonings. Then, dip each chicken strip in the 1 cup of flour, then in the buttermilk; finally, dredge them in the cornmeal mixture.
- Cook the chicken strips in the air fryer baking pan for 16 minutes at 365 degrees F. Serve garnished with green onions. Bon appétit!

76. Chive, Feta and Chicken Frittata

Ready in about 10 minutes
Servings 4

This frittata is easy to prepare and requires just one baking dish that fits your Air fryer. You can add a few dashes of chili powder to kick things up a notch!

Per serving: 176 Calories; 7.7g Fat; 2.4g Carbs; 22.8g Protein; 1.5g Sugars

Ingredients

1/3 cup Feta cheese, crumbled
1 teaspoon dried rosemary
½ teaspoon brown sugar
2 tablespoons fish sauce
1 ½ cup cooked chicken breasts, boneless and shredded
1/2 teaspoon coriander sprig, finely chopped
3 medium-sized whisked eggs
1/3 teaspoon ground white pepper
1 cup fresh chives, chopped
1/2 teaspoon garlic paste
Fine sea salt, to taste
Nonstick cooking spray

Directions

- Grab a baking dish that fit in your air fryer.
- Lightly coat the inside of the baking dish with a non-stick cooking spray of choice. Stir in all ingredients, minus Feta cheese. Stir to combine well.
- Set your machine to cook at 335 degrees for 8 minutes; check for doneness. Scatter crumbled Feta over the top and eat immediately!

77. Grilled Chicken Tikka Masala

Ready in about 35 minutes +
marinating time
Servings 4

Warm up with this surprisingly simple yet delicious dish. This aromatic, grilled chicken might become your new staple!

Per serving: 319 Calories; 20.1g Fat; 1.9g Carbs; 30.5g Protein; 0.1g Sugars

Ingredients

1 teaspoon Tikka Masala
1 teaspoon fine sea salt
2 heaping teaspoons whole grain mustard
2 teaspoons coriander, ground
2 tablespoon olive oil
2 large-sized chicken breasts, skinless and halved lengthwise
2 teaspoons onion powder
1 ½ tablespoons cider vinegar
Basmati rice, steamed
1/3 teaspoon red pepper flakes, crushed

Directions

- Preheat the air fryer to 335 degrees for 4 minutes.
- Toss your chicken together with the other ingredients, minus basmati rice. Let it stand at least 3 hours.
- Cook for 25 minutes in your air fryer; check for doneness because the time depending on the size of the piece of chicken.
- Serve immediately over warm basmati rice. Enjoy!

78. Award Winning Breaded Chicken

Ready in about 10 minutes +
marinating time
Servings 4

Have you ever tried an oven "fried" breaded chicken? If so, you will be pleasantly surprised that you can get an even better taste in your Air fryer. Amazing!

Per serving: 262 Calories; 14.9g Fat; 2.7g Carbs; 27.5g Protein; 0.3g Sugars

Ingredients

For the Marinade:
1 1/2 teaspoons olive oil
1 teaspoon red pepper flakes, crushed
1/3 teaspoon chicken bouillon granules
1/3 teaspoon shallot powder
1 1/2 tablespoons tamari soy sauce
1/3 teaspoon cumin powder
1 ½ tablespoons mayo
1 teaspoon kosher salt

For the chicken:
2 beaten eggs
Breadcrumbs
1 ½ chicken breasts, boneless and skinless
1 ½ tablespoons plain flour

Directions

- Butterfly the chicken breasts, and then, marinate them for at least 55 minutes.
- Coat the chicken with plain flour; then, coat with the beaten eggs; finally, roll them in the breadcrumbs.
- Lightly grease the cooking basket. Air-fry the breaded chicken at 345 degrees F for 12 minutes, flipping them halfway.

79. Cheese and Garlic Stuffed Chicken Breasts

Ready in about 20 minutes
Servings 2

Stuffed chicken breasts are one of the family's favorite main courses! Anyway, chicken is a staple in many kitchens worldwide. If you don't have Cottage cheese on hand, just use Ricotta.

Per serving: 424 Calories; 24.5g Fat; 7.5g Carbs; 43.4g Protein; 5.3g Sugars

Ingredients

1/2 cup Cottage cheese
2 eggs, beaten
2 medium-sized chicken breasts, halved
2 tablespoons fresh coriander, chopped
1teaspoon fine sea salt
Seasoned breadcrumbs
1/3teaspoon freshly ground black pepper, to savor
3 cloves garlic, finely minced

Directions

- Firstly, flatten out the chicken breast using a meat tenderizer.
- In a medium-sized mixing dish, combine the Cottage cheese with the garlic, coriander, salt, and black pepper.
- Spread 1/3 of the mixture over the first chicken breast. Repeat with the remaining ingredients. Roll the chicken around the filling; make sure to secure with toothpicks.
- Now, whisk the egg in a shallow bowl. In another shallow bowl, combine the salt, ground black pepper, and seasoned breadcrumbs.
- Coat the chicken breasts with the whisked egg; now, roll them in the breadcrumbs.
- Cook in the air fryer cooking basket at 365 degrees F for 22 minutes. Serve immediately.

80. Dinner Avocado Chicken Sliders

Ready in about 10 minutes
Servings 4

Ground chicken has never tasted so good! Vitamin-packed avocado gives an amazing taste and adds a nutritional value to these sliders.

Per serving: 321 Calories; 18.7g Fat; 15.8g Carbs; 23.5g Protein; 1.2g Sugars

Ingredients

½ pounds ground chicken meat
4 burger buns
1/2 cup Romaine lettuce, loosely packed
½ teaspoon dried parsley flakes
1/3 teaspoon mustard seeds
1 teaspoon onion powder
1 ripe fresh avocado, mashed
1 teaspoon garlic powder
1 ½ tablespoon extra-virgin olive oil
1 cloves garlic, minced
Nonstick cooking spray
Salt and cracked black pepper (peppercorns), to taste

Directions

- Firstly, spritz an air fryer cooking basket with a non-stick cooking spray.
- Mix ground chicken meat, mustard seeds, garlic powder, onion powder, parsley, salt, and black pepper until everything is thoroughly combined. Make sure not to overwork the meat to avoid tough chicken burgers.
- Shape the meat mixture into patties and roll them in breadcrumbs; transfer your burgers to the prepared cooking basket. Brush the patties with the cooking spray.
- Air-fry at 355 F for 9 minutes, working in batches. Slice burger buns into halves. In the meantime, combine olive oil with mashed avocado and pressed garlic.
- To finish, lay Romaine lettuce and avocado spread on bun bottoms; now, add burgers and bun tops. Bon appétit!

81. Peanut Butter and Chicken Bites

Ready in about 10 minutes
Servings 8

Leftover chicken gets a lift with mellowly soft cheese and flavorful peanut butter. Nutty, tasty and yummy!

Per serving: 150 Calories; 9.7g Fat; 2.1g Carbs; 12.9g Protein; 1.6g Sugars

Ingredients

1 ½ tablespoons soy sauce
1/2 teaspoon smoked cayenne pepper
8 ounces soft cheese
1 1/2 tablespoons peanut butter
1/3 leftover chicken
1 teaspoon sea salt
32 wonton wrappers
1/3 teaspoon freshly cracked mixed peppercorns
1/2 tablespoon pear cider vinegar

Directions

- Combine all of the above ingredients, minus the wonton wrappers, in a mixing dish.
- Lay out the wrappers on a clean surface. Now, spread the wonton wrappers with the prepared chicken filling.
- Fold the outside corners to the center over the filling; after that, roll up the wrappers tightly; you can moisten the edges with a little water.
- Set the air fryer to cook at 360 degrees F. Air fry the rolls for 6 minutes, working in batches. Serve with marinara sauce. Bon appétit!

82. Tangy Paprika Chicken

Ready in about 30 minutes
Servings 4

Enrich this weeknight staple by tossing it in paprika, mustard powder and ground cumin. You can discard the skin and fat or simply use the chicken fillets.

Per serving: 312 Calories; 17.6g Fat; 2.6g Carbs; 30.4g Protein; 1.2g Sugars

Ingredients

1 ½ tablespoons freshly squeezed lemon juice
2 small-sized chicken breasts, boneless
1/2 teaspoon ground cumin
1 teaspoon dry mustard powder
1 teaspoon paprika
2 teaspoons cup pear cider vinegar
1 tablespoon olive oil
2 garlic cloves, minced
Kosher salt and freshly ground mixed peppercorns, to savor

Directions

- Warm the olive oil in a nonstick pan over a moderate flame. Sauté the garlic for just 1 minutes.
- Remove your pan from the heat; add cider vinegar, lemon juice, paprika, cumin, mustard powder, kosher salt, and black pepper. Pour this paprika sauce into a baking dish.
- Pat the chicken breasts dry; transfer them to the pre-pared sauce. Bake in the preheated air fryer for about 28 minutes at 335 degrees F; check for doneness using a thermometer or a fork.
- Allow to rest for 8 to 9 minutes before slicing and serving. Serve with dressing.

83. Super-Easy Chicken with Tomato Sauce

Ready in about 20 minutes + marinating time
Servings 4

A tangy, homemade tomato sauce pairs perfectly with chicken breast in this 5-star recipe! We added bucatini in this recipe, but you can use your favorite spaghetti.

Per serving: 377 Calories; 24.8g Fat; 6.5g Carbs; 31.6g Protein; 4.1g Sugars

Ingredients

1 tablespoon balsamic vinegar
½ teaspoon red pepper flakes, crushed
1 fresh garlic, roughly chopped
2 ½ large-sized chicken breasts, cut into halves
1/3 handful fresh cilantro, roughly chopped
2 tablespoons olive oil
4 Roma tomatoes, diced
1 ½ tablespoons butter
1/3 handful fresh basil, loosely packed, sniped
1 teaspoon kosher salt
2 cloves garlic, minced
Cooked bucatini, to serve

Directions

- Place the first seven ingredients in a medium-sized bowl; let it marinate for a couple of hours.
- Preheat the air fryer to 325 degrees F. Air-fry your chicken for 32 minutes and serve warm.
- In the meantime, prepare the tomato sauce by pre-heating a deep saucepan. Simmer the tomatoes until you make a chunky mixture. Throw in the garlic, basil, and butter; give it a good stir.
- Serve the cooked chicken breasts with the tomato sauce and the cooked bucatini. Bon appétit!

84. Mouthwatering Chicken Cheese Burgers

Ready in about 10 minutes
Servings 8

These chicken burgers deserve a place of honor at your table. Forget on classic burgers, chicken is the new beef!

Per serving: 257 Calories; 16.6g Fat; 2.4g Carbs; 23.9g Protein; 0.2g Sugars

Ingredients

8 slices Pimiento Cheese
1/2 teaspoon dried marjoram
1 teaspoon porcini powder
2 teaspoons cumin powder
1 ½ pound chicken meat, ground
3 cloves garlic, minced
A few dashes of hot sauce
2 teaspoons onion powder
½ tablespoon Worcestershire sauce
1/2 teaspoon dried parsley flakes
Thinly sliced red onion, to serve
1 teaspoon kosher salt
1 teaspoon freshly cracked black pepper

Directions

- Generously grease an air fryer cooking basket with a thin layer of vegetable oil.
- In a mixing dish, combine all of the above items, minus cheese and red onion.
- Shape into eight patties and coat them with your favorite breadcrumbs.
- Air fry the burgers at 355 F for 19 to 10 minutes, working in batches. Place one slice of Pimiento Cheese on each burger.
- To serve, add cheeseburgers to the burger buns and garnish with red onion. Bon appétit!

85. Herbed Passila Chicken

Ready in about 25 minutes
Servings 2

The pungent taste of pasilla chili powder will enrich your chicken and surprise your taste buds. Give your dish an additional twist with a dash of red pepper flakes and finely chopped aromatics.

Per serving: 330 Calories; 7.7g Fat; 2.4g Carbs; 58g Protein; 0g Sugars

Ingredients

2 sprigs thyme, finely chopped
A pinch of Pasilla chili powder
1 ½ large-sized chicken breast, cut into halves
1 sprig rosemary, finely chopped
1 teaspoon kosher salt
3 cloves garlic, finely chopped
1 teaspoon ground black pepper
Sesame oil, for drizzling
A pinch red pepper flakes

Directions

- Preheat your air fryer to 345 degrees F.
- Toss the chicken breasts with the remaining ingredients.
- Roast for 26 minutes in the preheated air fryer. Serve with your favorite salad. Bon appétit!

86. Indian-Style Baked Eggs with Chicken

Ready in about 15 minutes
Servings 6

Eat a rich breakfast for a party dinner! If you don't have garam masala on hand, just add 2 bay leaves and a dash of the following spices: ground cumin, coriander seeds, green cardamom pods and freshly grated nutmeg. A dash of ground dried red chile is optional.

Per serving: 377 Calories; 15.2g Fat; 2.4g Carbs; 54.5g Protein; 0.6g Sugars

Ingredients

6 medium-sized eggs, beaten
1/2 teaspoon garam masala
1 cup scallions, finely chopped
3 cloves garlic, finely minced
1 1/2 cup leftover chicken, shredded
2 tablespoons sesame oil
Hot sauce, for drizzling
1 teaspoon turmeric
1 teaspoon mixed peppercorns, freshly cracked
1 teaspoon kosher salt
1/3 teaspoon smoked paprika

Directions

- Warm sesame oil in a sauté pan over a moderate flame; then, sauté the scallions together with garlic until just fragrant; it takes about 5 minutes. Now, throw in leftover chicken and stir until thoroughly warmed.
- In a medium-sized bowl or a measuring cup, thoroughly combine the eggs with all seasonings.
- Then, coat the inside of six oven safe ramekins with a nonstick cooking spray. Divide the egg/chicken mixture among your ramekins.
- Air-fry approximately 18 minutes at 355 degrees F. Drizzle with hot sauce and eat warm.

87. Dad's Yummy Chicken Frittata

Ready in about 15 minutes
Servings 2

Here's a good idea to get hooked on chicken. Your family will ask you to make this chicken-flavored recipe again and again.

Per serving: 389 Calories; 30.6g Fat; 4.7g Carbs; 24.2g Protein; 1.9g Sugars

Ingredients

3 eggs, well whisked
½ heaping tablespoon sesame seeds
½ teaspoon garlic paste
2 ½ ounces leftover chicken, skin and bones removed, chopped or shredded
1 teaspoon kosher salt
1 teaspoon cayenne pepper
1/2 cup scallion, finely chopped
1/3 teaspoon turmeric powder
1 ½ tablespoons sesame oil
A pinch of freshly grated nutmeg
1/3 teaspoon freshly cracked black peppercorns

Directions

- Simply combine all of the above ingredients in a baking dish that fits in your air fryer.
- Preheat the machine to 345 degrees F; now, cook for 9 to 10 minutes.
- Eat warm, garnished with a dollop of sour cream if desired, and enjoy!

88. Skinny Chicken and Carrot Meatballs

Ready in about 55 minutes
Servings 4

These old-fashioned meatballs are cheap and easy to make. They are really good to serve with your favorite homemade flavored mayo.

Per serving: 275 Calories; 18.6g Fat; 2.7g Carbs; 22.9g Protein; 1.2g Sugars

Ingredients

1/2 pound ground chicken
3 cloves garlic
1 ½ cup plain flour
1/2 cup seasoned breadcrumbs
3 medium-sized carrots
2 eggs
1/2 tablespoon honey
2 medium-sized shallots
1 teaspoon dried oregano
1/3 teaspoon ground cinnamon
1 teaspoon seasoned salt
1 teaspoon black pepper, or to taste

Directions

- In a food processor, blitz the carrots, shallots and garlic for 50 seconds; transfer the pureed vegetable mixture to a mixing bowl. Add ground chicken and mix to combine well.
- Then, add the remaining ingredients in the order listed above, minus the flour; place in your refrigerator for about 40 minutes. Roll the balls over plain flour.
- Finally, air-fry the balls at 355 degrees F approximately 18 minutes, turning occasionally. Serve with your favorite sauce for dipping.

89. Saucy Orange Marinated Chicken

Ready in about 25 minutes + marinating time
Servings 4

This recipe calls for a zesty and flavorful marinade that is incredibly easy to make. This marinade features a stone-ground mustard and fresh orange juice for a more vibrant flavor; it goes well with chicken breasts.

Per serving: 255 Calories; 13.5g Fat; 1.7g Carbs; 30.3g Protein; 0.8g Sugars

Ingredients

1/2 teaspoon stone-ground mustard
1/2 teaspoon minced fresh oregano
1/3 cup freshly squeezed orange juice
2 small-sized chicken breasts, skin-on
1 teaspoon kosher salt
1teaspoon freshly cracked mixed peppercorns

Directions

- Preheat your air fryer to 345 degrees F.
- Toss all of the above ingredients in a medium-sized mixing dish; allow it to marinate overnight.
- Cook in the preheated air fryer for 26 minutes. Bon appétit!

90. Hot Spicy Chicken Burgers

Ready in about 20 minutes
Servings 4

To save your time, you can cook some extra chicken burgers for lunch and pack the rest for dinner. It is easy to double this recipe and work in batches when you have a magical kitchen appliance like an Air fryer!

Per serving: 366 Calories; 9.6g Fat; 4.4g Carbs; 61.6g Protein; 2.3g Sugars

Ingredients

1/3 teaspoon paprika
1/3 cup scallions, peeled and chopped
3 cloves garlic, peeled and minced
1 teaspoon ground black pepper, or to taste
1/2 teaspoon fresh basil, minced
1 ½ cups chicken, minced
1 ½ tablespoons soy sauce
1/2 teaspoon grated fresh ginger
1/2 tablespoon chili sauce
3 tablespoons breadcrumbs
1 teaspoon salt

Directions

- Thoroughly combine all ingredients in a mixing dish. Then, form into 4 patties.
- Cook in the preheated air fryer for 18 minutes at 355 degrees F. Serve on sandwich buns and garnish with toppings of choice.

91. Parsley Lime Grilled Chicken

Ready in about 25 minutes
Servings 2

In this healthy chicken recipe, lime and parsley are added to produce a flavorful, zesty dish. You can add a dash of paprika to emphasize the flavors.

Per serving: 390 Calories; 20.6g Fat; 4.7g Carbs; 46.9g Protein; 0.6g Sugars

Ingredients

1 1/2 handful fresh parsley, roughly chopped
Fresh juice of 1/2 lime
1 teaspoon ground black pepper
1 1/2 large-sized chicken breasts, cut into halves
1 teaspoon kosher salt
Zest of 1/2 lime

Directions

- Preheat your air fryer to 335 degrees F.
- Toss the chicken breasts with the other ingredients and let it marinate a couple of hours.
- Roast for 26 minutes and serve warm. Bon appétit!

92. Tangy Tomato Chicken Drumsticks

Ready in about 20 minutes
Servings 6

Recipes with chicken drumsticks are endless. If you want to emphasize a smoky flavor, use liquid smoke or a dark smoky beer. Their smoky flavor pairs well with fresh, tangy tomatoes.

Per serving: 390 Calories; 15.6g Fat; 7.2g Carbs; 51.9g Protein; 2.8g Sugars

Ingredients

2 leeks, sliced
2 large-sized tomatoes, chopped
3 cloves garlic, minced
½ teaspoon dried oregano
6 chicken legs, boneless and skinless
½ teaspoon smoked cayenne pepper
2 tablespoons olive oil
A freshly ground nutmeg

Directions

- In a mixing dish, thoroughly combine all ingredients, minus the leeks. Place in the refrigerator and let it marinate overnight.
- Lay the leeks onto the bottom of an air fryer cooking basket. Top with the chicken legs.
- Roast chicken legs at 375 degrees F for 18 minutes, turning halfway through. Serve with hoisin sauce.

93. Sweet-Chili Chicken Breasts with Asiago Cheese

Ready in about 10 minutes
Servings 4

Say YES to your favorite chicken food! Air-frying is one of the best and easiest ways to cook the perfect stuffed chicken rolls. Meanwhile, just whip up your favorite salad and enjoy!

Per serving: 490 Calories; 47.6g Fat; 6.8g Carbs; 33.9g Protein; 4.5g Sugars

Ingredients

2 ounces Asiago cheese, cut into sticks
1/3 cup tomato paste
1/2 teaspoon garlic paste
2 chicken breasts, cut in half lengthwise
1/2 cup green onions, chopped
1 tablespoon sweet chili sauce
1/2 cup roasted vegetable stock
1 tablespoon sesame oil
1 teaspoon salt
2 teaspoons unsweetened cocoa
1/2 teaspoon sweet paprika, or more to taste

Directions

- Sprinkle chicken breasts with the salt and sweet paprika; drizzle with sweet chili sauce. Now, place a stick of Asiago cheese in the middle of each chicken breast.
- Then, tie the whole thing using a kitchen string; give a drizzle of sesame oil.
- Transfer the stuffed chicken to the cooking basket. Add the other ingredients in the order listed above; toss to coat the chicken.
- Afterward, cook for about 11 minutes at 395 degrees F. Serve the chicken on two serving plates, garnish with fresh or pickled salad and serve immediately. Bon appétit!

94. Butter and Cider Chicken Drumsticks

Ready in about 20 minutes
Servings 4

These guilt-free chicken legs have a little amount of fat but they are still tasty like those that have been fried in oil.

Per serving: 264 Calories; 18.6g Fat; 0.9g Carbs; 23.6g Protein; 0.3g Sugars

Ingredients

½ tablespoon brown sugar
½ tablespoon Worcestershire sauce
1 teaspoon finely grated orange zest
2 tablespoons melted butter
½ teaspoon smoked paprika
4 chicken drumsticks, rinsed and halved
1 teaspoon sea salt flakes
1 tablespoon cider vinegar
1/2 teaspoon mixed peppercorns, freshly cracked

Directions

- Firstly, pat the chicken drumsticks dry. Coat them with the melted butter on all sides. Toss the chicken drumsticks with the other ingredients.
- Transfer them to the air fryer cooking basket and roast for about 13 minutes at 345 degrees F. Bon appétit!

95. Tortilla Chip-Crusted Chicken

Ready in about 10 minutes
Servings 4

Instead of the common breading, use crushed tortilla chips to make a crunchy, super yummy chicken. If you tend to prepare a kid-friendly version of this chicken, just omit hot paprika. And don't worry, it's still really, really, tasty.

Per serving: 347 Calories; 23.6g Fat; 1.5g Carbs; 30.5g Protein; 0.5g Sugars

Ingredients

2 tablespoons melted butter
3 eggs, beaten
1 pound chicken breast, ground
1/2 cup crushed tortilla chips
1 teaspoon hot paprika
2 teaspoon sages, ground
1/3 teaspoon powdered ginger
1/2 teaspoon dried thyme
1/3 teaspoon ground black pepper, to taste
1 teaspoon kosher salt

Directions

- Mix the first six ingredients in a shallow bowl. After that, stir in the melted butter; mix to combine well.
- Whisk the two eggs and the thyme. Add the third beaten egg to a shallow bowl.
- Form the mixture into chicken nugget shapes; now, coat them with the beaten eggs; then, dredge them in the seasoned tortilla chips.
- Cook in the preheated air fryer at 405 degrees F for 8 minutes. Bon appétit!

96. Tamarind Chicken Bubble & Squeak

Ready in about 25 minutes
Servings 4

When it comes to the vegetables, use bell peppers, thinly sliced zucchini and carrots; they are the convenient choice because it will all cook at about the same rate.

Per serving: 356 Calories; 21.2g Fat; 8.5g Carbs; 20.3g Protein; 2.9g Sugars

Ingredients

3 eggs, whisked
½ teaspoon dried marjoram
1/3 cup Fontina cheese, grated
1 teaspoon sea salt
1/3 teaspoon red pepper flakes, crushed
1/2 cup leftover vegetables of choice
1/2 red onion, thinly sliced
1/2 tablespoon tamarind puree
2 cups cooked chicken, shredded or chopped
3 cloves garlic, finely minced

Directions

- Simply mix all of the above ingredients with a wide spatula.
- Scrape the mixture into a previously greased baking dish.
- Set your air fryer to cook at 365 degrees F for 22 minutes. Air-fry until everything is bubbling. Serve warm on individual plates. Bon appétit!

97. Melt-In-Your-Mouth Chicken Rolls

Ready in about 10 minutes
Servings 10

You can prepare these saucy rolls for a family lunch or an elegant supper. This is a sophisticated, protein-packed meal so you can't go wrong.

Per serving: 450 Calories; 6g Fat; 70g Carbs; 16.1g Protein; 4.2g Sugars

Ingredients

½ large-sized chicken breasts, cooked and shredded
1/3 cup soy sauce
40 wonton wrappers
9 ounces Ricotta cheese
2 tablespoons rice vinegar
2 tablespoon molasses
Salt and ground black pepper, to taste

Directions

- Combine all of the above ingredients, minus wonton wrappers, in a mixing dish.
- Lay out wrappers on a clean surface. Spread wonton wrappers with the prepared filling.
- Fold the outside corners to the center over the filling and roll up every wonton wrapper tightly; you can moisten the edges with a little water.
- Set the air fryer to cook at 380 degrees F. Air-fry the rolls for 3 to 4 minutes, working in batches. Serve with favorite sauce and enjoy!

98. Hawaiian-Style Pineapple Chicken

Ready in about 30 minutes
Servings 4

Here's a great idea for Sunday lunch! This is a protein-packed meal so you can serve it as a muscle-building dinner, too.

Per serving: 339 Calories; 21.6g Fat; 2.4g Carbs; 31.8g Protein; 1.2g Sugars

Ingredients

1/2 teaspoon grated fresh ginger
1/3 cup pineapple juice
1/2 teaspoon sea salt flakes
3 medium-sized boneless chicken breasts, cut into small pieces
1 ½ tablespoons sesame oil
3 green garlics, finely chopped
1/2 cup dry white wine
1/2 small-sized pineapple, peeled, cored and cut into wedges
1/2 teaspoon fresh thyme leaves, minced
1/3 teaspoon freshly cracked black pepper

Directions

* Warm the sesame oil in a deep sauté pan over a moderate heat. Then, sauté the green garlic until just fragrant.
* Remove the pan from the heat and pour in the pineapple juice and the white wine. After that, add the thyme, sea salt, fresh ginger, and freshly cracked black pepper. Scrape this mixture into a baking dish.
* Stir in the chicken chunks. Tuck the pineapple wedges among the chicken chunks.
* Cook in the preheated air fryer for 28 minutes at 335 degrees F. Serve on individual plates and eat warm.

99. Chicken Sausage with Eggs and Vegetables

Ready in about 20 minutes
Servings 6

The Air fryer can turn an ordinary chicken sausage into an amazing restaurant-style main dish. If this sounds appealing to you, try this irresistible combination of the eggs, chicken sausage cheese, bell peppers, and shallots.

Per serving: 211 Calories; 14.6g Fat; 5.9g Carbs; 14.7g Protein; 1.4g Sugars

Ingredients

6 eggs
2 bell peppers, seeded and sliced
1 teaspoon dried oregano
1 teaspoon hot paprika
1 teaspoon dried oregano
1 teaspoon freshly cracked black pepper
6 chicken sausages
1 teaspoon sea salt
1 1/2 shallots, cut into wedges
1 teaspoon dried basil

Directions

* Take four ramekins and divide chicken sausages, shallot, and bell pepper among those ramekins. Cook at 315 degrees F for about 12 minutes.
* Now, crack an egg into each ramekin. Sprinkle the eggs with hot paprika, basil, oregano, salt, and cracked black pepper. Cook for 5 more minutes at 405 degrees F.
* Serve with English muffins if desired. Bon appétit!

100. Spicy Ground Chicken Omelet

Ready in about 10 minutes
Servings 2

This ground chicken omelet is perfect for any occasion. A hot sauce gives it a spicy, piquant flavor.

Per serving: 292 Calories; 20.9g Fat; 3g Carbs; 21.6g Protein; 1g Sugars

Ingredients

1 clove garlic, finely minced
3 eggs, whisked
1 teaspoon ground black pepper
A dash of hot sauce
1 teaspoon salt
3 ounces ground chicken
1/3 cup scallions, finely chopped

Directions

- Thoroughly combine all ingredients in a mixing dish. Now, scrape the egg mixture into the air fryer baking dish.
- Set your machine to cook at 355 degrees F; air fry for 8 minutes or until thoroughly cooked. Serve immediately.

101. Chicken Sausage and Roasted Garlic Frittata

Ready in about 10 minutes
Servings 6

In this fragrant frittata recipe, you will use nutrient-rich eggs, your favorite style of chicken sausage and goat cheese. It doubles easily by using your Air fryer. Serve with lots of rustic whole-grain bread.

Per serving: 291 Calories; 14.1g Fat; 3.5g Carbs; 35.9g Protein; 1.7g Sugars

Ingredients

6 large-sized eggs
2 tablespoons butter, melted
3 tablespoons cream
1 cup chicken sausage, chopped
2 tablespoons roasted garlic, pressed
1/3 cup goat cheese such as Caprino, crumbled
1 teaspoon smoked cayenne pepper
1 teaspoon freshly ground black pepper
1/2 red onion, peeled and chopped
1 teaspoon fine sea salt

Directions

- First of all, grease six oven safe ramekins with melted butter. Then, divide roasted garlic and red onion among your ramekins. Add chicken sausage and toss to combine.
- Beat the eggs with cream until well combined and pale; sprinkle with cayenne pepper, salt, and black pepper; beat again.
- Scrape the mixture into your ramekins and air-fry for about 13 minutes at 355 degrees F.
- Top with crumbled cheese and serve immediately.

102. Easy Nacho Chicken Burgers

Ready in about 15 minutes
Servings 4

Cooking the ground chicken meat with all these aromatics adds rich and incredible flavor to these one-dish burgers. Serve with Dijon mustard, mayo and fresh salad.

Per serving: 360 Calories; 10.3g Fat; 38.4g Carbs; 30.1g Protein; 1.2g Sugars

Ingredients

1 palmful dried basil
1/3 cup crushed tortilla chips
2 teaspoons dried marjoram
1/3 teaspoon ancho chili powder
4 whole-wheat tortillas, to serve
2 teaspoons dried parsley flakes
1/2 teaspoon onion powder
Toppings, to serve
1/3 teaspoon porcini powder
1 teaspoon sea salt flakes
1 pound chicken meat, ground
2 teaspoons cumin powder
1/3 teaspoon red pepper flakes, crushed
1 teaspoon freshly cracked black pepper

Directions

- Generously grease an air fryer cooking basket with a thin layer of vegetable oil.
- In a mixing dish, combine chicken meat with all seasonings. Shape into 4 patties and coat them with crushed tortilla chips.
- Cook chicken burgers in the preheated air fryer for 15 minutes at 345 degrees F, working in batches, flipping them once.
- Serve in tortillas and add toppings of choice. Bon appétit!

103. Mozzarella and Chicken Rolls

Ready in about 10 minutes
Servings 10

Mild and tender mozzarella combines well with leftover chicken (especially white meat). Inspired by versatile wonton wrappers, you can come up with this recipe that is just scrumptious!

Per serving: 433 Calories; 18.6g Fat; 2.7g Carbs; 22.9g Protein; 1.2g Sugars

Ingredients

8 ounces Mozzarella cheese, shredded
40 wonton wrappers
1/3 cup hot sauce
1/2 pound leftover chicken
1/2 teaspoon dried dill weed
1 teaspoon freshly cracked mixed peppercorns
1 teaspoon sea salt

Directions

- To make the filling, combine the leftover chicken, salt, cracked peppercorns, dill weed, and hot sauce in a mixing dish; mix until everything is well incorporated.
- Lay out wrappers on a clean surface. Now, divide the chicken filling among wonton wrappers. Divide shredded Mozzarella among wonton wrappers.
- Fold the outside corners to the center over the filling; after that, roll up each wrapper; you can moisten the edges with a little water.
- Air fry in the preheated machine at 370 degrees F for 8 minutes; working with batches. To finish, arrange them on a nice serving platter. Bon appétit!

104. Chicken Thighs with Mustard-Rosemary Sauce

Ready in about 15 minutes +
marinating time
Servings 4

Try these heavenly delicious chicken thighs with rich and flavorful mayo-based sauce! Kewpie mayonnaise is a Japanese-style mayo that has a thinner consistency and tangier flavor than American mayo. Hon-dashi powder and malt vinegar give the sauce an authentic character.

Per serving: 146 Calories; 10.9g Fat; 6.7g Carbs; 5.9g Protein; 0.5g Sugars

Ingredients

1/2 cup full fat sour cream
1 teaspoon ground cinnamon
½ teaspoon whole grain mustard
1 ½ tablespoons Kewpie mayonnaise
½ chicken thighs, boneless, skinless, and cut into pieces
1 ½ tablespoons olive oil
2 heaping tablespoons fresh rosemary, minced
½ cup white wine
3 cloves garlic, minced
1/2 teaspoon smoked paprika
Salt and freshly cracked black pepper, to taste

Directions

- Firstly, in a mixing dish, combine chicken thighs with olive oil and white wine; stir to coat.
- After that, throw in the garlic, smoked paprika, ground cinnamon, salt, and black pepper; cover and refrigerate for 1 to 3 hours.
- Set the air fryer to cook at 375 degrees F. Roast the chicken thighs for 18 minutes, turning halfway through and working in batches.
- To make the sauce, combine the sour cream, whole grain mustard, Kewpie mayonnaise and rosemary. Serve the turkey with the mustard/rosemary sauce and enjoy!

105. Amazing Sage and Parmesan Chicken

Ready in about 20 minutes
Servings 6

Using a crisp cooking wine and a freshly grated Parmigiano-Reggiano is one of the easiest ways to transform a good-enough chicken recipe into an outstanding family meal! Chardonnay and Pinot Grigio work well too.

Per serving: 231 Calories; 9.6g Fat; 1.9g Carbs; 32.3g Protein; 0.1g Sugars

Ingredients

3 boneless and skinless chicken breasts, cut into small pieces
1/3 cup cooking wine (such as Sauvignon Blanc)
1teaspoon fresh sage leaves, minced
1 teaspoon freshly cracked black pepper
1/3 cup Parmigiano-Reggiano cheese, freshly grated
3 cloves garlic, minced
2 tablespoons olive oil
1 teaspoon seasoned salt
1 teaspoon fresh rosemary leaves, minced

Directions

- Warm the oil in a sauté pan over a moderate flame. Then, sauté the garlic until just fragrant.
- Next, remove the pan from the heat; pour in the cooking wine. Add the seasonings in the order listed above and toss until everything is well combined. Pour this mixture into a lightly-oiled baking dish.
- Toss in the pieces of chicken breasts; roast in the preheated air fryer at 325 degrees F for 32 minutes. Scatter grated cheese over the chicken and serve on individual plates.

106. Restaurant-Style Roasted Drumsticks with Potatoes

Ready in about 25 minutes
Servings 5

This is a great idea for your next dinner party. Bear in mind that Aleppo pepper has that perfectly rich and a little smoky taste.

Per serving: 421 Calories; 17.8g Fat; 37.2g Carbs; 28.4g Protein; 3.4g Sugars

Ingredients

5 chicken drumsticks
2 sprigs thyme
3 red potatoes, quartered
1 teaspoon granulated garlic
1 teaspoon Aleppo chili
½ cup shallots, chopped
1/2 teaspoon celery seeds
1/2 teaspoon onion powder
3 sprigs rosemary
2 tablespoons sesame oil
1/2 teaspoon sea salt
1/3 teaspoon red pepper flakes, crushed

Directions

- In a small-sized bowl or a measuring cup, make the rub by mixing sesame oil, red pepper, salt, celery seeds, onion powder, granulated garlic, and Aleppo chili. Mix to combine well.
- After that, evenly coat each chicken leg with the prepared rub mixture. Sprinkle your potatoes with thyme and rosemary.
- Lower the potatoes onto the bottom of the baking dish that is greased with a nonstick cooking spray. Now, add the shallots and top with the seasoned chicken drumsticks.
- Roast in the preheated air fryer for 28 minutes at 355 degrees F, turning occasionally; work in batches. Bon appétit!

107. Berbere Chicken Drumsticks with Cauliflower

Ready in about 25 minutes
Servings 6

This recipe doesn't call for any extra fat and it is a proof that you don't need it for amazing flavor. The Air fryer is really fabulous!

Per serving: 234 Calories; 12.3g Fat; 4.7g Carbs; 25.4g Protein; 1.4g Sugars

Ingredients

2 handful fresh Italian parsleys, roughly chopped
½ cup fresh chopped chives
2 sprigs thyme
6 chicken drumsticks
1 ½ small-sized head cauliflowers, broken into large-sized florets

For the Berbere Spice Rub Mix:
2 teaspoons mustard powder
1/3 teaspoon porcini powder
1 ½ teaspoons berbere spice
1/3teaspoon sweet paprika
1/2 teaspoon shallot powder
1teaspoon granulated garlic
1 teaspoon freshly cracked pink peppercorns
1/2 teaspoon sea salt

Directions

- Simply combine all items for the berbere spice rub mix. After that, coat the chicken drumsticks with this rub mix on all sides. Transfer them to the baking dish.
- Now, lower the cauliflower onto the chicken drumsticks. Add thyme, chives and Italian parsley and spritz everything with a pan spray. Transfer the baking dish to the preheated air fryer.
- Next step, set the timer for 28 minutes; roast at 355 degrees F, turning occasionally. Bon appétit!

TURKEY

108. Cheesy Turkey Meatballs 65

109. Turkey Sliders with Chive Mayonnaise 65

110. Honey-Glazed Thanksgiving Turkey Breast 66

111. Crowd-Pleasing Turkey and Quinoa Skewers 66

112. Holiday Colby Turkey Meatloaf 67

113. Sweet Italian Turkey Sausage with Vegetables 67

114. Prune-Stuffed Turkey Tenderloins 68

115. Quinoa and Ground Turkey Stuffed Peppers 68

116. Cajun and Mustard Turkey Fingers 69

117. Must-Serve Roasted Turkey Thighs with
     Vegetables 69

118. Hot Peppery Turkey Sandwiches 70

119. Hoisin-Glazed Turkey Drumsticks 70

120. Thai Sticky Turkey Wings 71

121. Finger-Lickin' Vermouth and Honey Turkey 71

122. Spiced Scallion Stuffed Turkey Roulade 72

123. Spaghetti with Turkey and Porcini Sauce 72

124. Italian-Style Turkey and Asparagus Casserole 73

125. Sherry Dijon Turkey Drumstick 73

126. Cocoa-Roasted Herbed Turkey Thighs 74

127. Finger-Lickin' Grilled Turkey 74

128. Last Minute Turkey with Potatoes 75

129. Curried Turkey Drumsticks 75

130. Easiest Turkey Meatloaf Ever 76

131. Turkey Breasts in Scallion Sauce 76

132. Vermouth and Honey Turkey Breast 77

133. Turkey Drumsticks with Hoisin Glaze 77

134. Cheesy Pasilla Turkey 78

135. Festive Turkey Drumsticks with Gala Apples 78

136. Roasted Turkey Sausage with Potatoes 79

137. Dinner Turkey Sandwiches 79

138. Dijon and Curry Turkey Cutlets 80

139. Super Easy Sage and Lime Wings 80

140. Creamy Lemon Turkey 81

141. Turkey Wontons with Garlic-Parmesan Sauce 81

142. Cajun Turkey Meatloaf 82

143. Wine-Braised Turkey Breasts 82

144. Turkey in Yogurt-Mint Sauce 83

145. Turkey Sausage with Cauliflower 83

146. Mom's Juicy Turkey Breasts 84

147. Hot Spicy Turkey Meatloaf 84

148. Mustard and Sage Turkey Breasts 85

149. Wine and Coriander Turkey Wings 85

150. Baked Eggs with Ground Turkey 86

151. Winter Turkey Breasts with Leeks 86

152. Easy Honey Mustard Turkey Breast 87

153. Asiago Turkey Wrapped in Bacon 87

154. Eggs with Turkey Sausage 88

155. Turkey with Honey Applesauce 88

156. Rustic Turkey Breast with Walnuts 89

157. Country Turkey and Pepper Frittata 89

158. Lemony Turkey with Mustard Sauce 90

159. Turkey Tortilla Wraps 90

160. Zesty Air Fried Turkey Leg 91

161. Lime Turkey Tortilla Roll-Ups 91

162. Curried Turkey Drumsticks 92

108. Cheesy Turkey Meatballs

Ready in about 15 minutes
Servings 6

These crowd-pleasing and child-friendly meatballs are perfect for any occasion. They are delicious eye catching!

Per serving: 241 Calories; 17.5g Fat; 1.1g Carbs; 23.0g Protein; 0.0 g Sugars

Ingredients

1 pound ground turkey
1 tablespoon fresh mint leaves, finely chopped
1 teaspoon onion powder
1 ½ teaspoons garlic paste
1 teaspoon crushed red pepper flakes
1/4 cup melted butter
3/4 teaspoon fine sea salt
1/4 cup grated Pecorino Romano

Directions

- Simply place all of the above ingredients into the mixing dish; mix until everything is well incorporated.
- Use an ice cream scoop to shape the meat into golf ball sized meatballs.
- Air fry the meatballs at 380 degrees F for approximately 7 minutes; work in batches, shaking them to ensure evenness of cooking.
- Serve with simple tomato sauce garnished with fresh basil leaves. Bon appétit!

109. Turkey Sliders with Chive Mayonnaise

Ready in about 20 minutes
Servings 6

Stuck on what to make for dinner? Treat your family to these restaurant-style, addictive turkey sliders. If you are short of time, just serve mayo and mustard instead of preparing the chive mayo. Easy!

Per serving: 252 Calories; 15.9g Fat; 10.0g Carbs; 17.1g Protein; 2.7g Sugars

Ingredients

For the Turkey Sliders:
3/4 pound turkey mince
1/4 cup pickled jalapeno, chopped
1 tablespoon oyster sauce
1-2 cloves garlic, minced
1 tablespoon chopped fresh cilantro
2 tablespoons chopped scallions
Sea salt and ground black pepper, to savor

For the Chive Mayo:
1 cup mayonnaise
1 tablespoon chives
1 teaspoon salt
Zest of 1 lime

Directions

- In a mixing bowl, thoroughly combine all ingredients for the turkey sliders.
- Mold the mixture into 6 even-sized slider patties. Then, air-fry them at 365 degrees F for 15 minutes.
- Meanwhile, make the Chive Mayo by mixing the rest of the above ingredients. Assemble the sandwiches with burger buns and serve warm.

110. Honey-Glazed Thanksgiving Turkey Breast

Ready in about 55 minutes
Servings 6

A tasty holiday main dish that has all the best flavors of the season, prepared with ingredients your family and guests would love. Enjoy!

Per serving: 386 Calories; 8.2g Fat; 24.5g Carbs; 51.7g Protein; 22.2g Sugars

Ingredients

2 teaspoons butter, softened
1 teaspoon dried sage
2 sprigs rosemary, chopped
1 teaspoon salt
1/4 teaspoon freshly ground black pepper, or more to taste
1 whole turkey breast
2 tablespoons turkey broth
1/4 cup honey
2 tablespoons whole-grain mustard
1 tablespoon butter

Directions

- Start by preheating your Air Fryer to 360 degrees F.
- To make the rub, combine 2 tablespoons of butter, sage, rosemary, salt, and pepper; mix well to combine and spread it evenly over the surface of the turkey breast.
- Roast for 20 minutes in an Air Fryer cooking basket. Flip the turkey breast over and cook for a further 15 to 16 minutes. Now, flip it back over and roast for 12 minutes more.
- While the turkey is roasting, whisk the other ingredients in a saucepan. After that, spread the glaze all over the turkey breast.
- Return to the Air Fryer for another 5 minutes; let the turkey rest for a few minutes before carving. Bon appétit!

111. Crowd-Pleasing Turkey and Quinoa Skewers

Ready in about 15 minutes
Servings 8

These great meatballs get a nutrition boost from amazing quinoa that is one of the healthiest foods on the Earth. Quinoa is packed with vitamins, minerals, useful fiber, protein, etc.

Per serving: 236 Calories; 12.1g Fat; 15.6g Carbs; 18.2g Protein; 0.0g Sugars

Ingredients

1 cup red quinoa, cooked
1 ½ cups of water
14 ounces ground turkey
2 small eggs, beaten
1 teaspoon ground ginger
2 ½ tablespoons vegetable oil
1 cup chopped fresh parsley
2 tablespoons seasoned breadcrumbs
3/4 teaspoon salt
1 heaping teaspoon fresh rosemary, finely chopped
1/2 teaspoon ground allspice

Directions

- Mix all of the above ingredients in a bowl. Knead the mixture with your hands.
- Then, take small portions and gently roll them into balls.
- Now, preheat your Air Fryer to 380 degrees F. Air fry for 8 to 10 minutes in the Air Fryer basket. Serve on a serving platter with skewers and eat with your favorite dipping sauce.

112. Holiday Colby Turkey Meatloaf

Ready in about 50 minutes
Servings 6

Soft, moist meatloaf that is loaded with fragrant herbs and cheese. Keep in mind that Colby cheese is a perfect match for turkey but you can use another semi-hard cheese as needed.

Per serving: 252 Calories; 11.5g Fat; 8.7g Carbs; 27.5g Protein; 3.2g Sugars

Ingredients

1 pound turkey mince
1/2 cup scallions, finely chopped
2 garlic cloves, finely minced
1 teaspoon dried thyme
1/2 teaspoon dried basil
3/4 cup Colby cheese, shredded
3/4 cup crushed saltines
1 tablespoon tamari sauce
Salt and black pepper, to your liking
1/4 cup roasted red pepper tomato sauce
1 teaspoon brown sugar
3/4 tablespoons olive oil
1 medium-sized egg, well beaten

Directions

- In a nonstick skillet, that is preheated over a moderate heat, sauté the turkey mince, scallions, garlic, thyme, and basil until just tender and fragrant.
- Then set your Air Fryer to cook at 360 degrees. Combine sautéed mixture with the cheese, saltines and tamari sauce; then form the mixture into a loaf shape.
- Mix the remaining items and pour them over the meatloaf. Cook in the Air Fryer baking pan for 45 to 47 minutes. Eat warm.

113. Sweet Italian Turkey Sausage with Vegetables

Ready in about 40 minutes
Servings 4

Sweet Italian turkey sausages are combined with a mild mix of spices in this colorful, delicious recipe. Keep in mind that you can swap Sweet Italian turkey sausage for turkey sausage patties.

Per serving: 413 Calories; 27.2g Fat; 22.6g Carbs; 19.0g Protein; 3.9g Sugars

Ingredients

1 onion, cut into wedges
2 carrots, trimmed and sliced
1 parsnip, trimmed and sliced
2 potatoes, peeled and diced
1 teaspoon dried thyme
1/2 teaspoon dried marjoram
1 teaspoon dried basil
1/2 teaspoon celery seeds
Sea salt and ground black pepper, to taste
1 tablespoon melted butter
3/4 pound sweet Italian turkey sausage

Directions

- Mix the vegetables with all seasonings and melted butter. Arrange the vegetables on the bottom of the Air Fryer cooking basket. Lower the sausage onto the top of the vegetables.
- Roast at 360 degrees F for 33 to 37 minutes or until the sausages are no longer pink. Work in batches as needed, shaking halfway through the roasting time. Bon appétit!

114. Prune-Stuffed Turkey Tenderloins

Ready in about 1 hour
Servings 4

Turkey stuffed with a tangy filling of prunes, spices and butter – this tastes like a holiday! Just soak prunes in water to make them soft before cutting. Enjoy!

Per serving: 467 Calories; 25.4g Fat; 20.7g Carbs; 43.1g Protein; 12.2g Sugars

Ingredients

3/4 cup prunes, pitted and chopped
1/2 teaspoon dried marjoram
1 sprig thyme, leaves only, crushed
2 tablespoons fresh coriander, minced
1/4 teaspoon ground allspice
1/2 cup softened butter
1 ½ pounds turkey tenderloins
2 tablespoons dry white wine

Directions

- In a mixing bowl, thoroughly combine the first 6 ingredients; stir with a spoon until everything is well shared.
- Cut the "pockets" into the sides of the turkey tenderloins. Stuff them with prepared prune mixture. Now, tie each "pocket" with a cooking twine. Sprinkle them with white wine.
- Cook the stuffed turkey in the preheated Air Fryer at 385 degrees F for 48 to 55 minutes, checking periodically.
- Afterward, remove cooking twine, cut each turkey tenderloin into 2 slices and serve immediately.

115. Quinoa and Ground Turkey Stuffed Peppers

Ready in about 30 minutes
Servings 4

These peppers are full of rich, old-fashioned flavor, reminding us of grandma's cooking. Try to use the peppers of different colors to express your artistic side!

Per serving: 384 Calories; 22.6g Fat; 27.6g Carbs; 21.7g Protein; 8.5g Sugars

Ingredients

1/4 cup canola oil
7 ounces ground turkey
1/2 cup onion, finely chopped
2 cloves garlic, peeled and finely minced
1/2 cup quinoa, cooked
1 tablespoon fresh cilantro, chopped
1 tablespoon fresh parsley, chopped
1 ½ cups chopped tomatoes
1 teaspoon dried basil
Salt and black pepper, to taste
4 bell peppers, slice off the tops, deveined
1/2 cup fat-free chicken broth
1 tablespoon cider vinegar
1/3 cup shredded three-cheese blend

Directions

- Preheat the oil in a saucepan over a moderate heat. Now, sauté the turkey, onion and garlic for 4 to 5 minutes or until they have softened.
- Add cooked quinoa, cilantro, parsley, 1 cup of tomatoes, basil, salt, and black pepper.
- Stuff the peppers with the prepared meat filling. Transfer them to a baking dish.
- After that, thoroughly combine the remaining tomatoes with chicken broth and cider vinegar. Add the sauce to the baking dish.
- Cook covered at 360 degrees F for 18 minutes. Uncover, top with cheese and cook for 5 minutes more or until cheese is bubbling. Serve right away.

116. Cajun and Mustard Turkey Fingers

Ready in about 20 minutes
Servings 4

Turkey fingers are one of our greatest guilty pleasures. These ones aren't deep-fried so you can relax and enjoy them to the fullest. Cajun spice mix makes them irresistible!

Per serving: 240 Calories; 2.6g Fat; 28.2g Carbs; 27.1g Protein; 4.6g Sugars

Ingredients

1/2 cup cornmeal mix
1/2 cup all-purpose flour
1 ½ tablespoons Cajun seasoning
1 ½ tablespoons whole-grain mustard
1 ½ cups buttermilk
1 teaspoon soy sauce
3/4 pound turkey tenderloins, cut into finger-sized strips
Salt and ground black pepper, to your liking

Directions

- Grab three bowls. Combine the cornmeal, flour, and Cajun seasoning in the first bowl. Mix the whole-grain mustard, buttermilk and soy sauce in the second one.
- Season the turkey fingers with the salt and black pepper. Now, dip each strip into the buttermilk mix; after that, cover them with the cornmeal mixture on all sides.
- Transfer the prepared turkey fingers to the Air Fryer baking pan and cook for 15 minutes at 360 degrees F. Serve with hot tomato ketchup and enjoy!

117. Must-Serve Roasted Turkey Thighs with Vegetables

Ready in about 1 hour 15 minutes
Servings 4

Roasted turkey thighs with vegetables are a fantastic alternative to cooking a whole bird for Christmas or Thanksgiving. Keep it simple and save your time in the kitchen. You deserve it!

Per serving: 218 Calories; 5.6g Fat; 8.7g Carbs; 31.9g Protein; 4.0g Sugars

Ingredients

1 red onion, cut into wedges
1 carrot, trimmed and sliced
1 celery stalk, trimmed and sliced
1 cup Brussel sprouts, trimmed and halved
1 cup roasted vegetable broth
1 tablespoon apple cider vinegar
1 teaspoon maple syrup
2 turkey thighs
1/2 teaspoon mixed peppercorns, freshly cracked
1 teaspoon fine sea salt
1 teaspoon cayenne pepper
1 teaspoon onion powder
1/2 teaspoon garlic powder
1/3 teaspoon mustard seeds

Directions

- Take a baking dish that easily fits into your device; place the vegetables on the bottom of the baking dish and pour in roasted vegetable broth.
- In a large-sized mixing dish, place the remaining ingredients; let them marinate for about 30 minutes. Lay them on the top of the vegetables.
- Roast at 330 degrees F for 40 to 45 minutes. Bon appétit!

118. Hot Peppery Turkey Sandwiches

Ready in about 25 minutes
Servings 4

This Air Fryer recipe is a great way to use leftover turkey. Combine it with your favorite vegetables, serve in hamburger buns and you will have a delicious dinner. It freezes well, too.

Per serving: 207 Calories; 8.7g Fat; 19.9g Carbs; 13.5g Protein; 4.2g Sugars

Ingredients

1 cup leftover turkey, cut into bite-sized chunks
2 bell peppers, deveined and chopped
1 Serrano pepper, deveined and chopped
1 leek, sliced
1/2 cup sour cream
1 teaspoon hot paprika
3/4 teaspoon kosher salt
1/2 teaspoon ground black pepper
1 heaping tablespoon fresh cilantro, chopped
A few dashes of Tabasco sauce
4 hamburger buns

Directions

- Toss all ingredients, without the hamburger buns, in an Air Fryer baking pan; toss until everything is well coated.
- Now, roast it for 20 minutes at 385 degrees F. Serve on hamburger buns; add some extra sour cream and Dijon mustard if desired. Bon appétit!

119. Hoisin-Glazed Turkey Drumsticks

Ready in about 40 minutes +
marinating time
Servings 4

Hoisin sauce is commonly used as a glaze for meat because of its thick texture. Add some mustard and honey and you will get a perfect glaze for your festive meat main course.

Per serving: 397 Calories; 18.5g Fat; 9.6g Carbs; 44.3g Protein; 7.3g Sugars

Ingredients

2 turkey drumsticks
2 tablespoons balsamic vinegar
2 tablespoons dry white wine
1 tablespoon extra-virgin olive oil
1 sprig rosemary, chopped
Salt and ground black pepper, to your liking
2 ½ tablespoons butter, melted

For the Hoisin Glaze:
2 tablespoons hoisin sauce
1 tablespoon honey
1 tablespoon honey mustard

Directions

- Add the turkey drumsticks to a mixing dish; add the vinegar, wine, olive oil, and rosemary. Let them marinate for 3 hours.
- Then, preheat the Air Fryer to 350 degrees F.
- Season the turkey drumsticks with salt and black pepper; spread the melted butter over the surface of drumsticks.
- Cook turkey drumsticks at 350 degrees F for 30 to 35 minutes, working in batches. Turn the drumsticks over a few times during the cooking.
- While the turkey drumsticks are roasting, prepare the Hoisin glaze by mixing all the glaze ingredients. After that, drizzle the turkey with the glaze mixture; roast for a further 5 minutes. Let it rest about 10 minutes before carving and serving. Bon appétit!

120. Thai Sticky Turkey Wings

Ready in about 40 minutes
Servings 4

Try this recipe and you will find that air-frying is one of the best ways to make perfect sticky wings. Use a few dashes of Tabasco sauce for spicier wings.

Per serving: 284 Calories; 14.1g Fat; 18.8g Carbs; 19.4g Protein; 13.9g Sugars

Ingredients

3/4 pound turkey wings, cut into pieces
1 teaspoon ginger powder
1 teaspoon garlic powder
3/4 teaspoon paprika
2 tablespoons soy sauce
1 handful minced lemongrass
Sea salt flakes and ground black pepper, to savor
2 tablespoons rice wine vinegar
1/4 cup peanut butter
1 tablespoon sesame oil
1/2 cup Thai sweet chili sauce

Directions

- In a saucepan with boiling water, cook the turkey wings for 20 minutes.
- Transfer the turkey wings to a large-sized mixing dish; toss with the remaining ingredients, without Thai sweet chili sauce.
- Air-fry them for 20 minutes at 350 degrees F or until they are thoroughly cooked; make sure to flip them over during the cooking time.
- Serve with Thai sweet chili sauce and lemon wedges. Bon appétit!

121. Finger-Lickin' Vermouth and Honey Turkey

Ready in about 55 minutes +
marinating time
Servings 4

Marinated turkey tenderloin is delicious any time of the year. Serve with sautéed Brussels sprouts and a glass of rosé wine. Enjoy!

Per serving: 256 Calories; 9.2g Fat; 5.4g Carbs; 33.4g Protein; 4.7g Sugars

Ingredients

1 teaspoon marjoram
1 teaspoon dried oregano
1 tablespoon honey
1/4 cup vermouth
2 tablespoons lemon juice
1 turkey tenderloin, quartered
1 tablespoon sesame oil
Sea salt flakes, to savor
1/2 teaspoon freshly ground pepper, or to savor
3/4 teaspoon smoked paprika
1 teaspoon crushed sage leaves, dried

Directions

- Place the first 6 ingredients in a mixing dish; let it marinate for 3 hours at least.
- Then, drizzle the turkey breasts with sesame oil and add the other ingredients.
- Lastly, roast in the Air Fryer cooking basket about 50 to 55 minutes at 355 degrees F; make sure to turn them over a few times during the cooking time.

122. Spiced Scallion Stuffed Turkey Roulade

Ready in about 50 minutes
Servings 4

A meat roulade is always a good idea for an elegant party dinner but you can't go wrong if you serve it for any occasion.

Per serving: 227 Calories; 10.8g Fat; 1.5g Carbs; 29.7g Protein; 0.0g Sugars

Ingredients

1 turkey fillet
Salt and garlic pepper, to your liking
1/3 teaspoon onion powder
1/2 teaspoon dried basil
1/3 teaspoon ground red chipotle pepper
1 ½ teaspoons mustard seeds
1/2 teaspoon fennel seeds
2 tablespoons melted butter
3 tablespoons coriander, finely chopped
1/2 cup scallions, finely chopped
2 clove garlic, finely minced

Directions

- Place the turkey fillets on a clean and dry surface. Then, flatten the fillets to a thickness of about 1/2-inch using a meat mallet. Sprinkle them with salt, garlic pepper, and onion powder.
- Then, mix the basil, chipotle pepper, mustard seeds, fennel seeds and butter in a small-sized bowl. Spread this mixture over the fillets, leaving an inch border.
- Top with coriander, scallions and garlic. Roll the fillets towards the border. Lastly, secure the rolls with a cooking twine and transfer them to the Air Fryer cooking basket.
- Roast at 350 degrees F for about 50 minutes; turn it halfway through the roasting time. Check for doneness and serve warm.

123. Spaghetti with Turkey and Porcini Sauce

Ready in about 30 minutes
Servings 2

From now onwards, you have no excuse to not make a pasta. This recipe is loaded with mushrooms, tomato paste and Mediterranean-inspired spices. It's a flavor bomb.

Per serving: 315 Calories; 9.3g Fat; 36.5g Carbs; 27.8g Protein; 5.5g Sugars

Ingredients

1/2 package spaghetti, cooked
1/2 cup tomato paste
1/3 teaspoon marjoram
2 cloves garlic, finely minced
1 tablespoon tomato ketchup
1pound ground turkey
1/3 pound Porcini mushrooms
1 teaspoon dried dill weed
1/2 cup scallions, finely chopped
1 teaspoon rosemary
1 teaspoon seasoned salt
1/3 teaspoon mixed peppercorns, freshly cracked

Directions

- Start by preheating your air fryer to 375 degrees F.
- Simply throw the ground turkey along with the mushrooms, scallions, and the garlic into a lightly greased casserole dish; air-fry for 14 minutes at 375 degrees F.
- Then, stir in the remaining items, minus the spaghetti; air-fry for a further 14 minutes. Serve over spaghetti on individual plates. Bon appétit!

124. Italian-Style Turkey and Asparagus Casserole

Ready in about 20 minutes
Servings 2

Using Pecorino Romano cheese is one of the easiest ways to transform a good-enough turkey recipe into an outstanding royal meal.

Per serving: 361 Calories; 13.8g Fat; 31.2g Carbs; 27.2g Protein; 2.9g Sugars

Ingredients

1 cup ground turkey
1/3 cup Pecorino Romano cheese, freshly grated
1 cup Italian parsley, roughly chopped
5 slices of Italian bread, crust removed and cubed
5 asparagus spears, roughly chopped
1/3 cup yogurt
1 teaspoon thyme, dried or fresh
2 large-sized eggs, lightly beaten
1/3 teaspoon paprika
½ teaspoon ground black pepper
1/3 teaspoon sea salt
Nonstick cooking spray

Directions

- Use a cooking spray to lightly grease a baking dish. Arrange the Italian bread cubes on the bottom of the prepared baking dish.
- In a mixing dish, whisk the yogurt and the two eggs. Stir in the grated Pecorino Romano cheese; add the black pepper, salt, paprika, and thyme. Pour 3/4 of the egg/cheese mixture over the bread cubes.
- Add the ground turkey and the fresh parsley; top with the chopped asparagus spears. Spread the remaining egg/cheese mixture over the top; lastly, add the remaining Pecorino Romano cheese. Bake at 345 degrees F for about 13 minutes. Eat warm.

125. Sherry Dijon Turkey Drumstick

Ready in about 30 minutes
Servings 2

These turkey drumsticks always turn out incredibly juicy and succulent! You can easily double or triple the recipe according to the amount of people you will be serving.

Per serving: 181 Calories; 12.3g Fat; 7.7g Carbs; 11.9g Protein; 4.8g Sugars

Ingredients

2 tablespoons Dijon mustard
1/2 tablespoon ginger, minced
1/3 cup milk
4 turkey drumsticks
Sea salt flakes and ground black pepper
1/3 cup cream sherry wine
1/3 teaspoon smoked paprika

Directions

- Place all of the above ingredients in a bowl; toss to coat the drumsticks on all sides.
- Let it marinate for at least 2 hours or preferably overnight in the refrigerator.
- Roast in the preheated air fryer at 380 degrees F for 28 minutes; flip turkey drumsticks over at half-time. Bon appétit!

126. Cocoa-Roasted Herbed Turkey Thighs

Ready in about 35 minutes
Servings 4

Your family will love this outstanding turkey recipe. The secret ingredient is a raw cocoa powder, that is used to make the flavorful coating.

Per serving: 175 Calories; 1.6g Fat; 8.7g Carbs; 10.9g Protein; 1g Sugars

Ingredients

For the Spice Rub Mix:
1/3 teaspoon porcini powder
1 teaspoon garlic powder
1 teaspoon mixed peppercorns, freshly cracked
1/2 teaspoon shallot powder
1/3 teaspoon sweet paprika
1/2 teaspoon fine sea salt

For Turkey Thighs:
1/2 handful fresh Italian parsley, roughly chopped
2 sprigs thyme, roughly chopped
6 turkey thighs
1/2 palmful raw cocoa powder, unsweetened
1 sprig rosemary, roughly chopped
3 coriander sprigs, roughly chopped

Directions

- Simply combine all the items for the spice rub mix. Now, coat the turkey thighs with this rub mix on all sides. Lay them on the bottom of a lightly greased baking dish.
- Add the herbs and cocoa powder. Transfer the baking dish to the preheated air fryer.
- Finally, set the timer to 32 minutes; air-fry at 365 degrees F, turning periodically. Bon appétit!

127. Finger-Lickin' Grilled Turkey

Ready in about 30 minutes +
marinating time
Servings 4

Ever wish you could get that restaurant-style turkey breast at home? This recipe will surprise you! It would be great if you could marinate the turkey overnight.

Per serving: 402 Calories; 12.9g Fat; 41.2g Carbs; 38.2g Protein; 32g Sugars

Ingredients

1/3 teaspoon cumin powder
1/2 tablespoon Worcestershire sauce
1/2 teaspoon dried savory
1/3 cup honey
1 1/2 pounds turkey breasts, sliced
Salt and pepper, to savor
1/3 cup ketchup
2 teaspoons orange zest
1/2 teaspoon garlic powder
1/3 cup fresh orange juice

Directions

- Firstly, place the turkey in a mixing dish; add all of the above ingredients; toss until the turkey breasts are well coated. Let it marinate for at least 3 hours.
- Place the turkey breast in the air fryer grill pan; grill your turkey at 400 degrees F approximately 28 minutes. Work in batches. Bon appétit!

128. Last Minute Turkey with Potatoes

Ready in about 25 minutes
Servings 2

For the best results and a reduction in overall cooking time, you should cook the potatoes before adding the remaining ingredients. Lastly, check your potatoes for doneness by using a fork; they should be crumbly on the outside and fluffy on the inside.

Per serving: 271 Calories; 10.9g Fat; 34.8g Carbs; 9.3g Protein; 2.5g Sugars

Ingredients

1/3 cup turkey stock
2/3 cup leftover turkey, shredded or chopped
1/2 teaspoon dried rosemary
2 medium-sized potatoes, peeled and diced
1 tablespoon olive oil
2 bay leaves
1/2 yellow onion, chopped
1 green garlic, finely chopped
1 teaspoon shallot powder
1/2 teaspoon hot paprika
1/3 teaspoon mixed peppercorns, freshly cracked
1 teaspoon kosher salt

Directions

- Firstly, cook the potatoes in the preheated air fryer at 355 degrees F for 8 minutes. Transfer them to a baking dish.
- Add the remaining ingredients; toss to coat; cook for 8 more minutes or until everything is thoroughly heated. Serve and enjoy!

129. Curried Turkey Drumsticks

Ready in about 25 minutes
Servings 2

A nice and easy meal for two. Serve with a crisp Sauvignon Blanc to organize a memorable, romantic evening.

Per serving: 240 Calories; 9.6g Fat; 16.2g Carbs; 19.9g Protein; 2.3g Sugars

Ingredients

1 ½ tablespoons red curry paste
1/2 teaspoon cayenne pepper
1 ½ tablespoons minced ginger
2 turkey drumsticks
1/3 cup coconut milk
1 teaspoon kosher salt, or more to taste
1/3 teaspoon ground pepper, to more to taste

Directions

- First of all, place the turkey drumsticks with all the ingredients in your refrigerator; let it marinate overnight.
- Cook the turkey drumsticks at 390 degrees F for 22 minutes; make sure to flip them over at half-time. Serve with a salad on the side.

130. Easiest Turkey Meatloaf Ever

Ready in about 50 minutes
Servings 6

Here's a must-try meatloaf recipe! Serve this great-tasting meatloaf on a plate, on a bun, or accompanied by vegetables.

Per serving: 425 Calories; 21.6g Fat; 3.6g Carbs; 41g Protein; 2.2g Sugars

Ingredients

½ cup breadcrumbs
1/3 pound Pecorino Romano cheese, cubed
3 whole eggs
1 cup tomato ketchup
1 pound ground turkey
1/2 teaspoon seasoned salt
1/2 cup milk
1 teaspoon garlic pepper
1/2 teaspoon cayenne pepper

Directions

- Preheat your air fryer to 375 degrees F.
- Place all the ingredients, minus the cheese and ketchup, in a large-sized mixing dish; mix to combine well.
- Now, fold the cubes of Pecorino Romano cheese cubes into the meat mixture. Shape into the meatloaf and top with ketchup.
- Air-fry for 50 minutes. Let it rest 7-8 minutes before slicing and eat warm!

131. Turkey Breasts in Scallion Sauce

Ready in about 2 hours 35 minutes
Servings 2

These turkey breasts are irresistible! As a matter of fact, scallions bring their full flavors to the fore. They are delicious for eye and palate!

Per serving: 243 Calories; 15g Fat; 12.7g Carbs; 16.9g Protein; 1.2g Sugars

Ingredients

1/3 cup vegetable or turkey stock
1/2 cup scallions, thinly sliced
1 ½ tablespoons plain flour
1/3 teaspoon smoked cayenne pepper
2 turkey breasts, sliced
1/3 cup dry white wine
Sea salt flakes and ground black pepper, to taste
1 ½ tablespoons sesame oil
1/3 teaspoon dried rosemary
3 cloves garlic, minced

Directions

- Place the turkey breast in a large-sized bowl; add the white wine, smoked cayenne pepper, salt, and black pepper. Cover and allow it to marinate at least 1 hour.
- Drain the turkey and transfer it to a lightly oiled baking dish; air-fry for 18 minutes at 365 degrees F.
- Then, pause the machine, and add the other ingredients; toss to coat well. Cook for another 14 minutes. Bon appétit!

132. Vermouth and Honey Turkey Breast

Ready in about 35 minutes
Servings 2

Stuck on what to make for dinner? Treat your beloved one to these appetizing, addictive turkey breasts. In addition, they are ready in no time.

Per serving: 299 Calories; 4.6g Fat; 10 Carbs; 21g Protein; 3.6g Sugars

Ingredients

1 teaspoon smoked paprika
1 turkey breast, halved and marinated for 2 hours
1/2 teaspoon dried oregano
1 teaspoon dried basil
1 ½ tablespoon sesame oil
1/2 teaspoon marjoram
Sea salt flakes, to taste
1/2 tablespoon honey
1/2 tablespoon lemon juice
1 tablespoon vermouth
1 teaspoon freshly ground pepper, or to savor

Directions

- Firstly, pat the turkey breasts dry. Then, coat them with the sesame oil.
- Next, add the remaining ingredients in the order listed above.
- Afterward, bake in the air fryer cooking basket about 28 minutes at 335 degrees F. Serve warm with your favorite sauce for dipping.

133. Turkey Drumsticks with Hoisin Glaze

Ready in about 30 minutes
Servings 6

Try this outstanding main dish, made with ingredients your family will love. It begins with an unexpected flavor of fresh herbs and cider vinegar and ends with a sticky, zingy sauce.

Per serving: 199 Calories; 15.4g Fat; 4.5g Carbs; 8.3g Protein; 3.7g Sugars

Ingredients

1/3 cup pear or apple cider vinegar
2 palmful fresh or dried sage leaves, roughly chopped
Salt and pepper, to taste
2 sprigs rosemary, chopped
3 turkey drumsticks
1 sprig thyme, chopped
1 ½ tablespoons butter
1 ½ tablespoons olive oil

For the Glaze:
1/2 tablespoon honey mustard
1 ½ tablespoons hoisin sauce
1/2 tablespoon honey

Directions

- Place turkey drumsticks in a mixing dish; add cider vinegar, olive oil, thyme, rosemary, and sage. Let it marinate at least 7 hours or overnight.
- Set your air fryer to cook at 355 degrees F.
- Coat the turkey drumsticks with melted butter and sprinkle with salt and pepper to savor.
- Cook turkey drumsticks at 355 degrees F for 28 minutes, working in batches. Now, pause the machine and flip turkey drumsticks once during the cooking time.
- While the turkey drumsticks are cooking, make the glaze by mixing all glaze items. Brush the turkey with the glaze mixture and air-fry for a further 4 minutes. Let it rest before carving.

134. Cheesy Pasilla Turkey

Ready in about 30 minutes
Servings 2

Pasilla pepper is actually a dried form of the chilaca chili pepper. It is also called "Mexican negro", "little raisin" and "pasilla chile".
Wonder what to bring for a potluck? Check this out!

Per serving: 259 Calories; 19.1g Fat; 7.6g Carbs; 14g Protein; 1.5g Sugars

Ingredients

1/3 cup Parmesan cheese, shredded
2 turkey breasts, cut into four pieces
1/3 cup mayonnaise
1 ½ tablespoons sour cream
1/2 cup crushed crackers
1 dried Pasilla peppers
1 teaspoon onion salt
1/3 teaspoon mixed peppercorns, freshly cracked

Directions

- In a shallow bowl, mix the crushed crackers, Parmesan cheese, onion salt, and the cracked mixed peppercorns together.
- In a food processor, blitz the mayonnaise, along with the cream and dried Pasilla peppers until there are no lumps.
- Coat the turkey breasts with this mixture, ensuring that all sides are covered.
- Then, coat each piece of turkey in the Parmesan/cracker mix.
- Now, preheat the air fryer to 365 degrees F; cook for 28 minutes until thoroughly cooked.

135. Festive Turkey Drumsticks with Gala Apples

Ready in about 30 minutes +
marinating time
Servings 6

Anything red meat can do, poultry can do better! Don't miss this outstanding turkey recipe and make your holiday a memorable one.

Per serving: 100 Calories; 3.6g Fat; 14.7g Carbs; 4.9g Protein; 10.4g Sugars

Ingredients

3 Gala apples, cored and diced
1/2 tablespoon Dijon mustard
2 sprigs rosemary, chopped
3 turkey drumsticks
1/3 cup cider vinegar
2 teaspoons olive oil
1/2cup tamari sauce
1/2 teaspoon smoked cayenne pepper
Kosher salt and ground black pepper, to taste

Directions

- Dump drumsticks, along with cider vinegar, tamari, and olive oil, into a mixing dish. Let it marinate overnight or at least 3 hours.
- Set your air fryer to cook at 355 degrees F. Spread turkey drumsticks with Dijon mustard.
- Season turkey drumsticks with salt, black pepper, smoked cayenne pepper, and rosemary;
- Place the prepared drumstick in a lightly greased baking dish; scatter diced apples over them; work in batches, one drumstick at a time.
- Pause the machine after 13 minutes; flip turkey drumstick and continue to cook for a further 10 minutes. Bon appétit!

136. Roasted Turkey Sausage with Potatoes

Ready in about 40 minutes
Servings 6

It's easy to create a fantastic family lunch when you have turkey sausages and potatoes on hand. Sausage lovers take note.

Per serving: 212 Calories; 17.1g Fat; 6.3g Carbs; 8g Protein; 0.5g Sugars

Ingredients

1/2 pound red potatoes, peeled and diced
1/2 teaspoon onion salt
1/2 teaspoon dried sage
1/2pound ground turkey
1/3 teaspoon ginger, ground
1 sprig rosemary, chopped
1 ½ tablespoons olive oil
1/2 teaspoon paprika
2 sprigs thyme, chopped
1 teaspoon ground black pepper

Directions

- In a bowl, mix the first six ingredients; give it a good stir. Heat a thin layer of vegetable oil in a nonstick skillet that is placed over a moderate flame.
- Form the mixture into patties; fry until they're browned on all sides, or about 12 minutes.
- Arrange the potatoes at the bottom of a baking dish. Sprinkle with the rosemary and thyme; add a drizzle of olive oil. Top with the turkey.
- Roast for 32 minutes at 365 degrees F, turning once halfway through. Eat warm.

137. Dinner Turkey Sandwiches

Ready in about 4 hours 30 minutes
Servings 4

The star of these turkey breasts is a condensed cream of onion soup. It gives them an extra burst of flavor!

Per serving: 114 Calories; 5.6g Fat; 3.6g Carbs; 13.1g Protein; 0.2g Sugars

Ingredients

1/2 pound turkey breast
1 teaspoon garlic powder
7 ounces condensed cream of onion soup
1/3 teaspoon ground allspice
BBQ sauce, to savor

Directions

- Simply dump the cream of onion soup and turkey breast into your crock-pot. Cook on HIGH heat setting for 3 hours.
- Then, shred the meat and transfer to a lightly greased baking dish.
- Pour in your favorite BBQ sauce. Sprinkle with ground allspice and garlic powder. Air-fry an additional 28 minutes.
- To finish, assemble the sandwiches; add toppings such as pickled or fresh salad, mustard, etc.

138. Dijon and Curry Turkey Cutlets

Ready in about 30 minutes +
marinating time
Servings 4

This French spin on classic turkey meat will blow your mind. You can substitute turmeric for curry powder and lime juice for lemon juice.

Per serving: 190 Calories; 16.8g Fat; 2.5g Carbs; 7.4g Protein; 0.8g Sugars

Ingredients

1/2 tablespoon Dijon mustard
1/2 teaspoon curry powder
Sea salt flakes and freshly cracked black peppercorns, to savor
1/3pound turkey cutlets
1/2 cup fresh lemon juice
1/2 tablespoons tamari sauce

Directions

- Set the air fryer to cook at 375 degrees. Then, put the turkey cutlets into a mixing dish; add fresh lemon juice, tamari, and mustard; let it marinate at least 2 hours.
- Coat each turkey cutlet with the curry powder, salt, and freshly cracked black peppercorns; roast for 28 minutes; work in batches. Bon appétit!

139. Super Easy Sage and Lime Wings

Ready in about 30 minutes + marinating time
Servings 4

Thought turkey wings were less tasty than the rest of the bird? Think again. Well, with two tablespoons of fresh chopped sage and freshly squeezed lime juice, these wings are super addicting.

Per serving: 127 Calories; 7.6g Fat; 3.7g Carbs; 11.9g Protein; 0.2g Sugars

Ingredients

1 teaspoon onion powder
1/3 cup fresh lime juice
1/2 tablespoon corn flour
1/2 heaping tablespoon fresh chopped parsley
1/3 teaspoon mustard powder
1/2 pound turkey wings, cut into smaller pieces
2 heaping tablespoons fresh chopped sage
1/2 teaspoon garlic powder
1/2 teaspoon seasoned salt
1 teaspoon freshly cracked black or white peppercorns

Directions

- Simply dump all of the above ingredients into a mixing dish; cover and let it marinate for about 1 hours in your refrigerator.
- Air-fry turkey wings for 28 minutes at 355 degrees F. Bon appétit!

140. Creamy Lemon Turkey

Ready in about 2 hours 25 minutes
Servings 4

Mouth-watering, juicy turkey breasts with all amazing flavors of tomatoes, garlic, and cream! You just want to dig your fork in there.

Per serving: 260 Calories; 15.3g Fat; 8.9g Carbs; 28.6g Protein; 1.9g Sugars

Ingredients

1/3 cup sour cream
2 cloves garlic, finely minced
1/3 teaspoon lemon zest
2 small-sized turkey breasts, skinless and cubed
1/3 cup thickened cream
2 tablespoons lemon juice
1 teaspoon fresh marjoram, chopped
Salt and freshly cracked mixed peppercorns, to taste
1/2 cup scallion, chopped
1/2 can tomatoes, diced
1 ½ tablespoons canola oil

Directions

- Firstly, pat dry the turkey breast. Mix the remaining items; marinate the turkey for 2 hours.
- Set the air fryer to cook at 355 degrees F. Brush the turkey with a nonstick spray; cook for 23 minutes, turning once. Serve with naan and enjoy!

141. Turkey Wontons with Garlic-Parmesan Sauce

Ready in about 15 minutes
Servings 8

In this recipe, you can make homemade wonton wrappers but if you are in a hurry, store-bought ones will fit the bill.

Per serving: 362 Calories; 13.5g Fat; 40.4g Carbs; 18.5g Protein; 1.2g Sugars

Ingredients

8 ounces cooked turkey breasts, shredded
16 wonton wrappers
1 ½ tablespoons butter, melted
1/3 cup cream cheese, room temperature
8 ounces Asiago cheese, shredded
3 tablespoons Parmesan cheese, grated
1 teaspoon garlic powder
Fine sea salt and freshly ground black pepper, to taste

Directions

- In a small-sized bowl, mix the butter, Parmesan, garlic powder, salt, and black pepper; give it a good stir.
- Lightly grease a mini muffin pan; lay 1 wonton wrapper in each mini muffin cup. Fill each cup with the cream cheese and turkey mixture.
- Air-fry for 8 minutes at 335 degrees F. Immediately top with Asiago cheese and serve warm. Bon appétit!

142. Cajun Turkey Meatloaf

Ready in about 45 minutes
Servings 6

Cajun spice mix contains garlic powder, onion powder, cayenne pepper, oregano and thyme. Need we say more? You will want to grab a napkin or two and indulge in these incredible flavors.

Per serving: 429 Calories; 31.6g Fat; 8.3g Carbs; 25.3g Protein; 2.2g Sugars

Ingredients

1 1/3 pounds turkey breasts, ground
½ cup vegetable stock
2 eggs, lightly beaten
1/2 sprig thyme, chopped
1/2 teaspoon Cajun seasonings
1/2 sprig coriander, chopped
½ cup seasoned breadcrumbs
2 tablespoons butter, room temperature
1/2 cup scallions, chopped
1/3 teaspoon ground nutmeg
1/3 cup tomato ketchup
1/2 teaspoon table salt
2 teaspoons whole grain mustard
1/3 teaspoon mixed peppercorns, freshly cracked

Directions

- Firstly, warm the butter in a medium-sized saucepan that is placed over a moderate heat; sauté the scallions together with the chopped thyme and coriander leaves until just tender.
- While the scallions are sautéing, set your air fryer to cook at 365 degrees F.
- Combine all the ingredients, minus the ketchup, in a mixing dish; fold in the sautéed mixture and mix again.
- Shape into a meatloaf and top with the tomato ketchup. Air-fry for 50 minutes. Bon appétit!

143. Wine-Braised Turkey Breasts

Ready in about 30 minutes +
marinating time
Servings 4

Yes, dry white wine is one of the secret ingredients in this recipe. However, adding a teaspoon of two of a high-quality honey enhances crispiness and adds colors.

Per serving: 230 Calories; 11.6g Fat; 15.2g Carbs; 16.1g Protein; 2.2g Sugars

Ingredients

1/3 cup dry white wine
1½ tablespoon sesame oil
1/2 pound turkey breasts, boneless, skinless and sliced
1/2 tablespoon honey
1/2 cup plain flour
2 tablespoons oyster sauce
Sea salt flakes and cracked black peppercorns, to taste

Directions

- Set the air fryer to cook at 385 degrees. Pat the turkey slices dry and season with the sea salt flakes and the cracked peppercorns.
- In a bowl, mix the other ingredients together, minus the flour; rub your turkey with this mixture. Set aside to marinate for at least 55 minutes.
- Coat each turkey slice with the plain flour. Cook for 27 minutes; make sure to flip once or twice and work in batches. Bon appétit!

144. Turkey in Yogurt-Mint Sauce

Ready in about 35 minutes
Servings 4

This is just one of zillion ways to cook with yogurt. It gives you meat just enough of sourness whilst fresh mint adds a fragrance and a touch of nature.

Per serving: 325 Calories; 5.1g Fat;19.6g Carbs; 21.9g Protein; 6.2g Sugars

Ingredients

1 1/2 turkey breast, quartered
1/2 teaspoon hot paprika
1/2 cup dry sherry
1 teaspoon kosher salt
1/3 teaspoon shallot powder
2 cloves garlic, peeled and halved
Freshly cracked pink or green peppercorns, to taste

For the Yogurt-Mint Sauce:
1/3 cup sour cream
1 ½ tablespoons fresh roughly chopped mint
1 cup plain yogurt

Directions

- Firstly, rub the garlic halves evenly over the surface of the turkey breast.
- Add the dry sherry, shallot powder, hot paprika, salt, and cracked peppercorns. Allow it to marinate in your refrigerator for at least 1½ hours.
- Set your air fryer to cook at 365 degrees F. Roast the turkey for 32 minutes, turning halfway through; roast in batches.
- Meanwhile, prepare your sauce by mixing all the ingredients for the Yogurt-Mint Sauce. Serve warm the roasted turkey with the Yogurt-Mint sauce. Bon appétit!

145. Turkey Sausage with Cauliflower

Ready in about 45 minutes
Servings 4

You won't mind swapping the ground chicken for turkey in this recipe. The seasonings are all the indulgence this dish needs.

Per serving: 289 Calories; 25.4g Fat; 3.2g Carbs; 11.9g Protein; 1g Sugars

Ingredients

1 teaspoon garlic pepper
1 teaspoon garlic powder
1/3 teaspoon dried oregano
1/2 pound ground turkey
1/2 teaspoon salt
1/3 cup onions, chopped
1/3 teaspoon dried basil
1/2 teaspoon dried thyme, chopped
Nonstick cooking spray
1/2 head cauliflower, broken into florets

Directions

- In a mixing bowl, thoroughly combine the first six ingredients; stir well to combine. Spritz a nonstick skillet with pan spray; form the mixture into 4 sausages.
- Then, cook the sausage over medium heat until they are no longer pink, approximately 12 minutes.
- Arrange the cauliflower florets at the bottom of a baking dish. Sprinkle with thyme and basil; spritz with pan spray. Top with the turkey sausages.
- Roast for 28 minutes at 375 degrees F, turning once halfway through. Eat warm.

146. Mom's Juicy Turkey Breasts

Ready in about 25 minutes +
marinating time
Servings 2

With the exception of the marinating time, this turkey recipe is quick to prepare. You can use these turkey breasts to make grab-and-go quick sandwiches or an elegant party dinner.

Per serving: 345 Calories; 18.2g Fat; 1.8g Carbs; 40.9g Protein; 0.7g Sugars

Ingredients

1/2 tablespoon minced fresh parsley
1 ½ tablespoons Worcestershire sauce
Sea salt flakes and cracked black peppercorns, to savor
1 ½ tablespoons olive oil
1/3 turkey breasts, halved
1 ½ tablespoons rice vinegar
1/2 teaspoon marjoram

Directions

- Set the air fryer to cook at 395 degrees. In a bowl, mix all ingredients together; make sure to coat turkey breast well. Set aside to marinate for at least 3 hours.
- Roast each turkey piece for 23 minutes; make sure to pause the machine and flip once to roast evenly. Bon appétit!

147. Hot Spicy Turkey Meatloaf

Ready in about 55 minutes
Servings 6

Need more ideas for what to make with ground turkey breast? It is better the next day, so, you'll be eating this meatloaf all day long.

Per serving: 373 Calories; 20.9g Fat; 10.6g Carbs; 35.7g Protein; 4.8g Sugars

Ingredients

1½ pounds turkey breasts, ground
1/2 pound Cheddar cheese, cubed
1/2 cup hot spicy ketchup
1/2 cup turkey or chicken stock
1/3 teaspoon hot paprika
3 eggs, lightly beaten
1 ½ tablespoon olive oil
2 cloves garlic, pressed
1 ½ teaspoons dried rosemary
1/2 cup yellow onion, chopped
1/3 cup ground quick oats
1/2 teaspoon pepper
A few dashes of Tabasco sauce
1 teaspoon seasoned salt

Directions

- Heat the olive oil in a medium-sized saucepan that is placed over a moderate flame; now, sauté the onions, garlic, and dried rosemary until just tender, or about 3 to 4 minutes.
- In the meantime, set the air fryer to cook at 385 degrees F.
- Place all the ingredients, minus the hot spicy ketchup, in a mixing dish together with the sautéed mixture; thoroughly mix to combine.
- Shape into meatloaf and top with the hot spicy ketchup. Air-fry for 47 minutes. Bon appétit!

148. Mustard and Sage Turkey Breasts

Ready in about 30 minutes
Servings 4

Looking for inspiring and creative ways to cook with turkey breasts? These turkey breasts are both healthy and gourmet!

Per serving: 373 Calories; 19.9g Fat; 5g Carbs; 41.9g Protein; 1.8g Sugars

Ingredients

1/2 teaspoon smoked paprika
1 1/2 tablespoons mustard
1 ½ tablespoons soy sauce
1/3 cup chopped fresh sage
1 ½ tablespoons sesame oil
1/3 cup lemon juice
1/3 turkey breast, quartered lengthwise
1/2 teaspoon marjoram
Sea salt flakes, to taste
1 teaspoon freshly ground pepper, or to savor

Directions

- Firstly, pat the turkey breast dry; brush it with the sesame oil. Now, add the soy sauce, lemon juice, fresh sage, and the mustard; let it marinate for at least 2 hours.
- After that, discard the marinade; season the turkey breasts with the paprika, salt, black pepper, and marjoram.
- Now, bake in the air fryer cooking basket for about 22 minutes at 365 degrees F.

149. Wine and Coriander Turkey Wings

Ready in about 2 hours 30 minutes
Servings 4

Lots of aromatics and white wine, make this recipe a winner for your family lunch! Be inspired by turkey wings and experiment with oriental seasonings, crushed herbs and cooking wine in this recipe.

Per serving: 126 Calories; 7g Fat; 2.8g Carbs; 12.2g Protein; 1.2g Sugars

Ingredients

1 teaspoon freshly cracked pink peppercorns
1 ½ teaspoons all-purpose flour
½ pound turkey wings, cut into smaller pieces
2 teaspoon garlic powder
1/3 cup white wine
1/2 teaspoon garlic salt
1/2 tablespoon coriander, ground

Directions

- Toss all of the above ingredients in a mixing dish. Let it marinate at least 3 hours.
- Air-fry turkey wings for 28 minutes at 355 degrees F. Bon appétit!

150. Baked Eggs with Ground Turkey

Ready in about 30 minutes
Servings 6

Make room for this 5-star meal! Feel free to adjust a number of spices to your own personal taste.

Per serving: 234 Calories; 15.6g Fat; 6.2g Carbs; 16g Protein; 1.9g Sugars

Ingredients

1 ½ pounds ground turkey
6 whole eggs, well beaten
1/3 teaspoon smoked paprika
2 egg whites, beaten
Tabasco sauce, for drizzling
2 tablespoons sesame oil
2 leeks, chopped
3 cloves garlic, finely minced
1 teaspoon ground black pepper
1/2 teaspoon sea salt

Directions

- Warm the oil in a pan over moderate heat; then, sweat the leeks and garlic until tender; stir periodically.
- Next, grease 6 oven safe ramekins with pan spray. Divide the sautéed mixture among six ramekins.
- In a bowl, beat the eggs and egg whites using a wire whisk. Stir in the smoked paprika, salt and black pepper; whisk until everything is thoroughly combined. Divide the egg mixture among the ramekins.
- Air-fry approximately 22 minutes at 345 degrees F. Drizzle Tabasco sauce over each portion and serve.

151. Winter Turkey Breasts with Leeks

Ready in about 35 minutes
Servings 4

This is a filling and comforting one-pot meal that is chock-full of aromatics and protein-packed meat. It is perfect for windy nights when you need something satisfying and warming.

Per serving: 176 Calories; 8.6g Fat; 9.1g Carbs; 9g Protein; 3.1g Sugars

Ingredients

4 turkey breasts, boneless and skinless
1/2 palmful chopped fresh sage leaves
1 ½ tablespoons freshly squeezed lemon juice
1/3 teaspoon dry mustard
1/3 cup dry white wine
3 cloves garlic, minced
2 leeks, cut into thick slices
1/2 teaspoon smoked paprika
2 tablespoons olive oil

Directions

- Combine the first six ingredients in a small-sized mixing bowl; mix thoroughly until everything is well combined
- Then, smear this mixture on the turkey breast. Add white wine and let it marinate about 2 hours.
- Transfer to the cooking basket along with the leeks.
- Bake at 375 degrees F for 48 minutes, turning once or twice. Bon appétit!

152. Easy Honey Mustard Turkey Breast

Ready in about 40 minutes
Servings 4

These finger-licking turkey breasts will delight your senses! Sweet and tangy honey mustard makes everything better!

Per serving: 201 Calories; 9.6g Fat; 4.7g Carbs; 20.6g Protein; 1.5g Sugars

Ingredients

1/2 teaspoon dried thyme
4 medium-sized turkey breasts
1/2 teaspoon dried sage
3 whole star anise
1 ½ tablespoons olive oil
1 ½ tablespoons honey mustard
1 teaspoon smoked cayenne pepper
1 teaspoon fine sea salt

Directions

- Set your air fryer to cook at 365 degrees F.
- Brush the turkey breast with olive oil and sprinkle with seasonings.
- Cook at 365 degrees F for 45 minutes, turning twice. Now, pause the machine and spread the cooked breast with honey mustard.
- Air-fry for 6 to 8 more minutes. Let it rest before slicing and serving.

153. Asiago Turkey Wrapped in Bacon

Ready in about 10 minutes
Servings 12

Some kind of magic happens when you take a piece of turkey breast and wrap it in a nice slice of a high-quality bacon.

Per serving: 306 Calories; 30.6g Fat; 1g Carbs; 43.9g Protein; 0.6g Sugars

Ingredients

1 ½ small-sized turkey breast, chop into 12 pieces
12 thin slices Asiago cheese
Paprika, to taste
Fine sea salt and ground black pepper, to savor
12 rashers bacon

Directions

- Lay out the bacon rashers; place 1 slice of Asiago cheese on each bacon piece.
- Top with turkey, season with paprika, salt, and pepper, and roll them up; secure with a cocktail stick.
- Air-fry at 365 degrees F for 13 minutes. Bon appétit!

154. Eggs with Turkey Sausage

Ready in about 20 minutes
Servings 6

Loaded with fresh bell pepper and flavorful turkey sausage, this deliciously satisfying eggs are just as good as a family breakfast, as it is served on weeknights. Hot Italian turkey sausage works well in this recipe.

Per serving: 290 Calories; 10.1g Fat; 28.5g Carbs; 21.9g Protein; 2.2g Sugars

Ingredients

6 English muffins
1 teaspoon dried dill weed
1 teaspoon mustard seeds
6 turkey sausages
3 bell peppers, seeded and thinly sliced
6 medium-sized eggs
1/2 teaspoon fennel seeds
1 teaspoon sea salt
1/3 teaspoon freshly cracked pink peppercorns

Directions

- Set your air fryer to cook at 325 degrees F. Cook the sausages and bell peppers in the air fryer cooking basket for 8 minutes.
- Crack the eggs into the ramekins; sprinkle them with salt, dill weed, mustard seeds, fennel seeds, and peppercorns. Cook an additional 12 minutes at 395 degrees F.
- Serve on English muffins and enjoy!

155. Turkey with Honey Applesauce

Ready in about 30 minutes +
marinating time
Servings 2

Roasted turkey? Boring. Consider adding some apples, honey and freshly cracked pink peppercorns. Better?

Per serving: 378 Calories; 24.1g Fat; 23.7g Carbs; 16g Protein; 18.2g Sugars

Ingredients

1/3 teaspoon mustard powder
1/3 cup apple cider vinegar
1 apple, peeled, cored and diced
1/2 pound turkey, sliced
1 garlic clove, peeled and halved
1/2 teaspoon shallot powder
1 tablespoon honey
1 tablespoons melted butter
1 teaspoon freshly cracked pink peppercorns
1 teaspoon onion salt
1/3 teaspoon ground allspice

Directions

- Rub turkey slices with the garlic halves and transfer them to a mixing dish. Now, stir in seasonings and cider vinegar. Allow it to marinate at least 2 hours.
- After that, roast your turkey for 28 minutes at 395 degrees F.
- In the meantime, place the apples, honey, and butter in a sauté pan that is preheated over a moderate heat. Cook for 9 minutes or until apples have softened.
- Pour the apple sauce over warm turkey breasts and serve on a serving platter.

156. Rustic Turkey Breast with Walnuts

Ready in about 1 hour 30 minutes
Servings 2

Old-fashioned turkey breasts just like grandma used to make! You can use pine nuts instead of walnuts. The aim is to achieve a rustic and rich flavor.

Per serving: 388 Calories; 20.5g Fat; 16g Carbs; 34.6g Protein; 10.2g Sugars

Ingredients

1 ½ tablespoons soy sauce
1/2 tablespoon cornstarch
2 bay leaves
1/3 cup dry sherry
1 ½ tablespoons chopped walnuts
1 teaspoon shallot powder
2 turkey breasts, sliced
1 teaspoon garlic powder
2 teaspoons olive oil
1/2 teaspoon onion salt
1/2 teaspoon red pepper flakes, crushed
1 teaspoon ground black pepper

Directions

- Begin by preheating your air fryer to 395 degrees F. Place all ingredients, minus chopped walnuts, in a mixing bowl and let them marinate at least 1 hour.
- After that, cook the marinated turkey breast approximately 23 minutes or until heated through.
- Pause the machine, scatter chopped walnuts over the top and air-fry an additional 5 minutes. Bon appétit!

157. Country Turkey and Pepper Frittata

Ready in about 5 minutes
Servings 1

Prepare an easy peppery frittata with little effort in no time! You can use the peppers of different colors to make it a feast for the eyes!

Per serving: 342 Calories; 27.1g Fat; 4g Carbs; 19.4g Protein; 2.2g Sugars

Ingredients

1/2 red bell pepper, seeded and chopped
1 clove garlic, finely minced
1/3 teaspoon parsley flakes
1/2 green bell pepper, seeded and chopped
3 eggs, whisked
2 ounces ground turkey
1/2 small-sized leek, finely chopped
1 teaspoon garlic pepper
1/2 teaspoon fine sea salt

Directions

- Simply whisk all of the above ingredients in a mixing dish. Now, scrape the mixture into the air fryer baking tray.
- Set the machine to cook at 355 degrees F; air-fry approximately 8 minutes. Eat warm, garnished with hot sauce, if desired.

158. Lemony Turkey with Mustard Sauce

Ready in about 1 hour 10 minutes
Servings 4

Top-notch chefs make turkey breasts with mustard and a drizzle of freshly squeezed lemon. Thanks to the Air fryer, you can relax and enjoy a glass of wine as the entire house fills with the wonderful smells.

Per serving: 175 Calories; 9.6g Fat; 1.7g Carbs;10.9g Protein; 0.8g Sugars

Ingredients

½ teaspoon cumin powder
4 turkey breasts, quartered
2 cloves garlic, smashed
½ teaspoon hot paprika
2 tablespoons melted butter
1 teaspoon fine sea salt
Freshly cracked mixed peppercorns, to savor
Fresh juice of 1 lemon

For the Mustard Sauce:
1 ½ tablespoons mayonnaise
1 ½ cups Greek yogurt
1/2 tablespoon yellow mustard

Directions

- Grab a medium-sized mixing dish and combine together the garlic and melted butter; rub this mixture evenly over the surface of the turkey.
- Add the cumin powder, followed by paprika, salt, peppercorns, and lemon juice. Place in your refrigerator at least 55 minutes.
- Set your air fryer to cook at 375 degrees F. Roast the turkey for 18 minutes, turning halfway through; roast in batches.
- In the meantime, make the mustard sauce by mixing all ingredients for the sauce. Serve warm roasted turkey with the mustard sauce. Bon appétit!

159. Turkey Tortilla Wraps

Ready in about 2 hours + 20 minutes
Servings 4

There are ordinary tortilla wraps and extraordinary air fryer tortilla wraps. Try it yourself and you'll see a difference; you'll feel a difference.

Per serving: 195 Calories; 9.1g Fat; 23.3g Carbs; 6g Protein; 0.4g Sugars

Ingredients

8 corn tortillas
1/2 tablespoon Dijon mustard
½ small-sized red onion, thinly sliced
1 ½ tablespoons vegetable oil
1/3 cup Mexican blend cheese, shredded
1 turkey breasts, halved
1/2 teaspoon Tabasco
1 teaspoon garlic powder
2 teaspoons white vinegar
1/3 teaspoon kosher salt
1/3 teaspoon black pepper

Directions

- Combine the turkey, Tabasco, black pepper, kosher salt, garlic powder, white vinegar, and vegetable oil in a mixing bowl. Cover and let it marinate at least 2 hours.
- After that, preheat the air fryer to 355 degrees F; drain the turkey and air-fry for 23 minutes. Allow it to cool slightly.
- Shred the turkey with meat claws. To assemble your wraps, microwave the tortillas. Spread the tortillas with Dijon mustard.
- Divide the turkey filling among warm tortillas; add Mexican blend cheese and red onion; roll them tightly. Bon appétit!

160. Zesty Air Fried Turkey Leg

Ready in about 30 minutes
Servings 6

These amazing turkey legs are absolutely worth the time invested. In terms of the herb seasoning blend, you can add cayenne pepper, crushed dry rosemary, marjoram, ground bay leaves, etc.

Per serving: 244 Calories; 16g Fat; 8g Carbs; 11g Protein; 3.9g Sugars

Ingredients

1 ½ tablespoons yellow mustard
1 ½ tablespoons herb seasoning blend
1/3 cup tamari sauce
1 ½ tablespoons olive oil
1/2 lemon, juiced
3 turkey drumsticks
1/3 cup pear or apple cider vinegar
2 sprigs rosemary, chopped

Directions

- Dump all ingredients into a mixing dish. Let it marinate overnight.
- Set your air fryer to cook at 355 degrees F.
- Season turkey drumsticks with salt and black pepper and roast them at 355 degrees F for 28 minutes. Cook one drumstick at a time.
- Pause the machine after 14 minutes and flip turkey drumstick. Serve warm with a plum sauce. Bon appétit!

161. Lime Turkey Tortilla Roll-Ups

Ready in about 2 hours + 25 minutes
Servings 8

Corn tortillas are everything bread will never be. This recipe is kid-friendly but it can be served for a party dinner. Serve with a generous spoonful of Greek yogurt.

Per serving: 347 Calories; 14.6g Fat; 19g Carbs; 34.1g Protein; 0.8g Sugars

Ingredients

8 corn tortillas
1/3 Colby cheese, thinly sliced
1/2 large-sized turkey breasts, halved
1 teaspoon cumin powder
1/3 small-sized onion, chopped
1/3 cup lime juice
3 cloves garlic, minced
1 teaspoon garlic powder
Kosher salt, to savor
1 ½ tablespoons olive oil

Directions

- Combine the turkey, cumin powder, garlic powder, lime juice, and olive oil in a mixing bowl. Cover and marinate it at least 2 hours.
- After that, preheat the air fryer to 355 degrees F; discard the marinade, drain the turkey and air-fry for 23 minutes. Allow it to cool slightly.
- Now, shred the turkey with meat claws. Now, stir in the minced garlic and mix to combine well. To finish, heat your tortillas in a microwave until pliable.
- Divide the turkey filling among the tortillas; add the cheese, onion, and salt, and roll them tightly; secure with toothpicks. Bon appétit!

162. Curried Turkey Drumsticks

Ready in about 25 minutes
Servings 2

Marinated in coconut milk and seasonings, these turkey drumsticks become incredibly tender, surprisingly delicious! Serve with a cold glass of quality beer.

Per serving: 240 Calories; 9.6g Fat; 16.2g Carbs; 19.9g Protein; 2.3g Sugars

Ingredients

1 ½ tablespoons red curry paste
1/2 teaspoon cayenne pepper
1 ½ tablespoons minced ginger
2 turkey drumsticks
1/3 cup coconut milk
1 teaspoon kosher salt, or more to taste
1/3 teaspoon ground pepper, to more to taste

Directions

- First of all, place turkey drumsticks with all ingredients in your refrigerator; let it marinate overnight.
- Cook turkey drumsticks at 380 degrees F for 23 minutes; make sure to flip them over at half-time. Serve with the salad on the side.

PORK

163. Smoky Bacon and Gruyere Crescents with Herbs . 94

164. Aromatic Pork with Root Veggies............................ 94

165. Tangy Fried Pork Balls.. 95

166. Rich Filled Mexican Wraps....................................... 95

167. Grandma's Garlicky Pork Tenderloin 96

168. Asian-Style Pork Strips 96

169. Sunday Pork Roast 97

170. Marjoram Tortilla Burgers with Mint Dip.............. 97

171. Flavorsome Barbecue Pork Chops 98

172. Parmesan Pork Sausage Meatballs 98

173. Pork Slices with Coriander-Garlic Sauce 99

174. Lip-Smacking Pork Ribs with Classic Sauce........... 99

175. Grilled Sage Rack of Pork 100

176. Classic Rosemary Pork Meatloaf........................... 100

177. Three-Pepper Roast Pork Loin 101

178. Tangy Hannah Sweet Potatoes with Bacon 101

179. Rich Pork Sausage and Egg Breakfast 102

180. Grandma's Famous Pork Chops 102

181. Mediterranean Crescent Squares 103

182. Cheesy Meatball and Mushroom Casserole 103

183. Salami Rolls with Homemade Mustard Spread ... 104

184. Peppery Roasted Potatoes with Smoked Bacon .. 104

185. Cornbread with Pulled Pork 105

186. Famous Cheese and Bacon Rolls 105

187. Baked Eggs with Kale and Ham 106

188. Easiest Pork Chops Ever 106

189. Onion Rings Wrapped in Bacon 107

190. Easy Pork Burgers with Blue Cheese 107

191. Sausage, Pepper and Fontina Frittata 108

192. Country-Style Pork Meatloaf 108

193. Grilled Lemony Pork Chops 109

194. Sweet and Spicy Bacon 109

195. Perfect Restaurant-Style Pork Burgers 110

196. Pizza-Style English Muffins 110

197. Herbed Pork Fries 111

198. Hearty Pork with Vegetables 111

199. Pork Sausage with Eggs and Peppers 112

200. Saucy Pork Meatballs with Fennel 112

201. Sautéed Mixed Greens with Bacon 113

202. Easy Family Dinner Rolls 113

203. Chinese-Style Pork Bites 114

204. Old-Fashioned Pork Pasta Sauce 114

205. Rosemary Pork Sausage Balls 115

206. Potato and Ground Pork Casserole 115

207. Mediterranean-Style Pork Chops with

Petite Potatoes... 116

208. Barbeque Pork Strips 116

209. Morning Bubble & Squeak with Pork 117

210. Delicious Red Gold Potatoes with Bacon 117

211. Pork Chops with Kale 118

212. Herbed and Breaded Pork Schnitzel...................... 118

213. Spicy Pork Kebabs 119

214. Pork Sausage with Vidalia Onions and Celery 119

215. Saucy Hoisin Pork 120

216. Bubble & Squeak with Pork Sausage 120

217. Basil-Vermouth Pork Chops................................. 121

163. Smoky Bacon and Gruyere Crescents with Herbs

Ready in about 50 minutes
Servings 8

For the most beautiful dinner parties, try these easy, puffy rolls that melt in your mouth. A feast for all senses!

Per serving: 428 Calories; 28.8g Fat; 14.3g Carbs; 26.8g Protein; 2.1g Sugars

Ingredients

1 (8-ounce) can crescent dinner rolls
1 heaping tablespoon fresh basil leaves, finely chopped
1 heaping tablespoon fresh parsley, finely chopped
1 (8-ounce) package smoked Gruyere cheese, grated
3/4 pound smoked bacon, coarsely chopped
1 medium-sized egg, well-beaten

Directions

- Begin by preheating your Air Fryer to 325 degrees F.
- Next, separate crescent dough into 8 triangles. Divide the fresh herbs among crescents and press them lightly into dough.
- Then, add the cheese and the bacon. Roll up each crescent, starting at longest side. After that, firmly pinch edges to seal; brush them with the egg. Afterwards, gently stretch each crescent.
- Transfer them to the Air Fryer basket and press the power button; bake about 7 minutes. Now, pause the machine, turn the temperature to 385 degrees F and cook for further 4 minutes. Eat warm.

164. Aromatic Pork with Root Veggies

Ready in about 30 minutes
Servings 6

One of the favorite "fix-it-and-forget-it" recipes. Try to cut the meat and vegetables all the same size so that they can roast evenly.

Per serving: 585 Calories; 30.7g Fat; 14.1g Carbs; 53.9g Protein; 2.0g Sugars

Ingredients

1 ½ pounds pork belly
2 medium-sized carrots, cut into thick slices
2 Russet potatoes, peeled and diced
2 cloves garlic, finely minced
2 green onions, quartered, white and green parts
1/4 cup cooking wine
Kosher salt and ground black pepper, to taste
1 teaspoon cayenne pepper
1 tablespoon coriander
1 teaspoon celery seeds

Directions

- Blanch the pork belly in boiling water for approximately 15 minutes. Then, cut it into chunks.
- Arrange the pork chunks, carrots, and potatoes in the Air Fryer basket. Add the minced garlic and green onions. Drizzle everything with cooking wine of your choice.
- Sprinkle with salt, black pepper, cayenne pepper, fresh coriander, and celery seeds. Toss to coat well.
- Roast in the preheated Air Fryer at 330 degrees F for 30 minutes.
- Serve on individual serving plates. Bon appétit!

165. Tangy Fried Pork Balls

Ready in about 20 minutes
Servings 4

This is a new twist of an old-fashioned favorite. Just add a turmeric powder and fresh ginger to these balls for an ambrosial flavor and enjoy them submerged in your favorite sauce. Yummy!

Per serving: 175 Calories; 4.1g Fat; 2.8g Carbs; 30.3g Protein; 0.6g Sugars

Ingredients

1 pound ground pork
1 cup scallions, finely chopped
2 cloves garlic, finely minced
1 ½ tablespoons Worcester sauce
1 tablespoon oyster sauce
1 teaspoon turmeric powder
1/2 teaspoon freshly grated ginger root
1 tablespoon breadcrumbs
1 small sliced red chili, for garnish

Directions

- Mix all of the above ingredients, apart from the red chili. Knead with your hands to ensure an even mixture.
- Roll into equal balls and transfer them to the Air Fryer cooking basket.
- Set the timer for 15 minutes and push the power button. Air-fry at 350 degrees F. Sprinkle with sliced red chili; serve immediately with your favorite sauce for dipping. Enjoy!

166. Rich Filled Mexican Wraps

Ready in about 20 minutes
Servings 10

This life-changing bites can be served as an amazing dinner or tempting snacks. Don't replace Mexican cheese blend in order to perfect your wraps.

Per serving: 314 Calories; 7.5g Fat; 40.4g Carbs; 19.7g Protein; 2.3g Sugars

Ingredients

1/4 pound ground pork
1/2 pound ground beef
2 rashers bacon
1 ½ teaspoons Mexican spice mix
1 ounce tomato ketchup
9 ounces canned crushed tomatoes, drained
1 chipotle pepper, deveined and chopped
20 wonton wrappers
3/4 cup Mexican cheese blend, fine cut shredded

Directions

- In a large-sized skillet that is preheated over a moderate flame, brown the pork, beef and the bacon. Then, using a spatula, crumble the browned meat and crush the bacon; then drain.
- Stir in Mexican spice mix, ketchup, crushed tomatoes, and chipotle pepper.
- Lightly grease a mini muffin tin with a pan spray; add wonton wrappers to the muffin tin and press to form the cups. Fill them with the meat mixture; top each cup with cheese.
- Bake in the preheated device at 360 degrees F approximately 11 minutes. Bon appétit!

167. Grandma's Garlicky Pork Tenderloin

Ready in about 20 minutes +
marinating time
Servings 4

Flavorsome pork with garlic and fragrant herbs – just like grandma used to make it! To tuck garlic slivers into the slits, you can also score the meat i.e. cut small slits in a criss-cross pattern.

Per serving: 168 Calories; 4.1g Fat; 1.4g Carbs; 29.9g Protein; 0.0g Sugars

Ingredients

1 pound pork tenderloin
4-5 garlic cloves, peeled and halved
1 teaspoon kosher salt
1/3 teaspoon ground black pepper
1 teaspoon dried basil
1/2 teaspoon dried oregano
1/2 teaspoon dried rosemary
1/2 teaspoon dried marjoram
2 tablespoons cooking wine

Directions

- Rub the pork with garlic halves; add the seasoning and drizzle with the cooking wine. Then, cut slits completely through pork tenderloin. Tuck the remaining garlic into the slits.
- Wrap the pork tenderloin with foil; let it marinate overnight.
- Roast at 360 degrees F for 15 to 17 minutes. Serve warm with roasted potatoes. Bon appétit!

168. Asian-Style Pork Strips

Ready in about 50 minutes
Servings 6

This is very simple but delicious weeknight meal. Soaking the strips into a marinade only for half an hour will make them tender. After that, they need to be fried for 7 to 8 minutes.

Per serving: 409 Calories; 20.5g Fat; 29.6g Carbs; 22.0g Protein; 2.8g Sugars

Ingredients

1 pound boneless center-cut loin pork chops, cut into 1/2-inch strips
2 tablespoons bourbon
1 teaspoon honey
1/2 teaspoon chili powder
1 teaspoon celery seeds
1/2 teaspoon mustard seeds
1 teaspoon peeled fresh ginger, freshly grated
Salt and freshly ground black pepper, to your liking
1/2 cup all-purpose flour
6 ounces seasoned breadcrumbs

Directions

- Place the pork strips together with the bourbon, honey, chili powder, celery seeds, mustard seeds and the ginger in a zip-top plastic bag; seal and place in your refrigerator 30 to 45 minutes.
- After that, remove the pork from the marinade and season with salt and pepper. Coat with flour and finally dip it into the breadcrumbs.
- Set your Air Fryer to cook at 380 degrees F. Press the power button and air-fry for 4 minutes; pause the machine, shake the basket and cook for 3 more minutes.
- Serve with warm rice noodles.

169. Sunday Pork Roast

Ready in about 55 minutes
Servings 6

If you are lucky enough to own an Air Fryer, then, you can prepare your Sunday pork roast in the easiest possible way. To serve it up, add wild rice to each serving plate. Ta-Da! Delight your family and guests!

Per serving: 278 Calories; 16.0g Fat; 0.3g Carbs; 31.2g Protein; 0.0g Sugars

Ingredients

1 ½ pounds boneless pork loin roast, washed
1 teaspoon mustard seeds
1 teaspoon garlic powder
1 teaspoon porcini powder
1 teaspoon shallot powder
3/4 teaspoon sea salt flakes
1 teaspoon red pepper flakes, crushed
2 dried sprigs thyme, crushed
2 tablespoons lime juice

Directions

- Firstly, score the meat using a small knife; make sure to not cut too deep.
- In a small-sized mixing dish, combine all seasonings in the order listed above; mix to combine well.
- Massage the spice mix into the pork meat to evenly distribute. Drizzle with lemon juice.
- Then, set your Air Fryer to cook at 360 degrees F. Place the pork in the Air Fryer basket; roast for 25 to 30 minutes. Pause the machine, check for doneness and cook for 25 minutes more.

170. Marjoram Tortilla Burgers with Mint Dip

Ready in about 40 minutes
Servings 4

These tortillas stand out from all the others thanks to a tangy mint spread, aromatic marjoram, and flavorsome pork mince. Don't forget to microwave your tortillas before serving!

Per serving: 302 Calories; 10.8g Fat; 15.7g Carbs; 34.8g Protein; 1.5g Sugars

Ingredients

For the Pork Sliders:
1 pound pork, ground
1 onion, peeled and finely chopped
2 garlic cloves, minced
1 ½ teaspoons whole-grain mustard
Salt and ground black pepper, to taste
1/2 teaspoon cumin powder
1 tablespoon marjoram
1/4 cup Gruyère cheese, shredded

For the Mint Spread:
1/4 cup sour cream
1/4 soft cheese
1/4 cup fresh mint, coarsely chopped
4 whole-wheat tortillas

Directions

- Thoroughly combine all the ingredients for the pork balls; knead with your hands for better results.
- Shape into 4 patties. Air-fry for 35 to 40 minutes at 370 degrees, cooking in batches. Make sure to flip them over halfway through the cooking time.
- While the sliders are cooking, combine the sour cream with soft cheese and mint leaves.
- Then, warm and soften the tortillas in the microwave; divide the mint spread among tortillas. Add cooked pork sliders and serve immediately.

171. Flavorsome Barbecue Pork Chops

Ready in about 20 minutes
Servings 6

In this recipe, you can marinate the chops with seasonings for about 3 hours or overnight; it will certainly add flavor. However, if you are short on time, don't worry; feel free to skip that step.

Per serving: 285 Calories; 20.0g Fat; 6.2g Carbs; 18.8g Protein; 0.7g Sugars

Ingredients

6 pork chops
Hickory-smoked salt, to savor
Ground black pepper, to savor
1 teaspoon onion powder
1/2 teaspoon garlic powder
1/2 teaspoon cayenne pepper
1 teaspoon packed brown sugar
1/3 cup all-purpose flour

Directions

- Simply place all of the above ingredients into a zip-top plastic bag; shake them up to coat well.
- Spritz the chops with a pan spray (canola spray works well here) and transfer them to the Air Fryer cooking basket.
- Roast them for 20 minutes at 375 degrees F. Serve with sautéed vegetables. Bon appétit!

172. Parmesan Pork Sausage Meatballs

Ready in about 20 minutes
Servings 4

If you have only 20 minutes, you can easily cook these heavenly meatballs with a touch of Parmesan cheese with delightful marinara sauce. Sounds tasty? Okay, let's get cooking!

Per serving: 207 Calories; 11.1g Fat; 16.6g Carbs; 10.1g Protein; 4.3g Sugars

Ingredients

1 cup pork sausage meat
1 shallot, finely chopped
2 garlic cloves, finely minced
1/2 teaspoon fine sea salt
1/4 teaspoon ground black pepper, or more to taste
3/4 teaspoon paprika
1 ½ tablespoons parmesan cheese, preferably freshly grated
1/2 cup seasoned breadcrumbs
1/2 jar marinara sauce

Directions

- Mix all of the above ingredients, except the marinara sauce, in a large-sized dish, until everything is well incorporated.
- Shape into meatballs. Air-fry them at 360 degrees F for 10 minutes; pause the Air Fryer, shake them up and cook for additional 6 minutes or until the balls are no longer pink in the middle.
- Meanwhile, heat the marinara sauce over a medium flame. Serve the pork sausage meatballs with marinara sauce. Bon appétit!

173. Pork Slices with Coriander-Garlic Sauce

Ready in about 30 minutes + marinating time
Servings 4

Pork slices with crispy crackling are a culinary version of the little black dress! Air-frying is one of the best ways to achieve this extraordinary, vivid impression.

Per serving: 408 Calories; 27.9g Fat; 2.1g Carbs; 36.8g Protein; 0.0g Sugars

Ingredients

1 pound pork butt, cut into pieces 2-inches long
1 teaspoon cornstarch
1 egg white, well whisked
Salt and ground black pepper, to taste
1 tablespoon olive oil
1 tablespoon soy sauce
1 teaspoon lemon juice, preferably freshly squeezed

For the Coriander-Garlic Sauce:
3 garlic cloves, peeled
1/3 cup fresh parsley leaves
1/3 cup fresh coriander leaves
1/2 tablespoon salt
1 teaspoon lemon juice
1/3 cup extra-virgin olive oil

Directions

- Combine the pork strips with cornstarch, egg white, salt, pepper, olive oil, soy sauce, and lemon juice. Cover and refrigerate for 30 to 45 minutes.
- After that, spritz the pork strips with a nonstick cooking spray.
- Set your Air Fryer to cook at 380 degrees F. Press the power button and air-fry for 15 minutes; pause the machine, shake the basket and cook for 15 more minutes.
- Meanwhile, puree the garlic in a food processor until finely minced. Now, puree the parsley, coriander, salt, and lemon juice. With the machine running, carefully pour in the olive oil.
- Serve chilled sauce with pork slices and enjoy!

174. Lip-Smacking Pork Ribs with Classic Sauce

Ready in about 15 minutes + marinating time
Servings 4

Pork ribs in classic red wine sauce – it smells like holiday happiness! This classic sauce will improve the flavor and presentation of the pork ribs.

Per serving: 438 Calories; 27.3g Fat; 3.8g Carbs; 32.2g Protein; 1.5g Sugars

Ingredients

For the Pork Ribs:
1 pound pork ribs
2 tablespoons olive oil
1/2 teaspoon freshly cracked black peppercorns
1/2 teaspoon Hickory-smoked salt
1 tablespoon Dijon honey mustard
1/4 cup soy sauce
1 clove garlic, minced

For the Red Wine Sauce:
1 ½ cups beef stock
1 cup red wine
1 teaspoon brown sugar
1 teaspoon balsamic vinegar
1/4 teaspoon salt

Directions

- Place all ingredients for the pork ribs in a large-sized mixing dish. Cover and marinate in your refrigerator overnight or at least 3 hours.
- Air-fry the pork ribs for 10 minutes at 320 degrees F.
- Meanwhile, make the sauce. Add a beef stock to a deep pan that is preheated over a moderate flame; boil until it is reduced by half.
- Add the remaining ingredients and increase the temperature to high heat. Let it cook for further 10 minutes or until your sauce is reduced by half.
- Serve the pork ribs with red wine sauce. Bon appétit!

175. Grilled Sage Rack of Pork

Ready in about 15 minutes +
marinating time
Servings 4

An elegant entrée for a special dinner. Serve with buttered green beans, Waldorf salad, dinner rolls and rose wine.

Per serving: 295 Calories; 4.2g Fat; 32.5g Carbs; 30.2g Protein; 25.9g Sugars

Ingredients

1 rib rack of pork, chine bone cut off
1 teaspoon shallot powder
1/2 teaspoon cumin powder
2 gloves garlic, finely minced
Salt and pepper, to your liking
1 ½ tablespoons Teriyaki sauce
1 cup BBQ sauce
2 tablespoons honey
1 heaping tablespoon fresh sage, snipped

Directions

- Put all the ingredients, except the fresh sage leaves, into a mixing dish; let it marinate for at least 30 minutes.
- Then, set your Air Fryer to cook at 360 degrees F; air-fry the marinated pork using the Air Fryer grill pan for 15 minutes. Check for doneness and serve sprinkled with snipped fresh sage.

176. Classic Rosemary Pork Meatloaf

Ready in about 30 minutes
Servings 6

Spicy pork sausage and ground turkey with aromatic rosemary, make this a sumptuous meal for any occasion! What about leftovers? Try to make the sandwiches; just add a crisp lettuce and pickled red onions, and enjoy!

Per serving: 282 Calories; 19.2g Fat; 9.2g Carbs; 18.3g Protein; 5.1g Sugars

Ingredients

Non-stick cooking spray
1 shallot, finely chopped
1 rib celery, finely chopped
2 gloves garlic, minced
1 tablespoon Worcestershire sauce
3/4 pound spicy ground pork sausage
1/4 pound ground turkey
2 sprigs rosemary, leaves only, crushed
1/4 cup minced fresh parsley
1 egg, lightly whisked
3 tablespoons fresh panko
Salt and freshly ground pepper, to your liking
1/3 cup tomato ketchup

Directions

- Spritz a cast-iron skillet with a cooking spray. Then, sauté the shallots, celery and garlic until just tender and fragrant.
- Now, add Worcestershire sauce and both kinds of meat to the sautéed mixture. Remove from the heat. Add the rosemary, parsley, egg, fresh panko, salt, and pepper; mix to combine well.
- Transfer the mixture to the baking pan and shape into a loaf. Cover the prepared meatloaf with tomato ketchup.
- Air-fry at 390 degrees F for 25 minutes or until thoroughly warmed.

177. Three-Pepper Roast Pork Loin

Ready in about 30 minutes
Servings 6

The key to this sophisticated roast – cut slits to hold the chunks of peppers and massage the seasoning into the meat. You'll thank us later.
Per serving: 241 Calories; 14.4g Fat; 5.3g Carbs; 22.2g Protein; 3.3g Sugars

Ingredients

1 tablespoon olive oil
1 pound pork loin
1 teaspoon dried basil
1/2 teaspoon dried oregano
1⁄4 teaspoon crushed red pepper flakes
1 teaspoon dried thyme
1/4 teaspoon freshly grated nutmeg
Sea salt flakes and freshly ground black pepper, to taste
1 Pimento chili pepper, deveined and chopped
1 Yellow wax pepper, deveined and chopped
1 sweet bell pepper, deveined and chopped
1 tablespoon peanut butter
1/4 cup beef broth
1/2 tablespoon whole-grain mustard
1 bay leaf

Directions

- Lightly grease the inside of an Air Fryer baking dish with a thin layer of olive oil. Then, cut 8 slit down the center of pork (about 3x3"). Sprinkle with the seasonings and massage them into the meat to evenly distribute
- Then, tuck peppers into the slits and transfer the meat to the Air Fryer baking dish. Scatter remaining peppers around the roast.
- In a mixing dish, whisk the peanut butter, beef broth, and mustard; now, pour broth mixture around the roast.
- Add the bay leaf and roast the meat for 25 minutes at 390 degrees F; turn the pork over halfway through the roasting time. Bon appétit!

178. Tangy Hannah Sweet Potatoes with Bacon

Ready in about 23 minutes
Servings 4

Quick and tasty, this dish is perfect for your next family lunch. The combo of Hannah potatoes, bacon and pepper has never tasted better!

Per serving: 394 Calories; 30.3g Fat; 25.3g Carbs; 5.7g Protein; 6.5g Sugars

Ingredients

1/2 green or yellow bell pepper, seeded and cut into strips
5 Hannah sweet potatoes, peeled and diced
5 slices bacon, diced
1 teaspoon ground black pepper
½ tablespoon honey
½ teaspoon fennel seeds
1teaspoon grated nutmeg, preferably freshly grated
2 tablespoons melted butter
1/2 red bell pepper, seeded and cut into strips
2 shallots, cut into wedges
½ teaspoon sea salt
1 teaspoon garlic powder
½ tablespoon balsamic vinegar

Directions

- Begin by preheating your air fryer to 355 degrees F.
- Next, arrange the sweet potatoes on the bottom of the air fryer baking tray. Add the bell peppers and the shallot.
- Sprinkle with all the seasonings and drizzle with the vinegar, honey, and the melted butter. Cook for 12 minutes in the preheated air fryer.
- Pause the machine and place the bacon on the top; cook an additional 4 minutes or until everything is heated through. Bon appétit!

179. Rich Pork Sausage and Egg Breakfast

Ready in about 20 minutes
Servings 5

Treat your body like the amazing temple with this rich protein breakfast. This combination of pork sausages, bacon and eggs will give you the energy you need to start a day.

Per serving: 385 Calories; 32.4g Fat; 1.77g Carbs; 20.7g Protein; 1.1g Sugars

Ingredients

1/2 teaspoon ground black pepper, or more to taste
1/2 teaspoon mustard seeds
10 slices of bacon
1/3 teaspoon fennel seeds
5 eggs
10 pork sausages
1/3 teaspoon kosher salt

Directions

- Divide the sausages and bacon among five ramekins; crack an egg into each ramekin. Sprinkle with seasonings.
- Cook for 18 minutes at 345 degrees F or until your eggs reach desired texture.
- Serve warm with some extra Dijon mustard and spicy tomato ketchup. Bon appétit!

180. Grandma's Famous Pork Chops

Ready in about 1 hour 12 minutes
Servings 4

Pork chops are a staple in a grandma's kitchen, right?! This recipe is proof that she was right. These pork chops are coated with butter crackers, eggs and seasonings for a delicious family lunch.

Per serving: 473 Calories; 28.5g Fat; 6g Carbs; 45.6g Protein; 2.5g Sugars

Ingredients

3 eggs, well-beaten
1 ½ cup crushed butter crackers
2 teaspoons mustard powder
1 ½ tablespoons olive oil
1/2 tablespoon soy sauce
2 tablespoons Worcestershire sauce
½ teaspoon dried rosemary
4 large-sized pork chops
½ teaspoon dried thyme
2 teaspoons fennel seeds
Salt and freshly cracked black pepper, to taste
1 teaspoon red pepper flakes, crushed

Directions

- Add the pork chops along with olive oil, soy sauce, Worcestershire sauce, and seasonings to a resealable plastic bag. Allow pork chops to marinate for 50 minutes in your refrigerator.
- Next step, dip the pork chops into the beaten eggs; then, coat the pork chops with the butter crackers on both sides.
- Cook in the air fryer for 18 minutes at 405 degrees F, turning once. Bon appétit!

181. Mediterranean Crescent Squares

Ready in about 20 minutes
Servings 6

A combination of prosciutto and herbs gives these rolls a wonderful burst of flavor. Nutty, subtle and creamy Asiago cheese adds them a touch of Italy. Bon appétit!

Per serving: 281 Calories; 20.8g Fat; 4.1g Carbs; 18.6g Protein; 1.2g Sugars

Ingredients

6 slices Asiago cheese
1/2 teaspoon oregano
1/3 teaspoon fresh or dried rosemary, chopped
6 slices prosciutto
1 teaspoon salt
1/2 teaspoon basil
1 teaspoon freshly ground black pepper
1/3teaspoon smoked paprika
½ can crescent roll, refrigerated
1/3 teaspoon fresh or dried thyme, chopped
1/2 tablespoon fresh coriander, minced
6 well-beaten eggs

Directions

- Unroll the crescent rolls and form six rectangles. Gently fold up the edges of each rectangle and transfer them to the air fryer basket.
- Now, crack 1 egg into each rectangle. Sprinkle with the rosemary, thyme, basil, oregano, salt, ground black pepper, paprika, and minced coriander.
- Add 1 piece of prosciutto and top with 1 slice of Asiago cheese. Repeat with the remaining rectangles.
- Bake for 12 minutes at 292 degrees F and serve warm.

182. Cheesy Meatball and Mushroom Casserole

Ready in about 41 minutes
Servings 4

If you don't have Italian breadcrumbs on hand, you can make them in your own kitchen. Just combine plain breadcrumbs with sea salt, black pepper, dried parsley flakes, oregano, basil, garlic powder and onion powder.

Per serving: 238 Calories; 12.2g Fat; 11.2g Carbs; 21.9g Protein; 3.9g Sugars

Ingredients

2 tablespoons Italian breadcrumbs
10 ounces lean ground pork
1 ½ cup mushrooms, sliced
3 carrots, peeled and shredded
1 teaspoon saffron
2 teaspoons fennel seeds
1/3 cup Monterey Jack cheese, preferably freshly grated
1/3 cup cream
2 medium-sized leeks, finely chopped
1/teaspoon dried dill weed
2 small-sized egg
1/2 teaspoon cumin
½ teaspoon fine sea salt
Freshly ground black pepper, to taste

Directions

- Begin by preheating the air fryer to 400 degrees F.
- In a bowl, mix the ingredients for the meatballs. Shape the mixture into mini meatballs.
- In an air fryer baking dish, toss the carrots and mushrooms with the cream; cook for 23 minutes in the preheated air fryer.
- Pause the machine and place the reserved meatballs in a single layer on top of the carrot/mushroom mixture.
- Top with the grated Monterey Jack cheese; bake for 9 minutes longer. Serve warm.

183. Salami Rolls with Homemade Mustard Spread

Ready in about 10 minutes
Servings 4

Rich in flavor and sinfully delicious, these rolls could also be made with another type of cheese like Asiago or Pecorino Romano. Also, you can substitute pepperoni for salami.

Per serving: 375 Calories; 17.6g Fat; 27.4g Carbs; 26.7g Protein; 8g Sugars

Ingredients

7 ounces Manchego cheese, grated
2/3 pound pork salami, chopped
7 ounces canned crescent rolls

For the Mustard Spread:
1 tablespoon sour cream
1/3 teaspoon garlic powder
1/3 cup mayonnaise
2 ½ tablespoons spicy brown mustard
Salt, to taste

Directions

- Start by preheating your air fryer to 325 degrees F. Now, form the crescent rolls into "sheets".
- Place the chopped Manchego and pork salami in the middle of each dough sheet.
- Shape the dough into the rolls; bake the rolls for 8 minutes. Then, decrease the temperature and bake at 290 degrees F for 5 more minutes.
- In the meantime, combine all of the ingredients for the mustard spread. Arrange the warm rolls on a serving platter and serve with the mustard spread on the side. Enjoy!

184. Peppery Roasted Potatoes with Smoked Bacon

Ready in about 15 minutes
Servings 2

As you can see, there's more than one way to cook potatoes in your Air fryer. As a matter of fact, the possibilities are endless. Let your imagination run wild!

Per serving: 242 Calories; 11.6g Fat; 15,4g Carbs; 14.9g Protein; 5.7g Sugars

Ingredients

5 small rashers smoked bacon
1/3 teaspoon garlic powder
1 teaspoon sea salt
2 teaspoons paprika
1/3 teaspoon ground black pepper
1 bell pepper, seeded and sliced
1 teaspoon mustard
2 habanero peppers, halved

Directions

- Simply toss all the ingredients in a mixing dish; then, transfer them to your air fryer's basket.
- Air-fry at 375 degrees F for 10 minutes. Serve warm.

185. Cornbread with Pulled Pork

Ready in about 24 minutes
Servings 2

Cornbread is a cinch to make in the Air fryer. This rustic cornbread, loaded with pulled pork and scallions, will amaze your family.

Per serving: 239 Calories; 7.6g Fat; 6.3g Carbs; 34.6g Protein; 4g Sugars

Ingredients

2 ½ cups pulled pork, leftover works well too
1 teaspoon dried rosemary
1/2 teaspoon chili powder
3 cloves garlic, peeled and pressed
1/2 recipe cornbread
1/2 tablespoon brown sugar
1/3 cup scallions, thinly sliced
1 teaspoon sea salt

Directions

- Preheat a large-sized nonstick skillet over medium heat; now, cook the scallions together with the garlic and pulled pork.
- Next, add the sugar, chili powder, rosemary, and salt. Cook, stirring occasionally, until the mixture is thickened.
- Preheat your air fryer to 335 degrees F. Now, coat two mini loaf pans with a cooking spray. Add the pulled pork mixture and spread over the bottom using a spatula.
- Spread the previously prepared cornbread batter over top of the spiced pulled pork mixture.
- Bake this cornbread in the preheated air fryer until a tester inserted into the center of it comes out clean, or for 18 minutes. Bon appétit!

186. Famous Cheese and Bacon Rolls

Ready in about 10 minutes
Servings 6

Take your dinner party to the completely new level with these fluffy and yummy bacon rolls. Swiss cheese adds depth and a specific savory note to these rolls.

Per serving: 386 Calories; 16.2g Fat; 29.7g Carbs; 14.7g Protein; 4g Sugars

Ingredients

1/3 cup Swiss cheese, shredded
10 slices of bacon
10 ounces canned crescent rolls
2 tablespoons yellow mustard 6

Directions

- Start by preheating your air fryer to 325 degrees F.
- Then, form the crescent rolls into "sheets". Spread mustard over the sheets. Place the chopped Swiss cheese and bacon in the middle of each dough sheet.
- Create the rolls and bake them for about 9 minutes.
- Then, set the machine to 385 degrees F; bake for an additional 4 minutes in the preheated air fryer. Eat warm with some extra yellow mustard.

187. Baked Eggs with Kale and Ham

Ready in about 15 minutes
Servings 2

Each serving starts with steamed kale and sliced ham, and then it's topped with an egg. Lastly, you'll add seasonings. Yummy!

Per serving: 417 Calories; 17.8g Fat; 3g Carbs; 61g Protein; 0.9g Sugars

Ingredients

2 eggs
1/4 teaspoon dried or fresh marjoram
2 teaspoons chili powder
1/3 teaspoon kosher salt
½ cup steamed kale
1/4 teaspoon dried or fresh rosemary
4 pork ham slices
1/3 teaspoon ground black pepper, or more to taste

Directions

- Divide the kale and ham among 2 ramekins; crack an egg into each ramekin. Sprinkle with seasonings.
- Cook for 15 minutes at 335 degrees F or until your eggs reach desired texture.
- Serve warm with spicy tomato ketchup and pickles. Bon appétit!

188. Easiest Pork Chops Ever

Ready in about 22 minutes
Servings 6

Cajun seasoning blend makes everything better. Don't miss these buttery, juicy and flavorsome pork chops!

Per serving: 398 Calories; 21g Fat; 4.7g Carbs; 44.2g Protein; 0.5g Sugars

Ingredients

1/3 cup Italian breadcrumbs
Roughly chopped fresh cilantro, to taste
2 teaspoons Cajun seasonings
Nonstick cooking spray
2 eggs, beaten
3 tablespoons white flour
1 teaspoon seasoned salt
Garlic & onion spice blend, to taste
6 pork chops
1/3 teaspoon freshly cracked black pepper

Directions

- Coat the pork chops with Cajun seasonings, salt, pepper, and the spice blend on all sides.
- Then, add the flour to a plate. In a shallow dish, whisk the egg until pale and smooth. Place the Italian bread-crumbs in the third bowl.
- Dredge each pork piece in the flour; then, coat them with the egg; finally, coat them with the breadcrumbs. Spritz them with cooking spray on both sides.
- Now, air-fry pork chops for about 18 minutes at 345 degrees F; make sure to taste for doneness after first 12 minutes of cooking. Lastly, garnish with fresh cilantro. Bon appétit!

189. Onion Rings Wrapped in Bacon

Ready in about 25 minutes
Servings 4

Crispy and spicy onion rings for a romantic weeknight dinner or an elegant cocktail party! Double the recipe if desired. Just remember to add a sprinkling of fresh parsley. Enjoy!

Per serving: 317 Calories; 16.8g Fat; 22.7g Carbs; 20.2g Protein; 2.7g Sugars

Ingredients

12 rashers back bacon
1/2 teaspoon ground black pepper
Chopped fresh parsley, to taste
1/2 teaspoon paprika
1/2 teaspoon chili powder
1/2 tablespoon soy sauce
½ teaspoon salt

Directions

- Start by preheating your air fryer to 355 degrees F.
- Season the onion rings with paprika, salt, black pepper, and chili powder. Simply wrap the bacon around the onion rings; drizzle with soy sauce.
- Bake for 17 minutes, garnish with fresh parsley and serve. Bon appétit!

190. Easy Pork Burgers with Blue Cheese

Ready in about 44 minutes
Servings 6

Are you eager to try something new? Toss ground pork with tomato puree and seasonings and make these country-style burgers in no time!

Per serving: 383 Calories; 19.5g Fat; 24.7g Carbs; 25.7g Protein; 4g Sugars

Ingredients

1/3 cup blue cheese, crumbled
6 hamburger buns, toasted
2 teaspoons dried basil
1/3 teaspoon smoked paprika
1 pound ground pork
2 tablespoons tomato puree
2 small-sized onions, peeled and chopped
1/2 teaspoon ground black pepper
3 garlic cloves, minced
1 teaspoon fine sea salt

Directions

- Start by preheating your air fryer to 385 degrees F.
- In a mixing dish, combine the pork, onion, garlic, tomato puree, and seasonings; mix to combine well.
- Form the pork mixture into six patties; cook the burgers for 23 minutes. Pause the machine, turn the temperature to 365 degrees F and cook for 18 more minutes.
- Place the prepared burger on the bottom bun; top with blue cheese; assemble the burgers and serve warm.

191. Sausage, Pepper and Fontina Frittata

Ready in about 14 minutes
Servings 5

This tasty frittata features flavorful sausages, Fontina cheese and fresh peppers. Serve with a dollop of sour cream and a homemade crusty bread.

Per serving: 420 Calories; 19.6g Fat; 3.7g Carbs; 41g Protein; 2g Sugars

Ingredients

3 pork sausages, chopped
5 well-beaten eggs
1 ½ bell peppers, seeded and chopped
1 teaspoon smoked cayenne pepper
2 tablespoons Fontina cheese
1/2 teaspoon tarragon
1/2 teaspoon ground black pepper
1 teaspoon salt

Directions

- In a cast-iron skillet, sweat the bell peppers together with the chopped pork sausages until the peppers are fragrant and the sausage begins to release liquid.
- Lightly grease the inside of a baking dish with pan spray.
- Throw all of the above ingredients into the prepared baking dish, including the sautéed mixture; stir to combine.
- Bake at 345 degrees F approximately 9 minutes. Serve right away with the salad of choice.

192. Country-Style Pork Meatloaf

Ready in about 25 minutes
Servings 4

Elevate an ordinary meatloaf with fresh and dried herbs, tomato puree and green garlic. A perfect mix of flavor and textures will amaze your family and friends.

Per serving: 460 Calories; 26.6g Fat; 3.9g Carbs; 48.9g Protein; 2g Sugars

Ingredients

1/2 pound lean minced pork
1/3 cup breadcrumbs
1/2 tablespoons minced green garlic
1½ tablespoon fresh cilantro, minced
1/2 tablespoon fish sauce
1/3 teaspoon dried basil
2 leeks, chopped
2 tablespoons tomato puree
1/2 teaspoons dried thyme
Salt and ground black pepper, to taste

Directions

- Add all ingredients, except for breadcrumbs, to a large-sized mixing dish and combine everything using your hands.
- Lastly, add the breadcrumbs to form a meatloaf.
- Bake for 23 minutes at 365 degrees F. Afterward, allow your meatloaf to rest for 10 minutes before slicing and serving. Bon appétit!

193. Grilled Lemony Pork Chops

Ready in about 34 minutes
Servings 5

Pork chops are always a good idea for a family lunch. An air-fried pork is one of the best ways to comfort yourself and your family. Enjoy!

Per serving: 400 Calories; 23g Fat; 4.1g Carbs; 40.5g Protein; 1.5g Sugars

Ingredients

5 pork chops
1/3 cup vermouth
1/2 teaspoon paprika
2 sprigs thyme, only leaves, crushed
1/2 teaspoon dried oregano
Fresh parsley, to serve
1 teaspoon garlic salt½ lemon, cut into wedges
1 teaspoon freshly cracked black pepper
3 tablespoons lemon juice
3 cloves garlic, minced
2 tablespoons canola oil

Directions

- Firstly, heat the canola oil in a sauté pan over a moderate heat. Now, sweat the garlic until just fragrant.
- Remove the pan from the heat and pour in the lemon juice and vermouth. Now, throw in the seasonings. Dump the sauce into a baking dish, along with the pork chops.
- Tuck the lemon wedges among the pork chops and air-fry for 27 minutes at 345 degrees F. Bon appétit!

194. Sweet and Spicy Bacon

Ready in about 10 minutes
Servings 4

Drizzled with maple syrup and sprinkled with cayenne pepper, these bacon slices are really delicious! Your family and guests won't be able to resist.

Per serving: 337 Calories; 25.2g Fat; 5.8g Carbs; 9.8g Protein; 5.2g Sugars

Ingredients

1/3 teaspoon smoked cayenne pepper
12 slices thick-cut bacon slices
1 ½ tablespoons maple syrup

Directions

- Thoroughly combine all ingredients in a mixing dish.
- Transfer the glazed bacon slices to an air fryer cooking basket.
- Cook the bacon for 5 minutes at 353 degrees F. Serve with muhammara sauce if desired and enjoy!

195. Perfect Restaurant-Style Pork Burgers

Ready in about 48 minutes
Servings 5

Looking for a last-minute recipe for a family dinner? These stunning pork burgers will fit the bill! Serve with Unoaked Chardonnay.

Per serving: 225 Calories; 9g Fat; 22.5g Carbs; 13.4g Protein; 6.7g Sugars

Ingredients

1 teaspoon Italian mixed herbs
1/3 pound ground pork
5 hamburger buns
3 garlic cloves, minced
2 teaspoons Worcestershire sauce
1/2 teaspoon ground black pepper
2 tablespoons tomato puree, preferably homemade
1/2 onion, peeled and chopped
Fine sea salt, to taste

Directions

- Preheat your air fryer to 385 degrees F.
- In a mixing dish, thoroughly combine all ingredients, except for the hamburger buns.
- Shape the prepared mixture into 5 burgers and cook them in the air fryer cooking basket for 27 minutes. Pause the machine, decrease the temperature to 355 degrees F and cook for further 22 minutes.
- Tuck the prepared burgers into the warm hamburger buns, add your favorite toppings, and enjoy!

196. Pizza-Style English Muffins

Ready in about 9 minutes
Servings 6

Never underestimate the power of good English muffins. These outstanding muffins are ready in 10 minutes or less, so you can get breakfast on the table quickly and effortlessly.

Per serving: 490 Calories; 21.9g Fat; 26g Carbs; 48g Protein; 1.2g Sugars

Ingredients

6 English muffins, split
1 ½ tablespoons tapenade
6 small-sized pork sausages, thinly sliced
1 teaspoon ground black pepper
1 teaspoon dried oregano
1/2 cup goat cheese, crumbled
1 ½ teaspoon sea salt

Directions

- Place English muffins on a clean surface. Spread tapenade over your muffins. Add the sausage. Top with cheese and season with salt and pepper to taste, as well as dried oregano.
- Turn the machine to 380 degrees F; set the timer for 8 minutes. Eat warm.

197. Herbed Pork Fries

Ready in about 13 minutes
Servings 4

Try this heavenly delicious combination of pork, eggs, and seasonings. You can use Mediterranean-style breadcrumbs in this recipe.

Per serving: 275 Calories; 4.4g Fat; 30.4g Carbs; 22.2g Protein; 3.8g Sugars

Ingredients

1/2 pound pork meat, cut into strips
1/2 cup all-purpose flour
2 teaspoons cumin powder
1/2 teaspoon rosemary, chopped
4 ounces seasoned breadcrumbs
2 medium-sized eggs
2 teaspoons dried basil, chopped
Salt and ground black pepper, to taste

Directions

- Start by preheating your air fryer to 375 degrees F.
- Take three shallow bowls. Whisk the eggs in the first shallow bowl. Mix the rosemary, basil, cumin, and flour in the second mixing bowl.
- Then, add the breadcrumbs to the third bowl. Sprinkle the meat strips with the salt and pepper. Now, dip each pork strip into the flour/seasoning mixture; then, dip them in the egg mixture; finally, coat the pork strips with breadcrumbs.
- Cook the pork fries for 7 minutes until they are golden brown. Serve with a sauce such as Hoisin sauce if desired.

198. Hearty Pork with Vegetables

Ready in about 20 minutes
Servings 2

This surprisingly easy pork dinner recipe is both classy and delicious! This is nice spooned over polenta or spaghetti.

Per serving: 147 Calories; 3.7g Fat; 11.9g Carbs; 17g Protein; 1.2g Sugars

Ingredients

½ cup cream of onion soup
½ bell pepper, seeded and diced
Fine sea salt and black pepper, to taste
1/3 cup carrots, chopped
4 ounces pork tenderloin, diced
1/3 cup onions, chopped
2 teaspoons cayenne pepper
2 garlic cloves, halved

Directions

- Begin by preheating your air fryer to 385 degrees F.
- Add all ingredients to a baking dish that is previously greased with a thin layer of canola oil; cook about 5 minutes.
- Gently stir the ingredients and cook an additional 12 minutes. Bon appétit!

199. Pork Sausage with Eggs and Peppers

Ready in about 24 minutes
Servings 6

Peppers are one of the healthiest foods under the Sun. And this recipe uses them creatively.

Per serving: 400 Calories; 21.6g Fat; 2.8g Carbs; 45.6g Protein; 1.2g Sugars

Ingredients

1 green bell pepper, seeded and thinly sliced
6 medium-sized eggs
1 Habanero pepper, seeded and minced
1/2 teaspoon sea salt
2 teaspoons fennel seeds
1 red bell pepper, seeded and thinly sliced
1 teaspoon tarragon
1/2 teaspoon freshly cracked black pepper
6 pork sausages

Directions

- Place the sausages and all peppers in the air fryer cooking basket. Cook at 335 degrees F for 9 minutes.
- Divide the eggs among 6 ramekins; sprinkle each egg with the seasonings. Cook for 11 more minutes at 395 degrees F. Serve warm.

200. Saucy Pork Meatballs with Fennel

Ready in about 25 minutes
Servings 4

Fresh, sliced fennel adds an extra layer of deliciousness to these saucy meatballs. It's no shocker that meatballs are one of the most popular dishes in the world!

Per serving: 372 Calories; 24g Fat; 12.7g Carbs; 25g Protein; 6.9g Sugars

Ingredients

10 ounces ground pork
½ cup tomato paste
1/2 tablespoon fresh chopped thyme
2 fennels, thinly sliced
2 eggs
1 ½ cups fresh scallions, chopped
3 tablespoons breadcrumbs, preferably homemade
1 ½ tablespoon vegetable oil
1 teaspoon freshly ground black pepper
1 teaspoon fine sea salt

Directions

- In a saucepan that is placed over a moderate heat, cook the sliced fennel in the hot vegetable oil. Sauté the fennel until tender and reserve.
- Mix the other ingredients, except for the tomato paste. Shape the mixture into 10 small balls.
- Now, cook the meatballs in the air fryer for 6 minutes at 395 degrees F. Arrange the cooked meatballs in the bottom of an oven proof dish; pour in the tomato paste.
- Add the reserved fennel and cook in your air fryer at 335 degrees F for an additional 4 more minutes. Bon appétit!

201. Sautéed Mixed Greens with Bacon

Ready in about 7 minutes
Servings 2

Here's a great, luscious combo of mixed greens and bacon. It seems that leafy greens (kale, Swiss chard, collards, Dandelion greens…) are a natural pairing for pork.

Per serving: 259 Calories; 16.4g Fat; 9.8g Carbs; 18.5g Protein; 2.7g Sugars

Ingredients

7 ounces mixed greens
8 thick slices pork bacon
2 shallots, peeled and diced
Nonstick cooking spray

Directions

- Begin by preheating the air fryer to 345 degrees F.
- Now, add the shallot and bacon to the air fryer cooking basket; set the timer for 2 minutes. Spritz with a nonstick cooking spray.
- After that, pause the air fryer; throw in the mixed greens; give it a good stir and cook an additional 5 minutes. Serve warm.

202. Easy Family Dinner Rolls

Ready in about 14 minutes
Servings 5

Made with ground pork, these rolls will inspire you and lead to some new ideas. However, these rolls go with another combo of spices.

Per serving: 284 Calories; 17.4g Fat; 15.4g Carbs; 17.2g Protein; 1.3g Sugars

Ingredients

5 slices Colby cheese
1 teaspoon ground black pepper
½ pound ground pork
5 dinner rolls
1/2 teaspoon shallot powder
1 teaspoon fine sea salt
½ teaspoon smoked cayenne pepper
1/3 teaspoon porcini powder
3 cloves garlic

Directions

- Start by preheating your air fryer to 405 degrees F. Mix the ground pork with the garlic, shallot powder, porcini powder, fine sea salt, smoked cayenne pepper, and black pepper.
- Form the ground pork mixture into 5 patties and transfer to the air fryer cooking basket. Now, cook for 8 minutes in the preheated air fryer.
- Next, pause your machine; immediately place the cheese slices on top of the warm burgers; return them to the air fryer and continue to cook for 2 more minutes.
- Place the cheeseburgers in dinner rolls, add your favorite toppings and eat warm!

203. Chinese-Style Pork Bites

Ready in about 14 minutes
Servings 4

This combination of ground pork, cider vinegar and five-spice powder is marvelous! A few clever choices will turn boring ground pork into something deeply satisfying.

Per serving: 147 Calories; 7.9g Fat; 8g Carbs; 10.7g Protein; 4.2g Sugars

Ingredients

1 teaspoon five-spice powder
1/2 onion, peeled and finely chopped
1/2 teaspoon fine sea salt
1 ½ tablespoons Worcester sauce
1/2 teaspoon ground black pepper, to taste
1/2 tablespoon apple cider vinegar
1/3 pound ground pork
3 cloves garlic, minced

Directions

- Firstly, mix all of the above ingredients in a large-sized bowl.
- Shape into bite-sized balls and cook in your air fryer for 13 minutes at 365 degrees F. Serve on a nice platter with cocktail picks and enjoy!

204. Old-Fashioned Pork Pasta Sauce

Ready in about 19 minutes
Servings 4

There are a few good reasons to make this sauce in your Air fryer. It is simple set-it-an-forget-it sauce. It is delicious and it won't heat up your kitchen. Use fresh, ripe tomatoes when they're in the season.

Per serving: 394 Calories; 25.3g Fat; 10.1g Carbs; 31g Protein; 5.5g Sugars

Ingredients

1 teaspoon kosher salt
1/2 tablespoon tomato ketchup
1/3 teaspoon cayenne pepper
1½ pounds ground pork
1/3 cup tomato paste
3 cloves garlic, minced
1/2 medium-sized white onion, peeled and chopped
1/3 tablespoon fresh cilantro, chopped
1/2 tablespoon extra-virgin olive oil
1/3 teaspoon freshly cracked black pepper
1/2 teaspoon grated fresh ginger

Directions

- Begin by preheating your air fryer to 395 degrees F.
- Then, thoroughly combine all the ingredients until the mixture is uniform.
- Transfer the meat mixture to the air fryer baking dish and cook for about 14 minutes. Serve with the cooked pasta and enjoy.

205. Rosemary Pork Sausage Balls

Ready in about 19 minutes
Servings 4

What could be better than rich, sinfully delicious sausage bites that are ready in less than 20 minutes? This is a must-try recipe for your next cocktail party!

Per serving: 192 Calories; 9.2g Fat; 17.9g Carbs; 11.6g Protein; 3g Sugars

Ingredients

3 garlic cloves, peeled and minced
2 tablespoons fresh or dried rosemary
3 cups scallions, finely chopped
7 ounces sausage meat
1/3 cup seasoned breadcrumbs
Salt and ground black pepper, to taste

Directions

* Place all of the above ingredients in a mixing dish; mix until everything is thoroughly combined.
* Roll into small balls and air-fry at 355 degrees F for 13 minutes. Serve with toothpicks and your favorite sauce. Bon appétit!

206. Potato and Ground Pork Casserole

Ready in about 37 minutes
Servings 6

Cheddar cheese is the key to this pork's deliciousness. Cutting the potatoes into similarly sized pieces will help them cook at the same rate in your Air fryer.

Per serving: 429 Calories; 8g Fat; 67g Carbs; 21.9g Protein; 4.2g Sugars

Ingredients

2 eggs
1/3 cup Cheddar cheese, grated
5 potatoes, peeled and shredded
1/3 cup cream
1/2 shallot, peeled and chopped
11 ounces lean ground pork
1/2 tablespoon fresh cilantro leaves
3 tablespoons seasoned breadcrumbs
1/2 teaspoon ground black pepper
1/3 teaspoon ground allspice
1 teaspoon fresh thyme leaves
1 teaspoon fine sea salt

Directions

* Start by preheating your air fryer to 395 degrees F. Prepare two mixing bowls.
* Now, mix the shallot, ground pork, thyme, cilantro, and the egg; then, stir in the seasoned breadcrumbs, salt and black pepper. Mix well, shape into mini meatballs and reserve.
* In another bowl, toss the potatoes with the cream and allspice. Now, cook the potato mixture for 23 minutes in the preheated air fryer.
* Once the cooking is done, place the reserved mini meatballs in a single layer on top of the potato mixture.
* Top with Cheddar cheese and cook an additional 9 minutes or until the cheese has browned. Serve warm in individual plates.

207. Mediterranean-Style Pork Chops with Petite Potatoes

Ready in about 33 minutes
Servings 4

If you can't find petite potatoes, fingerling potatoes or red bliss work well too. With a fresh iceberg salad, this is a complete meal.

Per serving: 512 Calories; 12g Fat; 65.7g Carbs; 49g Protein; 2.9g Sugars

Ingredients

11 petite potatoes, quartered into wedges
1/2 teaspoon fine sea salt
3 garlic cloves, pressed
1 tablespoon fresh rosemary, chopped
1/2 tablespoon fresh thyme, chopped
Zest of 1 medium-sized orange
3 boneless pork chops
2 tablespoons canola oil, divided
1/2 teaspoon dried basil
1 teaspoon ground black pepper, divided

Directions

- Rub the pork with canola oil; add the thyme, rosemary, basil, black pepper, salt, and orange zest; toss to combine. Set aside.
- Now, combine the potatoes and minced garlic; add the salt and ground black pepper to taste.
- Add the potatoes to a baking dish. Place the chops on top of the potatoes.
- Bake at 365 degrees F for 27 minutes, turning halfway through.

208. Barbeque Pork Strips

Ready in about 30 minutes
Servings 4

An air fryer makes everything better! Even if you use a store-bought barbecue sauce. Serve these pork strips with a chunky pasta or egg noodles.

Per serving: 141 Calories; 5.3g Fat; 6.3g Carbs; 16.1g Protein; 5.1g Sugars

Ingredients

2 tablespoons tomato purée
2 tablespoons brown sugar
2 teaspoons ground ginger
2 teaspoons soy sauce
2 tablespoons dry white wine
½ pound pork loin steak, cut into strips
2 teaspoons crushed red pepper flakes
2 teaspoons sesame oil
A few drops liquid smoke
Salt and ground black pepper, to taste

Directions

- Start by preheating your air fryer to 385 degrees F.
- Toss the pork with other ingredients; let it marinate at least 20 minutes in a fridge.
- Then, air-fry the pork strips for 7 minutes. Bon appétit!

209. Morning Bubble & Squeak with Pork

Ready in about 31 minutes
Servings 4

After you mix all ingredients, you'll gently bake them in your Air fryer. Spoon over homemade biscuits or toast.

Per serving: 219 Calories; 12.9g Fat; 3.2g Carbs; 21.6g Protein; 1g Sugars

Ingredients

1/3 cup Colby cheese, grated
1 teaspoon fine sea salt
2 cups pulled pork
1/3 teaspoon marjoram
1/2 large-sized shallot, thinly sliced
3 cloves garlic, finely minced
3 eggs, whisked
1/2 teaspoon thyme
1/3 teaspoon ground black pepper
Leftover stuffing or vegetables
A pinch of grated nutmeg

Directions

- Begin by preheating your air fryer to 345 degrees F.
- In a mixing dish, thoroughly combine all the ingredients using a wide spatula.
- Dump the mixture into a baking dish. Then, bake in the preheated air fryer for about 26 minutes or until it's bubbling. Work in batches as needed. Bon appétit!

210. Delicious Red Gold Potatoes with Bacon

Ready in about 17 minutes
Servings 6

This quick-fix pork recipe may become one of the family's favorite! It is almost perfect, quick, easy and budget-friendly.

Per serving: 400 Calories; 14.3g Fat; 60.4g Carbs; 10.5g Protein; 5g Sugars

Ingredients

1 teaspoon onion powder
1 ½ tablespoons canola oil
4 garlic cloves, peeled and smashed
6 Red Gold potatoes, peeled and diced
1/2 teaspoon caraway seeds
1 teaspoon sea salt
6 slices bacon, diced
1/2 teaspoon whole grain mustard
1 teaspoon ground black pepper

Directions

- Begin by preheating your air fryer to 365 degrees F. Then, throw diced potatoes into a baking pan. Now, cook them for 8 minutes, checking for doneness and stirring once.
- Add the rest of the above ingredients; cook an additional 4-5 minutes. Serve and enjoy!

211. Pork Chops with Kale

Ready in about 25 minutes
Serving 6

Combine pork chops and leafy greens in your Air fryer and you'll have dinner on the table in 25 minutes. You can use Swiss chard if desired.

Per serving: 440 Calories; 16.2g Fat; 13.4g Carbs; 56g Protein; 10g Sugars

Ingredients

3 center-cut loin pork chops
1/2 teaspoon fresh thyme
1/3 tablespoon honey
1/2 apple, cored and cut into
1/3 teaspoon dried basil
3 cups kale leaves, torn into pieces
1 1/2 teaspoons olive oil
1/3 cup pear cider vinegar
1/2 teaspoon yellow mustard
Ground black pepper and fine sea salt, to your liking

Directions

- To make the dressing, combine the olive oil, pear cider vinegar, yellow mustard, and honey. Now, stir in ground black pepper and fine sea salt.
- In another bowl, mix the kale and apple; toss with the dressing to coat well. Season the pork chops on all sides with thyme and basil.
- Roast the pork chops at 405 degrees F for 18 minutes, turning halfway through. Serve warm.

212. Herbed and Breaded Pork Schnitzel

Ready in about 15 minutes
Servings 2

Pork schnitzel is probably one of the most convenient foods to cook in your Air fryer – and this entire meal pulls together in 15 minutes.

Per serving: 275 Calories; 18.6g Fat; 2.7g Carbs; 22.9g Protein; 1.2g Sugars

Ingredients

1 pork schnitzel, halved
1 teaspoon garlic salt
1/2 heaping tablespoon fresh parsley
1 cup breadcrumbs of choice, preferably homemade
1/3 tablespoon pear cider vinegar
1/2 teaspoon mustard
2 eggs, beaten
1/2 teaspoon fennel seed
1/3 teaspoon ground black pepper

Directions

- Blitz the breadcrumbs, vinegar, black pepper, garlic salt, mustard, fennel seeds, and fresh parsley in your food processor until uniform and smooth. Dump the blended mixture into a shallow bowl.
- Add the beaten egg to another shallow bowl.
- Coat the pork with the beaten egg; then, dredge them in the herb mixture.
- Bake at 355 degrees F for about 14 minutes. Bon appétit!

213. Spicy Pork Kebabs

Ready in about 22 minutes
Servings 3

If you're a fan of pork kebabs, you'll love this recipe! Your taste buds will thank you for that.

Per serving: 330 Calories; 16.9g Fat; 3g Carbs; 39.3g Protein; 1.3g Sugars

Ingredients

5 tablespoons breadcrumbs
2 tablespoons tomato puree
1/2 fresh serrano, minced
1/3 teaspoon paprika
1/2 pound pork, ground
½ cup green onions, finely chopped
3 cloves garlic, peeled and finely minced
1 teaspoon ground black pepper, or more to taste
1 teaspoon salt, or more to taste

Directions

- Thoroughly combine all ingredients in a mixing dish. Then, form your mixture into sausage shapes.
- Cook for 18 minutes at 355 degrees F. Mound salad on a serving platter, top with air fried kebabs and serve warm.

214. Pork Sausage with Vidalia Onions and Celery

Ready in about 28 minutes
Servings 6

Pork always pairs well with remarkable aromas of onions and celery. You can substitute Mayan sweets or Creole onions for Vidalia.

Per serving: 216 Calories; 5.6g Fat; 31.6g Carbs; 11.3g Protein; 3.5g Sugars

Ingredients

6 English muffins
1 teaspoon red pepper flakes, crushed
6 pork sausages
3 Vidalia onions, peeled and cleaned
3 celery stalks, thinly sliced
6 medium-sized eggs
2 teaspoons cumin seeds
1 teaspoon sea salt

Directions

- Place the sausages, celery, and Vidalia onions in an air fryer cooking basket. Cook at 325
- degrees F for 10 minutes; taste for doneness and cook for 3 more minutes as needed.
- Divide the eggs among 6 ramekins; sprinkle them with red pepper, cumin seeds and sea salt. Now, turn the temperature to 395 degrees F; cook for 12 more minutes.
- Serve with English muffins and some extra toppings of choice. Enjoy!

215. Saucy Hoisin Pork

Ready in about 30 minutes
Servings 4

Here's a simple twist on the traditional way of preparing a pork loin. Honey and wine add rich and zingy flavor to this hearty meal.

Per serving: 219 Calories; 8.1g Fat; 19.5g Carbs; 17.1g Protein; 14.5g Sugars

Ingredients

2 tablespoons honey
2 tablespoons dry white wine
1/3 cup hoisin sauce
2 teaspoons smoked cayenne pepper
3 potatoes, peeled and cubed
3 garlic cloves, pressed
1/2 pound pork loin steak, cut into strips
3 teaspoons fresh lime juice
Salt and ground black pepper, to taste

Directions

- Start by preheating your air fryer to 395 degrees F.
- Toss the pork with other ingredients; let it marinate at least 20 minutes in a fridge.
- Then, air-fry the pork strips for 5 minutes. Bon appétit!

216. Bubble & Squeak with Pork Sausage

Ready in about 30 minutes
Servings 6

This traditional English dish is the perfect way of using up your leftovers after holidays or big family lunch. This bubble & squeak features mashed potatoes but you can add almost any vegetables you have leftover in the refrigerator.

Per serving: 485 Calories; 27.6g Fat; 8.2g Carbs; 49g Protein; 1.2g Sugars

Ingredients

1 ½ cup potato mash
1/2 teaspoon tarragon
1/3 cup Colby cheese
1/2 teaspoon ground black pepper
1/2 onion, peeled and sliced
1 teaspoon cumin powder
1/2 teaspoon sea salt
3 beaten eggs
6 pork sausages, chopped

Directions

- Grab a mixing dish and mix all ingredients in the order listed above.
- Divide the prepared mixture among 6 ramekins; now, place ramekins in your air fryer.
- Cook for 27 minutes at 365 degrees F. Eat warm.

217. Basil-Vermouth Pork Chops

Ready in about 22 minutes
Servings 6

Flavorful pork chops are made incredibly tasty thanks to the magic of the Air fryer. If you don't have vermouth on hand, use dry white wine or even pear cider.

Per serving: 393 Calories; 15.4g Fat; 2.6g Carbs; 56g Protein; 0.2g Sugars

Ingredients

2 tablespoons vermouth
6 center-cut loin pork chops
1/2 tablespoon fresh basil, minced
1/3 teaspoon freshly ground black pepper, or more to taste
2 tablespoons whole grain mustard
1 teaspoon fine kosher salt

Directions

- Toss pork chops with other ingredients until they are well coated on both sides.
- Air-fry your chops for 18 minutes at 405 degrees F, turning once or twice.
- Mound your favorite salad on a serving plate; top with pork chops and enjoy.

BEEF

218. Asian-Style Beef Burgers 123

219. Christmas Smoked Beef Roast 123

220. Country-Style Beef Meatloaf 124

221. Japanese-Style Marinated Flank Steak................... 124

222. Dinner Ciabatta Cheeseburgers 125

223. Perfect Thai Meatballs 125

224. Herbed Crumbed Filet Mignon 126

225. The Best London Broil Ever 126

226. Old-Fashioned Beef Stroganoff 127

227. Tender Beef Chuck with Brussels Sprouts 127

228. All-In-One Spicy Spaghetti with Beef 128

229. Beer-Braised Short Loin 128

230. Leftover Beef and Kale Omelet 129

231. Hearty Beef Cubes with Vegetables 129

232. Easy Grilled Beef Ribs 130

233. Festive Teriyaki Beef 130

234. Must-Serve Cajun Beef Tenderloin....................... 131

235. Filet Mignon with Hot Roasted Garlic Sauce 131

236. Chinese-Style Creamed Beef 132

237. Cheeseburger Frittata with Baby Spinach 132

238. Beef in Hoisin-Wine Sauce 133

239. Whisky Sirloin Steak 133

240. Beef in Cheesy Tomato Sauce 134

241. Winter Beef Sausage and Vegetables 134

242. Herbed Marinated Beef in Garlic Sauce 135

243. Beef and Vegetable Appetizer Rolls 135

244. Beef and Goat Cheese Frittata 136

245. Beef Medallions with Red Potatoes 136

246. Classic Old-Fashioned Beef with Vegetables 137

247. Steaks with Herbed Butter 137

248. Beef and Goat Cheese Frittata 138

249. Tangy Tender Beef Steak 138

250. Italian Beef in Creamy Chive Sauce 139

251. Italian-Style Dinner Rolls 139

252. Parmesan Beef Schnitzel 140

253. Beef Medallions with Porcini Mushrooms Sauce 140

254. Award-Winning Steaks 141

255. Famous Beef Sloppy Joes...................................... 141

256. Mom's Mouthwatering Beef Medallions 142

257. Beef in Creamy Jalapeño Sauce 142

258. Tuscan Beef Chops 143

259. Beef with Beer Mustard and Tomato Sauce.......... 143

260. Classic Meatballs with Tomato Sauce................... 144

261. Flank Steak Beef in Cascabel-Cumin Sauce 144

262. Holiday Spicy and Garlicky Steak 145

263. Beef Chops with Parmesan-Kale Salad 145

264. Tender Beef Chops with English Mustard 146

265. Saucy Lemony Beef Steaks 146

266. Easy Cocktail Rolls 147

267. Chili & Dark Chocolate Beef Meatballs 147

268. Butter Crumbed Beef Schnitzel............................ 148

269. Melt-in-Your-Mouth Beef 148

270. Shallot and Carrot Steak 149

271. Tender Spicy Beef with Cotija Cheese................... 149

272. Easiest Breaded Steaks Ever 150

273. Chipotle and Beef Pastry Rolls 150

274. Mouthwatering Minute Steaks 151

275. Teriyaki Beef with Sautéed Broccoli 151

276. Barbeque Minute Steaks 152

277. Beef and Cheese Puff Pastry 152

278. Herby and Honey Beef Steaks 153

218. Asian-Style Beef Burgers

Ready in about 20 minutes
Servings 4

This recipe looks like the American classic but it is inspired by Asian soy sauce and fresh scallions. Serve with spicy homemade sauce and enjoy!

Per serving: 167 Calories; 5.5g Fat; 1.4g Carbs; 26.4g Protein; 0.0g Sugars

Ingredients

3/4 pound lean ground beef
1 tablespoon soy sauce
1 teaspoon Dijon mustard
A few dashes of liquid smoke
1 teaspoon shallot powder
1 clove garlic, minced
1/2 teaspoon cumin powder
1/4 cup scallions, minced
1/3 teaspoon sea salt flakes
1/3 teaspoon freshly cracked mixed peppercorns
1 teaspoon celery seeds
1 teaspoon parsley flakes

Directions

- Mix all of the above ingredients in a bowl; knead until everything is well incorporated.
- Shape the mixture into four patties. Next, make a shallow dip in the center of each patty to prevent them puffing up during air-frying.
- Spritz the patties on all sides using a non-stick cooking spray. Cook approximately 12 minutes at 360 degrees F. Check for doneness – an instant read thermometer should read 160 degrees F. Serve them on butter rolls with toppings of choice. Bon appétit!

219. Christmas Smoked Beef Roast

Ready in about 45 minutes
Servings 8

If you probably already know, the beef roast can be a tough meat if it is not cooked properly. Air-frying in one of the best ways to cook a moist and tender beef. Give it a try!

Per serving: 243 Calories; 10.6g Fat; 0.4g Carbs; 34.5g Protein; 0.0g Sugars

Ingredients

2 pounds roast beef, at room temperature
2 tablespoons extra-virgin olive oil
1 teaspoon sea salt flakes
1 teaspoon black pepper, preferably freshly ground
1 teaspoon smoked paprika
A few dashes of liquid smoke
2 jalapeño peppers, thinly sliced

Directions

- Start by preheating the Air Fryer to 330 degrees F.
- Then, pat the roast dry using kitchen towels. Rub with extra-virgin olive oil and all seasonings along with liquid smoke.
- Roast for 30 minutes in the preheated Air Fryer; then, pause the machine and turn the roast over; roast for additional 15 minutes.
- Check for doneness using a meat thermometer and serve sprinkled with sliced jalapeños. Bon appétit!

220. Country-Style Beef Meatloaf

Ready in about 30 minutes
Servings 4

The elusive flavor in this meatloaf comes from the seasonings and their zesty touch. It is important to add eggs and plain milk, which keep it moist and gooey.

Per serving: 206 Calories; 7.9g Fat; 15.9g Carbs; 17.6g Protein; 0.8g Sugars

Ingredients

3/4 pound ground chuck
1/4 pound ground pork sausage
1 cup shallot, finely chopped
2 eggs, well beaten
3 tablespoons plain milk
1 tablespoon oyster sauce
1 teaspoon porcini mushrooms
1/2 teaspoon cumin powder
1 teaspoon garlic paste
1 tablespoon fresh parsley
Seasoned salt and crushed red pepper flakes, to taste
1 cup crushed saltines

Directions

- Simply place all ingredients in a large-sized mixing dish; mix until everything is thoroughly combined.
- Press the meatloaf mixture into the Air Fryer baking dish; set your Air Fryer to cook at 360 degrees F for 25 minutes. Press the power button and cook until heated through.
- Check for doneness and serve with your favorite wine!

221. Japanese-Style Marinated Flank Steak

Ready in about 15 minutes
Servings 4

This amazing Japanese-style marinade will enhance flavor and tenderize the meat. It makes meat slightly springy and so tender!

Per serving: 367 Calories; 15.1g Fat; 6.4g Carbs; 48.6g Protein; 3.4g Sugars

Ingredients

3/4 pound flank steak
1 ½ tablespoons sake
1 tablespoon brown miso paste
1 teaspoon honey
2 garlic cloves, pressed
1 tablespoon olive oil

Directions

- Place all the ingredients in a sealable food bag; shake until completely coated and place in your refrigerator for at least 1 hour.
- Then, spritz the steak with a non-stick cooking spray; make sure to coat on all sides. Place the steak in the Air Fryer baking pan.
- Set your Air Fryer to cook at 400 degrees F. Roast for 12 minutes, flipping twice. Serve immediately.

222. Dinner Ciabatta Cheeseburgers

Ready in about 15 minutes
Servings 4

*Here are the decadent and flavorsome burgers...
mmmm! Everybody loves comfort food but burgers will
always have their special place in our hearts.*

Per serving: 271 Calories; 13.3g Fat; 21.9g Carbs;
15.3g Protein; 2.9g Sugars

Ingredients

3/4 pound ground chuck
1 envelope onion soup mix
Kosher salt and freshly ground black pepper, to taste
1 teaspoon paprika
4 slices Monterey-Jack cheese
4 ciabatta rolls
Mustard and pickled salad, to serve

Directions

- In a mixing dish, thoroughly combine ground chuck, onion soup mix, salt, black pepper, and paprika.
- Then, set your Air Fryer to cook at 385 degrees F. Shape the mixture into 4 patties. Air-fry them for 10 minutes.
- Next step, place the slices of cheese on the top of the warm burgers. Air-fry one minute more.
- Serve on ciabatta rolls garnished with mustard and pickled salad of choice. Bon appétit!

223. Perfect Thai Meatballs

Ready in about 20 minutes
Servings 4

*Finger-lickin' customizable meatballs! You can serve
these bouncy meatballs as a main course with warm
rice or egg noodles. You can also serve them as an appetizer with a dipping sauce.*

Per serving: 242 Calories; 10.5g Fat; 0.2g Carbs; 34.4g
Protein; 0.0g Sugars

Ingredients

1 pound ground beef
1 teaspoon red Thai curry paste
1/2 lime, rind and juice
1 teaspoon Chinese spice
2 teaspoons lemongrass, finely chopped
1 tablespoon sesame oil

Directions

- Thoroughly combine all ingredients in a mixing dish.
- Shape into 24 meatballs and place them into the Air Fryer cooking basket. Cook at 380 degrees F for 10 minutes; pause the machine and cook for a further 5 minutes, or until cooked through.
- Serve accompanied by the dipping sauce. Bon appétit!

224. Herbed Crumbed Filet Mignon

Ready in about 20 minutes
Servings 4

This crunchy filet mignon is sure to become your holiday favorite! You can also experiment with seasonings and create your unique recipe!

Per serving: 268 Calories; 14.5g Fat; 1.0g Carbs; 32.0g Protein; 0.0g Sugars

Ingredients

1/2 pound filet mignon
Sea salt and ground black pepper, to your liking
1/2 teaspoon cayenne pepper
1 teaspoon dried basil
1 teaspoon dried rosemary
1 teaspoon dried thyme
1 tablespoon sesame oil
1 small-sized egg, well-whisked
1/2 cup seasoned breadcrumbs

Directions

- Season the filet mignon with salt, black pepper, cayenne pepper, basil, rosemary, and thyme. Brush with sesame oil.
- Put the egg in a shallow plate. Now, place the breadcrumbs in another plate.
- Coat the filet mignon with the egg; then, lay it into the crumbs. Set your Air Fryer to cook at 360 degrees F.
- Cook for 10 to 13 minutes or until golden. Serve with mixed salad leaves and enjoy!

225. The Best London Broil Ever

Ready in about 30 minutes + marinating time
Servings 8

This is a great recipe for chilly winter days. Serve this mouthwatering London broil with German potato salad and enjoy with your family!

Per serving: 257 Calories; 9.2g Fat; 0.1g Carbs; 41.0g Protein; 0.4g Sugars

Ingredients

2 pounds London broil
3 large garlic cloves, minced
3 tablespoons balsamic vinegar
3 tablespoons whole-grain mustard
2 tablespoons olive oil
Sea salt and ground black pepper, to taste
1/2 teaspoon dried hot red pepper flakes

Directions

- Score both sides of the cleaned London broil.
- Thoroughly combine the remaining ingredients; massage this mixture into the meat to coat it on all sides. Let it marinate for at least 3 hours.
- Set the Air Fryer to cook at 400 degrees F; Then cook the London broil for 15 minutes. Flip it over and cook another 10 to 12 minutes. Bon appétit!

226. Old-Fashioned Beef Stroganoff

Ready in about 20 minutes
Servings 4

The key to this amazing hearty stew – use fresh leek and garlic! In this recipe, please skip the extra lean steak and choose the one with a bit more fat.

Per serving: 352 Calories; 20.8g Fat; 10.0g Carbs; 29.8g Protein; 1.4g Sugars

Ingredients

3/4 pound beef sirloin steak, cut into small-sized strips
1/4 cup balsamic vinegar
1 tablespoon brown mustard
2 tablespoons all-purpose flour
1 tablespoon butter
1 cup beef broth
1 cup leek, chopped
2 cloves garlic, crushed
1 teaspoon cayenne pepper
Sea salt flakes and crushed red pepper, to taste
1 cup sour cream
2 ½ tablespoons tomato paste

Directions

- Place the beef along with the balsamic vinegar and the mustard in a mixing dish; cover and marinate in your refrigerator for about 1 hour.
- Then, coat the beef strips with the flour; butter the inside of a baking dish and put the beef into the dish.
- Add the broth, leeks and garlic. Cook at 380 degrees for 8 minutes. Pause the machine and add the cayenne pepper, salt, red pepper, sour cream and tomato paste; cook for additional 7 minutes.
- Check for doneness and serve with warm egg noodles, if desired. Bon appétit!

227. Tender Beef Chuck with Brussels Sprouts

Ready in about 25 minutes +
marinating time
Servings 4

If you have to choose among thousands and thousands of beef recipes, you would probably choose this one. Why is it so? Keep on reading...

Per serving: 302 Calories; 14.2g Fat; 6.5g Carbs; 36.6g Protein; 1.6g Sugars

Ingredients

1 pound beef chuck shoulder steak
2 tablespoons vegetable oil
1 tablespoon red wine vinegar
1 teaspoon fine sea salt
1/2 teaspoon ground black pepper
1 teaspoon smoked paprika
1 teaspoon onion powder
1/2 teaspoon garlic powder
1/2 pound Brussels sprouts, cleaned and halved
1/2 teaspoon fennel seeds
1 teaspoon dried basil
1 teaspoon dried sage

Directions

- Firstly, marinate the beef with vegetable oil, wine vinegar, salt, black pepper, paprika, onion powder, and garlic powder. Rub the marinade into the meat and let it stay at least for 3 hours.
- Air fry at 390 degrees F for 10 minutes. Pause the machine and add the prepared Brussels sprouts; sprinkle them with fennel seeds, basil, and sage.
- Turn the machine to 380 degrees F; press the power button and cook for 5 more minutes. Pause the machine, stir and cook for further 10 minutes.
- Next, remove the meat from the cooking basket and cook the vegetables a few minutes more if needed and according to your taste. Serve with your favorite mayo sauce.

228. All-In-One Spicy Spaghetti with Beef

Ready in about 30 minutes
Servings 4

Ground beef in a palatable spicy sauce over warm spaghetti! This staple food of Italy would win your heart!

Per serving: 359 Calories; 5.5g Fat; 59.9g Carbs; 16.9g Protein; 2.7g Sugars

Ingredients

3/4 pound ground chuck
1 onion, peeled and finely chopped
1 teaspoon garlic paste
1 bell pepper, chopped
1 small-sized habanero pepper, deveined and finely minced
1/2 teaspoon dried rosemary
1/2 teaspoon dried marjoram
1 ¼ cups crushed tomatoes, fresh or canned
1/2 teaspoon sea salt flakes
1/4 teaspoon ground black pepper, or more to taste
1 package cooked spaghetti, to serve

Directions

- In the Air Fryer baking dish, place the ground meat, onion, garlic paste, bell pepper, habanero pepper, rosemary, and the marjoram.
- Air-fry, uncovered, for 10 to 11 minutes. Next step, stir in the tomatoes along with salt and pepper; cook 17 to 20 minutes. Serve over cooked spaghetti. Bon appétit!

229. Beer-Braised Short Loin

Ready in about 15 minutes
Servings 4

There are many ways to tenderize beef cuts. You can use soda, coffee, tea, tomato based sauce, buttermilk, yogurt, and so on. If you prefer an acid based marinade, use glass dishes to prevent any chemical reactions.

Per serving: 379 Calories; 16.4g Fat; 3.7g Carbs; 46.0g Protein; 0.0g Sugars

Ingredients

1 ½ pounds short loin
2 tablespoons olive oil
1 bottle beer
2-3 cloves garlic, finely minced
2 Turkish bay leaves

Directions

- Pat the beef dry; then, tenderize the beef with a meat mallet to soften the fibers. Place it in a large-sized mixing dish.
- Add the remaining ingredients; toss to coat well and let it marinate for at least 1 hour.
- Cook about 7 minutes at 395 degrees F; after that, pause the Air Fryer. Flip the meat over and cook for another 8 minutes, or until it's done.

230. Leftover Beef and Kale Omelet

Ready in about 20 minutes
Servings 4

Too busy to cook? You can simply whip up leftovers, vegetable and eggs for lunch. For this recipe, utilize leftover beef like beef burgers, steak, pulled beef brisket, etc.

Per serving: 236 Calories; 13.7g Fat; 4.0g Carbs; 23.8g Protein; 1.0g Sugars

Ingredients

Non-stick cooking spray
1/2 pound leftover beef, coarsely chopped
2 garlic cloves, pressed
1 cup kale, torn into pieces and wilted
1 tomato, chopped
1/4 teaspoon brown sugar
4 eggs, beaten
4 tablespoons heavy cream
1/2 teaspoon turmeric powder
Salt and ground black pepper, to your liking
1/8 teaspoon ground allspice

Directions

- Spritz the inside of four ramekins with a cooking spray.
- Divide all of the above ingredients among the prepared ramekins. Stir until everything is well combined.
- Air-fry at 360 degrees F for 16 minutes; check with a wooden stick and return the eggs to the Air Fryer for a few more minutes as needed. Serve immediately.

231. Hearty Beef Cubes with Vegetables

Ready in about 20 minutes +
marinating time
Servings 4

This recipe adds a whole new dimension to the art of air-frying! You can prepare a full meal using just one machine. Incredible!

Per serving: 325 Calories; 17.4g Fat; 3.5g Carbs; 37.8g Protein; 1.1g Sugars

Ingredients

1 pound top round steak, cut into cubes
2 tablespoons olive oil
1 tablespoon apple cider vinegar
1 teaspoon fine sea salt
1/2 teaspoon ground black pepper
1 teaspoon shallot powder
3/4 teaspoon smoked cayenne pepper
1/2 teaspoon garlic powder
1/4 teaspoon ground cumin
1/4 pound broccoli, cut into florets
1/4 pound mushrooms, sliced
1 teaspoon dried basil
1 teaspoon celery seeds

Directions

- Firstly, marinate the beef with olive oil, vinegar, salt, black pepper, shallot powder, cayenne pepper, garlic powder, and cumin. Toss to coat well and let it stay for at least 3 hours.
- Place the beef cubes in the Air Fryer cooking basket; cook at 365 degrees F for 12 minutes. Pause the machine, check the cubes for doneness and transfer them to a bowl.
- Now, clean the cooking basket and place the vegetables in; sprinkle them with basil and celery seeds; toss to coat.
- Set the temperature to 400 degrees F; cook for 5 to 6 minutes or until the vegetables are warmed through.
- Serve with reserved meat cubes. Bon appétit!

232. Easy Grilled
Beef Ribs

Ready in about 20 minutes +
marinating time
Servings 4

This could be the only recipe for beef ribs you'll ever need! Quick, easy and delicious!

Per serving: 459 Calories; 34.4g Fat; 1.0g Carbs; 34.7g Protein; 0.0g Sugars

Ingredients

1 pound meaty beef ribs
3 tablespoons apple cider vinegar
1 cup coriander, finely chopped
1 heaping tablespoon fresh basil leaves, chopped
2 garlic cloves, finely chopped
1 chipotle powder
1 teaspoon fennel seeds
1 teaspoon hot paprika
Kosher salt and black pepper, to your liking
1/2 cup vegetable oil

Directions

- First of all, rinse the ribs and dry them using paper towels.
- Place all of the above ingredients in a mixing dish; toss to coat well.
- Cover and refrigerate for at least 3 hours. Discard the marinade and place your ribs on an Air Fryer grill pan.
- Now, set your Air Fryer to cook at 360 degrees F. Cook for 8 minutes; check for doneness and cook for another 3 to 5 minutes. Garnish with the remaining marinade and serve right away!

233. Festive Teriyaki
Beef

Ready in about 40 minutes
Servings 4

Sometimes, a true comfort food such as a roasted beef rump steak and a slice or two of homemade crusty bread is all you really need. When it comes to the sauce, you can use sweet marsala wine or dry sherry instead of mirin (Japanese sweet rice wine).

Per serving: 284 Calories; 20.6g Fat; 0.1g Carbs; 22 Protein; 0.4g Sugars

Ingredients

2 heaping tablespoons fresh parsley, roughly chopped
1 pound beef rump steaks
2 heaping tablespoons fresh chives, roughly chopped
Salt and black pepper (or mixed peppercorns), to savor

For the Sauce:
½ cup grapefruit juice
1/3 cup hoisin sauce
1 tablespoon fresh ginger, grated
1 ½ tablespoons mirin
3 garlic cloves, minced
2 tablespoon rice bran oil
½ cup soy sauce
1/3 cup brown sugar

Directions

- Firstly, steam the beef rump steaks for 8 minutes (use the method of steaming that you prefer). Season the beef with salt and black pepper; scatter the chopped parsley and chives over the top.
- Roast the beef rump steaks in an air fryer basket for 28 minutes at 345 degrees, turning halfway through.
- While the beef is cooking, combine the ingredients for the teriyaki sauce in a sauté pan. Then, let it simmer over low heat until it has thickened.
- Toss the beef with the teriyaki sauce until it is well covered and serve.

234. Must-Serve Cajun Beef Tenderloin

Ready in about 60 minutes
Servings 2

Whether it is a family lunch or celebratory dinner, beef tenderloin is always a good idea! If you like to experiment in the kitchen, add 1 teaspoon of white sugar to enhance a sweet-tangy flavor.

Per serving: 336 Calories; 19.1g Fat; 6.5g Carbs; 31.3g Protein; 1.2g Sugars

Ingredients

1/3 cup beef broth
2 tablespoons Cajun seasoning, crushed
1/2 teaspoon garlic powder
7 ounce beef tenderloins
½ tablespoon pear cider vinegar
1/3 teaspoon cayenne pepper
1 ½ tablespoon olive oil
1/2 teaspoon freshly ground black pepper
1 teaspoon salt

Directions

- Firstly, coat the beef tenderloins with salt, cayenne pepper, and black pepper.
- Mix the remaining items in a medium-sized bowl; let the meat marinate for 40 minutes in this mixture.
- Roast the beef for about 22 minutes at 385 degrees F, turning it halfway through the cooking time. Bon appétit!

235. Filet Mignon with Hot Roasted Garlic Sauce

Ready in about 15 minutes
Servings 6

If you are looking for a festive beef dish, here's an ideal option for you! For a next-day lunch, you can wrap leftovers in a warm tortilla.

Per serving: 493 Calories; 40.5g Fat; 1.7g Carbs; 35.6g Protein; 1.1g Sugars

Ingredients

1/3 stick butter, at room temperature
1/2 cup cream
1/2 medium-sized garlic bulb, peeled and pressed
6 filet mignon steaks
2 teaspoons mixed peppercorns, freshly cracked
1 ½ tablespoons apple cider
A dash of hot sauce
1 ½ teaspoons sea salt flakes

Directions

Season the mignon steaks with the cracked peppercorns and salt flakes. Roast the mignon steaks in the preheated air fryer for 24 minutes at 385 degrees F, turning once. Check for doneness and set aside, keeping it warm.
In a small nonstick saucepan that is placed over a moderate flame, mash the garlic to a smooth paste. Whisk in the rest of the above ingredients. Whisk constantly until it has a uniform consistency.
To finish, lay the filet mignon steaks on serving plates; spoon a little sauce onto each filet mignon. Bon appétit!

236. Chinese-Style Creamed Beef

Ready in about 19 minutes
Servings 4

This is the perfect dish for those days when you're craving a homemade, rich meal. Best of all, the complete meal is ready in less than 20 minutes.

Per serving: 353 Calories; 5.4g Fat; 55g Carbs; 20.4g Protein; 3.4g Sugars

Ingredients

Cooked rice noodles
1/3 pound beef tenderloin, cut into strips
1/2 teaspoon balsamic vinegar
½ cup corn meal mix
1 cup buttermilk
1/3 teaspoon ground black pepper, or to taste
1½ cup plain flour
Seven spice powder
1/2 teaspoon ground cinnamon
1 teaspoon hot paprika
1/3 teaspoon salt

Directions

- Grab three mixing bowls. Combine the corn meal mix, 3/4cup flour, and seven spice powder in the first mixing bowl.
- Whisk the buttermilk and balsamic vinegar in the second bowl. Add the remaining 3/4 cup flour to the third shallow bowl.
- Sprinkle the beef strips with black pepper, salt, ground cinnamon, and hot paprika. Coat each strip with the remaining flour; then, dip them in the buttermilk mixture; lastly, cover them with the spiced cornmeal mixture.
- Cook in the air fryer baking tray for about 12 minutes at 365 degrees F or until ready. Serve over the hot rice noodles. Bon appétit!

237. Cheeseburger Frittata with Baby Spinach

Ready in about 40 minutes
Servings 4

This is the perfect weeknight comfort food. Tasty family dish doesn't have to be time-consuming and complicated.

Per serving: 428 Calories; 21.4g Fat; 9.7g Carbs; 31.5g Protein; 1.2g Sugars

Ingredients

5 tablespoons feta cheese, crumbled
1 handful of baby spinach
5 eggs
5 cups lean ground beef
1 ½ red onions, finely chopped
3 cloves garlic, finely minced
1 ½ tablespoons corn oil
2 teaspoons dried dill weed
1/2 teaspoon porcini mushroom powder
Generous pinches of salt and ground black pepper

Directions

- Firstly, set the air fryer to cook at 345 degrees F.
- Heat the oil in a skillet over a moderate flame. Now, cook the onion and garlic until they start to soften.
- Stir in the ground beef; cook until it's browned, crumbling with a fork.
- In a mixing dish or a suitable measuring cup, whisk the eggs with salt, pepper, dill, and the porcini powder.
- Coat the inside of a baking dish with pan spray. Scrape the beaten egg mixture into the baking dish, followed by the reserved sautéed mixture and baby spinach. Add crumbled feta.
- Bake for about 28 minutes or until the frittata is set. Serve on individual plates. Bon appétit!

238. Beef in Hoisin-Wine Sauce

Ready in about 24 minutes
Servings 4

Flank steak is very versatile food so you can just combine the spices you have on hand. Serve on a bed of long-grain rice.

Per serving: 287 Calories; 21.4g Fat; 10.6g Carbs; 13.1g Protein; 6g Sugars

Ingredients

1/2 pound flank steak, cut into small pieces
1 teaspoon fresh sage leaves, minced
1/3 cup olive oil
3 tablespoons cooking wine
1 teaspoon seasoned salt
3 cloves garlic, minced
1 teaspoon fresh rosemary leaves, finely minced
1/3 cup Hoisin sauce
1/2 teaspoon freshly cracked black pepper

Directions

- Warm the oil in a sauté pan over a moderate heat. Now, sauté the garlic until just tender and fragrant.
- Then, pour in the Hoisin sauce and the cooking wine. Now, add the remaining ingredients. Toss to coat well.
- Then, roast for about 18 minutes at 345 degrees F. Eat warm garnished with roasted potatoes.

239. Whisky Sirloin Steak

Ready in about 15 minutes +
marinating time
Servings 6

You could try adding diced jalapeno peppers to give your dish an extra kick. Serve with grilled corn on the cob.

Per serving: 260 Calories; 12.3g Fat; 1.8g Carbs; 33.5g Protein; 1.2g Sugars

Ingredients

3 sirloin steaks
½ teaspoon sugar
1 ½tablespoons tamari sauce
1/3 teaspoon cayenne pepper
1/3 teaspoon ground ginger
2 garlic cloves, thinly sliced
1 ½ tablespoons whiskey
2 tablespoons olive oil
Fine sea salt, to taste

Directions

- Firstly, add all the ingredients, minus the olive oil and the steak, to a resealable plastic bag.
- Throw in the steak and let it marinate for a couple of hours. After that, drizzle the sirloin steaks with 2 tablespoons olive oil.
- Roast for approximately 22 minutes at 395 degrees F, turning it halfway through the time. Bon appétit!

240. Beef in Cheesy Tomato Sauce

Ready in about 27 minutes
Servings 3

What's the secret to a great beef dish? Choosing the best beef cuts, of course! Beef tenderloin is the best choice for a festive family lunch.

Per serving: 440 Calories; 24g Fat; 15.3g Carbs; 41.4 g Protein; 1.2g Sugars

Ingredients

2 ounces Cotija cheese, cut into sticks
2 teaspoons paprika
2 teaspoons dried thyme
1/2 cup shallots, peeled and chopped
3 beef tenderloins, cut in half lengthwise
2 teaspoons dried basil
1/3 cup homemade bone stock
2 tablespoon olive oil
3 cloves garlic, minced
1 ½ cups tomato puree
1 teaspoon ground black pepper, or more to taste
1 teaspoon fine sea salt, or more to taste

Directions

- Firstly, season the beef tenderloin with the salt, ground black pepper, and paprika; place a piece of the Cotija cheese in the middle.
- Now, tie each tenderloin with a kitchen string; drizzle with olive oil and reserve.
- Stir the garlic, shallots, bone stock, tomato puree into an oven safe bowl; cook in the preheated air fryer at 375 degrees F for 7 minutes.
- Add the reserved beef along with basil and thyme. Set the timer for 14 minutes. Eat warm and enjoy!

241. Winter Beef Sausage and Vegetables

Ready in about 25 minutes
Servings 4

For an over-the-top family lunch, make sure to find extra quality beef sausages. Their smoky and rich flavor will match beautifully with Idaho potatoes, peppers, celery and carrots.

Per serving: 185 Calories; 11.6g Fat; 13.7g Carbs; 7.9g Protein; 1.6g Sugars

Ingredients

1/2 pound beef sausage
2 red bell peppers, cut lengthwise
1 sprig rosemary, chopped
3 medium-sized carrots, sliced
2 shallots, cut into wedges
½ pound Idaho potatoes, cut into chunks
½ celery stalk, sliced
½ teaspoon caraway seeds
1 teaspoon salt

Directions

- Place all the ingredients on the bottom of the air fryer basket. Toss until everything is well combined.
- Roast for approximately 32 minutes at 385 degrees F, stirring once halfway through. Serve warm on a serving platter.

242. Herbed Marinated Beef in Garlic Sauce

Ready in about 1 hour 22 minutes
Servings 4

For this saucy and buttery beef, you can use bottom eye roast, top chuck or rump roast. Thanks to the Air fryer, you will keep a great texture of the meat and shorten the cooking time as well.

Per serving: 275 Calories; 18.6g Fat; 2.7g Carbs; 22.9g Protein; 1.2g Sugars

Ingredients

1½ pounds beef, cubed
½ cup full fat sour cream
1/2 cup white wine
2 teaspoons dried rosemary
1½ tablespoon herb vinegar
1 teaspoon sweet paprika
3 cloves garlic, minced
2 tablespoons extra-virgin olive oil
2 teaspoons dried basil
1 tablespoons mayonnaise
Salt and ground black pepper, to taste

Directions

- In a large-sized mixing bowl, whisk together the oil, wine, and beef. Now, stir in the seasonings and herb vinegar. Cover and marinate at least 50 minutes.
- Then, preheat your air fryer to 375 degrees F. Roast the marinated beef for about 18 minutes, turning halfway through.
- Meanwhile, make the sauce by mixing the sour cream with the mayonnaise and garlic. Serve the warm beef with the garlic sauce and enjoy!

243. Beef and Vegetable Appetizer Rolls

Ready in about 10 minutes
Servings 6

What's for dinner? Well, everyone loves puff pastry rolls! You can cut them into halves and serve as party canapés too!

Per serving: 138 Calories; 10.2g Fat;1.7g Carbs; 9.9g Protein; 0.2g Sugars

Ingredients

1/2 teaspoon cumin powder
7 ounces ground beef
Fine sea salt and crushed red pepper flakes, to savor
1/2 yellow onion, peeled and finely chopped
1 ½ tablespoons olive oil
1 sheet puff pastry
1 ½ zucchinis, grated
1/2 teaspoon garlic powder
1/3 teaspoon smoked cayenne pepper

Directions

- Begin by preheating a cast-iron skillet over a moderate heat; then, warm the oil and sauté the onions and zucchini until they have softened.
- Throw in the beef and stir until it has browned. Sprinkle with garlic powder, cumin powder, salt, black pepper, and cayenne pepper.
- Then, cut the puff pastry into rectangular strips (1-inch x 1.5-inch). Spread the vegetable/beef filling on pastry strips. Now, pierce the edges of the puff pastry using a fork.
- Cook for 5 to 6 minutes at 325 degrees F, working in batches. Bon appétit!

244. Beef and Goat Cheese Frittata

Ready in about 25 minutes
Servings 2

Reinvent a classic egg dish by swapping a bacon for the lean ground beef - just add your favorite salad and a teaspoon of spicy mustard.

Per serving: 506 Calories; 44.9g Fat; 6.7g Carbs; 33g Protein; 3.2g Sugars

Ingredients

3 tablespoons goat cheese, crumbled
2 cups lean ground beef
1 ½ tablespoons olive oil
1/2 teaspoon dried marjoram
3 eggs
1/2 onion, peeled and chopped
1/2 teaspoon paprika
1/2 teaspoon kosher salt
1 teaspoon ground black pepper

Directions

- Set your air fryer to cook at 345 degrees F.
- Melt the oil in a skillet over a moderate flame; then, sweat the onion until it has softened. Add ground beef and cook until browned; crumble with a fork and set aside, keeping it warm.
- Whisk the eggs with all the seasonings.
- Spritz the inside of a baking dish with a pan spray. Pour the beaten egg mixture into the baking dish, followed by the reserved beef/onion mixture. Top with the crumbled goat cheese.
- Bake for about 27 minutes or until a tester comes out clean and dry when stuck in the center of the frittata. Bon appétit!

245. Beef Medallions with Red Potatoes

Ready in about 30 minutes
Servings 4

Treat your family with the most tender and elegant beef cut. Beef medallions are lean yet flavorful and succulent. Thanks to the Air fryer, beef medallions retain their great texture and compact shape.

Per serving: 217 Calories; 10.4g Fat; 17.2g Carbs; 14.8g Protein; 4.7g Sugars

Ingredients

2 tablespoons olive oil
2 small bunch parsley, roughly chopped
1/2 cup sweet onions, cut into wedges
½ pound beef medallions
½ pound red potatoes, cut into large chunks
3 bell peppers, seeded and sliced
2 sprigs thyme
1 sprig rosemary
Umami dust seasoning, to taste
Salt and ground black pepper, to taste

Directions

- Firstly, arrange the vegetables on the bottom of the air fryer basket; add seasonings and drizzle with olive oil. Roast for 8 minutes and pause the machine.
- Now, place beef medallions on top of the vegetables.
- Roast for 18 minutes longer at 375 degrees, stirring once halfway through. To serve, sprinkle with umami dust seasoning and enjoy!

246. Classic Old-Fashioned Beef with Vegetables

Ready in about 20 minutes
Servings 6

For the best results, marinate your steaks a couple of hours. When it comes to s carving, slice them against the grain.

Per serving: 439 Calories; 14.3g Fat; 63.5g Carbs; 16.1g Protein; 18.1g Sugars

Ingredients

3 parsnips, cut into thick slices
1/2 cup cream of shallot soup
3 leeks, cut into thick slices
1 teaspoon kosher salt
2 tablespoons Dijon mustard
1/2 teaspoon tarragon
1/3 teaspoon ground black pepper, or to taste
6 small-sized lean steaks
2 tablespoons dried mint
1/2 can tomatoes, crushed
2 teaspoons freshly grated lemon rind
3 carrots, cut into thick slices

Directions

- Add all the ingredients to the air fryer baking tray; toss to coat well.
- Roast in the preheated air fryer for 14 minutes at 400 degrees F.
- Work in batches and make sure to stir halfway through the cooking time. Bon appétit!

247. Steaks with Herbed Butter

Ready in about 15 minutes +
marinating time
Servings 4

Want to amaze your family for holidays? Then, give this recipe a try! Serve with sourdough buns and Dijon sauce.

Per serving: 275 Calories; 18.6g Fat; 2.7g Carbs; 22.9g Protein; 1.2g Sugars

Ingredients

1/3 stick butter, room temperature
1 ½ teaspoon dried thyme, finely minced
2 teaspoons fresh rosemary, minced
3 green onions, white and green parts, chopped
4 beef steaks
1/3 teaspoon freshly cracked black pepper, or more to taste
2 teaspoons dried parsley flakes
1/3 teaspoon fine sea salt
2 cloves garlic, finely minced

Directions

- Roast beef steaks in the preheated air fryer for 18 minutes at 405 degrees F, turning once.
- In a mixing bowl, combine the other items in the order listed above; mix to combine well. Refrigerate until serving time.
- Don't forget to take it out of your refrigerator 28 minutes before using. Freeze the herbed butter for up to 3 months.

248. Beef and Goat Cheese Frittata

Ready in about 25 minutes
Servings 2

This classic frittata, filled with cheese, beef and seasonings, makes a delicious, high protein breakfast for two. You can swap goat cheese for Feta if desired.

Per serving: 506 Calories; 44.9g Fat; 6.7g Carbs; 33g Protein; 3.2g Sugars

Ingredients

3 tablespoons goat cheese, crumbled
2 cups lean ground beef
1 ½ tablespoons olive oil
½ teaspoon dried marjoram
3 eggs
½ onion, peeled and chopped
½ teaspoon paprika
½ teaspoon kosher salt
1 teaspoon ground black pepper

Directions

- Set your air fryer to cook at 345 degrees F.
- Melt the oil in a skillet over a moderate flame; then, sweat the onion until it has softened. Add ground beef and cook until browned; crumble with a fork and set aside, keeping it warm.
- Whisk the eggs with all the seasonings.
- Spritz the inside of a baking dish with a pan spray. Pour the beaten egg mixture into the baking dish, followed by the reserved beef/onion mixture. Top with the crumbled goat cheese.
- Bake for about 27 minutes or until a tester comes out clean and dry when stuck in the center of the frittata. Bon appétit!

249. Tangy Tender Beef Steak

Ready in about 15 minutes
Servings 4

This homey steak might become your favorite in winter months! Simple and ready in just 15 minutes. Couldn't ask for more.

Per serving: 380 Calories; 15.6g Fat; 5.7g Carbs; 50.6g Protein; 1.6g Sugars

Ingredients

1 ½ tablespoons hoisin sauce
2 pinches grated nutmeg
2 tablespoons whole grain mustard
4 beef steaks
2 teaspoons freshly chopped ginger, peeled
3 tablespoons Whisky
Fine kosher salt and freshly ground black pepper, to taste

Directions

- Toss beef steaks with other ingredients until everything is well coated.
- Cook for 18 minutes at 405 degrees F, turning once or twice.
- Serve warm with egg noodles.

250. Italian Beef in Creamy Chive Sauce

Ready in about 25 minutes
Servings 4

Get ready for juicy tenderness and outstanding appearance! This beef dish is perfect for any family gathering.

Per serving: 254 Calories; 17.9g Fat; 3.5g Carbs; 19g Protein; 1.1g Sugars

Ingredients

½ pound beef tenderloin
2 teaspoons freshly squeezed lime juice
1/2 cup sour cream
2 heaping tablespoons chives, chopped
2 tablespoons sesame oil
1 teaspoon salt
1 teaspoon brown sugar
½ cup white wine
2 1/2 tablespoons mayonnaise
2 teaspoons dried Italian herbs
Freshly cracked pink peppercorns, to taste

Directions

- In a large-sized mixing bowl, whisk together the wine, sesame oil, and lime juice; add the seasonings and sugar; finally, add the beef. Cover and let your beef marinate for at least 50 minutes in the fridge.
- Then, preheat the air fryer to 385 degrees F; set the timer for 18 minutes; cook until thoroughly warmed, stirring halfway through.
- In the meantime, make the sauce by mixing the mayonnaise, cream, and chives. Serve the prepared beef with the sauce. Bon appétit!

251. Italian-Style Dinner Rolls

Ready in about 15 minutes
Servings 8

If you like dinner rolls, try this recipe that is satisfying yet light and delicious. Everyone loves beef burgers without an excess fat and calories!

Per serving: 393 Calories; 22.6g Fat; 16.4g Carbs; 29.9g Protein; 3.2g Sugars

Ingredients

8 slices Pecorino Toscano cheese
2 teaspoons Italian seasonings
8 dinner rolls
1 ½ pounds ground beef
Generous pinches of salt and ground black pepper

Directions

- Start by preheating the air fryer to 395 degrees F. Mix ground beef with salt, black pepper and Italian seasonings; knead to combine well.
- Shape the ground beef mixture into 8 equal patties. Now, air-fry your burgers in the preheated machine for 9 minutes.
- Top each burger with 1 slice of Pecorino Toscano cheese; return to the air fryer to cook for one more minute.
- Serve your burgers in dinner rolls and enjoy!

252. Parmesan Beef Schnitzel

Ready in about 25 minutes
Servings 4

Majestic tender, sinfully delicious and juicy schnitzel! Consider adding a chipotle powder that will give your schnitzel a hint of spiciness and heat.

Per serving: 403 Calories; 34.6g Fat; 2.7g Carbs; 46.9g Protein; 0.2g Sugars

Ingredients

2 eggs, well whisked
1/2 cup breadcrumbs
1 ½ teaspoons garlic powder
4 beef schnitzels
1 ½ tablespoons sesame oil
1/3 cup grated Parmesan cheese
1 teaspoon shallot powder
Table salt and ground black pepper, to taste

Directions

- Preheat your air fryer to 365 degrees F. Season the beef schnitzels with salt and ground black pepper.
- In a mixing dish, combine the oil, breadcrumbs, garlic powder, shallot powder, and Parmesan cheese. Stir until the mixture becomes crumbly.
- Add the whisked eggs to a shallow plate.
- Dip each schnitzel into the egg; then, dip it into the Parmesan/crumb mix, making sure it is well covered.
- Cook in the preheated air fryer for 14 minutes or until crispy. Serve immediately with a sauce or salad and enjoy!

253. Beef Medallions with Porcini Mushrooms Sauce

Ready in about 25 minutes
Servings 4

The grand champion of beef cuts, the air-fried beef medallions will become your family favorite. These beef medallions are juicy and fabulous.

Per serving: 249 Calories; 16.6g Fat; 0g Carbs; 23.7g Protein; 0g Sugars

Ingredients

1 ½ tablespoons vegetable oil
½ pound beef medallions
Salt and crushed red pepper flakes, to taste

For the Sauce:
2 tablespoons dry white wine
1/2 cup Porcini mushrooms, thinly sliced
1 ½ shallots, minced
1 tablespoon butter, softened
2 sprigs dried rosemary, crushed
1 garlic cloves, minced
2 sprigs dried thyme, crushed
1/3teaspoon freshly cracked black peppercorns
Fine sea salt, to taste

Directions

- Toss beef medallions with salt, red pepper flakes, and vegetable oil. Cook in the preheated air fryer at 355 degrees F for 20 minutes.
- In the meantime, prepare the mushroom sauce. Firstly, melt the butter in the pan that is placed over a moderate heat.
- Now, sauté the shallots until tender and fragrant. Next, add the sliced mushrooms and cook until just fragrant; it will take about 5 minutes.
- Add the other ingredient for the sauce and stir until everything is thoroughly warmed.
- To serve, lay beef medallion on a serving plate; ladle the sauce over it. Repeat with the remaining servings and eat warm.

254. Award-Winning Steaks

Ready in about 20 minutes
Servings 4

Set back and look forward to the incredible beef steak ahead! By using this new cooking technique, your steak remains succulent and so flavorful that all you need is a tablespoon or two of horseradish sauce to make it magnificent.

Per serving: 420 Calories; 22.3g Fat; 2.7g Carbs; 50.3g Protein; 0.9g Sugars

Ingredients

2 tablespoons Worcestershire sauce
1/2 teaspoon dried parsley flakes
1 ½ heaping tablespoons fresh cilantro
1 teaspoon ground cinnamon
4 tablespoons dry white wine
2 tablespoons canola oil
4 small-sized beef steaks
2 teaspoons ground cumin
1/3 teaspoon dried thyme
1 teaspoon sea salt, or more to taste
1/3 teaspoon freshly ground pepper, or more to taste

Directions

- Firstly, coat the steaks with the cumin, parsley flakes, black pepper, salt, thyme, and ground cinnamon.
- Drizzle the steaks with the white wine, canola oil, and Worcestershire sauce.
- Lastly, roast your steaks for 16 minutes at 325 degrees F. Serve garnished with fresh cilantro. Bon appétit!

255. Famous Beef Sloppy Joes

Ready in about 15 minutes
Servings 2

Stunning cooking aromas are coming from your kitchen… An air fryer will bring a spirit of good old times into your home!

Per serving: 475 Calories; 24.7g Fat; 28.3g Carbs; 34.2g Protein; 7.2g Sugars

Ingredients

2 hamburger buns
½ pound ground beef
8 ounces canned tomatoes
2 teaspoons olive oil
1 garlic clove, peeled and finely minced
1/2 teaspoon parsley flakes
Lettuce, to serve
1/2 tablespoon Worcestershire sauce
1/3 cup tomato ketchup
½ bell pepper, seeded and chopped

Directions

- Begin by preheating your air fryer to 355 degrees F. Heat the oil and cook the garlic and beef until browned; it will take 4 to 5 minutes.
- Crumble the beef with a spatula.
- Throw in Worcestershire sauce, canned tomatoes, ketchup, parsley flakes, and bell pepper; air fry for 14 minutes; make sure to stir halfway through.
- To serve, assemble the sandwiches using the hamburger buns and lettuce leaves. Bon appétit!

256. Mom's Mouthwatering Beef Medallions

Ready in about 25 minutes
Servings 4

Everyone can become a great chef with an Air fryer! In addition, beef medallions are so versatile, so flavorful, so that you can't go wrong with them.
Serve with lots of homemade crusty bread or penne pasta.

Per serving: 149Calories; 7.6g Fat; 1.4g Carbs; 17.9g Protein; 0.2g Sugars

Ingredients

2 tablespoons Creole mustard
½ tablespoon apple cider vinegar
1 ½ tablespoons extra-virgin olive oil
½ pounds beef tenderloin, trimmed and sliced into thick medallions
2 teaspoon cumin seeds, ground
½ teaspoon seasoned salt
1/3 teaspoon freshly cracked black peppercorns, or multi-color peppercorns

Directions

● Toss the beef medallions with all the other items until well coated. Cook in your air fryer for 13 minutes at 365 degrees F.
● Check for doneness and cook for 4 to 5 minutes longer as needed.
● To finish, mound the wilted kale onto a serving plate. Top with the beef medallions and serve immediately.

257. Beef in Creamy Jalapeño Sauce

Ready in about 15 minutes +
marinating time
Servings4

If you have the opportunity to choose, shop for organic beef. For a complete holiday meal, serve with roasted seasonal vegetables on the side.

Per serving: 232 Calories; 15.1g Fat; 4.7g Carbs; 18.9g Protein; 1.3g Sugars

Ingredients

2 tablespoons Creole mustard
½ pound beef tenderloin
1/3 teaspoon sea salt
½ teaspoon onion powder
1/3 cup white wine
½ teaspoon brown sugar
2 tablespoons olive oil
2 teaspoons fresh orange juice
½ teaspoon garlic powder
Freshly cracked green peppercorns, to taste
½ tablespoon jalapeño pepper, finely minced
½ cup sour cream

Directions

● Add the first 9 ingredients to a mixing bowl; whisk until everything is well incorporated. Now, throw in the beef and marinate at least 50 minutes in your refrigerator.
● After that, preheat your air fryer to 375 degrees F; set the timer for 18 minutes; cook the beef until cooked through.
● Meanwhile, mix sour cream with jalapeño pepper; mix to combine well and serve with warm beef. Bon appétit!

258. Tuscan Beef Chops

Ready in about 20 minutes
Servings 3

Regardless of whether you are a very beginner or an old hand, you must try this recipe. Bring Italy to your kitchen with Tuscan seasoning mix.

Per serving: 241 Calories; 15.1g Fat; 4.8g Carbs; 22.9g Protein; 0.5g Sugars

Ingredients

3 sprigs fresh thyme, chopped
1/3 cup herb vinegar
2 teaspoons Tuscan seasoning
3 beef chops
2 teaspoons garlic powder
Kosher salt and ground black pepper, to taste

Directions

- Toss the beef chops with the other ingredients.
- Roast at 395 degrees F for 16 minutes, turning once or twice. Afterward, taste for doneness, add the seasonings and serve warm. Bon appétit!

259. Beef with Beer Mustard and Tomato Sauce

Ready in about 10 minutes
Servings 4

Looking for a stress-free family dish? Richly flavored and amazingly tender, this beef tenderloin is guaranteed to make your lunch so much better.

Per serving: 228 Calories; 18.9g Fat; 0.7g Carbs; 13.4g Protein; 0.5g Sugars

Ingredients

2 teaspoons beer mustard
1teaspoon kosher salt, or more to taste
1 ½ small-sized beef tenderloin, cut in half lengthwise
2 tablespoons olive oil
2 teaspoons ground cumin
1 teaspoon crushed red pepper flakes, or more to taste

For Tomato Sauce:
1 teaspoon salt
2 garlic cloves, pressed
½ tablespoon olive oil
3 large-sized tomatoes, chopped
2 rosemary sprigs, finely chopped

Directions

- Firstly, sprinkle beef tenderloins with all seasonings listed above. Now, drizzle each tenderloin with olive oil and beer mustard.
- Next step, air-fry for 13 minutes at 355 degrees F.
- Meanwhile, prepare the tomato sauce by preheating a nonstick sauté pan over a moderate flame. Add all ingredients for the sauce to the pan, bringing to a boil; now, lower the heat to a brisk simmer.
- Cook until the sauce has reduced by almost half. Serve the prepared beef with the tomato sauce. Bon appétit!

260. Classic Meatballs with Tomato Sauce

Ready in about 20 minutes
Servings 4

This easy family dish features beef sausage meat that is versatile and economical. For parties, transfer the meatballs along with the sauce to a crock pot to keep them warm.

Per serving: 75 Calories; 5.4g Fat; 5g Carbs; 4.5g Protein; 0.2g Sugars

Ingredients

4 tablespoons quick oats
1/3 cup green onion
3 ounces beef sausage meat
3 garlic cloves, minced
1/3 teaspoon ground black pepper
Sea salt, to taste

For the sauce:
2 tablespoons Worcestershire sauce
1/3 yellow onion, minced
Dash of Tabasco sauce
1/3 cup tomato paste
1 teaspoon cumin powder
1/2 tablespoon balsamic vinegar

Directions

- Knead all of the above ingredients until everything is well incorporated.
- Roll into balls and cook in the preheated air fryer at 365 degrees for 13 minutes.
- In the meantime, in a saucepan, cook the ingredients for the sauce until thoroughly warmed. Serve your meatballs with the tomato sauce and enjoy!

261. Flank Steak Beef in Cascabel-Cumin Sauce

Ready in about 15 minutes
Servings 4

Treat your family to a comforting plate of something fabulous like this flank steak in Mexican-inspired spicy sauce. Cascabel chili pepper is also known as chile bola.

Per serving: 135 Calories; 5.6g Fat; 7.7g Carbs; 13.7g Protein; 4.9g Sugars

Ingredients

2 teaspoons brown mustard
2 tablespoons mayonnaise
8 ounces beef flank steak, trimmed and cubed
2 teaspoons minced cascabel
½ cup scallions, finely chopped
1/3 cup Crème fraîche
2 teaspoons cumin seeds
3 cloves garlic, pressed
Pink peppercorns to taste, freshly cracked
1 teaspoon fine table salt
1/3 teaspoon black pepper, preferably freshly ground

Directions

- Firstly, fry the cumin seeds just about 1 minute or until they pop.
- After that, season your beef flank steak with fine table salt, black pepper and the fried cumin seeds; arrange the seasoned beef cubes on the bottom of your baking dish that fits in the air fryer.
- Throw in the minced cascabel, garlic, and scallions; air-fry approximately 8 minutes at 390 degrees F.
- Once the beef cubes start to tender, add your favorite mayo, Crème fraîche, freshly cracked pink peppercorns and mustard; air-fry 7 minutes longer. Serve over hot wild rice. Bon appétit!

262. Holiday Spicy and Garlicky Steak

Ready in about 20 minutes
Servings 2

This steak is not very spicy but it has a smoky, rustic flavor thanks to the peppers and smoked paprika.

Per serving: 450 Calories; 25.6g Fat; 3.4g Carbs; 50.8g Protein; 0.3g Sugars

Ingredients

1/2 Ancho chili pepper, soaked in hot water before using
½ tablespoon brandy
2 teaspoons smoked paprika
1 1/2 tablespoons olive oil
2 beef steaks
Kosher salt, to taste
1 teaspoon ground allspice
3 cloves garlic, sliced

Directions

- Sprinkle the beef steaks with salt, paprika, and allspice. Add the steak to a baking dish that fits your fryer. Scatter the sliced garlic over the top.
- Now, drizzle it with brandy and olive oil; spread minced Ancho chili pepper over the top.
- Bake at 385 degrees F for 14 minutes, turning halfway through.

263. Beef Chops with Parmesan-Kale Salad

Ready in about 10 minutes
Servings 2

Looking for a main dish that doesn't take a lot of time? Look no further! These beef chops are not only easy to prepare, they serve up amazingly too.

Per serving: 206 Calories; 18g Fat; 1.7g Carbs; 9.8g Protein; 0.4g Sugars

Ingredients

1/2 cup vegetable stock
1/3 cup scallions, chopped
1 cloves garlic, minced
2 beef chops
½ tablespoon melted butter
Table salt and ground black pepper, to savor

For the Salad:
1 ½ tablespoons freshly grated Parmesan
1 tablespoon apple cider vinegar
2 tablespoons extra-virgin olive oil
2 cups very finely chopped or slivered curly kale
1/3 teaspoon ground black pepper, or more to taste
1 teaspoon table salt

Directions

- Take an oven safe dish and toss beef chops with salt, pepper, butter, scallions, and garlic; pour in the stock; gently stir to coat.
- Now, roast your chops at 395 degrees F for 12 to 14 minutes.
- Meanwhile, make the parmesan-kale salad by mixing all salad components. Serve warm beef chops with the prepared kale salad.

264. Tender Beef Chops with English Mustard

Ready in about 40 minutes
Servings 3

Using English mustard with beef chops is a good idea. However, it's not the secret ingredient in this recipe – it's a grated rind of 1/2 small-sized lime.

Per serving: 402 Calories; 44.5g Fat; 1.7g Carbs; 52.9g Protein; 0.3g Sugars

Ingredients

1 ½ teaspoon English mustard
3 boneless beef chops
1/3 teaspoon garlic pepper
3 new potatoes, quartered
2 teaspoons oregano, dried
2 tablespoons vegetable oil
1 ½ tablespoons fresh coriander, chopped
1/2 teaspoon onion powder
1/2 teaspoon basil, dried
Grated rind of 1/2 small-sized lime
1/2 teaspoon fine sea salt

Directions

- Firstly, make the rub for the beef chops by mixing all the ingredients, except the chops and the new potatoes.
- Now, evenly spread the beef chops with the English mustard rub.
- Then, arrange the new potatoes in the bottom of the air fryer cooking basket. Top them with the prepared beef chops.
- Roast for about 27 minutes at 365 degrees F, turning halfway through. Serve on individual plates with couscous salad on the side if desired.

265. Saucy Lemony Beef Steaks

Ready in about 15 minutes
Servings 2

There are a million ways to turn a regular steak into a romantic dinner for two! This recipe is only one of them. When it comes to the seasonings, mustard seeds and cumin power work well too.

Per serving: 400 Calories; 20g Fat; 2.3g Carbs; 50.8g Protein; 0.6g Sugars

Ingredients

3 beef steaks
4 tablespoons white wine
2 teaspoons crushed coriander seeds
½ teaspoon fennel seeds
1/3 cup beef broth
2 tablespoons lemon zest, grated
2 tablespoons canola oil
1/2 lemon, cut into wedges
Salt flakes and freshly ground black pepper, to taste

Directions

- Heat the oil in a saucepan over a moderate flame. Then, cook the garlic for 1 minute, or until just fragrant.
- Remove the pan from the heat; add the beef broth, wine, lemon zest, coriander seeds, fennel, salt flakes, and freshly ground black. Pour the mixture into a baking dish.
- Add beef steaks to the baking dish; toss to coat well. Now, tuck the lemon wedges among the beef steaks.
- Bake for 18 minutes at 335 degrees F. Serve warm.

266. Easy Cocktail Rolls

Ready in about 15 minutes
Servings 4

These melt-in-your-mouth cocktail rolls are a wonderful make-ahead snack for your next holiday party! Beer mustard is the perfect addition to these rolls.

Per serving: 183Calories; 5.6g Fat; 3.4g Carbs; 12.9g Protein; 0g Sugars

Ingredients

2 tablespoons beer mustard
8 ounces beef cocktail smokies
1 sheet puff pastry

Directions

- Firstly, drain the beef cocktail smokies and pat them dry on a kitchen towel. Cut the puff pastry into even rectangular strips.
- Spread the strips with beer mustard. Roll the strips around the smokies; let them stand for 4 to 5 minutes in a freezer. Preheat your air fryer to 335 degrees F.
- Cook for 5 to 6 minutes, working in batches. Serve with beer and enjoy the party!

267. Chili & Dark Chocolate Beef Meatballs

Ready in about 25 minutes
Servings 4

Easy to make and easy to eat, these meatballs are always a hit! Give them your own twist by using chocolate gourmet sausages.

Per serving: 201 Calories; 8.7g Fat; 26.5g Carbs; 3.6g Protein; 14g Sugars

Ingredients

1 cup green onion, finely minced
1/2 teaspoon parsley flakes
2 teaspoons onion flakes
6 ounces chili & dark chocolate sausage, crumbled
2 tablespoons seasoned breadcrumbs
3 cloves garlic, finely minced
Fine sea salt and ground black pepper, to taste
½ tablespoon fresh chopped sage

Directions

- Mix all ingredients in a bowl until the mixture has a uniform consistency.
- Roll into bite-sized balls and transfer them to a baking dish.
- Cook in the preheated air fryer at 345 degrees for 18 minutes. Serve on wooden sticks and enjoy!

268. Butter Crumbed Beef Schnitzel

Ready in about 10 minutes
Servings 2

Besides being delicious, this schnitzel is easy to prepare. Making this your favorite just got even easier thanks to the Air fryer.

Per serving: 271 Calories; 16.3g Fat; 22g Carbs; 9.3g Protein; 2.5g Sugars

Ingredients

2 medium-sized eggs
1 teaspoon cayenne pepper, or more to taste
1/2 cup buttered crumbs
1/3 freshly ground black pepper, or more to taste
Wedges of 1 fresh lemon, to serve
2 beef schnitzels
1 teaspoon fine sea salt
1 ½ tablespoons canola oil

Directions

- Season beef schnitzel with salt, cayenne pepper, and ground black pepper.
- In a mixing dish, whisk the oil with buttered crumbs. In another bowl, whisk the eggs until pale and frothy.
- Firstly, coat beef schnitzels with the whisked eggs; then, coat it with the crumb/oil mixture.
- Air-fry for 10 minutes at 355 degrees F. Serve warm, garnished with lemon wedges and enjoy!

269. Melt-in-Your-Mouth Beef

Ready in about 13 minutes
Servings 2

The Air fryer ensures you get a moist and tender beef flank steak without sacrificing flavor and texture. Use a sour cream with a fat content of 20 %.

Per serving: 268 Calories; 13.1g Fat; 6.7g Carbs; 29.8g Protein; 0.9g Sugars

Ingredients

1/3 cup sour cream
½ cup green onion, chopped
1 tablespoon mayonnaise
3 cloves garlic, smashed
9 ounces beef flank steak, trimmed and cubed
2 tablespoons fresh sage, minced
½ teaspoon salt
1/3 teaspoon black pepper, or to taste

Directions

- Season your meat with salt and pepper; arrange beef cubes on the bottom of a baking dish that fits in your air fryer.
- Stir in green onions and garlic; air-fry for about 7 minutes at 385 degrees F.
- Once your beef starts to tender, add the cream, mayonnaise, and sage; air-fry an additional 8 minutes. Serve over cooked spaghetti if desired. Bon appétit!

270. Shallot and Carrot Steak

Ready in about 17 minutes
Servings 6

Steak pairs well with lager, pale ales and Syrah. In this recipe, you can also use the crushed ripe tomatoes instead of canned ones.

Per serving: 331 Calories; 10.4g Fat; 45.6g Carbs; 14.3g Protein; 12.8g Sugars

Ingredients

1/3 cup cream of shallot soup
2 sprigs fresh rosemary, chopped
4 carrots, sliced
1/2 can tomatoes, crushed
2 sprigs fresh thyme, chopped
1 teaspoon kosher salt
4 tablespoons dry white wine
1 teaspoon ground black pepper, or to taste
6 lean steaks, cut into strips
3 shallots, peeled and cut into wedges
1/2 teaspoon cayenne pepper

Directions

- Add all ingredients to an air fryer baking tray; then, cook for 13 minutes at 395 degrees F.
- Work in batches; pause the machine once or twice to shake your food. Bon appétit!

271. Tender Spicy Beef with Cotija Cheese

Ready in about 15 minutes
Servings 6

Air frying is one of the best cooking methods to achieve flavors that will blow you away! The aged version of Cotija cheese is similar to Parmesan. Therefore, you can swap them easily. A good alternative for soft Cotija cheese is Feta.

Per serving:397 Calories; 18.6g Fat; 3.9g Carbs; 53.2g Protein; 0.94g Sugars

Ingredients

3 eggs, whisked
1/3 cup finely grated cotija cheese
1 cup fresh Italian breadcrumbs
6 minute steaks
2 tablespoons berbere
1 ½ tablespoons olive oil
Fine sea salt and ground black pepper, to taste

Directions

- Begin by sprinkling minute steaks with berbere, salt and pepper.
- Take a mixing dish and thoroughly combine the oil, cotija cheese, and Italian breadcrumbs. In a separate mixing dish, beat the eggs.
- Firstly, dip minute steaks in the egg; then, dip them in breadcrumb/cheese mixture.
- Air-fry for 15 minutes at 345 degrees F; work in batches. Bon appétit!
- Note: If you can't find berbere spice, mix equal amount of sweet paprika, ground coriander, ground ginger, ground fenugreek, and ground allspice.

272. Easiest Breaded Steaks Ever

Ready in about 16 minutes
Servings 4

You're about to cook the best and the easiest steaks you've ever eaten! Homemade seasoned breadcrumbs are cost effective and they taste great. You just need a stale bread and a few pinches of your favorite seasonings.

Per serving: 474 Calories; 22.1g Fat; 8.7g Carbs; 54.7g Protein; 1.6g Sugars

Ingredients

1/3 cup seasoned breadcrumbs
2 eggs
2 teaspoons caraway seeds
4 beef steaks
2 teaspoons garlic powder
1 tablespoon melted butter
Fine sea salt and cayenne pepper, to taste

Directions

- Generously coat steaks with garlic powder, caraway seeds, salt, and cayenne pepper.
- In a mixing dish, thoroughly combine melted butter with seasoned crumbs. In another bowl, beat the eggs until they're well whisked.
- First, coat steaks with the beaten egg; then, coat beef steaks with the buttered crumb mixture.
- Place the steaks in the air fryer cooking basket; cook for 10 minutes at 355 degrees F. Serve with mashed potatoes. Bon appétit!

273. Chipotle and Beef Pastry Rolls

Ready in about 10 minutes
Servings 4

The light dough of puff bakes perfectly in your Air fryer. For an amazing golden-brown crust, make an egg wash and then, brush it over your rolls.

Per serving: 212 Calories; 14.6g Fat; 6.7g Carbs; 13.4g Protein; 2.2g Sugars

Ingredients

1 1/2 chipotle peppers, finely minced
7 ounces ground beef
2 tablespoons olive oil
3 cloves garlic, finely minced
1 ½ onion, peeled and finely chopped
1 sheet puff pastry
Fine sea salt and freshly ground black pepper, to taste

Directions

- To make the filling, preheat a pan over a moderate heat and add the oil; swirl to coat and add the onions and garlic. Now, cook until they're just tender.
- Throw in chipotle pepper and beef; cook until the beef has browned. Season with salt and pepper.
- Cut the puff pastry into rectangular strips (1-inch x 1.5-inch).
- Spread the filling among prepared pastry strips. Now, pierce the edges of the puff pastry using your hands and a fork.
- Cook for 5 to 6 minutes at 325 degrees F, working in batches. Bon appétit!

274. Mouthwatering Minute Steaks

Ready in about 10 minutes +
marinating time
Servings 4

There are so many creative ways to use minute steaks. This twisty combination of herb vinegar, seasonings and minute steak is sure to be a favorite at your next family lunch.

Per serving: 296 Calories; 14g Fat; 6.7g Carbs; 36.5g Protein; 0.6g Sugars

Ingredients

1 1/2 tablespoons extra-virgin olive oil
1/2 cup herb vinegar
1/3 teaspoon celery seed
4 minute steaks
1 teaspoon salt
2 teaspoons cayenne pepper
1/3 teaspoon ground black pepper, or to taste

Directions

- Toss all ingredients in a mixing dish. Cover the dish and marinate the steaks in the refrigerator for about 3 hours.
- Finally, cook minute steaks for 13 minutes at 355 degrees F. Eat warm with your favorite salad and French fries. Bon appétit!

275. Teriyaki Beef with Sautéed Broccoli

Ready in about 60 minutes
Servings 4

The best part of this beef dish is teriyaki marinade; it will make your beef buttery tender and sinfully flavorful.

Per serving: 220 Calories; 12.4g Fat; 8.3g Carbs; 19.8g Protein; 4.4g Sugars

Ingredients

½ had broccoli, broken into florets
1/3 cup teriyaki marinade
Fine sea salt and ground black pepper, to taste
½ pound rump steak
2 red capsicums, sliced
1 ½ teaspoon sesame oil

Directions

- Add rump roast and teriyaki marinade to a mixing dish; stir to coat. Let it marinate for about 40 minutes.
- Then, roast in the preheated air fryer for 13 minutes at 395 degrees F. Stir halfway through cooking time.
- Meanwhile, sauté the broccoli in the hot sesame oil along with sliced capsicum; cook until tender and season with salt and pepper to savor.
- Place the prepared rump steak on a serving platter and serve garnished with sautéed broccoli. Bon appétit!

276. Barbeque Minute Steaks

Ready in about 15 minutes
Servings 4

A barbecue sauce makes everything better! These delicious steaks will quickly become a lunch staple.

Per serving: 436 Calories; 20.1g Fat; 20g Carbs; 52.2g Protein; 4g Sugars

Ingredients

3 medium-sized eggs
2 ½ tablespoons barbecue sauce
1 cup ground rolled oats, crushed
2 dash hot peppers sauce
4 small beef steaks
1/3 teaspoon ground black pepper
1 ½ tablespoons butter
2 teaspoons cayenne pepper
1 teaspoon kosher salt

Directions

- Sprinkle minute steaks with cayenne pepper, ground black pepper, and kosher salt; drizzle them with hot pepper sauce and barbeque sauce.
- In a mixing dish, combine butter with ground rolled oats. In a separate bowl or a measuring cup, beat the eggs until frothy.
- Firstly, dip minute steaks in the egg; then, dip them in the butter/oat mixture.
- After that, fry your steaks for 9 minutes at 355 degrees F. Serve over cooked wild rice. Bon appétit!

277. Beef and Cheese Puff Pastry

Ready in about 10 minutes
Servings 4

If you are lucky enough to own an Air fryer, you can make the best cheesy pastry rolls ever. Serve with a salsa or red pepper chutney for a little something unexpected.

Per serving: 342 Calories; 23.6g Fat; 2.4g Carbs; 29.3g Protein; 0.7g Sugars

Ingredients

7 ounces soft cheese, softened
11 ounces ground beef
1/2 dash dried sage
3 sheets puff pastry
1 ½ small onions peeled and finely chopped
Salt and ground black pepper, to savor

Directions

- Preheat a nonstick skillet over a moderate flame; then, sauté ground beef along with the onion.
- Stir in the sage, salt, and pepper, and stir until ground beef is no longer pink and the onion is translucent.
- Cut the puff pastry into rectangular strips (1-inch x 1.5-inch).
- Spread the cheese and filling on prepared pastry strips. Now, pierce the edges of the puff pastry; you can use a fork.
- Cook for 6 to 7 minutes at 325 degrees F, working in batches. Bon appétit!

278. Herby and Honey Beef Steaks

Ready in about 20 minutes
Servings 4

Your family will adore this sticky, herby steak. Don't forget a garnish of chipotle peppers in adobo sauce for a little more kick.

Per serving: 473 Calories; 23.7g Fat; 11.3g Carbs; 51.1g Protein; 10.3g Sugars

Ingredients

2 tablespoons soy sauce
3 heaping tablespoons fresh chives
2 tablespoons olive oil
3 tablespoons dry white wine
4 small-sized beef steaks
2 teaspoons smoked cayenne pepper
1/2 teaspoon dried basil
1/2 teaspoon dried rosemary
2 tablespoons honey
1 teaspoon freshly ground pepper
1 teaspoon sea salt, or more to taste

Directions

- Firstly, coat the steaks with the cayenne pepper, black pepper, salt, basil, and rosemary.
- Drizzle the steaks with olive oil, white wine, soy sauce, and honey.
- Finally, roast in an air fryer basket for 20 minutes at 335 degrees F. Serve garnished with fresh chives. Bon appétit!

FISH & SEAFOOD

279. Crispy Snapper Fillets with Almond Sauce 155

280. Italian-Style Cod Fillets 155

281. Honey-Glazed Halibut Steaks 156

282. Crunchy Saltine Fish Fillets 156

283. Marinated Sardines with Roasted Potatoes 157

284. Garlicky Grilled Shrimp 157

285. Salmon Fillets with Sweet Potatoes 158

286. Fancy Coconut Curried Prawns 158

287. Tilapia Filets with Creamy Caper Sauce 159

288. Festive Sake-Glazed Flounder 159

289. Fish Fingers with Dijonnaise Sauce 160

290. Whitefish Cakes with Green Beans 160

291. Traditional Filipino Bistek 161

292. Chunky Fish and Celery Cakes 161

293. Jumbo Shrimp with Chipotle-Dijon Sauce 162

294. Super Easy Crunchy Grouper Fillets 162

295. Classic Cajun Shrimp 163

296. Za'atar Bacon Wrapped Shrimp 163

297. Salmon in Creamy Lime Sauce 164

298. Crispy Catfish Fillets 164

299. Cajun Fish Sticks 165

300. Crab and Carrot Cakes 165

301. Easy Herbed Shrimp 166

302. Quick-Fix Seafood Breakfast 166

303. Aromatic Egg Noodles with Shrimp 167

304. Sunday Shrimp in Roasted Garlic Sauce 167

305. Crispy Saucy Whitefish Fillets 168

306. Grouper Fillets with Jalapeño-Avocado Sauce 168

307. Hot Spicy Snapper Tacos 169

308. Easy Saucy Sage Halibut 169

309. Baked Prawns with Vegetables 170

310. The Ultimate Cod Fish Tacos 170

311. Hot Spicy Orange Roughy 171

312. Festive Milkfish Steak 171

313. Scallops with Zesty Cilantro Sauce 172

314. Mom's Special Chervil Shrimps 172

315. Curry and Paprika Fish Sticks 173

316. Soy and Ketchup Salmon Fillet 173

317. Lime and Caper Shrimp 174

318. Skinny Breaded Shrimp 174

319. Easiest Coconut Shrimp Ever 175

320. Eggs with Smoked Salmon and Asiago Cheese.... 175

321. Easiest and Healthiest Fish Nuggets Ever 176

322. Crab Cakes with Mustard and Capers 176

323. Mustard Lemon Cod Fillets 177

324. Brioche with Herring and Eggs 177

325. Salmon with Cilantro and Citrus Sauce 178

326. Rockfish Fillets with Avocado Cream 178

327. Easy Dill Crab Cakes 179

328. Grilled Sunday Shrimp 179

329. Delicious Restaurant-Style Fish Cakes 180

330. Cod Fillets in Creamy Citrus Sauce 180

331. Holiday Parmesan Baked Fish 181

332. One-More-Bite Whitefish and Eggs 181

333. Tarragon Fish Fillets 182

334. Tamari Scallops with Shallots 182

335. Chipotle Salmon Fish Cakes 183

336. Hot Spicy Halibut Fillets 183

337. Baked Spicy Tuna with Eggs 184

338. Cheesy Garlic Shrimp 184

339. Spaghetti with Minty Shrimp 185

279. Crispy Snapper Fillets with Almond Sauce

Ready in about 20 minutes
Servings 4

When it comes to the fried food, fish fillets are a must! The almond sauce will take these fillets over the top!

Per serving: 463 Calories; 20.3g Fat; 46.0g Carbs; 25.0g Protein; 2.3g Sugars

Ingredients

4 skin-on snapper fillets
Sea salt and ground pepper, to taste
1 cup breadcrumbs
2 tablespoons fresh cilantro, chopped
1 cup all-purpose flour
2 medium-sized eggs

For the Almond sauce:
1/4 cup almonds
2 garlic cloves, pressed
1 bread slice, chopped
1 cup tomato paste
1 teaspoon dried dill weed
1/2 teaspoon salt
1/4 teaspoon freshly ground mixed peppercorns
1/2 cup olive oil

Directions

- Season fish fillets with sea salt and pepper.
- In a shallow plate, thoroughly combine the breadcrumbs and fresh chopped cilantro.
- In another shallow plate, whisk the eggs until frothy; Place the sifted flour into a third plate.
- Dip the fish fillets in the flour, then in the egg; afterward, coat them with breadcrumbs. Set the Air Fryer to cook at 390 degrees F; air fry for 14 to 16 minutes or until crisp.
- To make the sauce, chop the almonds in a food processor. Add the remaining sauce ingredients, but not the olive oil.
- Blitz for 30 seconds; then, slowly and gradually pour in the oil; process until smooth and even. Serve with the prepared snapper fillets. Bon appétit!

280. Italian-Style Cod Fillets

Ready in about 15 minutes
Servings 4

There's nothing like fried fish fillets. This mouth-watering cod fish, coated with herby creamed sauce, is ready in about 15 minutes. Lovely!

Per serving: 181 Calories; 8.1g Fat; 3.0g Carbs; 23.8g Protein; 1.1g Sugars

Ingredients

4 cod fillets
1/4 teaspoon fine sea salt
1/4 teaspoon ground black pepper, or more to taste
1 teaspoon cayenne pepper
1/2 cup non-dairy milk
1/2 cup fresh Italian parsley, coarsely chopped
1 teaspoon dried basil
1/2 teaspoon dried oregano
1 Italian pepper, chopped
4 garlic cloves, minced

Directions

- Coat the inside of a baking dish with a thin layer of vegetable oil.
- Season the cod fillets with salt, pepper, and cayenne pepper.
- Next, puree the remaining ingredients in your food processor. Toss the fish fillets with this mixture.
- Set the Air Fryer to cook at 380 degrees F. Cook for 10 to 12 minutes or until the cod flakes easily. Bon appétit!

281. Honey-Glazed Halibut Steaks

Ready in about 15 minutes
Servings 4

*Halibut is a good source of omega-3 fatty acids, B vita-
mins, and many others essential nutrients. It is great for
your immune system and your cardiovascular system.*

Per serving: 304 Calories; 20.7g Fat; 8.8g Carbs; 22.1g
Protein; 8.7g Sugars

Ingredients

1 pound halibut steaks
Salt and pepper, to your liking
1 teaspoon dried basil
2 tablespoons honey
1/4 cup vegetable oil
2 ½ tablespoons Worcester sauce
1 tablespoon freshly squeezed lemon juice
2 tablespoons vermouth
1 tablespoon fresh parsley leaves, coarsely chopped

Directions

- Place all the ingredients in a large-sized mixing dish.
  Gently stir to coat the fish evenly.
- Set your Air Fryer to cook at 390 degrees F; roast for 5
  minutes. Pause the machine and flip the fish over.
- Then, cook for another 5 minutes; check for doneness
  and cook for a few more minutes as needed. Serve
  with a rich potato salad. Bon appétit!

282. Crunchy Saltine Fish Fillets

Ready in about 15 minutes
Servings 4

*This recipe works with any kind of white fish like floun-
der, cod, haddock, etc. Use a plastic bag and a rolling
pin to crush saltine crackers.*

Per serving: 236 Calories; 15.7g Fat; 8.6g Carbs; 16.5g
Protein; 0.0g Sugars

Ingredients

1 cup crushed saltines
1/4 cup extra-virgin olive oil
1 teaspoon garlic powder
1/2 teaspoon shallot powder
1 egg, well whisked
4 white fish fillets
Salt and ground black pepper, to taste
Fresh Italian parsley, to serve

Directions

- Thoroughly combine the crushed saltines and olive oil
  in a shallow bowl.
- In another bowl, combine the garlic powder, shallot
  powder, and the beaten egg.
- Generously season the fish fillets with salt and pepper.
  Dip each fillet into the beaten egg.
- Then, roll the fillets over the crumb mixture. Set your
  Air Fryer to cook at 370 degrees F. Air-fry for 10 to
  12 minutes. Serve garnished with fresh parsley and
  enjoy!

283. Marinated Sardines with Roasted Potatoes

Ready in about 1 hour 15 minutes
Servings 4

This is one of the family favorites, however, much healthier version! And the best part is – you can have a perfect fish with potatoes without slaving over a hot stove.

Per serving: 426 Calories; 27.2g Fat; 24.5g Carbs; 21.5g Protein; 2.1g Sugars

Ingredients

3/4 pound sardines, cleaned and rinsed
Salt and ground black pepper, to savor
1 teaspoon smoked cayenne pepper
1 tablespoon lemon juice
1 tablespoon soy sauce
2 tablespoons olive oil

For the Potatoes:
8 medium Russet potatoes, peeled and quartered
1/2 stick melted butter
Salt and pepper, to savor
1 teaspoon granulated garlic

Directions

- Firstly, pat the sardines dry with a kitchen towel. Add salt, black pepper, cayenne pepper, lemon juice, soy sauce, and olive oil; marinate them for 30 minutes.
- Air-fry the sardines at 350 degrees F for approximately 5 minutes. Increase the temperature to 385 degrees F and air-fry them for further 7 to 8 minutes. Then put the sardines in a nice serving platter.
- Clean the Air Fryer cooking basket; add the potatoes, butter, salt, pepper, and garlic. Roast at 390 degrees F for 30 minutes. Serve with the prepared sardines. Bon appétit!

284. Garlicky Grilled Shrimp

Ready in about 35 minutes
Servings 4

If you want to serve this amazing, briny-tasting shrimp as an appetizer, just add cocktail sticks. You can also serve it with warm angel hair pasta and create an extraordinary family lunch!

Per serving: 188 Calories; 8.9g Fat; 3.5g Carbs; 23.1g Protein; 0.0g Sugars

Ingredients

18 shrimps, shelled and deveined
2 tablespoons freshly squeezed lemon juice
1/2 teaspoon hot paprika
1/2 teaspoon salt
1 teaspoon lemon-pepper seasoning
2 tablespoons extra-virgin olive oil
2 garlic cloves, peeled and minced
1 teaspoon onion powder
1/4 teaspoon cumin powder
1/2 cup fresh parsley, coarsely chopped

Directions

- Place all the ingredients in a mixing dish; gently stir, cover and let it marinate for 30 minutes in the refrigerator.
- Air-fry in the preheated Air Fryer at 400 degrees F for 5 minutes or until the shrimps turn pink.
- Serve over cooked pasta if desired.

285. Salmon Fillets with Sweet Potatoes

Ready in about 45 minutes
Servings 4

If you are craving rich and satisfying dinner, serve salmon fillets with roasted sweet potato wedges. Classy and absolutely delicious. You can't go wrong.

Per serving: 321 Calories; 17.5g Fat; 8.2g Carbs; 34.0g Protein; 0.6g Sugars

Ingredients

For the Salmon Fillets:
4 (6-ounce) skin-on salmon fillets
1 tablespoon extra-virgin olive oil
1 teaspoon celery salt
1/4 teaspoon ground black pepper, or more to taste
2 tablespoons capers
A pinch of dry mustard
A pinch of ground mace
1 teaspoon smoked cayenne pepper

For the Potatoes:
4 sweet potatoes, peeled and cut into wedges
1 tablespoon sesame oil
Kosher salt and pepper, to taste

Directions

- Firstly, brush the salmon filets with the oil on all sides. Add all seasonings for the fillets.
- Air-fry at 360 degrees F for 5 minutes; pause the Air Fryer and cook for 5 more minutes.
- Toss the sweet potatoes with sesame oil, salt, and pepper; air-fry them at 380 degrees F for 15 minutes.
- Now, pause the machine, flip the potatoes over and cook additional 15 to 20 minutes. Serve with salmon fillets and enjoy!

286. Fancy Coconut Curried Prawns

Ready in about 10 minutes
Servings 4

This is a classic! Fresh, aromatic and delicious seafood at your fingertips! It would be a perfect dish for a cocktail party, family dinner, Sunday brunch...

Per serving: 239 Calories; 9.3g Fat; 18.6g Carbs; 19.1g Protein; 1.4g Sugars

Ingredients

12 prawns, cleaned and deveined
Salt and ground black pepper, to your liking
1/2 teaspoon cumin powder
1 teaspoon fresh lemon juice
1 medium-sized egg, whisked
1/3 cup of beer
1/2 cup all-purpose flour
1 teaspoon baking powder
1 tablespoon curry powder
1/2 teaspoon grated fresh ginger
1 cup flaked coconut

Directions

- Toss the prawns with salt, pepper, cumin powder, and lemon juice.
- In a mixing dish, place the whisked egg, beer, 1/4 cup of flour, baking powder, curry, and the ginger; mix to combine well.
- In another mixing dish, place the remaining 1/4 cup of flour; put the flaked coconut into a third bowl.
- Now, dip the prawns in the flour holding them by the tails. Then, dip them in the beer mix; afterwards, roll your prawns over flaked coconut.
- Air-fry at 360 degrees F for 5 minutes; turn them over, press the power button again and cook for additional 2 to 3 minutes. Bon appétit!

287. Tilapia Filets with Creamy Caper Sauce

Ready in about 15 minutes
Servings 4

This is 4-easy steps recipe that will take only 15 minutes. The sauce is so glamorous but super easy to put together!

Per serving: 215 Calories; 13.1g Fat; 3.5g Carbs; 21.5g Protein; 0.6g Sugars

Ingredients

4 tilapia fillets
1 tablespoon extra-virgin olive oil
Celery salt, to taste
Freshly cracked pink peppercorns, to taste

For the Creamy Caper Sauce:
1/2 cup crème fraîche
2 tablespoons mayonnaise
1/4 cup Cottage cheese, at room temperature
1 tablespoon capers, finely chopped

Directions

- Toss the tilapia fillets with olive oil, celery salt, and cracked peppercorns until they are well coated.
- Place the fillets in a single layer at the bottom of the Air Fryer cooking basket. Air-fry at 360 degrees F for about 12 minutes; turn them over once during cooking.
- Meanwhile, prepare the sauce by mixing the remaining items.
- Lastly, garnish air-fried tilapia fillets with the sauce and serve immediately!

288. Festive Sake-Glazed Flounder

Ready in about 15 minutes +
marinating time
Servings 4

For this recipe, use good sesame oil, mixed peppercorns, and fresh garlic, and you'll get a perfectly tender, flaky flounder. Serve with steamed asparagus if desired.

Per serving: 174 Calories; 6.3g Fat; 7.7g Carbs; 19.8g Protein; 3.2g Sugars

Ingredients

4 flounder fillets
Sea salt and freshly cracked mixed peppercorns, to taste
1 ½ tablespoons dark sesame oil
2 tablespoons sake
1/4 cup soy sauce
1 tablespoon grated lemon rind
2 garlic cloves, minced
1 teaspoon brown sugar
Fresh chopped chives, to serve

Directions

- Place all the ingredients, without the chives, in a large-sized mixing dish. Cover and allow it to marinate for about 2 hours in your fridge.
- Remove the fish from the marinade and cook in the Air Fryer cooking basket at 360 degrees F for 10 to 12 minutes; flip once during cooking.
- Pour the remaining marinade into a pan that is preheated over a medium-low heat; let it simmer, stirring continuously, until it has thickened.
- Pour the prepared glaze over flounder and serve garnished with fresh chives.

289. Fish Fingers with Dijonnaise Sauce

Ready in about 15 minutes
Servings 4

This is a child-friendly recipe so invite your child in the kitchen to help you cook these amazing fish fingers. Let's be creative!

Per serving: 377 Calories; 18.4g Fat; 31.9g Carbs; 20.9g Protein; 2.3g Sugars

Ingredients

For the Fish:
3/4 pound white fish, cut into strips
1 ½ tablespoons olive oil
1/2 teaspoon garlic salt
1 teaspoon red pepper flakes, crushed
1/2 teaspoon dried dill weed
1 cup all-purpose flour
2 medium-sized eggs, well whisked
3/4 cup tortilla chip crumbs

For the Dijonnaise Sauce:
1 ½ tablespoons Dijon mustard
1/2 cup mayonnaise
1/2 teaspoon lemon juice, freshly squeezed

Directions

- Rub the fish strips with olive oil, salt, red pepper and dill weed. Then, prepare three shallow bowls.
- Put the sifted flour into the first bowl. In another shallow bowl, place the eggs; in the third one, the tortilla chip crumbs.
- Meanwhile, preheat your machine to cook at 385 degrees F. Cover the fish strips with the flour, and then with the eggs; finally, roll each fish piece over the crumbs.
- Air-fry for 5 minutes, then pause the machine, flip them over and cook for another 5 minutes or until cooked through.
- In the meantime, make the Dijonnaise sauce by mixing together all sauce ingredients. Serve as a dipping sauce and enjoy!

290. Whitefish Cakes with Green Beans

Ready in about 1 hour 20 minutes
Servings 4

Use your blender or food processor to finely chop fish. These fish cakes are less gooey because they get their crisp crunch from the vegetables.

Per serving: 210 Calories; 4.5g Fat; 25.1g Carbs; 16.2g Protein; 3.5g Sugars

Ingredients

1 ½ cups whitefish fillets, minced
1 ½ cups green beans, finely chopped
1/2 cup scallions, chopped
1 chili pepper, deveined and minced
1 tablespoon red curry paste
1 teaspoon brown sugar
1 tablespoon fish sauce
2 tablespoons apple cider vinegar
1 teaspoon water
Sea salt flakes, to taste
1/2 teaspoon cracked black peppercorns
1 ½ teaspoons butter, at room temperature
Grated rind of 1 lemon
Breadcrumbs

Directions

- Add all ingredients in the order listed above to the mixing dish. Mix to combine well using a spatula or your hands.
- Form into small cakes and chill for 1 hour. Place a piece of aluminum foil over the cooking basket. Place the cakes on foil.
- Cook at 390 degrees F for 10 minutes; pause the machine, flip each fish cake over and air-fry for additional 5 minutes. Mound a cucumber relish onto the plates; add the fish cakes and serve warm.

291. Traditional Filipino Bistek

Ready in about 10 minutes +
marinating time
Servings 4

You will love this recipe even if you are not much of a fish lover. It would be great if you could use calamansi juice because of its mild taste but you can't go wrong with freshly squeezed lime juice.

Per serving: 242 Calories; 13.4g Fat; 9.2g Carbs; 22.7g Protein; 5.5g Sugars

Ingredients

A belly of 2 milkfish, deboned and sliced into 4 portions
3/4 teaspoon salt
1/4 teaspoon ground black pepper
1/4 teaspoon cumin powder
2 tablespoons calamansi juice
2 lemongrass, trimmed and cut crosswise into small pieces
1/2 cup tamari sauce
2 tablespoons fish sauce (Patis)
2 tablespoons brown sugar
1 teaspoon garlic powder
1/2 cup chicken broth
2 tablespoons olive oil

Directions

- Firstly, pat the fish dry using kitchen towels. Put the fish into a large-sized mixing dish; add the remaining ingredients and marinate for 3 hours in the refrigerator.
- Cook the fish steaks on an Air Fryer grill basket at 340 degrees F for 5 minutes.
- Pause the machine, flip the steaks over and set the timer for 4 more minutes. Cook until the color turns medium brown. Serve over steamed white rice.

292. Chunky Fish and Celery Cakes

Ready in about 10 minutes + chilling time
Servings 4

Turn a can of tuna or other fish into these delicious cakes for a quick and easy weeknight meal. They are great dipped in Dijonnaise sauce!

Per serving: 184 Calories; 7.5g Fat; 5.5g Carbs; 22.2g Protein; 0.9g Sugars

Ingredients

2 cans canned fish
2 celery stalks, trimmed and finely chopped
1 egg, whisked
1 cup soft bread crumbs
1 teaspoon whole-grain mustard
1/2 teaspoon sea salt
1/4 teaspoon freshly cracked black peppercorns
1 teaspoon paprika

Directions

- Mix all of the above ingredients in the order listed above; mix to combine well and shape into four cakes; chill for 50 minutes.
- Place on an Air Fryer grill pan. Spritz each cake with a non-stick cooking spray, covering all sides.
- Grill at 360 degrees F for 5 minutes; then, pause the machine, flip the cakes over and set the timer for another 3 minutes. Serve over mashed potatoes.

293. Jumbo Shrimp with Chipotle-Dijon Sauce

Ready in about 10 minutes
Servings 4

This sophisticated dish may become your weeknight favorite. A sharp-flavored chipotle-mustard sauce gives the dish a unique and irresistible flavor!

Per serving: 270 Calories; 12.2g Fat; 10.0g Carbs; 29.1g Protein; 2.1g Sugars

Ingredients

12 jumbo shrimps
1/2 teaspoon garlic salt
1/4 teaspoon freshly cracked mixed peppercorns

For the Sauce:
1 teaspoon Dijon mustard
4 tablespoons mayonnaise
1 teaspoon lemon rind, grated
1 teaspoon chipotle powder
1/2 teaspoon cumin powder

Directions

- Season your shrimp with garlic salt and cracked peppercorns.
- Now, air-fry them in the cooking basket at 395 degrees F for 5 minutes. After that, pause the machine. Flip them over and set the timer for 2 more minutes.
- Meanwhile, mix all ingredients for the sauce; whisk to combine well. Serve with the warm shrimps. Bon appétit!

294. Super Easy Crunchy Grouper Fillets

Ready in about 15 minutes
Servings 2

Cooking fish fillets in the Air fryer has a number of advantages to the traditional methods of frying and baking. Serve with mashed sweet potatoes.

Per serving: 370 Calories; 13.9g Fat; 1.5g Carbs; 56g Protein; 0.6g Sugars

Ingredients

2 medium-sized grouper fillets
1 tablespoon red wine vinegar
1tablespoons vegetable oil
1/3 teaspoon hot red pepper flakes, dried
2 medium-sized whole egg
1/2 cup crushed crackers
Sea salt and ground black pepper, to savor

Directions

- Set your air fryer to cook at 355 degrees F. Thoroughly combine the vegetable oil with the crushed crackers.
- In a separate shallow bowl, thoroughly beat the eggs. Drizzle each grouper fillet with red wine vinegar. Then, generously season the grouper fillets.
- Firstly, coat each grouper fillet with the beaten eggs; now, roll it in the crumb mix.
- Place in a single layer in the air fryer cooking basket. Air-fry for 14 minutes, turning periodically. Bon appétit!

295. Classic Cajun Shrimp

Ready in about 15 minutes
Servings 6

By cooking with your Air fryer, shrimp remains so succulent and so flavorful that you won't believe your eyes! With just the right seasoning and mustard balance, this shrimp recipe will make you forget about meat.

Per serving: 234 Calories; 13.6g Fat; 2g Carbs; 23.6g Protein; 0.2g Sugars

Ingredients

1 1/2 tablespoons extra-virgin olive oil
2 tablespoons Cajun seasoning
1½ pounds shrimp, deveined
2 tablespoons Dijon mustard
Sea salt flakes, to taste

Directions

- Start by preheating the air fryer to 385 degrees F.
- In a bowl, toss all ingredients together, coating the shrimp on all sides.
- Dump the shrimp into the cooking basket; air-fry for 7 to 8 minutes. Serve over naan. Bon appétit!

296. Za'atar Bacon Wrapped Shrimp

Ready in about 30 minutes
Servings 6

Make you own Za'atar seasoning blend by combining toasted sesame seeds, coarse salt, minced fresh thyme and ground sumac. Lovely!

Per serving: 193 Calories; 15.4g Fat; 0.6g Carbs; 12.7g Protein; 0.5g Sugars

Ingredients

½ pound thin bacon slices
1/2 tablespoon balsamic vinegar
½ pound shrimp, peeled and deveined
1/2 teaspoon Za'atar

Directions

- Drizzle each shrimp with balsamic vinegar; add the Za'atar.
- Next, wrap the bacon slices around the shrimps. Repeat with the remaining ingredients.
- Place in the refrigerator for 30 minutes. Meanwhile, set your air fryer to cook at 345 degrees F; air-fry for 8 minutes. Bon appétit!

297. Salmon in Creamy Lime Sauce

Ready in about 20 minutes
Servings 4

Why settle for an ordinary salmon dish when you can get extraordinary, juicy and flavorful salmon?! This surprisingly easy salmon dish is actually far easier to make than it sounds.

Per serving: 263 Calories; 12.6g Fat; 3.3g Carbs; 33.9g Protein; 1.4g Sugars

Ingredients

1/2 tablespoon fresh lime juice
1/2 teaspoon honey
1/2 teaspoon finely grated fresh lime zest
2 pieces salmon
1/3 cup sour cream
A pinch of salt and pepper
2 tablespoons extra-virgin olive oil
Salt and pepper, to taste

Directions

- Set the air fryer to cook at 265 degrees F. Season each salmon piece with the salt and pepper and then, drizzle with the extra-virgin olive oil.
- Place the seasoned salmon pieces in a single layer at the bottom of the cooking basket; cook for 12 minutes.
- While the salmon is cooking, prepare the sauce by mixing the other ingredients. Serve the salmon garnished with the creamy lime sauce.

298. Crispy Catfish Fillets

Ready in about 20 minutes
Servings 8

Looking for an easy family dish for the weeknight rush? These crispy fish fillets are just the dish you're looking for. If you are not a fan of catfish, use any other fish with a firm texture and mild flavor such as mahi mahi, halibut, grouper or monkfish.

Per serving: 127 Calories; 5g Fat; 4.1g Carbs; 15.7g Protein; 1.5g Sugars

Ingredients

4 catfish fillets, halved
2 eggs

For the Coating:
1/3 cup crushed saltines
2 tablespoons orange juice
2 tablespoons dry sherry
1 teaspoon onion salt
1 teaspoon garlic pepper
1/2 teaspoon red pepper flakes, crushed
1/2 teaspoon mustard seed
1 teaspoon dill weed, fresh or dried

Directions

- Firstly, beat the egg in a shallow bowl. Add the ingredients for the coating to another bowl.
- Coat the halves of catfish fillets with the egg; then, coat them with the coating mixture.
- Air-fry at 355 degrees F for about 13 minutes. Bon appétit!

299. Cajun Fish Sticks

Ready in about 20 minutes
Servings 6

Kids (and adults) will adore these flavorful sticks. Serve them for your cocktail party; also, they are great as an after-school snack.

Per serving: 209 Calories; 12.6g Fat;16.4g Carbs; 9g Protein; 1.3g Sugars

Ingredients

2 tablespoons olive oil
Cajun seasoning, to savor
1 pound fish sticks

Directions

- Set your air fryer to cook at 165 degrees F.
- Break the fish sticks into smaller pieces. Toss with the olive oil and the Cajun seasoning.
- Air fry for 11 minutes, flipping periodically. Serve with potato salad if desired. Bon appétit!

300. Crab and Carrot Cakes

Ready in about 20 minutes
Servings 4

Your guests will be impressed by this elegant dinner of crab, carrot and mayonnaise. Serve them with your choice of dipping sauce.

Per serving: 392 Calories; 7.6g Fat; 55.5g Carbs; 24.9g Protein; 4.9g Sugars

Ingredients

1 medium-sized egg, whisked
3 slices sourdough bread, crustless and torn into small pieces
1 teaspoon sea salt flakes, or more to taste
1/2 pound lump blue crab meat
1/3 teaspoon ground black pepper
3 cloves garlic, finely minced
1/2 tablespoon fresh lemon juice
2 tablespoons mayonnaise
1/3 teaspoon ground cumin
3 carrots, trimmed and shredded

Directions

- Mix all the ingredients thoroughly. Shape into 4 balls and press each ball to form the cakes.
- Then, spritz your cakes with cooking oil.
- Air-fry at 365 degrees F for 12 minutes, turning halfway through. Work in batches. Bon appétit!

301. Easy Herbed Shrimp

Ready in about 10 minutes
Servings 4

Shrimp and Mediterranean seasonings always go well. Serve with an onion-tomato dipping sauce.

Per serving: 364 Calories; 35.1g Fat; 0.5g Carbs; 11.9g Protein; 0.1g Sugars

Ingredients

1/2 teaspoon garlic powder
1/2 tablespoon fresh cilantro, finely chopped
1/3 teaspoon tarragon
1 1/2c tablespoons extra-virgin olive oil
1/2 pound shrimp, deveined
1/2 teaspoon dried rosemary
1/3 teaspoon basil, fresh or dried
1 teaspoon salt

Directions

- Set the air fryer to cook at 385 degrees F.
- In a mixing bowl, thoroughly combine all of the above ingredients; toss until everything is well coated.
- Transfer the shrimp mixture to the cooking basket; air-fry for about 6 minutes. Taste for doneness and serve right away.

302. Quick-Fix Seafood Breakfast

Ready in about 25 minutes
Servings 4

Fish is the key factor to a healthy diet. If you don't have dry sherry on hand, use Chardonnay, cream ales, pilsners or lagers.

Per serving: 306 Calories; 22g Fat; 2.4g Carbs; 23.2g Protein; 1.6g Sugars

Ingredients

1/3 cup rockfish pieces
5 eggs, well beaten
1 1/3 tablespoons scallions, chopped
1½ tablespoons soft cheese
1/2 teaspoon dried thyme
1/3 cup salmon pieces
1 tablespoon dry sherry
1/2 teaspoon dried basil
1½ tablespoons peanut oil
Fine sea salt and ground black pepper, to savor
1/2 teaspoon dried rosemary

Directions

- Warm the peanut oil in a nonstick skillet that is pre-heated over a moderate flame. Then, sauté the salmon, rockfish, and scallions; drizzle with the dry sherry and sauté for 4 minutes, turning occasionally.
- Meanwhile, lightly grease a baking dish with a pan spray. Throw in the sautéed seafood/scallion mix. Add the remaining ingredients in the order listed above.
- Bake for 12 minutes at 315 degrees F. Serve warm garnished with Tabasco sauce if desired.

303. Aromatic Egg Noodles with Shrimp

Ready in about 20 minutes
Servings 4

Prepare to become totally addicted to this seafood recipe! In addition, shrimp with noodles cooks very quickly in your Air fryer.

Per serving: 118 Calories; 5.6g Fat; 4g Carbs; 13g Protein; 2.4g Sugars

Ingredients

1/2 package egg noodles, cooked
1/2 teaspoon fennel seeds
1/2 cup pasta sauce of choice
1/3 teaspoon dry mustard
1/2 pound shrimp, deveined
1/3 teaspoon crushed red pepper flakes
1 teaspoon ground mace
1 tablespoon melted butter
1 teaspoon cardamom
1 tablespoon balsamic vinegar
1/3 teaspoon ground black pepper
1/2 teaspoon fine sea salt

Directions

- Start by preheating the air fryer to 385 degrees F.
- In a bowl, toss all ingredients, minus egg noodles and pasta sauce; make sure to coat the shrimp on all sides.
- Dump the shrimp into the cooking basket and air-fry for 7 to 8 minutes. Serve warm with egg noodles and pasta sauce of choice. Bon appétit!

304. Sunday Shrimp in Roasted Garlic Sauce

Ready in about 20 minutes
Servings 4

Skip the boring salad dinner and try this easy shrimp recipe instead. Enjoy this amazing combination of garlicky sauce and buttery shrimp.

Per serving: 160 Calories; 7.4g Fat; 0.9g Carbs; 23.9g Protein; 0.2g Sugars

Ingredients

1 pound shrimps, cleaned
1 teaspoon green peppercorns, freshly cracked
Freshly squeezed juice of 1/2 lemon
1/2 cup fresh parsley, chopped
1/2 tablespoon dry chili flakes
1/2 small-sized garlic head, minced
2 tablespoons peanut oil
Nonstick cooking spray
Sea salt flakes, to savor

Directions

- Firstly, spritz the garlic with nonstick cooking spray. Wrap up the greased garlic head in a piece of foil. Roast the garlic in the preheated air fryer at 395 degrees for about 12 minutes. Allow it to cool slightly.
- After that, squeeze the roasted garlic out of its peel; chop it finely and transfer it to a bowl. To make the sauce, add the remaining ingredients, minus the shrimps.
- In another larger bowl, place the shrimps and 1/2 of the sauce mixture. Toss to coat the shrimps on all sides.
- Bake at 375 degrees for 8 minutes, turning halfway; cook in batches. Serve right away with the remaining garlic sauce.

305. Crispy Saucy Whitefish Fillets

Ready in about 20 minutes
Servings 6

Try this healthy recipe that is ready in no time. If you like more intensive flavor, add a few dashes of chipotle pepper.

Per serving: 126 Calories; 5g Fat; 1.5g Carbs; 16.4g Protein; 0.9g Sugars

Ingredients

2 eggs, well-beaten
3 white fish fillets, halved

For the Coating:
2 tablespoons lime juice
2 tablespoons vermouth
1/3 teaspoon fennel seed
1/2 teaspoon dried thyme
1/3 cup crushed saltines
Salt and ground black pepper, to taste

Directions

- Coat white fish fillets with the beaten egg; make sure to coat on all sides.
- Add the ingredients for the coating to another bowl.
- Next step, cover the fish fillets with the coating mixture.
- Air-fry at 355 degrees F for about 13 minutes. Serve right away with a sauce such as tartar sauce. Bon appétit!

306. Grouper Fillets with Jalapeño-Avocado Sauce

Ready in about 20 minutes
Servings 8

Grouper, avocado and jalapeño are what contribute to the intense flavor of this fish recipe. Work in batches if needed.

Per serving: 388 Calories; 12.7g Fat; 19.6g Carbs; 42.5g Protein; 3.4g Sugars

Ingredients

6 grouper fillets
2 tablespoons olive oil
Sea salt and ground black pepper, to taste
2 eggs
1½ cup seasoned breadcrumbs

For the Avocado Sauce:
1/2 tablespoons lemon juice
1 teaspoon black pepper, preferably freshly ground
1/3 cup sour cream
1/2 jalapeño, remove seeds and vein
1 teaspoon salt
3 garlic cloves, minced
1/2 large-sized avocado, peeled, pitted, and quartered

Directions

- Set your air fryer to cook at 375 degrees F. Then, prepare two shallow bowls. In the first bowl, combine the breadcrumbs and the olive oil.
- In another shallow bowl, whisk the eggs. Next step, season the grouper fillets.
- Dip each grouper fillet into the egg mix; now, roll them over the breadcrumb mix to coat on all sides.
- Place in a single layer in the air fryer cooking basket. Air-fry for 9 to 10 minutes
- Meanwhile, blitz all the items for the avocado sauce in your food processor; puree until everything is smooth and uniform. Serve the air fried fillets on individual plates, dolloped with the avocado sauce. Bon appétit!

307. Hot Spicy Snapper Tacos

Ready in about 15 minutes
Servings 4

Three in one – fish, tortillas and tomato sauce. Skip the take-out and serve these low-calorie tacos. The best part – they come together in 15 minutes!

Per serving: 214 Calories; 2.8g Fat; 9.5g Carbs; 36.7g Protein; 5g Sugars

Ingredients

1/2 chili pepper, seeded and minced
1 tablespoon fresh sage, roughly chopped
1 ½ red onions, peeled and diced
1 garlic clove, minced
4 Roma tomatoes, diced
1 tablespoon fresh parsley, roughly chopped
1 teaspoon ground cumin
1 teaspoon coarse salt
1/3 teaspoon crushed red pepper
1 1/2 pounds snapper fillets, cut into chunks
16 corn tortillas
1/2 can beer
Batter, for coating

Directions

- Place the first 9 ingredients in a mixing bowl. Cover with a plastic wrap and place in the refrigerator.
- Preheat your air fryer to cook at 335 degrees F. Then, mix the beer with the batter.
- Next step, dip fish chunks into the beer/batter mixture. Then, air-fry, cooking in batches, for 7 minutes.
- Assemble your tacos with prepared snapper, warm tortillas, and prepared herbed tomato sauce. Enjoy!

308. Easy Saucy Sage Halibut

Ready in about 20 minutes
Servings 4

If you can never decide what to make for dinner, here's a great idea! Keep this recipe in your back pocket!

Per serving: 304 Calories; 19.3g Fat; 14.4g Carbs; 15g Protein; 2.5g Sugars

Ingredients

2 eggs
2 medium-sized halibut fillets
1/2 cup seasoned breadcrumbs
2 eggs
½ tablespoon fresh or dried sage, finely minced
2 tablespoons vegetable oil
1/2 teaspoon cayenne pepper
Sea salt and ground black pepper, to taste

Directions

- Set your air fryer to cook at 375 degrees F. Then, grab two mixing bowls. In the first bowl, combine the oil and the breadcrumbs.
- In the other bowl, whisk the egg. Next step, evenly sprinkle the halibut fillets with the cayenne pepper, salt, ground black pepper, and sage.
- Dip each fish fillet into the whisked egg; now, roll it over the breadcrumb mix.
- Place in a single layer in the air fryer cooking basket. Cook for about 8 to 10 minutes, working in batches. Serve with potato salad. Bon appétit!

309. Baked Prawns with Vegetables

Ready in about 15 minutes
Servings 4

Your new favorite way to eat prawns with vegetables. Parsnip, cabbage and sweet potatoes work well too. Serve with rosé wine.

Per serving: 45 Calories; 0.2g Fat; 5.7g Carbs; 2.9g Protein; 2.1g Sugars

Ingredients

8 prawns
1/2 tablespoon fish sauce
4 carrots, cut into matchsticks
1/2 teaspoon sugar
1/3 teaspoon cornstarch
1/2 tablespoon tamari sauce
2 celery stalks, cut into matchsticks
3 garlic cloves, chopped
1/2 cup water
1/3 teaspoon freshly ground pepper
1/2 shallot, thinly sliced
1/3 teaspoon coarse salt

Directions

- Simply dump the carrots, celery, shallot, and garlic into the cooking basket; then, air-fry for 5 minutes at 355 degrees F.
- Place the remaining ingredients in the baking dish; cook for 6 more minutes and serve with prepared vegetables. Bon appétit!

310. The Ultimate Cod Fish Tacos

Ready in about 15 minutes
Servings 8

This recipe is everything you love in fish tacos – warm tortillas, flaky white fish and salsa. Enjoy your Taco Tuesdays!

Per serving: 283 Calories; 6.4g Fat; 50.3g Carbs; 9g Protein; 7.2g Sugars

Ingredients

16 whole-wheat tortillas
1 1/3 pound codfish

For the Salsa:
1/3 cup green bell pepper, chopped
1 ½ finely minced fresh jalapeno peppers with seeds
7 tomatoes, diced
1/3 teaspoon crushed red pepper
1 ½ tablespoons fresh lime juice
1/2 red onion, peeled and diced
1/3 cup fresh cilantro, roughly chopped

For the Fish Batter:
1/7 cup baking powder
1/3 cup milk
1 teaspoon salt
1/3 cup all-purpose flour
1/3 cup water

Directions

- Cut the cod fish into bite-sized chunks. Microwave whole-wheat tortillas.
- Combine all of the above ingredients for the salsa and place the mixture in your refrigerator.
- Preheat your air fryer to cook at 335 degrees F. Then, combine all the ingredients for the batter.
- After that, dip the fish chunks into the batter mix. Then, air-fry, cooking in batches, for 6-7 minutes.
- Assemble your tacos with the prepared salsa and the warm tortillas; serve hot with the lime wedges.

311. Hot Spicy Orange Roughy

Ready in about 15 minutes
Servings 3

You can turn an ordinary fish fillet into something fantastic, adding carefully selected seasonings and crisp white wine. An Air fryer is really amazing!

Per serving: 364 Calories; 5.6g Fat; 24.1g Carbs; 14.2g Protein; 7.8g Sugars

Ingredients

2 large-sized eggs, well whisked
3 Orange roughy fillets, halved lengthwise

For the Coating:
1 ½ tablespoons dry white wine
A few drizzles of Tabasco sauce
Salt and ground black pepper, to taste
1 cup seasoned breadcrumbs
1 ½ tablespoons yellow cornmeal

Directions

- Coat fillets with the whisked egg; make sure to coat on all sides.
- Add the ingredients for the coating to another bowl.
- Next step, cover the fish fillets with the coating mixture.
- Air-fry at 355 degrees F for about 13 minutes. Bon appétit!

312. Festive Milkfish Steak

Ready in about 50 minutes
Servings 4

Thanks to its great, fatty texture, milkfish (also known as Chanos chanos), is very easy to cook in the Air fryer. Remember to pat your fish dry with a kitchen towel, and then, season it properly.

Per serving: 231 Calories; 76g Fat; 16.3g Carbs; 23.9g Protein; 13.2g Sugars

Ingredients

1/3 cup orange juice
1/4 cup brown sugar
1/3 cup dry sherry
1/2 pound milkfish steak
1 teaspoon ground ginger
1/3 cup tamari sauce
Fine sea salt and ground pepper, to taste

Directions

- To prepare the marinade, place all ingredients, minus the milkfish, in a saucepan. Bring to a boil over medium-high heat until the mixture is reduced by half. Let it cool.
- Now, marinate the milkfish steak for about 28 minutes in your refrigerator. Discard the marinade and transfer the fish steak to the preheated air fryer.
- Air-fry at 400 degrees F for 8 to 10 minutes. To finish, brush the hot fish steaks with the reserved marinade and enjoy!

313. Scallops with Zesty Cilantro Sauce

Ready in about 40 minutes
Servings 4

Scallops can be cooked in a variety of ways, but air-frying is one of the best and easiest methods; your seafood doesn't taste like fat, yet the texture of fried food is achieved.

Per serving: 254 Calories; 7.6g Fat; 11g Carbs; 36g Protein; 1.5g Sugars

Ingredients

1 1/2 pounds large sea scallops, cleaned
½ tablespoon lime juice
1 ½ tablespoons olive oil
1/3 cup fresh cilantro, chopped
1/2 teaspoon paprika
1/2 cup yogurt
½ tablespoon mustard sauce
1 teaspoon fine sea salt
1 teaspoon mixed peppercorns, freshly cracked

Directions

- Place all ingredients, minus scallops, in a large mixing dish; mix to combine well.
- Now, use 1/2 of the sauce to marinate your scallops; let it stand for 20 minutes. Remove scallops from marinade
- Bake at 375 degrees for 8 minutes, turning halfway; cook in batches. Serve right away with remaining cilantro sauce. Bon appétit!

314. Mom's Special Chervil Shrimps

Ready in about 10 minutes
Servings 4

Shrimps are a must-have during the summer season. When you want to please your family, simply toss your shrimp with seasonings and extra-virgin olive oil and dump them into the Air fryer. Lovely!

Per serving: 128 Calories; 3.6g Fat; 1g Carbs; 23.1g Protein; 0.2g Sugars

Ingredients

1 pound shrimps, deveined
1 teaspoon dried oregano
2 tablespoons extra-virgin olive oil
1 teaspoon dried basil
2 tablespoons fresh chervil, roughly chopped
1/4 teaspoon ground pepper
1/2 teaspoon salt
1 teaspoon paprika

Directions

- Set the air fryer to cook at 375 degrees F.
- In a mixing bowl, thoroughly combine all of the above ingredients; toss until everything is well coated.
- Transfer the shrimp mixture to the cooking basket; air-fry for about 7 minutes. Taste for doneness and serve right away.

315. Curry and Paprika Fish Sticks

Ready in about 20 minutes
Servings 4

Fish sticks pair perfectly with curry powder in this heavenly delicious finger food recipe. Serve with hot cooked rice for an additional hint of South Asian cuisine!

Per serving: 189 Calories; 12.6g Fat; 12.7g Carbs; 6.9g Protein; 0.9g Sugars

Ingredients

1/3 teaspoon curry powder
1/2 teaspoon smoked paprika
1/3 pound fish sticks
1 ½ tablespoon olive oil

Directions

- Set your air fryer to cook at 325 degrees F.
- Break the fish sticks into smaller pieces. Toss with olive oil, curry powder, and paprika.
- Ai- fry approximately 10 minutes; flip them occasionally using a pair of tongs. Bon appétit!

316. Soy and Ketchup Salmon Fillet

Ready in about 10 minutes +
marinating time
Servings 2

This salmon fillet is so simple and quick to make and contains great flavors of soy sauce, tomato ketchup and butter. Yummy!

Per serving: 380 Calories; 22.6g Fat; 12.7g Carbs; 42.9g Protein; 6.2g Sugars

Ingredients

1 ½ tablespoons melted butter
1/2 teaspoon cumin powder
1/3 cup vegetable stock
1 ½ tablespoons tomato ketchup
½ tablespoon brown sugar
1/3 teaspoon garlic powder
2 salmon fillets
1/3 cup soy sauce
1/3 teaspoon freshly ground black pepper
1 teaspoon fine sea salt

Directions

- Firstly, season the salmon fillets with the black pepper, salt, cumin, and garlic powder.
- In a separate bowl, combine the other ingredients to make the marinade.
- Allow the salmon to marinate in the refrigerator for at least 1 hour.
- Cook in the air fryer grill basket for 7 minutes at 345 degrees F.

317. Lime and Caper Shrimp

Ready in about 15 minutes
Servings 4

Shrimp are a cinch to make in the Air fryer. You'll find caper juice in Mediterranean dishes as well as French dishes. Capers, as a pea-sized dark green seasoning, offers a lot of possibilities in the kitchen.

Per serving: 95 Calories; 5.4g Fat; 0.7g Carbs; 11.5g Protein; 0.2g Sugars

Ingredients

1 1/2 tablespoon sesame oil
1 1/2 tablespoons fresh lime juice
1/2 pound shrimp, deveined
1/3 cup caper juice
Sea salt flakes, to savor
1/3 teaspoon green peppercorns, freshly cracked

Directions

- Set the air fryer to cook at 385 degrees F.
- In a bowl, thoroughly combine all ingredients, coating the shrimp on all sides.
- Dump the shrimp into the cooking basket; air-fry for 7 to 8 minutes. Bon appétit!

318. Skinny Breaded Shrimp

Ready in about 15 minutes
Servings 4

Coconut milk can help your recipe shine! With an addition of eggs and cornstarch, this is amazing, belly filling recipe.

Per serving: 204 Calories; 6.3g Fat; 14.9g Carbs; 17.6g Protein; 3.2g Sugars

Ingredients

For the Coating:
1 1/2 tablespoons cornstarch
1 teaspoon garlic paste
1/3 teaspoon white pepper, ground
1 teaspoon Sriracha
1/3 cup coconut milk
2 eggs, beaten
1/2 teaspoon chili powder
1 teaspoon onion salt

For the Breading:
1/2 pound jumbo shrimp, peeled and deveined
1/2 tablespoon lemon juice, freshly squeezed
1/2 cup seasoned breadcrumbs

Directions

- First, take 2 shallow dishes for breading.
- In the first dish, thoroughly combine all the coating ingredients. In another dish, place the seasoned breadcrumbs.
- Drizzle each shrimp with the fresh lemon juice; dip them in the batter; then, roll them over the prepared breadcrumbs. Spritz them with cooking spray and transfer to a cooking basket.
- Air-fry for 11 minutes at 385 degrees F, turning halfway through. Cook in batches and serve hot!

319. Easiest Coconut Shrimp Ever

Ready in about 25 minutes
Servings 4

Fresh-from-the-sea shrimp is a great dish for any occasion. Eat for a family dinner or a summer cocktail party; it will also enrich your holiday menu!

Per serving: 75 Calories; 0.6g Fat; 10.2g Carbs; 6.9g Protein; 0.9g Sugars

Ingredients

1/3 teaspoon paprika
3 egg whites
1/3 cup unsweetened coconut, shredded
1 teaspoon salt
12 large shrimps, peeled and de-veined
1/3 cup plain flour
Lime slices, for garnish
1/3 cup crushed saltine crackers
A pinch of ground allspice
Grated zest of 1/2 small-sized lime

Directions

- Set up a dredging station with three mixing bowls. Dump the flour into the first bowl. Beat the eggs whites in another bowl.
- In the third bowl, combine the saltines, coconut, lime zest, allspice, salt and paprika. Set the air fryer to cook at 395 degrees F.
- Dredge your shrimps in the flour; then, coat them with egg whites on all sides; lastly, press them into the saltine/coconut mixture. Make sure to coat well.
- Spritz each shrimp on all sides with cooking oil. Air-fry for 7 to 8 minutes, working in two batches.
- Turn the temperature to 335 degrees F. Air-fry an additional 3 minutes. Serve with lime slices on a nice serving platter. Bon appétit!

320. Eggs with Smoked Salmon and Asiago Cheese

Ready in about 25 minutes
Servings 4

This rich, family breakfast is simply adorable; salmon, eggs and Asiago cheese make a great blend.

Per serving: 153 Calories; 11.2g Fat; 2.4g Carbs; 10g Protein; 2g Sugars

Ingredients

1/3 cup Asiago cheese, grated
1/3 teaspoon dried dill weed
1/2 tomato, chopped
6 eggs
1/3 cup milk
Pan spray
1/2 cup smoked salmon, chopped
Fine sea salt and freshly cracked black pepper, to taste
1/3 teaspoon smoked cayenne pepper

Directions

- Set your air fryer to cook at 365 degrees F. In a mixing bowl, whisk the eggs, milk, smoked cayenne pepper, salt, black pepper, and dill weed.
- Lightly grease 4 ramekins with pan spray of choice; divide the egg/milk mixture among the prepared ramekins.
- Add the salmon and tomato; top with the grated Asiago cheese. Finally, air-fry for 16 minutes. Serve with a toast or English muffins. Bon appétit!

321. Easiest and Healthiest Fish Nuggets Ever

Ready in about 15 minutes
Servings 2

Who said fish nuggets can't be healthy?! These nuggets contain less oil, so they are will be loved by those on weight loss.

Per serving: 347 Calories; 18.2g Fat; 19.1g Carbs; 26.2g Protein; 1.6g Sugars

Ingredients

½ teaspoon cayenne pepper
½ cup crushed crackers
1/3 teaspoon salt
½ pound white fish, cut into sticks
1/3 cup plain flour
1 ½ tablespoons vegetable oil
1 egg, well beaten
Ground pepper, to taste

Directions

- Set the air fryer to cook at 395 degrees F.
- Take three bowls. Dump the sifted flour into the first bowl.
- Mix crushed crackers, oil, salt, ground pepper, and cayenne pepper in another bowl. Place the egg in the third bowl.
- Dip each fish piece into the flour; then, dip into the beaten egg. Roll them in the cracker mixture.
- Air-fry in the cooking basket for about 8 minutes. Bon appétit!

322. Crab Cakes with Mustard and Capers

Ready in about 20 minutes
Servings 8

Classic crab cakes made easy! Backfin is a mixture of jumbo lump crab and special grade crab meat. This is a fabulous appetizer and a wonderful party food too!

Per serving: 392Calories; 11.3g Fat; 49g Carbs; 23.1g Protein; 4.2g Sugars

Ingredients

1/3 teaspoon ground black pepper
1/2 tablespoon nonpareil capers
3 eggs, well whisked
½ teaspoon dried dill weed
1 1/2 tablespoons softened butter
1/2 teaspoon whole-grain mustard
1 1/2 pound backfin blue crabmeat
5 slices sourdough bread, crustless and torn into small pieces
2 ½ tablespoons mayonnaise
A pinch of salt

Directions

- Mix all the ingredients thoroughly. Shape into 4 balls and press each ball to form the cakes.
- Then, spritz your cakes with cooking oil.
- Air-fry at 365 degrees F for 12 minutes, turning halfway through. Bon appétit!

323. Mustard Lemon Cod Fillets

Ready in about 20 minutes
Servings 2

For brightly flavored cod fillets, use a freshly squeezed lemon juice and whole-grain mustard. Serve these gourmet fish fillets with a top–notch cheese to make them taste even more special!

Per serving: 501 Calories; 35.2g Fat; 32.4g Carbs; 30.9g Protein; 6.2g Sugars

Ingredients

2 medium-sized cod fillets
1/2 tablespoon fresh lemon juice
1 ½ tablespoons olive oil
1/2 tablespoon whole-grain mustard
Sea salt and ground black pepper, to savor
1/2 cup seasoned breadcrumbs
2 eggs

Directions

- Set your air fryer to cook at 355 degrees F. Thoroughly combine olive oil and breadcrumbs in a shallow bowl.
- In another shallow bowl, whisk the egg. Drizzle each cod fillet with lemon juice and spread with mustard. Then, sprinkle each fillet with salt and ground black pepper.
- Dip each fish fillet into the whisked egg; now, roll it in the olive oil/breadcrumb mix.
- Place in a single layer in the air fryer cooking basket. Cook for 10 minutes, working in batches, turning once or twice. Serve with potato salad. Bon appétit!

324. Brioche with Herring and Eggs

Ready in about 10 minutes
Servings 6

This salmon dish has the aroma of the Mediterranean! You can experiment with rosemary, capers, Kalamata olives and oregano in this recipe.

Per serving: 354 Calories; 20.3g Fat; 24.7g Carbs; 17.4g Protein; 4.5g Sugars

Ingredients

6 whole eggs
1/2 teaspoon smoked cayenne pepper
6 tablespoons soft cheese
1 teaspoon ground black pepper, to taste
1/2 cup herring fillets, marinated and chopped
6 brioche rolls
2 ½ teaspoons extra strong Dijon mustard
1/2 teaspoon dried thyme
2 tablespoons olive oil
1 teaspoon sea salt flakes

Directions

- Cut off the top of each brioche; then, scoop out the insides.
- Brush the inside of each brioche roll with the Dijon mustard and olive oil. Spread with the soft cheese.
- Place the prepared brioche shells in the cooking basket; add the herring fillets. Crack an egg into each brioche; add all the seasonings.
- Bake for 12 minutes at 325 degrees F. Bon appétit!

325. Salmon with Cilantro and Citrus Sauce

Ready in about 40 minutes
Servings 4

An appetizing, ambrosial salmon with a zingy, bright sauce! This fresh-tasting fish can be served on any occasion.

Per serving: 299 Calories; 14.2g Fat; 3.7g Carbs; 37.1g Protein; 2.7g Sugars

Ingredients

1 ½ pounds salmon steak
½ teaspoon grated lemon zest
1/2 tablespoon honey
Freshly cracked mixed peppercorns, to taste
1/3 cup lemon juice
Fresh chopped chives, for garnish
1/3 cup dry white wine
1/2 teaspoon fresh cilantro, chopped
Fine sea salt, to taste
1/3 cup Worcester sauce

Directions

- To prepare the marinade, place all ingredients, except for salmon steak and chives, in a deep pan. Bring to a boil over medium-high flame until it has reduced by half. Allow it to cool down.
- After that, allow salmon steak to marinate in the refrigerator approximately 40 minutes. Discard the marinade and transfer the fish steak to the preheated air fryer.
- Air-fry at 400 degrees F for 9 to10 minutes. To finish, brush hot fish steaks with the reserved marinade, garnish with fresh chopped chives, and serve right away!

326. Rockfish Fillets with Avocado Cream

Ready in about 2 hours 10 minutes
Servings 2

This recipe is a proof that avocado comes from a food heaven! It pairs wonderfully with the rockfish fillets.

Per serving: 403 Calories; 23.7g Fat; 9.7g Carbs; 36.7g Protein; 4.9g Sugars

Ingredients

For the Fish Fillets:
1 1/2 tablespoons balsamic vinegar
1/2 cup vegetable broth
1/3 teaspoon shallot powder
1/3 cup soy sauce
4 Rockfish fillets
1 teaspoon ground black pepper
1 ½ tablespoons olive oil
Fine sea salt, to taste
1/3 teaspoon garlic powder

For the Avocado Cream:
2 tablespoons Greek-style yogurt
1 clove garlic, peeled and minced
1 teaspoon ground black pepper
1/2 tablespoon olive oil
1/3 cup vegetable broth
2 avocados
1/2 teaspoon lime juice
1/3 teaspoon fine sea salt

Directions

- In a bowl, wash and pat the fillets dry using some paper towels. Add all the seasonings. In another bowl, stir in the remaining ingredients for the fish fillets.
- Add the seasoned fish fillets; cover and let the fillets marinate in your refrigerator at least 3 hours.
- Then, set your air fryer to cook at 325 degrees F. Cook marinated rockfish fillets in the air fryer grill basket for 9 minutes.
- In the meantime, prepare the avocado sauce by mixing all the ingredients with an immersion blender or regular blender. Serve the rockfish fillets topped with the avocado sauce. Enjoy!

327. Easy Dill Crab Cakes

Ready in about 10 minutes
Servings 4

Who said cooking is time-consuming? Here is an amazing recipe ready in 10 minutes! Crab cakes go well with potato salad, mashed vegetables, hot sauces and so forth.

Per serving: 235 Calories; 8.6g Fat; 22.7g Carbs; 20.4g Protein; 2.4g Sugars

Ingredients

1 ½ tablespoons mayonnaise
1/2 teaspoon whole-grain mustard
2 eggs, well beaten
1/3 teaspoon ground black pepper
3 slices bread, crustless and torn into small pieces
1/2 teaspoon dried dill weed
1/3 pound crabmeat
A pinch of salt
1 ½ tablespoons softened butter

Directions

- Mix all the ingredients thoroughly. Shape into 4 patties.
- Then, spritz your patties with cooking oil.
- Air-fry at 365 degrees F for 12 minutes, turning halfway through. Serve over boiled potatoes. Bon appétit!

328. Grilled Sunday Shrimp

Ready in about 10 minutes
Servings 4

This shrimp recipe matches quite well with mango salsa, pesto, harissa, and aioli. Get inspired and enjoy your Air fryer!

Per serving: 101 Calories; 5.6g Fat; 1.8g Carbs; 11.7g Protein; 0.7g Sugars

Ingredients

1 teaspoon crushed red pepper flakes, or more to taste
1 clove garlic, finely minced
Garlic pepper, to savor
1 ½ tablespoons fresh parsley, roughly chopped
1/2 pound shrimps, deveined
1 ½ tablespoons lemon juice
1 ½ tablespoons olive oil
Sea salt flakes, to taste

Directions

- Set the air fryer to cook at 385 degrees F.
- In a bowl, thoroughly combine all the ingredients, coating the shrimps on all sides.
- Dump the shrimps into the cooking basket; air-fry for 7 to 8 minutes in the grill pan. Bon appétit!

329. Delicious Restaurant-Style Fish Cakes

Ready in about 2 hours 20 minutes
Servings 4

You can't go wrong with air-fried and well-seasoned fish cakes. The perfect balance of potatoes and white fish makes these cakes irresistible!

Per serving: 106 Calories; 6.1g Fat;11.7g Carbs; 1.7g Protein; 0.8g Sugars

Ingredients

1 tablespoon plain flour
1/2 teaspoon English mustard
2 tablespoons butter, room temperature
1 ½ cup mashed potatoes
1/2 tablespoon cilantro, minced
2 tablespoons milk
2 ½ cups cooked white fish
Salt and freshly cracked black pepper, to savor

Directions

- In a large-sized bowl, combine the potatoes with the fish, cilantro, salt, and black pepper.
- Now, add the milk, English mustard, and butter; mix until everything's well incorporated. Now, throw in the flour; shape into patties.
- Place in the refrigerator for about 2 hours. Cook for 13 minutes at 395 degrees F. Serve with some extra English mustard.

330. Cod Fillets in Creamy Citrus Sauce

Ready in about 20 minutes
Servings 2

These cod fillets have a rich flavor and perfect texture. In addition, fish packs a nutritious punch in every recipe.

Per serving: 310 Calories; 22.1g Fat; 8.7g Carbs; 1.69g Protein; 0.9g Sugars

Ingredients

1 ½ tablespoons sesame oil
1/2 heaping teaspoon dried parsley flakes
1/3 teaspoon fresh lemon zest, finely grated
2 medium-sized cod fillets
1 teaspoon sea salt flakes
1/2 tablespoon fresh orange juice
A pinch of salt and pepper
1/3 teaspoon ground black pepper, or more to savor
1/2 tablespoon fresh lemon juice

Directions

- Set the air fryer to cook at 375 degrees F. Season each cod fillet with sea salt flakes, black pepper and dried parsley flakes. Now, drizzle them with sesame oil.
- Place the seasoned cod fillets in a single layer at the bottom of the cooking basket; air-fry approximately 10 minutes.
- While the fillets are cooking, prepare the sauce by mixing the other ingredients. Serve cod fillets on four individual plates garnished with the creamy citrus sauce. Bon appétit!

331. Holiday Parmesan Baked Fish

Ready in about 20 minutes
Servings 6

In this easy-to-prepare dish, fish fillets provide a rich flavor that contrasts with a zingy Parmesan/mayo coating. Feel free to use a full-fat mayo because there is no oil or another grease in this recipe.

Per serving: 432 Calories; 16.1g Fat; 53.7g Carbs; 16.9g Protein; 1g Sugars

Ingredients

6 saltines, crushed
1/2 cup Parmesan cheese, grated
1/3 teaspoon paprika
1 teaspoon dried dill weed
2 fish fillets
1/3 cup mayonnaise
1/2 tablespoon lime juice
Salt and ground black pepper, to taste

Directions

- Mix the mayonnaise, Parmesan, paprika, salt, black pepper, and dill weed until everything is thoroughly combined.
- Then, drizzle tilapia fillets with the lemon juice.
- Cover each fish fillet with Parmesan/mayo mixture; roll them in cracker crumbs. Bake at 335 for about 10 minutes. Eat warm and enjoy!

332. One-More-Bite Whitefish and Eggs

Ready in about 20 minutes
Servings 4

If you don't think you like smoked whitefish, think twice. Yogurt, herbs, eggs and scallions elevate this whitefish to awesome. Serve with a slice of rye bread and enjoy!

Per serving: 148 Calories; 8.6g Fat; 7.9g Carbs; 10.5 g Protein; 3.2g Sugars

Ingredients

1/2 tablespoon yogurt
1/3 cup spring garlic, finely chopped
Fresh chopped chives, for garnish
3 eggs, beaten
1/2 teaspoon dried dill weed
1 teaspoon dried rosemary
1/3 cup scallions, chopped
1/3 cup smoked whitefish, chopped
1 ½ tablespoons crème fraîche
1 teaspoon kosher salt
1 teaspoon dried marjoram
1/3 teaspoon ground black pepper, or more to taste
Cooking spray

Directions

- Firstly, spritz four oven safe ramekins with cooking spray. Then, divide smoked whitefish, spring garlic, and scallions among greased ramekins.
- Crack an egg into each ramekin; add the crème, yogurt and all seasonings.
- Now, air-fry approximately 13 minutes at 355 degrees F. Taste for doneness and eat warm garnished with fresh chives. Bon appétit!

333. Tarragon Fish Fillets

Ready in about 25 minutes
Servings 4

This is everything we want in Sunday meal: easy, delicious and well-seasoned. Serve with a glass of crisp and elegant white wine.

Per serving: 250 Calories; 15.4g Fat; 0.7g Carbs; 25.2g Protein; 0.3g Sugars

Ingredients

2 eggs, beaten
1/2 teaspoon tarragon
4 fish fillets, halved
2 tablespoons dry white wine
1/3 cup saltine crackers
1 teaspoon seasoned salt
1/3 teaspoon mixed peppercorns
1/2 teaspoon fennel seed

Directions

- Add the crackers, salt, peppercorns, fennel seeds, and tarragon to your food processor; blitz for about 20 seconds.
- Drizzle fish fillets with dry white wine. Dump the egg into a shallow dish.
- Now, coat the fish fillets with the beaten egg on all sides; then, coat them with the seasoned cracker mix.
- Air-fry at 345 degrees F for about 17 minutes. Bon appétit!

334. Tamari Scallops with Shallots

Ready in about 2 hour 12 minutes
Servings 2

Scallops are among the healthiest foods in the world. They are packed with protein, vitamin B12, iodine and omega-3 fats.

Per serving: 179 Calories; 10.7g Fat; 7g Carbs; 14g Protein; 1.3g Sugars

Ingredients

1 1/2 tablespoons tamari sauce
1/3 cup shallots, chopped
Belgian endive, for garnish
1/2 tablespoon balsamic vinegar
1 1/2 tablespoons olive oil
1 clove garlic, chopped
1/2 teaspoon ginger, grated
1/2 pound scallops, cleaned

Directions

- In a small-sized sauté pan that is placed over a moderate flame, simmer all ingredients, minus scallops and Belgian endive. Allow this mixture to cool down completely.
- After that, add the scallops and let them marinate for at least 2 hours in the refrigerator.
- Arrange the scallops in a single layer in the air fryer grill pan. Spritz with a cooking oil. Air-fry at 345 degrees for 10 minutes, turning halfway through. Serve immediately with Belgian endive. Bon appétit!

335. Chipotle Salmon Fish Cakes

Ready in about 3 hours 15 minutes
Servings 4

Poached salmon meets tamari sauce, milk and herbs in these amazing fish bites. You can fry them with tons of fat or utilize a hot air and make them healthy yet delicious in the Air fryer. It's up to you.

Per serving: 401 Calories; 19.4g Fat; 2g Carbs; 53g Protein; 0.9g Sugars

Ingredients

1/2 teaspoon chipotle powder
1/2 teaspoon butter, at room temperature
1/3 teaspoon smoked cayenne pepper
1/2 teaspoon dried parsley flakes
1/3 teaspoon ground black pepper
1/2 teaspoon tamari sauce
2 ½ cups poached salmon
1 1/2 tablespoon milk
1/2 white onion, peeled and finely chopped
1 teaspoon fine sea salt
Seasoned breadcrumbs

Directions

- Place all ingredients, minus breadcrumbs, in a large-sized mixing dish.
- Shape into cakes and roll each cake over seasoned breadcrumbs. After that, refrigerate for about 2 hours.
- Then, set your air fryer to cook at 395 degrees F for 13 minutes.
- Serve warm with a dollop of sour cream if desired. Bon appétit!

336. Hot Spicy Halibut Fillets

Ready in about 20 minutes
Servings 4

Are you obsessed with halibut fillets? If not, prepare to become one of those people! This fish dish is easy to make and tastes so good.

Per serving: 237 Calories; 17.7g Fat; 5g Carbs; 14.4g Protein; 0.7g Sugars

Ingredients

2 medium-sized halibut fillets
1 teaspoon curry powder
1/2 teaspoon ground coriander
Kosher salt and freshly cracked mixed peppercorns, to taste
1 ½ tablespoons olive oil
1/2 cup crushed crackers
2 eggs
1/2 teaspoon hot paprika
A few drizzles of tabasco sauce

Directions

- Set your air fryer to cook at 365 degrees F.
- Then, grab two mixing bowls. In the first bowl, combine the crushed crackers with olive oil.
- In another shallow bowl, thoroughly whisk the egg. Next step, evenly drizzle the halibut fillets with Tabasco sauce; add hot paprika, curry, coriander, salt, and cracked mixed peppercorns.
- Dip each fish fillet into the whisked egg; now, roll it over the crumb/oil mix.
- Place in a single layer in the air fryer cooking basket. Cook for 10 minutes, working in batches. Serve over creamed salad if desired. Bon appétit!

337. Baked Spicy Tuna with Eggs

Ready in about 20 minutes
Servings 4

So fresh, so tasty, this tuna recipe makes a great break-fast for your family. In case you didn't already know, tuna prevents heart diseases, lowers blood pressure and improves the immune system.

Per serving: 252 Calories; 15.6g Fat; 3.7g Carbs; 23.9g Protein; 1.1g Sugars

Ingredients

5 eggs, beaten
1/2 chili pepper, deveined and finely minced
1 ½ tablespoons sour cream
1/3 teaspoon dried oregano
1/2 tablespoon sesame oil
1/3 cup yellow onions, chopped
1 ½ cup canned tuna
1/2 sweet pepper, deveined and chopped
1/3 teaspoon dried basil
Fine sea salt and ground black pepper, to taste

Directions

- Warm sesame oil in a nonstick skillet that is preheated over a moderate flame. Then, sweat the onions and peppers for 4 minutes, or until they are just fragrant.
- Add chopped canned tuna and stir until heated through.
- Meanwhile, lightly grease a baking dish with a pan spray. Throw in sautéed tuna/pepper mix. Add the remaining ingredients in the order listed above.
- Bake for 12 minutes at 325 degrees F. Eat warm garnished with Tabasco sauce if desired.

338. Cheesy Garlic Shrimp

Ready in about 10 minutes
Servings 2

Garlic-flavored cheese is a great addition to this unique and cool shrimp recipe. Also, it is quick and easy enough to cook on a weeknight.

Per serving: 203 Calories; 10.8g Fat; 3.4g Carbs; 23g Protein; 2.1g Sugars

Ingredients

½ tablespoon fresh parsley, roughly chopped
1 ½ tablespoons balsamic vinegar
Sea salt flakes, to taste
1/2 pound shrimp, deveined
1 tablespoon orange juice
Garlic-flavored cheese, sliced
1/2 teaspoon garlic powder
1 ½ tablespoons olive oil
1/2 teaspoon smoked cayenne pepper
Salt and ground black peppercorns, to savor

Directions

- Set the air fryer to cook at 385 degrees F.
- In a bowl, thoroughly combine all ingredients, coating the shrimp on all sides.
- Dump the shrimp into the cooking basket; air-fry for 7 to 8 minutes. Bon appétit!

339. Spaghetti with Minty Shrimp

Ready in about 40 minutes
Servings 4

Is there anything better for summer lunch than a simple bowl of pasta with seafood? Try adding another combination of spices to satisfy your senses.

Per serving: 189 Calories; 6.4g Fat; 17g Carbs; 14.9g Protein; 0.4g Sugars

Ingredients

1 ½ packets spaghetti, cooked
1/2 tablespoon fresh basil leaves, chopped
½ pound shrimp, shelled and deveined
1 ½ tablespoons olive oil
3 cloves garlic, minced
1 teaspoon smoked cayenne pepper
1/2 teaspoon fresh mint, roughly chopped
½ teaspoon ginger, freshly grated
1 teaspoon sea salt

Directions

- Firstly, set your air fryer to cook at 395 degrees F.
- In a mixing dish, combine all of the above items; toss until everything is well combined and let it stand for about 28 minutes.
- Air-fry for 3 to 4 minutes. Serve with cooked spaghetti. Bon appétit!

FAST SNACKS & APPETIZERS

340. Spicy Brussels Sprout Snack 187

341. Crispy Eggplant Chips 187

342. Crispy Fried Leek Rings 188

343. Cheesy Broccoli Balls 188

344. Wings in Spicy Molasses Barbecue Sauce 189

345. Game Day Shrimp Bites 189

346. Buttery Sage Fingerling Potatoes 190

347. Pecorino Broccoli Melts 190

348. Homemade Cinnamon Banana Chips 191

349. Aromatic Roasted Squash Bites 191

350. Last Minute Brussels Sprout Appetizer 192

351. Quinoa and Dijon Cocktail Meatballs 192

352. Cheesy Mashed Potato Balls 193

353. Harissa and Basil Corn 193

354. Cocktail Sausage with Spicy Mayo Sauce 194

355. Garlic Kale Chips 194

356. The Easiest Zucchini Fries Ever 195

357. Movie Night Sweet Onion Snack 195

358. Brie, Arugula and Artichoke Dip 196

359. Vermouth Chicken Wings 196

360. Pork and Quinoa Cocktail Meatballs 197

361. Beef Meatballs in Blueberry Chipotle Sauce 197

362. Thai Chicken Wings 198

363. Potato Chips with Tangy Dipping Sauce 198

364. Brie and Pork Appetizer Meatballs 199

365. Restaurant-Style Onion Rings 199

366. Mayo-Cheese Jacket Potatoes 200

367. Cajun Kale Chips 200

368. Homemade Corn Tortilla Chips 201

369. Habanero Chicken Wings 201

370. Sweet Tortilla Chips 202

371. Must-Make Avocado Wrapped in Bacon 202

372. Meatballs with Mediterranean Dipping Sauce 203

373. Old-Fashioned Buffalo Wings 203

374. Party Parmesan Chicken Meatballs 204

375. Sticky Thai Turkey Wings 204

376. Cottage and Turkey Wonton Wrappers 205

377. Chinese-Style Turkey Wings 205

378. Buttermilk and Sage Chicken Wings 206

340. Spicy Brussels Sprout Snack

Ready in about 15 minutes
Servings 4

These Brussels sprouts are perfectly tender with a touch of mild fresh herbs and magical sesame oil. Try them as a perfect late night snack. Enjoy!

Per serving: 81 Calories; 3.9g Fat; 10.6g Carbs; 4.0g Protein; 2.5g Sugars

Ingredients

1 pound Brussels sprouts, ends and yellow leaves removed and halved lengthwise
Salt and black pepper, to taste
1 tablespoon toasted sesame oil
1 teaspoon fennel seeds
Chopped fresh parsley, for garnish

Directions

- Place the Brussels sprouts, salt, pepper, sesame oil, and fennel seeds in a resealable plastic bag. Seal the bag and shake to coat.
- Air-fry at 380 degrees F for 15 minutes or until tender. Make sure to flip them over halfway through the cooking time.
- Serve sprinkled with fresh parsley. Bon appétit!

341. Crispy Eggplant Chips

Ready in about 45 minutes
Servings 4

This is a great recipe for movie night at home. It is so addictive, so invite your friends over to keep yourself from eating the entire portion!

Per serving: 260 Calories; 14.1g Fat; 33.5g Carbs; 2.9g Protein; 9.0g Sugars

Ingredients

2 eggplants, peeled and thinly sliced
Salt
1/2 cup tapioca starch
1/4 cup canola oil
1/2 cup water
1 teaspoon garlic powder
1/2 teaspoon dried dill weed
1/2 teaspoon ground black pepper, to taste

Directions

- Salt the eggplant slices and let them stay for about 30 minutes. Squeeze the eggplant slices and rinse them under cold running water.
- Toss the eggplant slices with the other ingredients. Cook at 390 degrees F for 13 minutes, working in batches.
- Serve with a sauce for dipping. Bon appétit!

342. Crispy Fried Leek Rings

Ready in about 15 minutes
Servings 4

There's nothing better than crispy fried vegetables. But what about all the fat that actually goes with them? Simply make them in your Air Fryer and you'll get the same results with far fewer calories!

Per serving: 287 Calories; 7.8g Fat; 46.1g Carbs; 8.9g Protein; 5.9g Sugars

Ingredients

1 large-sized leek, cut into 1/2-inch wide rings
Salt and pepper, to taste
1/2 teaspoon mustard powder
1 cup milk
1 egg
1 cup self-rising flour
3/4 teaspoon baking powder
1 cup crushed saltines
1 tablespoon olive oil

Directions

- Toss your leeks with salt, pepper, and mustard powder. Grab three mixing bowls to set up a breading station.
- In a mixing bowl, whisk the milk and egg until frothy and pale. Now, combine the flour and baking powder in another mixing bowl. In the third bowl, combine the crushed saltines with olive oil.
- Coat the leek slices with the flour mixture. Dredge the floured leek slices into the milk/egg mixture, coating well. Finally, roll them over the crumb mixture.
- Air-fry for approximately 10 minutes at 370 degrees F. Bon appétit!

343. Cheesy Broccoli Balls

Ready in about 20 minutes
Servings 6

There is no wrong way to eat these veggie balls. You can serve them with cocktail sticks and a dipping sauce for full enjoyment!

Per serving: 328 Calories; 14.8g Fat; 32.2g Carbs; 16.3g Protein; 2.1g Sugars

Ingredients

2 eggs, well whisked
2 cups Colby cheese, shredded
1 cup all-purpose flour
Seasoned salt, to taste
1/4 teaspoon ground black pepper, or more to taste
1 head broccoli, chopped into florets
1 cup crushed saltines

Directions

- Thoroughly combine the eggs, cheese, flour, salt, pepper, and broccoli to make the consistency of dough.
- Chill for 1 hour and shape into small balls; roll the patties over the crushed saltines. Spritz them with cooking oil on all sides.
- Cook at 360 degrees F for 10 minutes. Check for doneness and return to the Air Fryer for 8 to 10 more minutes. Serve with a sauce for dipping. Bon appétit!

344. Wings in Spicy Molasses Barbecue Sauce

Ready in about 20 minutes
Servings 6

If you are looking for the recipe for Super Bowl Sunday, these spicy, sweet and sticky wings are a great idea! They get their heat from habanero hot sauce, which is simply delicious.

Per serving: 275 Calories; 10.9g Fat; 9.7g Carbs; 33.1g Protein; 7.9g Sugars

Ingredients

For the Sauce:
1 tablespoon yellow mustard
1 tablespoon apple cider vinegar
1 tablespoon olive oil
1/4 cup unsulfured blackstrap molasses
1/4 cup ketchup
2 tablespoons brown sugar
1 garlic clove, minced
Salt and ground black pepper, to your liking
1/8 teaspoon ground allspice
1/4 cup water

For the Wings:
2 pounds chicken wings
1/4 teaspoon celery salt
1/4 cup habanero hot sauce
Chopped fresh parsley, or garnish

Directions

- In a sauté pan that is preheated over a medium-high flame, place all the ingredients for the sauce and bring it to a boil. Then, reduce the temperature and simmer until it has thickened.
- Meanwhile, preheat your Air Fryer to 400 degrees F; cook the chicken wings for 6 minutes; flip them over and cook for additional 6 minutes. Season them with celery salt.
- Serve with the prepared sauce and habanero hot sauce, garnished with fresh parsley leaves. Bon appétit!

345. Game Day Shrimp Bites

Ready in about 45 minutes
Servings 10

This is an ultimate finger food and glorious game day snack! It pairs perfectly with a creamy homemade dipping sauce.

Per serving: 376 Calories; 24.8g Fat; 2.1g Carbs; 34.0g Protein; 0.0g Sugars

Ingredients

1 ¼ pounds shrimp, peeled and deveined
1 teaspoon paprika
1/2 teaspoon ground black pepper
1/2 teaspoon red pepper flakes, crushed
1 tablespoon salt
1 teaspoon chili powder
1 tablespoon shallot powder
1/4 teaspoon cumin powder
1 ¼ pounds thin bacon slices

Directions

- Toss the shrimps with all the seasoning until they are coated well.
- Next, wrap a slice of bacon around the shrimps, securing with a toothpick; repeat with the remaining ingredients; chill for 30 minutes.
- Air-fry them at 360 degrees F for 7 to 8 minutes, working in batches. Serve with cocktail sticks if desired. Enjoy!

346. Buttery Sage Fingerling Potatoes

Ready in about 45 minutes
Servings 8

These flavorful small potatoes are a guaranteed crowd pleaser. Sage protects your immune system, alleviates skin conditions and enhances your brain health.

Per serving: 178 Calories; 6.3g Fat; 28.6g Carbs; 3.5g Protein; 1.8g Sugars

Ingredients

1 ½ pounds fingerling potatoes, halved lengthwise
2 tablespoons melted butter
1/4 cup fresh sage leaves, finely chopped
2 sprigs thyme, chopped
1 teaspoon lemon zest, finely grated
1/4 teaspoon ground pepper
1 tablespoon sea salt flakes
1/2 teaspoon grated ginger

Directions

- Soak the potatoes in cold water for about 30 minutes. Then, pat them dry using a kitchen towel.
- After that, roast at 400 degrees F for 15 minutes. Serve in a nice serving bowl, accompanied by tomato ketchup and mayonnaise. Bon appétit!

347. Pecorino Broccoli Melts

Ready in about 20 minutes
Servings 6

If you are looking for healthy snack recipe, these broccoli bites are the answer! This recipe calls for Shoyu sauce – Japanese-style soy sauce that is made with soybeans and wheat. This sauce has less intensive flavor than Chinese soy sauce.

Per serving: 86 Calories; 4.2g Fat; 7.3g Carbs; 7.0g Protein; 1.8g Sugars

Ingredients

1 large-sized head of broccoli, broken into small florets
1/2 teaspoon sea salt
1/4 teaspoon ground black pepper, or more to taste
1 tablespoon Shoyu sauce
1 teaspoon groundnut oil
2 tablespoons Pecorino Toscano, freshly grated
Paprika, to taste

Directions

- Add the broccoli florets to boiling water; boil approximately 4 minutes; drain well.
- Season with salt and pepper; drizzle with Shoyu sauce and groundnut oil.
- Air-fry at 390 degrees F for 10 minutes; shake the Air Fryer basket, push the power button again, and continue to cook for 5 minutes more.
- Toss the fried broccoli with the cheese and paprika. Bon appétit!

348. Homemade Cinnamon Banana Chips

Ready in about 15 minutes
Servings 4

Before you start making this great guilt-free snack, don't forget to drizzle your bananas with fresh lemon juice. Otherwise, they will get brown quickly; further, you should add lemon juice for an extra hit of tangy, distinctive flavor. Win-Win!

Per serving: 114 Calories; 0.6g Fat; 29.4g Carbs; 1.6g Protein; 15.1g Sugars

Ingredients

4 medium-sized bananas, peeled and cut into 1/4-inch slices
Non-stick cooking spray
1/2 cup freshly squeezed lemon juice
1/2 teaspoon ground cinnamon
A pinch of kosher salt

Directions

- Lightly coat the bananas with olive oil; drizzle with the freshly squeezed lemon juice.
- Air-fry at 185 degrees F for 10 to 12 minutes.
- Take the banana slices out of the Air Fryer; sprinkle with cinnamon and salt. Place in an airtight container for storage.

349. Aromatic Roasted Squash Bites

Ready in about 20 minutes
Servings 6

Toss the winter squash with sugar and spices for an extraordinarily tasty appetizer! You will get all in one bite – zesty, sweet, and aromatic food!

Per serving: 110 Calories; 4.7g Fat; 18.5g Carbs; 1.0g Protein; 6.1g Sugars

Ingredients

1 ½ pounds winter squash, peeled and cut into 1/2-inch chunks
1/4 cup dark brown sugar
2 tablespoons melted coconut oil
A pinch of coarse salt
A pinch of pepper
2 tablespoons sage, finely chopped
Zest of 1 small-sized lemon
1/8 teaspoon ground allspice

Directions

- Toss the squash chunks with the other items.
- Roast in the Air Fryer's cooking basket at 350 degrees F for 10 minutes.
- Pause the machine, and turn the temperature to 400 degrees F; stir and roast for additional 8 minutes. Bon appétit!

350. Last Minute Brussels Sprout Appetizer

Ready in about 20 minutes
Servings 4

Prepare the healthiest chips ever and eat smart by using a rapid air technology! You can sprinkle Brussels sprout chips with lightly toasted sesame seeds if desired.

Per serving: 110 Calories; 7.4g Fat; 10.6g Carbs; 3.9g Protein; 2.5g Sugars

Ingredients

1 pound Brussels sprouts, trimmed and cut off the ends
1 teaspoon kosher salt
1 tablespoon lemon zest
Non-stick cooking spray

Directions

- Firstly, peel the Brussels sprouts using a small paring knife. Toss the leaves with salt and lemon zest; spritz them with a cooking spray, coating all sides.
- Bake at 380 degrees for 8 minutes; shake the cooking basket halfway through the cooking time and cook for 7 more minutes.
- Make sure to work in batches so everything can cook evenly. Taste and adjust the seasonings. Bon appétit!

351. Quinoa and Dijon Cocktail Meatballs

Ready in about 20 minutes
Servings 6

There are many exciting ways to cook meatballs. Air frying is a quick, easy, and healthy way to make these party favorites!

Per serving: 294 Calories; 8.6g Fat; 26.6g Carbs; 27.0g Protein; 7.1g Sugars

Ingredients

1/2 pound ground pork
1/2 pound ground beef
1 cup quinoa, cooked
1 beaten egg
2 scallions, finely chopped
1/2 teaspoon onion powder
1 ½ tablespoons Dijon mustard
3/4 cup ketchup
1 teaspoon ancho chili powder
1 tablespoon sesame oil
2 tablespoons tamari sauce
1/4 cup balsamic vinegar
2 tablespoons sugar

Directions

- Mix all the ingredients until everything is well incorporated.
- Roll into small meatballs.
- Cook at 370 degrees F for 10 minutes. Now, shake the basket and cook for 5 minutes more.

352. Cheesy Mashed Potato Balls

Ready in about 15 minutes
Servings 6

These appetizing balls are the perfect way to give new life to your leftovers. In this recipe, you can use Italian seasoning blend as well as a few tablespoons of ground pine nuts.

Per serving: 371 Calories; 24.4g Fat; 21.1g Carbs; 17.3g Protein; 0.6g Sugars

Ingredients

3 cups mashed potatoes
1 egg, slightly beaten
2 green onions, sliced
1/2 cup ham, finely chopped
1/2 cup Colby cheese, shredded
8 ounces soft cheese
1 cup seasoned breadcrumbs
2 ½ tablespoons canola oil

Directions

- Combine all the ingredients, except the breadcrumbs and canola oil, in a mixing dish. Roll the mixture into bite-sized balls.
- Thoroughly combine the breadcrumbs with canola oil. Roll the balls over the breadcrumb mix.
- Air-fry them at 390 degrees F for 5 minutes. Work in batches. Serve with toothpicks.

353. Harissa and Basil Corn

Ready in about 15 minutes
Servings 4

Corn on the cob is popular to eat as a fast snack or a brunch. This is a basic recipe. You can use your favorite mellow cheese, fragrant fresh herbs or a homemade dipping sauce.
Per serving: 168 Calories; 5.2g Fat; 29.8g Carbs; 5.3g Protein; 5.7g Sugars

Ingredients

4 ears corn, husked and cleaned
2 tablespoons harissa sauce
1 tablespoon melted ghee
1 teaspoon smoked cayenne pepper
Juice of 2 small-sized lemons
1 tablespoon fresh basil leaves, coarsely chopped

Directions

- Rub the corn with harissa sauce and melted ghee. Sprinkle with cayenne pepper. Arrange them on an Air Fryer grill pan.
- Air-fry them at 390 degrees F for 10 minutes. Pause the Air Fryer, turn the cobs over, and cook for additional 5 minutes.
- Drizzle warm corn with fresh lemon juice and garnish with fresh basil leaves. Bon appétit!

354. Cocktail Sausage with Spicy Mayo Sauce

Ready in about 15 minutes
Servings 4

It would be good if you could find high-quality pork sausages for this recipe. The tangy mayo dipping sauce gives them a special flavor twist!

Per serving: 304 Calories; 26.2g Fat; 4.5g Carbs; 12.4g Protein; 1.0g Sugars

Ingredients

1/2 pound pork cocktail sausages

For the Sauce:
1/4 cup mayonnaise
1/4 cup cream cheese
1 whole grain mustard
1 teaspoon balsamic vinegar
1 garlic clove, finely minced
1 teaspoon chili powder

Directions

- Take your sausages, give them a few pricks using a fork and place them on the Air Fryer grill pan.
- Set the timer for 15 minutes; after 8 minutes, pause the Air Fryer, turn the sausages over and cook for further 7 minutes.
- Check for doneness and take the sausages out of the machine.
- In the meantime, thoroughly combine all the ingredients for the sauce. Serve with warm sausages and enjoy!

355. Garlic Kale Chips

Ready in about 5 minutes
Servings 4

Here's an all-time favorite snack recipe. An air fryer helps you bring amazing flavors to your table with its revolutionary cooking technique.

Per serving: 91 Calories; 8.8g Fat; 3.2g Carbs; 1g Protein; 0g Sugars

Ingredients

2 ½ tablespoons olive oil
1 ½ teaspoons garlic powder
1 bunch of kale, torn into small pieces
2 tablespoons lemon juice
1 1/2 teaspoons seasoned salt

Directions

- Toss your kale with the other ingredients.
- Cook at 195 degrees F for 4 to 5 minutes, tossing kale halfway through.
- Serve with your favorite dipping sauce.

356. The Easiest Zucchini Fries Ever

Ready in about 26 minutes
Servings 4

Zucchini sticks with plenty of flavor! By substituting zucchini for potatoes, you will create a dish that's equally delicious as French fries, but it is creative and unexpected.

Per serving: 95 Calories; 3.7g Fat; 8.5g Carbs; 7.2g Protein; 2.7g Sugars

Ingredients

4 zucchinis, slice into sticks
2 teaspoons shallot powder
1/4 teaspoon dried dill weed
2 teaspoons garlic powder
1/2 cup Parmesan cheese, preferably freshly grated
1/3 teaspoon cayenne pepper
3 egg whites
1/3 cup crushed bran cereal
Cooking spray
Salt and ground black pepper, to your liking

Directions

- Pat the zucchini sticks dry using a kitchen towel.
- Grab a mixing bowl and beat the egg whites until pale; then, add all the seasonings in the order listed above and beat again
- Take another mixing bowl and mix together the crushed bran cereal and the Parmesan cheese.
- Then, coat the zucchini sticks with the seasoned egg mixture; then, roll them over the cereal/cheese mixture.
- Lay the breaded zucchini sticks in a single layer on the tray that is coated lightly with cooking spray.
- Bake at 375 degrees F for about 20 minutes until the sticks are golden brown. Serve with your favorite sauce for dipping.

357. Movie Night Sweet Onion Snack

Ready in about 32 minutes
Servings 2

A rosemary aioli is the perfect accompaniment to these simple onion rings. Chaat masala gives them an ample and unique flavor.

Per serving: 123 Calories; 0.35g Fat; 26g Carbs; 3.8g Protein; 1.3g Sugars

Ingredients

1 teaspoon chaat masala
2 large-sized dishes of ice water
1 teaspoon garlic pepper
1/3 teaspoon seasoned salt
3 large-sized sweet onions such as Mayan Sweets, thinly sliced
1/2 cup all-purpose flour

Directions

- Firstly, add the sweet onions and water to a bowl; let them soak for at least 15 minutes; after that drain them well.
- Place the remaining ingredients in a zip lock bag. Add the onion slices to the bag and shake it well.
- Transfer the onions to the air fryer cooking basket. Brush them with cooking spray.
- Bake for 12 minutes at 390 degrees F; turn them halfway through the cooking time. Serve with your favorite sauce for dipping.

358. Brie, Arugula and Artichoke Dip

Ready in about 22 minutes
Servings 10

Inspired by Brie cheese, the king among cheeses, you can come up with this guest-ready dip. The best part? This rich dipping sauce is ready in less than 25 minutes.

Per serving: 128 Calories; 10.2g Fat; 2.7g Carbs; 7.3g Protein; 0.5g Sugars

Ingredients

3 cups arugula leaves, torn into pieces
1/3 can artichoke hearts, drained and chopped
½ cup Mozzarella cheese, shredded
1/3 cup sour cream
3 cloves garlic, minced
1/3 teaspoon dried basil
1 teaspoon sea salt
7 ounces Brie cheese
1/2 cup mayonnaise
1/3 teaspoon ground black pepper, or more to taste
A pinch of ground allspice

Directions

- Combine together the Brie cheese, mayonnaise, sour cream, garlic, basil, salt, ground black pepper, and the allspice.
- Throw in the artichoke hearts and arugula; gently stir to combine. Transfer the prepared mixture to a baking dish. Now, scatter the Mozzarella cheese evenly over the top.
- Bake in your air fryer at 325 degrees F for 17 minutes. Serve with tortilla chips or veggie sticks. Bon appétit!

359. Vermouth Chicken Wings

Ready in about 1 hour 15 minutes
Servings 4

Your average chicken wings just got a makeover. A salt-pepper rub, vermouth and fish sauce give these chicken wings a beautiful amber crust.

Per serving: 184 Calories; 9.6g Fat; 5.5g Carbs; 13.7g Protein; 3.5g Sugars

Ingredients

2 teaspoons coriander seeds
1 ½ tablespoons soy sauce
1/3 cup vermouth
3/4 pound chicken wings
1 ½ tablespoons each fish sauce
½ teaspoon brown sugar
2 tablespoons melted butter
1 teaspoon seasoned salt
freshly ground black pepper, to taste

Directions

- Rub the chicken wings with the black pepper and seasoned salt; now, add the other ingredients.
- Next, soak the chicken wings in this mixture for 55 minutes in the refrigerator.
- Air-fry the chicken wings at 365 degrees F for 16 minutes or until warmed through. Bon appétit!

360. Pork and Quinoa Cocktail Meatballs

Ready in about 15 minutes
Servings 8

There are few things better than classic meatballs. Quinoa meatballs are one of them!

Per serving: 268 Calories; 14.3g Fat; 15g Carbs; 19g Protein; 0.38g Sugars

Ingredients

½ teaspoon fine sea salt
1½ cup quinoa, cooked
3 cloves garlic, minced
1½ pound ground pork
½ cup scallions, finely chopped
2 eggs, well whisked
1/3 teaspoon cumin powder
2/3 teaspoon ground black pepper, or more to taste
2 teaspoons basil

Directions

- Simply combine all the ingredients in a large-sized mixing bowl.
- Shape into bite-sized balls; cook the meatballs in the air fryer for 18 minutes at 345 degrees F. Serve with some tangy sauce such as marinara sauce if desired. Bon appétit!

361. Beef Meatballs in Blueberry Chipotle Sauce

Ready in about 25 minutes
Servings 4

Appetizer, anyone? Here's a decadent, a little sweet, a little savory recipe. You're never going back to boring meatballs again.

Per serving: 206 Calories; 9.6g Fat; 14.5g Carbs; 15g Protein; 12.8g Sugars

Ingredients

2 tablespoons Dijon mustard
1 ½ tablespoons Worcester sauce
2 tablespoons minced scallions
1/3 cup blueberry-chipotle ketchup
½ pound ground beef
1 ½ teaspoons minced green garlic
1/3 cup brown sugar
1/2 teaspoon cumin
1 tablespoons herb vinegar
Salt and ground black pepper, to savor

Directions

- In a large-sized mixing dish, place the meat, cumin, scallions, garlic, salt, and pepper; mix with your hands or a spatula so that everything is evenly coated.
- Form into meatballs and cook them in the preheated air fryer for 13 minutes at 375 degrees F. Air-fry until they are cooked in the middle.
- Meanwhile, add the other ingredients to a large saucepan that is placed over a medium-low heat; cook for 5 minutes.
- Next, add the meatballs and cook for a couple of minutes longer or until heated through. Bon appétit!

362. Thai Chicken Wings

Ready in about 25 minutes
Servings 6

These sticky Thai wings will improve your Super bowl Sunday! You can make a homemade Thai sweet chili sauce by mixing chili peppers, garlic, rice vinegar, sugar and salt.

Per serving: 75 Calories; 1.4g Fat; 5.7g Carbs; 8.9g Protein; 3.2g Sugars

Ingredients

2 ½ tablespoons dry sherry
2 teaspoons ginger powder
½ pound chicken wings
Lime wedges, to serve
2 teaspoons garlic powder
1/3 cup Thai sweet chili sauce
1 teaspoon smoked paprika
Sea salt and ground black pepper, to taste

Directions

- Toss the chicken wings with the ginger powder, garlic powder, paprika, sea salt, ground black pepper, and dry sherry.
- Air-fry the chicken wings for 16 minutes at 365 degrees F or until they are thoroughly heated.
- Serve with the Thai sweet chili sauce and the lemon wedges. Bon appétit!

363. Potato Chips with Tangy Dipping Sauce

Ready in about 56 minutes
Servings 6

Super easy, super yummy potato chips without excess fat. Is that possible? Sure, that's possible! Moreover, you can dip them into a homemade mayo-based sauce.

Per serving: 326 Calories; 8.4g Fat; 57.5g Carbs; 7.5g Protein; 2g Sugars

Ingredients

1/3 teaspoon red pepper flakes, crushed
1 ½ tablespoons mayonnaise
1 teaspoon seasoned salt
2 ½ tablespoons olive oil
5 Russet potatoes, cut into fries
1/3 cup sour cream
2 tablespoon garlic paste
1/3 teaspoon dried marjoram

Directions

- Soak the potatoes for 35 minutes in the water; you should change the water a couple of times to remove starch.
- Then, preheat your air fryer to 325 degrees F; air-fry your chips for 18 minutes or until they are golden brown.
- In the meantime, combine the remaining ingredients to make a dipping sauce. Serve your chips with the dipping sauce on the side and enjoy!

364. Brie and Pork Appetizer Meatballs

Ready in about 25 minutes
Servings 8

Why didn't we start putting cheese in our meatballs? Explore one of the best ways to serve pork meatballs at your party.

Per serving: 275 Calories; 18.6g Fat; 2.7g Carbs; 22.9g Protein; 1.2g Sugars

Ingredients

1 teaspoon cayenne pepper
2 teaspoons mustard
2 tablespoons Brie cheese, grated
5 garlic cloves, minced
2 small-sized yellow onions, peeled and chopped
1½ pounds ground pork
Sea salt and freshly ground black pepper, to taste

Directions

- Mix all of the above ingredients until everything is well incorporated.
- Now, form the mixture into balls (the size of golf a ball).
- Cook for 17 minutes at 375 degrees F. Serve with your favorite sauce.

365. Restaurant-Style Onion Rings

Ready in about 25 minutes
Servings 4

Just when we thought onion rings couldn't get any better... Onion rings in beer batter provide an endless array of flavors!

Per serving: 317 Calories; 1.6g Fat; 62.4g Carbs; 9.1g Protein; 1.3g Sugars

Ingredients

2/3 cup breadcrumbs
2 small-sized eggs
2 cups all-purpose flour
1/3 teaspoon baking powder
2/3 teaspoon red pepper flakes, crushed
1 large-sized onion, sliced into rings
2/3 cup beer
1/3 cup water
1/2 teaspoon fine sea salt

Directions

- Start by preheating the air fryer for 7 to 10 minutes.
- Then, use a medium-sized bowl to combine all-purpose flour with baking powder, sea salt, and crushed red pepper flakes.
- Dip onion rings into the prepared flour mixture; make sure to coat them on all sides. To make the batter, whisk in the egg, beer and water with a fork.
- Next, dip the rings into the prepared beer batter, coating them well. Now, coat them with the breadcrumbs.
- Afterward, cook the onion rings approximately 11 minutes at 345 degrees F. Eat warm.

366. Mayo-Cheese Jacket Potatoes

Ready in about 19 minutes
Servings 8

This recipe proves that your favorite potato dish is so much more than stuffed vegetable. You can use Colby, Longhorn or Brick instead of Cheddar cheese.

Per serving: 327 Calories; 7g Fat; 59g Carbs; 9.4g Protein; 2.2g Sugars

Ingredients

1/3 cup Cheddar cheese, grated
3 tablespoons mayonnaise
Sea salt, cayenne pepper and ground black pepper, to taste
2 heaping tablespoons roughly chopped chives
1 ½ tablespoons vegetable oil
7 Russet potatoes
1/3 cup scallions, chopped
1/2 cup soft cheese, softened

Directions

- Firstly, stab each potato with a fork. Preheat your air fryer to 360 degrees F. Set the timer for 10 minutes.
- Bake the potatoes in the air fryer cooking basket at 360 degrees F. Bake in batches.
- In the meantime, make the filling by mixing the rest of the above ingredients.
- Lastly, stuff your potatoes with the prepared filling. Arrange jacket potatoes on a nice serving platter and serve immediately. Bon appétit!

367. Cajun Kale Chips

Ready in about 7 minutes
Servings 4

Chips lovers take notice: Worchester sauce and Cajun spice mix are the key ingredients to this memorable family snack!

Per serving: 74 Calories; 7g Fat; 3g Carbs; 0.9g Protein; 1.3g Sugars

Ingredients

1 1/2 teaspoons Cajun spice mix
2 tablespoons sesame oil
Salt and pepper, to taste
3 heads of kale, torn into small pieces
2 tablespoons Worchester sauce

Directions

- Toss all ingredients together in a mixing bowl.
- Then, cook at 195 degrees F for about 4 minutes. Enjoy!

368. Homemade Corn Tortilla Chips

Ready in about 6 minutes
Servings 5

Homemade tortilla chips need little more than tortilla triangles. Pepper jack cheese that smells like freshly cut hay and chili powder that tastes like summer heat! Serve with fruity red wine.

Per serving: 79 Calories; 7.1g Fat; 0.6g Carbs; 2g Protein; 0.1g Sugars

Ingredients

1 ½ teaspoons chili powder
1/3 cup pepper jack cheese, grated
1 teaspoon dried basil
2 tablespoons olive oil
10 corn tortillas, cut into bite-sized triangles
1 teaspoon salt

Directions

- Start by preheating your air fryer to 385 degrees F.
- Brush tortilla triangles with olive oil. Bake tortilla triangles for 4 minutes until they're crispy.
- Toss with seasonings and pepper jack cheese; serve with your favorite sauce for dipping.

369. Habanero Chicken Wings

Ready in about 25 minutes
Servings 6

Hot, hot, hot! The appetizer is served, and it's full of sticky, spicy and yummy ingredients.

Per serving: 157 Calories; 4.6g Fat; 2.7g Carbs; 25.2g Protein; 1.8g Sugars

Ingredients

3 cloves garlic, peeled and halved
2 tablespoons habanero hot sauce
1/2 tablespoon soy sauce
1 ½ pounds chicken wings
1 teaspoon garlic salt
1 teaspoon smoked cayenne pepper
1 ½ teaspoons honey
1 teaspoon freshly ground black pepper, or to taste

Directions

- Rub the chicken wings with the garlic. Then, season them with the salt, black pepper, and the smoked cayenne pepper.
- Transfer the chicken wings to the food basket; add the soy sauce, habanero hot sauce, and honey; toss to coat on all sides.
- Air-fry the chicken wings at 365 degrees F for 16 minutes or until warmed through.

370. Sweet Tortilla Chips

Ready in about 7 minutes
Servings 6

Prepare this amazing snack food with common spices and corn goodness from your pantry. It might become a kids' lunchbox staple soon.

Per serving: 193 Calories; 5.7g Fat; 33.9g Carbs; 4.2g Protein; 0.5g Sugars

Ingredients

1/3 teaspoon caster sugar
2 tablespoons ground cinnamon
1 ½ tablespoon canola oil
9 corn tortillas, cut into bite-sized triangles
1/3 teaspoon ground allspice

Directions

- Start by preheating your air fryer to 380 degrees F.
- Brush tortilla triangles with canola oil. Bake tortilla triangles for 5 minutes until they're lightly browned and just crispy.
- Toss with cinnamon, allspice, and caster sugar. Bon appétit!

371. Must-Make Avocado Wrapped in Bacon

Ready in about 10 minutes
Servings5

Imagine a clean morning air and the scent of roses. You wake up to breakfast and see these wraps on your dining tables. Bon appétit!

Per serving: 450 Calories; 41.4g Fat; 20.7g Carbs; 8.5g Protein; 1.4g Sugars

Ingredients

2 teaspoons chili powder
5 small avocado dices
1 teaspoon salt
½ teaspoon garlic powder
1 teaspoon ground black pepper
5 rashers back bacon

Directions

- Lay the bacon rashers on a clean surface; then, place one piece of avocado slice on each bacon slice. Add the salt, black pepper, chili powder, and garlic powder.
- Then, wrap the bacon slice around the avocado and repeat with the remaining rolls; secure them with a cocktail sticks or toothpicks.
- Preheat your air fryer to 370 degrees F; cook in the preheated air fryer for 5 minutes and serve with your favorite sauce for dipping.

372. Meatballs with Mediterranean Dipping Sauce

Ready in about 15 minutes
Servings 4

Meatballs are awesome but adding a Mediterranean-inspired dip can be a game-changer! And this easy-to-make dipping sauce contains only six ingredients.
Per serving: 278 Calories; 21g Fat; 1.9g Carbs; 19.4g Protein; 0.5g Sugars

Ingredients

For the Meatballs:
1 1/2 tablespoons melted butter
2 teaspoons red pepper flakes, crushed
½ tablespoon fresh cilantro, finely chopped
2 eggs
2 tablespoons fresh mint leaves, finely chopped
1 teaspoon kosher salt
4 garlic cloves, finely minced
½ pound ground pork
2 tablespoons capers

For Mediterranean Dipping sauce:
1/3 cup black olives, pitted and finely chopped
2 tablespoons fresh Italian parsley
1/2 teaspoon lemon zest
1/3 cup Greek-style yogurt
1/2 teaspoon dill, fresh or dried and chopped
2 tablespoons fresh rosemary

Directions

- Start by preheating your air fryer to 395 degrees F.
- In a large-sized mixing dish, place all ingredients for the meatballs; mix to combine well. Shape the mixture into golf ball sized meatballs.
- Cook the meatballs for about 9 minutes, working in batches.
- In the meantime, make the dipping sauce by thoroughly whisking all the sauce ingredients. Serve warm meatballs with the prepared Mediterranean dipping sauce.

373. Old-Fashioned Buffalo Wings

Ready in about 25 minutes
Servings 4

Chicken wings are best when roasted or fried. This time, we will utilize the power of hot air for that crispy golden skin; in addition, even temperature ensures the wings are fried all the way through.

Per serving: 156 Calories; 10.7g Fat; 1.7g Carbs; 13.1g Protein; 0.2g Sugars

Ingredients

2 cloves garlic, smashed
3 tablespoons melted butter
Ground black pepper and fine sea salt, to taste
8 chicken wings
A few dashes of hot sauce

Directions

- First of all, steam chicken wings for 8 minutes; pat them dry and place in the refrigerator for about 55 minutes.
- Now, bake in the preheated air fryer at 335 degrees F for 28 minutes, turning halfway through. While the chicken wings are cooking, combine the other ingredients to make the sauce.
- To finish, toss air fried chicken wings with the sauce and serve immediately.

374. Party Parmesan Chicken Meatballs

Ready in about 10 minutes
Servings 4

These meatballs are made of chicken meat but they have an intense flavor you'll notice immediately. They are buttery, zingy and terrific!

Per serving: 266 Calories; 20g Fat; 3.1g Carbs; 17.7g Protein; 0.2g Sugars

Ingredients

1/2 cup whole-wheat bread crumbs
2 eggs
1 ½ tablespoons melted butter
1/3 teaspoon mustard seeds
1/2 pound ground chicken
3 garlic cloves, finely minced
1 teaspoon dried basil
1/2 teaspoon Hungarian paprika
1/3 cup Parmesan cheese, preferably freshly grated
1/2 lime, zested
1 teaspoon fine sea salt
1/3 teaspoon ground black pepper, or more to taste

Directions

- In a nonstick skillet that is preheated over a moderate flame, place the ground chicken and garlic; cook until the chicken is no longer pink and the garlic is just browned, about 3 minutes.
- Throw in the remaining ingredients; shape the mixture into balls (e.g. the size of a golf ball).
- Next step, roll each ball in plain flour and transfer them to the greased air fryer cooking basket.
- Set your air fryer to cook at 385 degrees F; cook for about 8 minutes, or till they're thoroughly heated.

375. Sticky Thai Turkey Wings

Ready in about 20 minutes
Servings 6

Comforting and inexpensive, turkey wings are perfect if you don't want to prepare the whole bird. Or maybe you just like the turkey wings.

Per serving: 180 Calories; 9.4g Fat; 7g Carbs; 16.9g Protein; 3g Sugars

Ingredients

1/2 teaspoon ginger powder
1/2 palmful minced lemongrass
1 teaspoon paprika
1/3 cup Thai sweet chili sauce
1/2 tablespoon fish sauce
1 ½ pounds turkey wings, cut into pieces
1/2 teaspoon garlic powder
1 ½ tablespoons rice wine vinegar
1 ½ tablespoon sesame oil
Sea salt flakes and ground black pepper, to savor

Directions

- Toss turkey wings with all of the above ingredients.
- Air-fry them for 18 minutes at 355 degrees or until they are thoroughly cooked.
- Serve with Thai sweet chili sauce and lemon wedges. Bon appétit!

376. Cottage and Turkey Wonton Wrappers

Ready in about 10 minutes
Servings 4

It takes a couple of minutes to mix the ingredients and fill the wontons – the Air fryer does the rest. Serve with a simple hot sauce on the side.

Per serving: 189 Calories; 3.9g Fat; 25.7g Carbs; 11.4g Protein; 1.1g Sugars

Ingredients

6 ounces turkey breasts, cooked and chopped
1 ½ tablespoons blue cheese dressing
8 wonton wrappers
1/3 cup Cottage cheese
Blue cheese, for topping
1 ½ tablespoons fish sauce
1/2 teaspoon dried rosemary

Directions

- In a large-sized mixing dish, combine together all items, minus wonton wrappers and blue cheese. Stir until everything is well combined.
- Grab a mini muffin pan and lay 1 wonton wrapper in each mini muffin cup. Fill each wrapper with the cottage/turkey mixture.
- Bake in the preheated air fryer for 8 minutes at 335 degrees F. Immediately top with crumbled blue cheese and serve. Bon appétit!

377. Chinese-Style Turkey Wings

Ready in about 2 hours 25 minutes
Servings 2

These well-seasoned wings are so tasty, so easy and they always bring back memories of childhood. In case you didn't know, Five spice powder consists of ground cloves, cinnamon, star anise, fennel seeds and Szechuan peppercorns.

Per serving: 216 Calories; 14.6g Fat; 4.7g Carbs; 15.6g Protein; 1.6g Sugars

Ingredients

1/2 teaspoon brown sugar
2 teaspoons sesame oil
1/2 teaspoon Five spice powder
1 ½ teaspoons soy sauce
1/2 teaspoon garlic powder
1 ½ tablespoons rice vinegar
1/2 tablespoon cornstarch
1/3 pound turkey wings, cut into pieces
1/2 teaspoon shallot powder
1/3 teaspoon sea salt flakes

Directions

- Begin by preheating the air fryer to 385 degrees F.
- Place all ingredients in a mixing dish and let it marinate at least 2 hours.
- Air-fry for 23 to 25 minutes. Serve warm.

378. Buttermilk and Sage Chicken Wings

Ready in about 1 hour 10 minutes
Servings 4

If you think about an affordable and nutritious meal, try these chicken wings. Round out the meal with a fresh salad.

Per serving: 266 Calories; 6.5g Fat; 9.7g Carbs; 39.4g Protein; 1.4g Sugars

Ingredients

1/3 cup flour
1/3 cup buttermilk
1 ½ pound chicken wings
2 tablespoons tamari sauce
1/3 teaspoon fresh sage
1 teaspoon mustard seeds
1/2 teaspoon garlic paste
1/2 teaspoon freshly ground mixed peppercorns
1/2 teaspoon seasoned salt
2 teaspoons fresh basil

Directions

- Place the seasonings along with the garlic paste, chicken wings, buttermilk, and tamari sauce in a large-sized mixing dish. Let it soak about 55 minutes; drain the wings.
- Dredge the wings in the flour and transfer them to the air fryer cooking basket.
- Air-fry for 16 minutes at 355 degrees F. Serve on a nice serving platter with a dressing on the side. Bon appétit!

RICE, GRAINS & BEANS

379. Garlic Rosemary Croutons 208

380. Ultimate Apricot French Toast 208

381. Corn and Scallion Cakes 209

382. Pumpkin and Pecan Breakfast Muffins 209

383. Mediterranean Polenta Rounds............................ 210

384. Nana's Rosemary Cornbread 210

385. Spiced Crumbed Beans 211

386. Indian-Style Roll-Ups... 211

387. Savory Burrata and Ham Muffins 212

388. Ham and Cheese Toast 212

389. Crispy Peppery Vegetable Fritters......................... 213

390. Mushroom Risotto Croquettes............................. 213

391. Aromatic Shrimp and Jasmine Risotto.................. 214

392. Golden Polenta Bites with Fried Veggies 214

393. Honey Buttery Dinner Rolls................................... 215

394. Spinach and Cheese Balls 215

395. Spicy Pork and Quinoa Stuffed Peppers................ 216

396. Pork Taco Balls with Currant Sauce 216

397. Beef and Baked Kidney Beans 217

398. Beef Franks and Baked Beans 217

399. Aromatic Chicken and Jasmine Rice Meatballs .. 218

400. Must Serve Turkey with Kidney Beans 218

401. Nacho Hash Browns 219

402. Turkey, Leek and Dark Beer Chili.......................... 219

403. Pasta with Ground Turkey Sauce 220

404. Jumbo Prawns with Green Beans 220

405. Spaghetti with Saucy Shrimp 221

406. Aromatic Turkey-Rice Balls................................... 221

407. Beef and Barley Stuffed Peppers 222

408. Rich Turkey and Chipotle Chili 222

409. Turkey Tortilla Wraps.. 223

410. Easiest Turkey Chili Ever 223

411. Pasta with Ground Turkey Sauce 224

412. Beef and Barley Meatballs 224

413. Fried Basmati Rice with Prawns 225

414. Festive Baked Green Beans 225

379. Garlic Rosemary Croutons

Ready in about 10 minutes
Servings 4

If you are a huge fan of the croutons, the good news is that you can make them in your Air Fryer. They are very versatile. This recipe calls for fresh garlic but you can freely experiment with fragrant herbs, organic oils, cheese, etc.

Per serving: 76 Calories; 6.1g Fat; 4.8g Carbs; 0.8g Protein; 0.0g Sugars

Ingredients

4 slices whole-wheat stale bread, edges trimmed and cut into 1/2-inch cubes
1 clove garlic, finely minced
2 tablespoons softened butter
1 sprig rosemary, chopped

Directions

- Toss the bread cubes with garlic, butter, and rosemary.
- Cook for 3 minutes at 285 degrees F. Shake the basket and cook for a further 3 minutes.
- Serve over favorite soups. Bon appétit!

380. Ultimate Apricot French Toast

Ready in about 10 minutes
Servings 6

If you're ready for the best breakfast prepared in an Air Fryer, try this recipe. You can substitute dried apples, pears, nectarines, or peaches for the apricot.

Per serving: 191 Calories; 6.7g Fat; 27.0g Carbs; 6.7g Protein; 9.6g Sugars

Ingredients

6 slices of French bread
2 tablespoons butter, at room temperature
1/3 cup milk
3 eggs, whisked
A pinch of ground allspice
A pinch of kosher salt
1/4 cup dried apricots, chopped
Confectioners' sugar, for garnish

Directions

- Start by preheating your Air Fryer to 380 degrees F.
- Coat the bread slices with butter on both sides. In a mixing bowl, whisk the milk, eggs, allspice, and salt.
- After that, soak buttered bread slices in the milk mixture for about 10 minutes. Transfer the bread slices to an Air Fryer baking dish.
- Scatter chopped apricots over the top of each slice of bread. Spritz with a non-stick cooking spray.
- Air-fry them for 2 minutes. Now, flip each bread slice over, spritz with the cooking spray, and cook for additional 3 minutes.
- Afterward, dust with confectioners' sugar and serve. Bon appétit!

381. Corn and Scallion Cakes

Ready in about 15 minutes
Servings 6

If you've never had corn fritters from an Air Fryer, you're missing the best and the most delicious fritters ever! You can substitute spring onions for the scallions.

Per serving: 168 Calories; 4.6g Fat; 27.4g Carbs; 5.2g Protein; 2.0g Sugars

Ingredients

1 ¼ cups all-purpose flour
1/2 teaspoon baking soda
1 teaspoon baking powder
1/4 teaspoon sugar
A pinch of kosher salt
A pinch of freshly grated nutmeg
1 teaspoon paprika
1/4 teaspoon white vinegar
1/2 cup milk
1 ½ tablespoons melted butter
1 whole egg
1 ¼ cups corn kernels
1/4 cup cilantro, chopped
1/4 cup scallions, chopped

Directions

- In a mixing bowl, combine the flour, baking soda, baking powder, sugar, salt, nutmeg, and paprika.
- In another bowl, combine the vinegar along with the milk, butter and egg. Add this mixture to the dry mixture.
- Preheat the Air Fryer to 380 degrees F. Stir in the corn kernels, cilantro, and the scallions. Then, shape the batter into the rounded fritters. Chill them in your freezer for 6 to 7 minutes.
- Air-fry them for about 5 minutes and serve warm with mayonnaise.

382. Pumpkin and Pecan Breakfast Muffins

Ready in about 20 minutes
Servings 4

This is a whole-grain breakfast in less than 20 minutes! It's one of the perks of owning an Air Fryer! Also, you can substitute banana for pumpkin puree.

Per serving: 247 Calories; 16.8g Fat; 24.1g Carbs; 2.2g Protein; 13.3g Sugars

Ingredients

4 tablespoons cake flour
1/3 teaspoon baking powder
1/4 cup oats
A pinch of salt
1/4 cup ghee, at room temperature
1/4 cup caster sugar
2 tablespoons pecans, ground
1/4 cup pumpkin puree
1/2 teaspoon freshly grated nutmeg
1/4 teaspoon crystalized ginger
1/4 teaspoon ground cinnamon

Directions

- Mix the first 4 ingredients in a bowl.
- In another bowl, beat the ghee with sugar; fold in the pecans and pumpkin puree, and stir again. Add this mixture to the dry flour mixture. Add the nutmeg, ginger and cinnamon, and mix again using a wide spatula.
- You can add a little water to make a batter. Then, prepare the muffin moulds by adding muffin liners to each of them.
- Bake the muffins at 320 degrees F for 10 minutes. Let them stay for 10 to 12 minutes before removing from the moulds. Bon appétit!

383. Mediterranean Polenta Rounds

Ready in about 2 hours 6 minutes
Servings 6

Let your imagination run wild and serve these polenta rounds as colorful canapes for your next cocktail party! You can add bocconcini, shaved cheese, mushrooms, olives, and so on.

Per serving: 203 Calories; 2.4g Fat; 40.8g Carbs; 3.9g Protein; 0.6g Sugars

Ingredients

1 tablespoon butter
2 cups polenta, pre-cooked
Salt and pepper, to your liking
1 sprig thyme, chopped
2 sprigs rosemary, chopped
1 teaspoon cayenne pepper
1/2 teaspoon dried basil
1/2 teaspoon dried oregano
Thin slices of prosciutto, to serve
Tomato ketchup, to serve

Directions

- Begin by preheating your Air Fryer to 360 degrees F. Then, butter the baking dish and set aside.
- Combine the polenta with all seasonings; scrape the mixture into the buttered baking dish and place in the refrigerator for 2 hours or until set.
- Then, cut equal discs from the polenta using a round pastry cutter. Air-fry approximately 6 minutes.
- Lastly, top each round with the slice of prosciutto and serve with the ketchup on the side. Bon appétit!

384. Nana's Rosemary Cornbread

Ready in about 1 hour
Servings 6

This cornbread turns out great every time. Spice it up and add smoky chipotles or other fiery peppers to this great recipe!

Per serving: 240 Calories; 8.0g Fat; 36.2g Carbs; 6.4g Protein; 5.0g Sugars

Ingredients

1 cup cornmeal
1 ½ cups of flour
1/2 teaspoon baking soda
1/2 teaspoon baking powder
1/4 teaspoon kosher salt
1 teaspoon dried rosemary
1/4 teaspoon garlic powder
2 tablespoons caster sugar
2 eggs
1/4 cup melted butter
1 cup buttermilk
1/2 cup corn kernels

Directions

- In a bowl, mix all dry ingredients until well combined. In another bowl, combine all liquid ingredients.
- Add the liquid mix to the dry mix. Fold in the corn kernels and stir to combine well.
- Press the batter into the round loaf pan that is lightly greased with a non-stick cooking spray.
- Air-fry for 1 hour at 380 degrees F. Bon appétit!

385. Spiced Crumbed Beans

Ready in about 10 minutes
Servings 4

Here's the perfect appetizer: hot, crispy beans with big flavors! This recipe calls for a cooking spray but a little melted ghee would be welcome too.

Per serving: 135 Calories; 3.1g Fat; 21.3g Carbs; 6.2g Protein; 1.2g Sugars

Ingredients

1/2 cup all-purpose flour
1 teaspoon smoky chipotle powder
1/2 teaspoon ground black pepper
1 teaspoon sea salt flakes
2 eggs, beaten
1/2 cup crushed saltines
10 ounces wax beans

Directions

- Mix the flour, chipotle powder, black pepper, and salt. Place the eggs in a second shallow bowl.
- Add the crushed saltines to a third bowl. Rinse the beans under running water and remove any tough strings.
- Dredge the beans into the flour mixture; then, coat with the beaten egg; finally, roll them over the crushed saltines.
- Spritz the beans with a non-stick cooking spray. Air-fry at 360 degrees F for 4 minutes. Shake the cooking basket and continue to cook for 3 minutes.

386. Indian-Style Roll-Ups

Ready in about 15 minutes
Servings 2

Who said you can't make bread rolls in an Air Fryer? Try these tender and delicious roll-ups chock full of aromatic Indian flavors. You will be delighted!

Per serving: 251 Calories; 3.6g Fat; 49.5g Carbs; 6.3g Protein; 4.2g Sugars

Ingredients

1 teaspoon vegetable oil
1/2 cup scallions, finely chopped
1/2 teaspoon curry powder
1/2 teaspoon cumin powder
2 large-sized russet potatoes, cooked and mashed
1/2 teaspoon mango powder
Salt and black pepper, to your liking
1/2 teaspoon chaat masala
1/3 teaspoon lal mirchs powder
6 slices multi-grain bread, cut the crusts off

Directions

- Heat the oil in a non-stick skillet over a moderate flame. Then, sauté the scallions until tender; add curry powder and cumin powder and cook for 30 seconds more, stirring constantly.
- Remove the skillet from the heat. Add mashed potatoes to the skillet and stir to combine well. Now, stir in the remaining ingredients, except the bread slices.
- Next, roll each slice of bread flat using a rolling pin. Divide the potato mixture among the bread slices and roll them up tightly. Secure with toothpicks. Spritz each roll with a cooking spray, coating on all sides.
- Place seam side down on the bottom of a cooking basket.
- Air-fry for 8 minutes at 390 degrees F. Pause the machine, flip them over and set the timer for additional 5 minutes. Eat warm with a sauce for dipping.

387. Savory Burrata and Ham Muffins

Ready in about 15 minutes
Servings 6

Burrata is a semi-soft Italian cheese that is very creamy, which makes it a perfect ingredient for these chewy muffins. Beyond brunch, you might want to consider this as an appetizer for your dinner party.

Per serving: 304 Calories; 2.2g Fat; 59.0g Carbs; 10.6g Protein; 2.4g Sugars

Ingredients

1 box muffin mix
1/2 cup fully cooked ham, chopped
1/4 cup spring onions, finely chopped
1 teaspoon garlic powder
1/2 teaspoon mustard powder
1/2 burrata ball

Directions

- Prepare the muffin mix as directed. Add the remaining ingredients and mix well.
- Lightly oil a mini muffin pan using cooking spray and divide out the mixture.
- Now, bake at 340 degrees F for about 10 minutes; pause the machine.
- After that, check for doneness and cook for 5 more minutes or until the muffins have risen; taste with a skewer. Bon appétit!

388. Ham and Cheese Toast

Ready in about 10 minutes
Servings 4

Every time you want warm and quick breakfast, you can make this toast that melts in your mouth. Add a pinch of nutmeg for a touch of sophistication!

Per serving: 293 Calories; 24.9g Fat; 4.7g Carbs; 12.9g Protein; 0.6g Sugars

Ingredients

4 slices of white sandwich bread
1/2 stick butter, at room temperature
1 teaspoon whole-grain mustard
8 ounces baked ham, thinly sliced
1 ½ cups Gruyere cheese, grated
A pinch of nutmeg

Directions

- Toast the bread slices; now, spread with butter and mustard.
- Add ham and top with Gruyere cheese; afterward, add a few sprinkles of freshly grated nutmeg.
- Air-fry them at 390 degrees F for 4 to 6 minutes. Serve warm with some extra mustard. Bon appétit!

389. Crispy Peppery Vegetable Fritters

Ready in about 15 minutes
Servings 4

If you don't have all day to make dinner, the fritters are a quick and effective solution! These fritters are child-friendly but if you want to spice them up, you can add chili powder or a few dashes of Tabasco sauce.

Per serving: 168 Calories; 8.5g Fat; 14.7g Carbs; 8.8g Protein; 1.8g Sugars

Ingredients

1 cup bell peppers, deveined and chopped
1 teaspoon sea salt flakes
1 teaspoon cumin
1/4 teaspoon paprika
1/2 cup shallots, chopped
2 cloves garlic, minced
1 ½ tablespoons fresh chopped cilantro
1 egg, whisked
3/4 cup Cheddar cheese, grated
1/4 cup cooked quinoa
1/4 cup self-rising flour

Directions

- Mix all the ingredients until everything is well incorporated. Shape into balls; then, slightly flatten each ball.
- Spritz the patties with a cooking spray. Place the patties in a single layer in your Air Fryer cooking basket.
- Cook at 340 degrees for 5 minutes; flip them over and cook another 5 minutes. Bon appétit!

390. Mushroom Risotto Croquettes

Ready in about 15 minutes
Servings 4

These protein-packed vegetarian balls are sure to please. In this recipe, try to use the mushrooms with a creamy texture and mild flavor like Oyster or Button mushrooms.

Per serving: 321 Calories; 6.9g Fat; 54.7g Carbs; 8.9g Protein; 2.0g Sugars

Ingredients

1 tablespoon rice bran oil
1 small-sized onion, finely chopped
2 garlic cloves, peeled and minced
1/2 cup mushrooms, finely chopped
6 ounces cooked rice
Sea salt, to savor
1/4 teaspoon ground black pepper, or more to taste
1/2 teaspoon dried dill weed
1 teaspoon paprika
1 tablespoon Colby cheese, grated
1 egg, beaten
1 cup breadcrumbs

Directions

- Warm the rice bran oil in a saucepan that is preheated over a moderate heat; sauté the onion and garlic until tender and fragrant.
- Add in the mushrooms and cook until the liquid has almost evaporated. Allow the sautéed mixture to cool slightly; fold in the cooked rice. Add the salt, black pepper, dill, and paprika.
- Fold in the cheese and mix again. Shape the mushroom/risotto mixture into bite-sized balls; gently flatten them with your hands. Dip them in the beaten egg; then, roll them over the breadcrumbs.
- Air-fry the risotto balls for 7 minutes at 390 degrees F. Check for doneness and cook for 2 to 3 more minutes as needed. Serve with marinara sauce. Bon appétit!

391. Aromatic Shrimp and Jasmine Risotto

Ready in about 15 minutes
Servings 4

Jasmine rice is a kind of fragrant rice named after the jasmine flower; it comes in two varieties – white and brown. You will love this risotto that reheats well too.

Per serving: 232 Calories; 7.5g Fat; 31.5g Carbs; 8.9g Protein; 1.2g Sugars

Ingredients

1 cup shrimps, deveined
1/2 cup green onion, finely chopped
2 cloves garlic, minced
1 celery stalk, trimmed and chopped
2 tablespoons peanut oil
1 tablespoon soy sauce
1 tablespoon oyster sauce
1 teaspoon brown sugar
1/2 teaspoon sea salt flakes
1/2 teaspoon red pepper flakes, crushed
5 ounces jasmine rice, pre-cooked
1 tablespoon fresh sage, chopped
1 tablespoon fresh thyme, chopped
1 tablespoon fresh basil, chopped
2 tablespoons fresh parsley, chopped

Directions

- Thoroughly combine the first ten ingredients; transfer the mixture to an Air Fryer baking dish. Air-fry for 7 minutes at 390 degrees F, cooking in batches as needed.
- Fold in the cooked rice; add the herbs and air-fry for further 7 minutes. Serve warm with sour cream. Bon appétit!

392. Golden Polenta Bites with Fried Veggies

Ready in about 50 minutes
Servings 6

Slices of crispy polenta are topped with roasted vegetable and Cheddar cheese – all-in-one vegetarian bites for a summer party.

Per serving: 313 Calories; 3.5 Fat; 62.7g Carbs; 7.6g Protein; 2.6g Sugars

Ingredients

1 cup onions, chopped
2 cloves garlic, finely minced
1/2 pound zucchini, cut into bite-sized chunks
1/2 pound potatoes, peeled and cut into bite-sized chunks
1 tablespoon olive oil
1 teaspoon paprika
1/2 teaspoon salt
1/2 teaspoon freshly ground black pepper, or more to taste
1/2 teaspoon dried dill weed, or more to taste
14 ounces pre-cooked polenta tube, cut into slices
1/4 cup Cheddar cheese, shaved

Directions

- Add the vegetables to an Air Fryer cooking basket. Sprinkle them with olive oil, paprika, salt, pepper, and dill.
- Now, set the machine to cook at 400 degrees F. Cook for 6 minutes.
- After that, pause the machine, shake the basket and set the timer for 6 minutes more. Set aside.
- Next, spritz the polenta slices with non-stick cooking oil. Spritz the cooking basket too. Set your Air Fryer to cook at 400 degrees F
- Air-fry for 20 to 25 minutes. Turn the polenta slices over and cook for another 10 minutes. Top each polenta slice with air-fried vegetables and shaved cheese. Enjoy!

393. Honey Buttery Dinner Rolls

Ready in about 3 hours 15 minutes
Servings 6

There's nothing like the warm, fluffy and moist bread rolls for family dinner. These buttery rolls will make your kitchen smell magnificent!

Per serving: 219 Calories; 9.0g Fat; 31.0g Carbs; 4.1g Protein; 9.5g Sugars

Ingredients

For the Rolls:
1 1/3 cups plain flour
1 ½ tablespoons white sugar
1 teaspoon of instant yeast
A pinch of kosher salt
2 tablespoons melted butter
1 egg yolk
1/3 cup milk
A pinch of nutmeg

For the Topping:
2 tablespoons softened butter
2 tablespoons honey

Directions

- Mix the flour, sugar, instant yeast, and salt using a stand mixer. Whisk on low speed for 1 minute or until smooth.
- Now, stir in the butter. Continue to mix for 1 more minute as it all combines.
- Lay the dough onto a lightly floured surface and knead several times. Transfer the dough to a large bowl, cover and place it in a warm room to rise until doubled in size.
- Now, whisk the egg yolk with milk and nutmeg. Coat the balls with the egg mixture.
- Shape into balls, loosely cover and allow the balls to rise until doubled; it takes about 1 hour.
- Then, bake them in the preheated Air Fryer at 320 degrees F for 14 to 15 minutes. In the meantime, make the topping by simply mixing the very soft butter with honey. Afterward, spread the topping onto each warm roll.
- Cover the leftovers and keep in your fridge. Bon appétit!

394. Spinach and Cheese Balls

Ready in about 15 minutes
Servings 4

What these balls lack in size they make up for in a flavor! This is the perfect way to trick kids into eating more spinach. So clever!

Per serving: 103 Calories; 9.1g Fat; 4.9g Carbs; 1.9g Protein; 1.2g Sugars

Ingredients

1/3 cup milk
1/2 cup cheese
1 ½ cups spinach, torn into pieces
1/3 cup rice flour
2 tablespoons canola oil
Salt and ground black pepper, to taste

Directions

- Add all the ingredients to a food processor or blender; then, puree the ingredients until it becomes dough.
- Next, roll the dough into small balls. Preheat your air fryer to 310 degrees F.
- Cook the balls in your air fryer for about 12 minutes or until they are crispy. Bon appétit!

395. Spicy Pork and Quinoa Stuffed Peppers

Ready in about 41 minutes
Servings 4

Serve these stuffed peppers as a main dish or as a starter along with a fresh salad. They are great paired with a bowl of warming soup on a windy winter day.

Per serving: 242 Calories; 15.6g Fat; 17.9g Carbs; 15g Protein; 4.8g Sugars

Ingredients

1 red bell pepper
5 ounces ground pork
1/3 cup dry white wine
1 orange bell pepper
1 teaspoon salsa
2 teaspoons rosemary, fresh or dried
1 ½ tablespoons canola oil
1 1/2 teaspoons fresh or dried oregano
3 cloves garlic, finely chopped
1/3 cup quinoa, rinsed and drained
1 1/3 cup crushed tomatoes
1 cup water
1/2 onion, peeled and finely chopped
½ tablespoon nutritional yeast

Directions

- Add the quinoa and 1 cup of water to a microwave safe bowl. Cover and cook your quinoa for 5 minutes. Remove the bowl from the microwave and give it a good stir.
- Place the bowl back in the microwave and cook an additional 3 minutes. After that, let your quinoa rest for an additional 6 minutes to absorb the liquid.
- In a sauté pan, warm canola oil over a moderate flame; sweat the onion, pork, and garlic for about 6 minutes; make sure to stir often.
- Add 1 cup of canned and crushed tomatoes; stir in the rosemary, oregano, and drained quinoa; give it a good stir and cook for 2 more minutes. Stir in nutritional yeast; stir again.
- Slice off the tops of your peppers and discard the seeds. Divide the prepared quinoa filling among your peppers; add tops and transfer them to a baking dish that is previously greased with a thin layer of vegetable oil.
- Whisk the remaining 1/3 cup of crushed tomatoes and 1/3 cup of white wine; add about 1 cup water; pour into the baking dish.
- Cover with foil and cook in the preheated air fryer at 365 degrees F for 22 minutes. Serve with your favorite salsa and enjoy!

396. Pork Taco Balls with Currant Sauce

Ready in about 14 minutes
Servings 6

To save your time, make a large batch of these balls, freeze half of them and keep in an airtight container. They are great for a savory snack or dinner party.

Per serving: 210 Calories; 6.2g Fat; 20.5g Carbs; 18.1g Protein; 3.2g Sugar

Ingredients

2 tablespoons mustard
2 onions, diced
2 teaspoons sesame oil
3 tablespoons dry red wine
3 cloves garlic, finely minced
15 ounces lean ground pork
Salt and ground black pepper, to taste
6 ounces tortilla crumbs
1/3 cup currant jelly

Directions

- Begin by preheating your air fryer to 335 degrees F.
- Next, thoroughly combine the pork, onions, sesame oil, garlic, salt, and black pepper. Form the mixture into bite-sized balls.
- Roll the balls in the tortilla crumbs and cook them for 7 minutes; work in batches.
- To make the sauce, mix red wine together with currant jelly and mustard; whisk well until everything is combined. Serve cooked meatballs with currant sauce and enjoy!

397. Beef and Baked Kidney Beans

Ready in about 20 minutes
Servings 6

You can experiment with this recipe and find your favorite version. Your version may be with canned tomatoes, jalapeno peppers, cannellini bean, etc.

Per serving: 405 Calories; 15.4g Fat; 12.7g Carbs; 51.6g Protein; 9.9g Sugars

Ingredients

2 red bell peppers, seeded and thinly sliced
1 ½ can tomatoes, crushed
1 teaspoon fine sea salt
3 bay leaves
6 beef steaks, trim the fat and cut into strips
1 ½ Habanero chili peppers
1 teaspoon paprika
Pink peppercorns, to taste
1 teaspoon dried basil
2 cups sweet onions such as Vidalia, peeled and chopped
3 cloves garlic, peeled and pressed
1 ½ can kidney beans
½ cup beef broth

Directions

- Combine the beef strips, sweet onions, garlic, chili pepper, and bell pepper; cook in your air fryer at 395 degrees F for 12minutes; work in batches.
- Throw in the other ingredients; set the timer for an additional 7 minutes; cook until thoroughly warmed. Bon appétit!

398. Beef Franks and Baked Beans

Ready in about 15 minutes
Servings 5

These beef frankfurters are so easy to make – try them at your next family lunch! Pasilla peppers give your beans a rich, smoky taste; they go well with mushrooms, garlic, fennel, and oregano too.

Per serving: 175 Calories; 10g Fat; 7.7g Carbs; 14.2g Protein; 0.8g Sugars

Ingredients

5 Pasilla chilies
1 1/2 can cannellini beans
5 beef frankfurters
Kosher salt and pepper, to savor
2 teaspoons dried rosemary

Directions

- Start by cooking the frankfurters in the air fryer for 5 minutes at 375 degrees F. Reserve frankfurters, keeping them warm.
- Then, dump the canned cannellini beans into an oven safe dish that fits in your air fryer. Add the other ingredients.
- Set the machine to cook at 305 degrees F for 6 minutes. Serve the warm frankfurters with baked beans and enjoy!

399. Aromatic Chicken and Jasmine Rice Meatballs

Ready in about 1 hour 10 minutes
Servings 10

Chicken and rice naturally go together. This is a great appetizer that tastes wonderful, but you can serve these meatballs with mashed potatoes and have a complete meal.

Per serving: 472 Calories; 34g Fat; 25 g Carbs; 20.8g Protein; 2.9g Sugars

Ingredients

5 eggs
1 ½ cups seasoned breadcrumbs
1 teaspoon dried oregano
1 1/2 cup Pecorino-Romano cheese, preferably freshly grated
1 teaspoon dried sage, chopped
1 ½ pounds ground chicken
1 teaspoon dried basil
2 cups jasmine rice, cooked
1/2 cup scallions, finely chopped
3 garlic cloves, finely minced
½ tablespoon herb-infused olive oil
1/2 teaspoon dried rosemary
1/3 cup melted butter
1 teaspoon garlic salt
1/3 teaspoon ground black pepper, or more to taste

Directions

- Cook the chicken along with the chopped scallions and garlic in a pan that is placed over a moderate flame.
- Throw in the jasmine rice, 4 whole eggs, herb-infused olive oil, butter, cheese, black pepper, and garlic salt. Let it rest in the refrigerator approximately 50 minutes.
- Shape the mixture into small balls. Beat the remaining 1 egg in a shallow bowl; in another bowl, combine all the remaining herbs with seasoned breadcrumbs.
- Coat each ball with the whisked egg on all sides; then, roll them over the herb/breadcrumb mixture.
- Air-fry at 385 degrees F for about 7 minutes, working in batches. Serve with toothpicks.

400. Must Serve Turkey with Kidney Beans

Ready in about 20 minutes
Servings 4

A freezer friendly dish that cooks up fast in your Air fryer! Let this recipe show you what turkey and beans can do!
Per serving: 210 Calories; 19.3g Fat; 6g Carbs; 6.9g Protein; 1.8g Sugars

Ingredients

1/2 can kidney beans
2 cups scallions, chopped
1 teaspoon dried oregano
1/2 can crushed tomatoes
1 teaspoon dried oregano
3 small-sized turkey breasts, cut into bite-sized chunks
1/3 cup roasted vegetable stock
1/2 teaspoon dried basil
1 teaspoon sea salt
Freshly cracked black peppercorns, to savor
3 bay leaves

Directions

- Add the turkey to the air fryer basket; then, cook at 375 degrees F for about 12 minutes, working in batches.
- Transfer the turkey to a lightly-oiled baking dish.
- Stir in the remaining ingredients in the order listed above; air-fry for a further 8 minutes; serve warm dolloped with sour cream. Bon appétit!

401. Nacho Hash Browns

Ready in about 17 minutes
Servings 4

This is a very creative recipe for hash browns because it uses tortilla chip crumbs as a topping and condensed nacho cheese soup to blend and enhance the flavors.

Per serving: 219 Calories; 16.3g Fat; 17.4g Carbs; 28g Protein; 2.2g Sugars

Ingredients

½ cup Cheddar cheese, shredded
½ cup refried beans
1 teaspoon cayenne pepper
1 cup hash brown potatoes, shredded
1 ½ tablespoons butter, melted
1/3 cup tortilla chip crumbs
2 shallots, peeled and chopped
1/3 cup cream cheese of choice
5 ounces condensed nacho cheese soup, undiluted
3 cloves garlic, peeled and finely minced
Fine sea salt and ground black pepper, to taste

Directions

- In a mixing bowl, beat cream cheese along with the nacho cheese soup, salt, ground black pepper, and cayenne pepper. Stir in hash brown potatoes, refried beans, shallot, garlic, and Cheddar cheese. Stir until everything is well combined.
- Spoon this mixture into a baking dish.
- Then, grab another mixing bowl, combine the tortilla chip crumbs with butter. Spread this mixture evenly over the top of hash brown mixture.
- Bake at 295 degrees approximately 10 minutes. Bon appétit!

402. Turkey, Leek and Dark Beer Chili

Ready in about 40 minutes
Servings 6

Here is a clever way to spice up your boring turkey meat. This flavor-filled chili is ready in 40 minutes.

Per serving: 322 Calories; 21.2g Fat; 11.3g Carbs; 24.9g Protein; 2.8g Sugars

Ingredients

1 ½ pounds ground turkey
1/2 can diced tomatoes
1/2 parsnip, coarsely chopped
1/3 cup vegetable stock
1 ½ teaspoons mustard powder
1/2 heaping tablespoon cilantro
1/2 cup dark beer
1/2 heaping tablespoon parsley
1/2 Habanero pepper, deveined minced
2 leeks, finely chopped
12 ounce canned beans, with liquid
1/3 teaspoon chili powder
2 cloves garlic, minced
1 teaspoon mixed peppercorns, ground
1/2 sweet pepper, deveined and thinly sliced
Kosher salt, to taste

Directions

- Spritz the inside of a baking dish with pan spray of your choice; throw in the leek, garlic, parsnip, sweet pepper, and Habanero pepper; air-fry for 4 minutes at 365 degrees F. Pause the machine.
- After that, throw in the turkey mince; continue to cook for 4-5 minutes or until meat is no longer pink. Then, add the stock, dark beer, chili powder, parsley, cilantro, and tomatoes. Cook for a further 18 minutes.
- Pause the machine again. Throw in the canned beans, mustard powder, peppercorns, and kosher salt; air-fry for 8 more minutes. Work in batches as needed. Bon appétit!

403. Pasta with Ground Turkey Sauce

Ready in about 30 minutes
Servings 4

Aromatic scents will fill your kitchen as this classic Italian-style dish cooks away in your Air fryer. Amazing!

Per serving: 302 Calories; 25.4g Fat; 6.4g Carbs; 11.9g Protein; 4g Sugars

Ingredients

1 ½ can chopped tomatoes
1 teaspoon red pepper flakes, crushed
1/2 pound ground turkey
1/2 onion, peeled and chopped
1/2 package elbow pasta, cooked
1/2 chipotle, finely minced
3 cloves garlic, finely minced
1 teaspoon mixed peppercorns, freshly cracked
1 teaspoon onion salt

Directions

- Simply throw the ground turkey along with garlic and onion into an oven safe bowl; air-fry for 10 minutes at 395 degrees F.
- After that, throw in the other ingredients, minus elbow pasta; air-fry for a further 17 minutes. Serve over warm elbow pasta and enjoy!

404. Jumbo Prawns with Green Beans

Ready in about 20 minutes
Servings 3

Enjoy restaurant-style jumbo prawns any day of the week. They're served with ultra-easy green beans for a fresh taste and a touch of spring.

Per serving: 44 Calories; 2.1g Fat; 6.3g Carbs; 1.4g Protein; 1.2g Sugars

Ingredients

9 jumbo prawns
1/2 tablespoon fish sauce
1/2 teaspoon mustard powder
1/2 teaspoon cornstarch
1/2 teaspoon sugar
1/2 pound green beans
1 teaspoon porcini powder
1/2 cup water
Sea salt flakes and celery seeds, to savor
1/2 teaspoon coarse salt
1/3 teaspoon freshly ground pepper

Directions

- Simply throw the green beans, sea salt flakes and the celery seeds into the cooking basket; then, air-fry at 385 degrees for 13 to 15 minutes.
- Place the remaining ingredients in the baking dish; cook for 6 more minutes and serve with the prepared green beans. Bon appétit!

405. Spaghetti with Saucy Shrimp

Ready in about 15 minutes
Servings 4

You don't have to cook as an Italian nonna to make the perfect spaghetti! Thanks to the Air fryer, this amazing, Italian-inspired dinner will turn out great and will be ready when you are.

Per serving: 318 Calories; 11.2g Fat; 15.6g Carbs; 37.6g Protein; 3.6g Sugars

Ingredients

1 teaspoon crushed red pepper flakes
1 teaspoon ground mace
1 1/4 package spaghetti
1/2 cup Italian dressing
1 ½ pound shrimps, deveined
1/3 teaspoon ground allspice
1 ½ tablespoons dry white wine
1 ½ tablespoons extra-virgin olive oil
1 teaspoon mixed peppercorns, freshly cracked
1/3 teaspoon dry mustard
1/2 teaspoon celery salt
1/3 teaspoon ground nutmeg

Directions

- Start by preheating the air fryer to 385 degrees F.
- In a bowl, toss all the ingredients, minus the spaghetti and the Italian dressing; make sure to coat the shrimps on all sides.
- Dump the shrimps into the cooking basket and air-fry for 7 to 8 minutes. Add the spaghetti and the Italian dressing. Bon appétit!

406. Aromatic Turkey-Rice Balls

Ready in about 2 hours 10 minutes
Servings 6

If you are aware how important it is to make smart food choices, you will love this recipe. Check out this spin on a classic family favorite.

Per serving: 346 Calories; 26g Fat; 24.2g Carbs; 19.9g Protein; 2g Sugars

Ingredients

2 cups jasmine rice, cooked
1/2 cup Cotija cheese, crumbled
1/2 cup crushed crackers
3 large-sized eggs, well beaten
1 pound turkey, ground
2 white onions, finely chopped
1/2 sprig thyme, roughly chopped
4 garlic cloves, finely minced
Salt and ground black pepper, to savor
1/3 melted butter

Directions

- Cook the turkey along with the onion, garlic, and thyme in a nonstick skillet over a moderate flame. Cook until the turkey is no longer pink.
- Stir in the other ingredients, minus the eggs and crushed crackers. Place in the refrigerator for 3 hours.
- Shape into bite-sized balls. Place the beaten egg in a shallow bowl. Throw the crushed crackers into another bowl.
- Coat each ball with the beaten eggs; then, roll them over the crushed crackers. Air-fry in the preheated air fryer at 375 degrees F for about 12 minutes, working in batches. Eat warm.

407. Beef and Barley Stuffed Peppers

Ready in about 25 minutes
Servings 4

Barley is a great source of vitamins, minerals, fiber, and antioxidants. It can help you fight heart diseases, lower high cholesterol levels and improve digestion.

Per serving: 452 Calories; 24g Fat; 46.4g Carbs; 15.8g Protein; 4.6g Sugars

Ingredients

1/3 cup beef stock
5 ounces lean ground beef
3 bell peppers
1 cup barley, cooked
2 teaspoons celery seeds
1 1/2 cups green onions, finely chopped
1 ½ cups crushed canned tomatoes
1/teaspoon dried marjoram
1/3 cup olive oil
1/3 teaspoon ground allspice
3 green garlic, finely minced
2 bay leaves

Directions

- Place a deep saucepan over a moderate flame and heat the oil until it starts to smoke; sweat green onion, green garlic and beef in the hot oil until the onion is translucent and the garlic is fragrant; afterward, drain off any excess grease.
- Stir in 1 cup of canned tomatoes followed by seasonings and cooked barley; stir until everything is well combined.
- Now, slice off the tops of your peppers and discard the seeds. Stuff your peppers with the prepared filling and add the reserved tops. Lay your peppers in a baking dish that is previously greased with a thin layer of vegetable oil.
- Whisk the remaining 1/2 cup of tomatoes with the beef stock and pour it into the dish. Cover with a piece of foil and cook for 12 minutes at 365degrees F. Now, remove the foil and cook an additional 11 minutes. Bon appétit!

408. Rich Turkey and Chipotle Chili

Ready in about 40 minutes
Servings 6

This amazing chili is packed with lean protein and a good amount of vegetables. Use lean ground turkey to reduce the fat but not the flavor.

Per serving: 388 Calories; 28.6g Fat; 17.6g Carbs; 15.7g Protein; 3.9g Sugars

Ingredients

2 medium-sized carrots, coarsely chopped
1/2 heaping tablespoon cilantro
1 ½ teaspoons ground cumin
1/2 can diced tomatoes
1 pound ground turkey
3 chipotles, deveined and minced
1 ½ cups chicken or turkey stock
2 stalks celery, coarsely chopped
1/2 red onion, finely chopped
14 ounce canned red kidney beans, with liquid
2 sweet peppers, deveined and thinly sliced
1 1/2 tablespoons canola oil
3 cloves garlic, minced
1/3 teaspoon chili powder
1/3 teaspoon hot sauce
2 bay leaves
Onion salt and ground black pepper, to taste
Lime slices, for garnish

Directions

- Grease the inside of a baking dish with 1 1/2 tablespoons of canola oil; throw in the garlic, onions, celery, carrots, chipotles, and sweet pepper; air-fry for 4 minutes at 355 degrees F. Pause the machine.
- After that, throw in the turkey mince; continue to cook for 7 minutes or until meat is no longer pink. Then, add stock, chili powder, cilantro, and tomatoes. Cook for a further 19 minutes.
- Pause the machine again. Throw in kidney beans, hot sauce, bay leaf, cumin, salt, and ground black pepper; air-fry for 9 more minutes. Serve garnished with sliced lime. Bon appétit!

409. Turkey Tortilla Wraps

Ready in about 2 hours + 20 minutes
Servings 4

Tortilla wraps in an Air fryer. Why not? As a matter of fact, this quick-fix version of family favorite turns out great every single time!

Per serving: 195 Calories; 9.1g Fat; 23.3g Carbs; 6g Protein; 0.4g Sugars

Ingredients

8 corn tortillas
1/2 tablespoon Dijon mustard
1/2 small-sized red onion, thinly sliced
1 ½ tablespoons vegetable oil
1/3 cup Mexican blend cheese, shredded
1 turkey breasts, halved
1/2 teaspoon Tabasco
1 teaspoon garlic powder
2 teaspoons white vinegar
1/3 teaspoon kosher salt
1/3 teaspoon black pepper

Directions

- Combine the turkey, Tabasco, black pepper, kosher salt, garlic powder, white vinegar, and vegetable oil in a mixing bowl. Cover and let it marinate at least 2 hours.
- After that, preheat the air fryer to 355 degrees F; drain the turkey and air-fry for 23 minutes. Allow it to cool slightly.
- Shred the turkey with meat claws. To assemble your wraps, microwave the tortillas. Spread the tortillas with Dijon mustard.
- Divide the turkey filling among warm tortillas; add Mexican blend cheese and red onion; roll them tightly. Bon appétit!

410. Easiest Turkey Chili Ever

Ready in about 45 minutes
Servings 6

This chili makes any Air-fryer skeptic a believer. You will go from cupboard to table in 45 minutes with this staple meal.

Per serving: 235 Calories; 20.5g Fat; 5g Carbs; 8.3g Protein; 1.9g Sugars

Ingredients

1/2 pounds turkey ground
1/2 can diced tomatoes
10 ounces canned beans, with liquid
1 1/3 cups vegetable broth
2 green bell peppers, seeded and diced
1 ½ tablespoons olive oil
1/2 red onion, finely chopped
1/3 teaspoon Tabasco sauce
1/2 teaspoon chili powder
2 red or orange bell peppers, seeded and diced
1/3 teaspoon dried parsley flakes
Kosher salt and freshly ground black pepper, to taste
3 cloves garlic, minced
3 bay leaves

Directions

- First of all, grease the bottom and sides of a baking dish with olive oil; throw in the garlic, onions, and bell pepper; air-fry for 4 minutes at 355 degrees F. Pause the machine.
- Stir in ground turkey and continue cooking for 3 minutes. Then, add vegetable broth, chili powder, dried parsley, and tomatoes. Cook for a further 18 minutes.
- Pause the machine again. Throw in the beans, Tabasco sauce, bay leaves, salt, and ground black pepper; let it cook for a further 9 minutes. Serve dolloped with sour cream if desired. Bon appétit!

411. Pasta with Ground Turkey Sauce

Ready in about 30 minutes
Servings 4

What is the onion salt? As its name suggests, it is the mixture of onions powder and table salt.

Per serving: 302 Calories; 25.4g Fat; 6.4g Carbs; 11.9g Protein; 4g Sugars

Ingredients

1 ½ can chopped tomatoes
1 teaspoon red pepper flakes, crushed
1/2 pound ground turkey
1/2 onion, peeled and chopped
1/2 package elbow pasta, cooked
1/2 chipotle, finely minced
3 cloves garlic, finely minced
1 teaspoon mixed peppercorns, freshly cracked
1 teaspoon onion salt

Directions

- Simply throw the ground turkey along with garlic and onion into an oven safe bowl; air-fry for 10 minutes at 395 degrees F.
- After that, throw in the other ingredients, minus elbow pasta; air-fry for a further 17 minutes. Serve over warm elbow pasta and enjoy!

412. Beef and Barley Meatballs

Ready in about 10 minutes
Servings 6

How to make meatballs even better? Make them in the Air fryer, and add barley!

Per serving: 440 Calories; 27g Fat; 15g Carbs; 34g Protein; 0.8g Sugars

Ingredients

2 eggs, well whisked
1/3 teaspoon sweet paprika
½ cup spent barley, wet
½ cup minced shallots
1 ½ pounds ground pork
1 teaspoon salt flakes
1/3 teaspoon coriander
4 cloves garlic, minced
½ teaspoon ground black pepper, or more to taste

Directions

- Simply mix all ingredients in a mixing dish.
- Shape into bite-sized balls; cook the meatballs in the air fryer for 13 minutes at 365 degrees F. Serve with mustard sauce if desired. Bon appétit!

413. Fried Basmati Rice with Prawns

Ready in about 15 minutes
Servings 3

As the combination of fresh from the sea prawns, honey and garlic wasn't enough for you, we added aromatic basmati rice for a fabulous, highly addictive meal.

Per serving: 218 Calories; 7.8g Fat; 34.2g Carbs; 5.3g Protein; 12.4g Sugars

Ingredients

3 parsnips, trimmed and chopped
1/2 tablespoon Worcestershire sauce
1/3 cup fresh parsley, chopped
1/2 tablespoon honey
3 ounces basmati rice, cooked
8 prawns, deveined
1 clove garlic, minced
1 ½ tablespoons peanut oil
1 carrot, trimmed and chopped
Salt and pepper, to your liking

Directions

- Mix the first eight ingredients in a baking tray that fits in your air fryer; cook in batches as needed. Air-fry for 9 minutes at 385 degrees F.
- Throw in basmati rice and air-fry for a further 6 minutes.
- Taste, adjust for seasonings and garnish with fresh parsley. Bon appétit!

414. Festive Baked Green Beans

Ready in about 16 minutes
Servings 4

With a trio of green beans, eggs and breadcrumbs, this great dish takes your holiday menu to a new level. Serve with bite-sized cubes of Feta cheese.

Per serving: 294 Calories; 17.7g Fat; 22.7g Carbs; 12.4g Protein; 2g Sugars

Ingredients

1/3 cup breadcrumbs
3 eggs
1 ½ tablespoon olive oil
1 teaspoon coarse ground black pepper
9 ounces green beans
2 teaspoons garlic paste
1 teaspoon fine sea salt
2 ½ tablespoons minced shallot
1/2 teaspoon cayenne pepper

Directions

- Take three shallow mixing dishes. In the first dish, thoroughly combine the flour, garlic paste, and minced shallot; mix well to combine.
- In the second dish, combine the breadcrumbs with the seasonings. Whisk the eggs in the third mixing dish.
- Next step, coat the beans with the flour mixture. Next, dip the beans in the whisked eggs; lastly, toss them in the breadcrumb mixture.
- Transfer the beans to the air fryer baking dish; drizzle with olive oil; bake at 345 degrees F for 10 minutes. Serve immediately.

VEGAN

415. Perfect Vegetable Kebabs..227

416. Cauliflower with Sesame and Corn 227

417. Indian-Style Fritters (Bhaji)..................................228

418. Roasted Sweet Potatoes with Garlic Mayo............228

419. Yummy Carrot Sticks with Hummus 229

420. Hearty Asparagus and Tofu Scramble..................229

421. Mediterranean Roasted Potatoes 230

422. Tofu Scramble Spring Rolls....................................230

423. Delicious Balls with Vegan Cheese 231

425. Super Yummy Veggie Sticks 231

426. Falafel with Vegan Tzatziki 232

427. Golden Crunchy Tofu Cubes..................................232

428. Homemade Potato Chips 233

429. Salsa and Veggie Wraps..233

430. Nutty and Spicy Corn on the Cob 234

415. Perfect Vegetable Kebabs

Ready in about 20 minutes
Servings 4

Colorful and delicious vegan kebabs! Make sure to soak the bamboo skewers in water at least 2 hours before using them.

Per serving: 249 Calories; 14.2g Fat; 29.1g Carbs; 3.0g Protein; 7.1g Sugars

Ingredients

3 medium-sized carrots, cut into thick slices
2 parsnips, cut into thick slices
1 fennel, diced
1 teaspoon whole grain mustard
2 cloves garlic, pressed
1 red onion, cut into wedges
2 tablespoons dry white wine
1/4 cup sesame oil
1 teaspoon sea salt flakes
1/2 teaspoon ground black pepper
1 teaspoon smoked paprika

Directions

- Place all of the above ingredients in a mixing dish; toss to coat well. Alternately thread vegetables onto the bamboo skewers.
- Cook on the Air Fryer grill pan for 15 minutes at 380 degrees F. Flip them over halfway through the cooking time.
- Taste, adjust the seasonings and serve warm.

416. Cauliflower with Sesame and Corn

Ready in about 25 minutes
Servings 4

To make cauliflower crumbles, you can use a cheese grater or a food processor. If you want to skip the rice, cauliflower rice is a perfect alternative. You will love it!

Per serving: 131 Calories; 5.1g Fat; 20.3g Carbs; 4.3g Protein; 4.5g Sugars

Ingredients

2 cups cauliflower crumbles
1 onion, peeled and finely chopped
1 tablespoon sesame oil
3 tablespoons tamari sauce
3 cloves garlic, peeled and pressed
1 tablespoon ginger, freshly grated
1 tablespoon fresh parsley, finely chopped
1/3 cup of lime juice
1 ½ cups frozen corn kernels
1 tablespoon sesame seeds

Directions

- Combine the cauliflower crumbles, onion, sesame oil, tamari sauce, garlic, and the ginger in a mixing dish; stir until everything's well incorporated.
- Air-fry at 400 degrees F for 12 minutes.
- Pause the Air Fryer. Add the parsley, lemon juice, and corn. Turn the machine to cook at 390 degrees F; cook additional 10 minutes.
- Meanwhile, toast the sesame seeds in a non-stick skillet; stir them constantly over a medium-low flame. Sprinkle over prepared cauliflower crumbles and serve warm.

417. Indian-Style Fritters (Bhaji)

Ready in about 40 minutes
Servings 4

This is such a comforting dish with gram flour, onions, and Indian green chili. Being vegan is so easy!

Per serving: 214 Calories; 4.0g Fat; 29.0g Carbs; 10.3g Protein; 6.7g Sugars

Ingredients

1 cup garbanzo bean flour (gram flour)
1/3 teaspoon baking powder
1 teaspoon curry paste
Salt and pepper, to your liking
2 red onions, chopped
1 Indian green chili, pureed
Non-stick cooking spray

Directions

- Place the first 4 ingredients in a mixing dish; to make the thick batter, add cold water
- Now, add onions and chili pepper; mix until everything is well incorporated.
- Shape the balls and slightly press them to make the patties. Spritz the patties with cooking oil on all sides.
- Place a sheet of aluminum foil in the Air Fryer food basket. Place the fritters on foil.
- Then, air-fry them at 360 degrees F for 15 minutes; flip them over, press the power button and cook for another 20 minutes. Serve right away!

418. Roasted Sweet Potatoes with Garlic Mayo

Ready in about 30 minutes
Servings 4

This cold-weather comfort food is simply irresistible! You can serve it as a warm appetizer but, it could probably become your main dish.

Per serving: 303 Calories; 11.2g Fat; 39.2g Carbs; 2.6g Protein; 2.7g Sugars

Ingredients

8 sweet potatoes, cut into wedges
1 teaspoon peanut oil
1/2 teaspoon celery salt
1/4 teaspoon red pepper flakes, crushed
1/2 cup vegan mayonnaise
1 clove garlic, minced
1 teaspoon lemon juice

Directions

- Toss sweet potatoes with peanut oil, celery salt, and red pepper flakes.
- Air-fry them at 380 degrees F for 10 minutes. Shake the cooking basket and cook for 20 minutes more.
- In the meantime, thoroughly combine the mayonnaise, garlic, and lemon juice.
- When the sweet potato wedges come out of the Air Fryer, check them for doneness. Serve with garlic mayonnaise and enjoy!

419. Yummy Carrot Sticks with Hummus

Ready in about 20 minutes
Servings 2

As a dinner or on-the-go combo, these carrots will satisfy your hunger during busy days. It will be ready in less than 20 minutes. Lovely!

Per serving: 137 Calories; 6.8g Fat; 18.4g Carbs; 1.6g Protein; 9.0g Sugars

Ingredients

5 carrots, washed, debris removed and sliced lengthways
1 teaspoon sea salt flakes
1/2 teaspoon white pepper
1/4 teaspoon dried dill weed
1 tablespoon sesame oil
Humus, for dipping

Directions

- Start by preheating your Air Fryer to cook at 370 degrees F.
- Toss the carrots with sea salt flakes, white pepper, dill, sesame oil, covering them on all sides.
- Now, air-fry them in the cooking basket for 12 minutes; shake the basket halfway through the cooking time.
- Serve warm with hummus (store-bought or homemade) for dipping. Bon appétit!

420. Hearty Asparagus and Tofu Scramble

Ready in about 15 minutes
Servings 2

If you like to experiment with scramble recipes, you should try this one. This whole dish comes together in the Air Fryer!

Per serving: 160 Calories; 10.8g Fat; 8.5g Carbs; 8.9g Protein; 3.5g Sugars

Ingredients

1 tablespoon sesame oil
10 ounces soft silken tofu, drained and chopped
6 ounces asparagus, chopped
2 garlic cloves, finely minced
1 teaspoon fresh lemon juice
1 tablespoon soy sauce
1/2 teaspoon paprika
1/2 teaspoon coarse salt
Freshly cracked mixed peppercorns, to taste
1/2 cup fresh basil, roughly chopped

Directions

- Grease a baking dish using the sesame oil. Now, add in the tofu and cook for 8 minutes at 370 degrees F.
- Stir in the other ingredients, except the basil leaves; cook for a further 6 minutes.
- Serve warm garnished with fresh basil leaves. Bon appétit!

421. Mediterranean Roasted Potatoes

Ready in about 15 minutes
Servings 2

A hot air circulates around potatoes so they get super crispy! Enjoy these outstanding, rich, Mediterranean flavors.

Per serving: 240 Calories; 10.9g Fat; 34.1g Carbs; 3.8g Protein; 2.4g Sugars

Ingredients

4 Russet potatoes, peeled and cut into wedges
1 tablespoon olive oil
1 teaspoon fresh lemon juice
2 sprigs thyme, chopped
1 sprig rosemary, chopped
1 teaspoon oregano
1/2 teaspoon basil
1/2 teaspoon seasoned salt
1/4 teaspoon freshly cracked peppercorns
Kalamata olives, for garnish

Directions

- Toss the potatoes with all the remaining ingredients but not the olives.
- Air-fry them at 360 degrees F for 10 minutes.
- Pause the machine and shake the basket; cook for additional 3 minutes. Serve warm with Kalamata olives.

422. Tofu Scramble Spring Rolls

Ready in about 25 minutes
Servings 4

This intensely flavored food makes a great breakfast for your family. Also, you can add chili peppers to spice them up.

Per serving: 335 Calories; 11.5g Fat; 41.5g Carbs; 20.4g Protein; 4.0g Sugars

Ingredients

4 pieces spring roll rice paper wrappers
1 (14-ounce) package extra-firm tofu, rinsed and pressed
1 sweet onion, diced
1 cup Cremini mushrooms, cleaned and sliced
1/4 cup fresh parsley, minced
Salt and black pepper, to taste
1/2 teaspoon turmeric powder
1/4 teaspoon cumin powder
1/2 teaspoon dried dill weed
1 sweet bell pepper, deveined and sliced
2 tablespoons nutritional yeast
2 tablespoons almond butter
2 tablespoons soy sauce
2 tablespoons coconut water

Directions

- Lightly grease an Air Fryer baking dish using non-stick cooking oil. Now, put the tofu in; stir and cook for 8 minutes at 370 degrees F. Make sure to stir once or twice so the tofu doesn't stick to the bottom of the dish.
- Then, put the sweet onions, mushrooms, parsley, salt, pepper, turmeric, cumin, dill, bell pepper, and nutritional yeasts; set the timer for 6 more minutes and press the power button.
- In the meantime, whisk the other ingredients in a small mixing dish. Lay the rice paper wrappers flat on a work surface and fill with the prepared veggie tofu scramble.
- Wrap the rolls and dip each one into the almond butter mixture. Air-fry at 355 degrees F for about 10 minutes; check for doneness and cook for a few minutes longer if needed. Bon appétit!

423. Delicious Balls with Vegan Cheese

Ready in about 30 minutes
Servings 6

Forget about fast food and make these homemade vegan balls! Cheap and delicious, these balls are ready in about 30 minutes.

Per serving: 313 Calories; 18.6g Fat; 31.9g Carbs; 4.3g Protein; 0.0g Sugars

Ingredients

2 cups of cake flour
A pinch of salt
1/2 cup canola oil
Water
1 cup vegan cheese, cubed
1/2 cup green coriander, minced
1/4 teaspoon cumin powder
1 teaspoon dried parsley flakes

Directions

- Firstly, make the dough by mixing the flour, salt, and canola oil; add water and knead it into dough. Let it stay for about 20 minutes.
- Divide the dough into equal size balls. Sprinkle cheese cubes with green coriander, cumin powder, and parsley.
- Now, press the cheese cubes down into the center of the dough balls. Then, pinch the edges securely to form a ball. Repeat with the rest of the dough.
- Lay the balls in the Air Fryer's cooking basket; spritz each ball with a cooking spray, coating on all sides. After that, cook for 8 to 10 minutes, shaking the basket once during the cooking time. Serve with your favorite vegan sauce for dipping. Bon appétit!

425. Super Yummy Veggie Sticks

Ready in about 20 minutes
Servings 4

You don't have to buy veggie sticks, you can make your own! These veggie sticks can be made with leftovers but, if you are able, try to use hearts of palm! You won't regret it.

Per serving: 167 Calories; 5.6g Fat; 24.4g Carbs; 6.3g Protein; 1.8g Sugars

Ingredients

14 ounces canned hearts of palm, drained
1/4 cup seasoned breadcrumbs
1 ½ teaspoons soy sauce
Salt and freshly ground black pepper, to taste
1 teaspoon cayenne pepper

For the Breading:
1 tablespoon olive oil
1 cup seasoned breadcrumbs
3/4 teaspoon dried dill weed

Directions

- Firstly, pulse the hearts of palm in your food processor; transfer them to a bowl and add 1/4 cup seasoned breadcrumbs, soy sauce, salt, black pepper, and cayenne pepper. Roll the mixture into veggie fingers shape.
- In another bowl, thoroughly combine the breading items.
- Now, coat the veggie fingers with the breading, covering completely.
- Air-fry for 15 minutes at 350 degrees F; turn them over once or twice during the cooking time. Eat with your favorite vegan sauce.

426. Falafel with Vegan Tzatziki

Ready in about 30 minutes
Servings 4

Falafel is an important part of Middle Eastern cuisine. It can be served with hummus, tahini sauce and salads. However, Greek Tzatziki works well too!

Per serving: 311 Calories; 12.5g Fat; 35.9g Carbs; 16.2g Protein; 8.0g Sugars

Ingredients

For the Falafel:
1 cup chickpea flour
1/4 teaspoon baking powder
1/3 cup warm water
1/2 teaspoon salt
1 tablespoon coriander leaves, finely chopped
2 tablespoons fresh lemon juice

For the Vegan Tzatziki:
12 ounces firm silken tofu
2 tablespoons lime juice, freshly squeezed
1/4 teaspoon ground black pepper, or more to taste
1/3 teaspoon sea salt flakes
1 teaspoon garlic powder
2 tablespoons olive oil
1 fresh cucumber, grated
1 tablespoon fresh dill, chopped

Directions

- In a bowl, thoroughly combine all the ingredients for the falafel. Allow the mixture to stay for approximately 10 minutes.
- Now, air-fry at 390 degrees F for 15 minutes; make sure to flip them over halfway through the cooking time.
- To make the Vegan Tzatziki, mix silken tofu, lime juice, black pepper, and salt in your food processor. Add the garlic powder and the olive oil and mix again.
- Stir in squeezed cucumber and dill; mix to combine well. Serve chilled with the warm falafel.

427. Golden Crunchy Tofu Cubes

Ready in about 40 minutes
Servings 4

These tofu cubes are perfect on sandwiches, herbed rice, or all by itself. If you have the time, marinate the tofu cubes longer than 30 minutes. The longer they sit in the marinade, the more flavorful they will be!

Per serving: 106 Calories; 5.4g Fat; 6.0g Carbs; 8.4g Protein; 2.0g Sugars

Ingredients

16 ounces firm tofu, pressed and cubed
Sea salt, to taste
2 tablespoons tamari sauce
1 tablespoon orange juice
3/4 teaspoon grated ginger root
1/2 teaspoon red chili powder
2 teaspoons dark toasted sesame oil
1 garlic clove, crushed
2 tablespoons tapioca starch

Directions

- Place all the ingredients, without the tapioca starch, in a mixing bowl; let it marinate for approximately 30 minutes.
- Next, sprinkle tapioca starch over the tofu cubes. Cook in the Air Fryer cooking basket at 375 degrees F for 10min.
- Then, pause the machine and shake the basket to ensure that the cubes cook evenly. Bon appétit!

428. Homemade Potato Chips

Ready in about 55 minutes
Servings 4

There's no need to use tons of fat to make delicious crispy potato chips — an Air Fryer is just fine. You can also experiment with spices and herbs and season them to your liking.

Per serving: 157 Calories; 1.4g Fat; 33.5g Carbs; 3.6g Protein; 2.5g Sugars

Ingredients

4 potatoes, peeled and sliced
1 teaspoon canola oil
Sea salt, to your liking

Directions

- Soak the potatoes in cold water for 25 minutes. Place the potato slices on paper towels to pat them dry.
- Toss them with canola oil and salt.
- Air-fry at 390 degrees F for 20 to 25 minutes.

429. Salsa and Veggie Wraps

Ready in about 15 minutes
Servings 4

Are you looking for more lunch options? Once you try these vegan wraps, you will make them over and over again. You can change the toppings and spices as well.

Per serving: 165 Calories; 5.9g Fat; 19.1g Carbs; 11.0g Protein; 3.8g Sugars

Ingredients

1 cup red onion, sliced
1 zucchini, chopped
1 poblano pepper, deveined and finely chopped
4 large-sized tortillas
1/2 cup salsa (homemade or store-bought)
4 tablespoons vegan mozzarella cheese
Iceberg lettuce, for garnish

Directions

- Begin by preheating your Air Fryer to 390 degrees F.
- In a sauté pan, cook red onion, zucchini, and poblano pepper until they are tender and fragrant.
- Divide the sautéed mixture among the 4 tortillas; spoon salsa over the top. Finish off with vegan mozzarella cheese. Wrap your tortillas around the filling.
- Air-fry them for 7 minutes in the preheated machine, flipping over halfway through the cooking time. Serve with fresh iceberg lettuce and enjoy!

430. Nutty and Spicy Corn on the Cob

Ready in about 15 minutes
Servings 4

One word: Corn! This amazing vegan dish goes either with vegan mayo or vegan mozzarella. Let your imagination run wild!

Per serving: 233 Calories; 13.5g Fat; 27.0g Carbs; 7.4g Protein; 4.3g Sugars

Ingredients

4 pieces corn on the cob, shucked
1 tablespoon sesame oil
1 tablespoon five-spice powder
1 teaspoon grated ginger root
Salt and pepper, to taste
1 teaspoon soy sauce
1/2 cup walnuts, chopped and toasted

Directions

- Brush corn with sesame oil. Now, in a small bowl, combine the five-spice powder, ginger, salt, pepper, and soy sauce.
- Rub the corn with the spiced mixture. Arrange them on an Air Fryer grill pan and set the machine to cook at 390 degrees F.
- Grill for 10 minutes, flipping over halfway through the cooking time. Serve garnished with chopped walnuts.

DESSERTS

431. Mini Strawberry Pies with Sugar Crust 236

432. Fudgy Coconut Brownies 236

433. Easiest Chocolate Lava Cake Ever 237

434. Chocolate Banana Cake 237

435. Butter Sugar Fritters 238

436. Father's Day Fried Pineapple Rings 238

437. Oaty Plum and Apple Crumble 239

438. Butter Lemon Pound Cake 239

439. Festive Double-Chocolate Cake 240

440. Apple and Pear Crisp with Walnuts 240

441. Family Coconut Banana Treat 241

442. Old-Fashioned Swirled German Cake 241

443. Vanilla and Banana Pastry Puffs 242

444. Party Hazelnut Brownie Cups 242

445. Sultana Cupcakes with Buttercream Icing 243

446. Last-Minute Cherry and Almond Dessert 243

447. Vegan Croissant Bread Pudding 244

448. Blackberry Chocolate Pound Cake 244

449. Dad's Orange Custards 245

450. Chocolate Cake with Pine Nuts 245

451. Strawberry Cheesecake Roll-Ups 246

452. Healthy Cinnamon Tortilla Chips 246

453. Old-Fashioned Fig Cake 247

454. Mother's Day Peanut Cupcakes 247

455. Apple Pie Roll-Ups with Walnuts 248

456. Easy Orange Fritters 248

457. Super Yummy Blueberry Tartlets 249

458. Creamed Peach and Almond Dessert 249

459. Mini Raspberry Tarts 250

460. Classic Raisin Bread Pudding 250

461. Apple Pie Bread Pudding with Pecans 251

462. Holiday Plum Clafoutis 251

463. Surprisingly Delicious Banana Beignets 252

464. Chocolate Mini Cheesecakes 252

465. Apple and Cranberry Dumplings 253

466. Aromatic Baked Plum Dessert 253

467. One-More-Bite Strawberry and Almond Cake ... 254

468. Ciabatta Chocolate Bread Pudding 254

469. Flavorsome Peach Cake 255

470. Lemon Mini Pies with Coconut 255

471. Cheesy Orange Fritters 256

472. Nana's Special Apricot Jam Dumplings 256

473. Baked Pears with Chocolate 257

474. Festive Baileys Brownie 257

475. Coconut Strawberry Fritters 258

476. Date and Hazelnut Cookies 258

477. Air Fried Apricots in Whiskey Sauce 259

478. Almond and Orange Cake 259

479. Delicious Fall Clafoutis 260

480. Coconut and Prune Cookies 260

481. Father's Day Cranberry and Whiskey Brownies . 261

482. Air Fried Pineapple in Macadamia Batter 261

483. Granny's Raisin Muffins 262

484. Cheap Bread Pudding with Sultanas 262

485. Easy Chocolate Raspberry Cake 263

486. Almond Butter Cookies 263

487. Country-Style Coconut and
     Macadamia Cookies 264

488. Chewy White Chocolate Cookies 264

489. Cranberry Pound Cake 265

490. Chocolate and Apricot Muffins 265

491. Almond Phyllo Dough Turnovers 266

492. Butter Walnut and Raisin Cookies 266

493. Sinfully Delicious Coconut and Orange Cake 267

494. Walnut and Prune Muffins 267

495. Rich Chocolate Espresso Brownies 268

431. Mini Strawberry Pies with Sugar Crust

Ready in about 15 minutes
Servings 8

There are many ways to use canned biscuit dough in an Air Fryer! You can make these delectable fresh pies for your family in 15 minutes. Incredible!

Per serving: 237 Calories; 12.8g Fat; 28.2g Carbs; 2.7g Protein; 8.9g Sugars

Ingredients

1/2 cup powdered sugar
1/4 teaspoon ground cloves
1/8 teaspoon cinnamon powder
1 teaspoon vanilla extract
1 (12-ounce) can biscuit dough
12 ounces strawberry pie filling
1/4 cup butter, melted

Directions

- Thoroughly combine the sugar, cloves, cinnamon, and vanilla.
- Then, stretch and flatten each piece of the biscuit dough into a round circle using a rolling pin.
- Divide the strawberry pie filling among the biscuits. Roll up tightly and dip each biscuit piece into the melted butter; cover them with the spiced sugar mixture.
- Brush with a non-stick cooking oil on all sides. Air-bake them at 340 degrees F for approximately 10 minutes or until they're golden brown. Let them cool for 5 minutes before serving.

432. Fudgy Coconut Brownies

Ready in about 15 minutes
Servings 8

Chop dark chocolate into small bits so it melts quickly in your microwave. For a more vibrant flavor, crumble gingersnaps over the brownies.

Per serving: 267 Calories; 15.4g Fat; 34.0g Carbs; 1.0g Protein; 27.5g Sugars

Ingredients

1/2 cup coconut oil
2 ounces dark chocolate
1 cup sugar
2 ½ tablespoons water
4 whisked eggs
1/4 teaspoon ground cinnamon
1/2 teaspoon ground anise star
1/4 teaspoon coconut extract
1/2 teaspoon vanilla extract
1 tablespoon honey
1/2 cup cake flour
1/2 cup desiccated coconut
Icing sugar, to dust

Directions

- Microwave the coconut oil along with dark chocolate. Stir in sugar, water, eggs, cinnamon, anise, coconut extract, vanilla, and honey.
- After that, stir in the flour and coconut; mix to combine thoroughly.
- Press the mixture into a lightly buttered baking dish. Air-bake at 355 degrees F for 15 minutes.
- Let your brownie cool slightly; then, carefully remove from the baking dish and cut into squares. Dust with icing sugar. Bon appétit!

433. Easiest Chocolate Lava Cake Ever

Ready in about 20 minutes
Servings 4

With a warm, gooey center, this is a perfect gourmet dessert for any festive occasion. Only one tablespoon of honey will add a deeper flavor to your dessert.

Per serving: 549 Calories; 37.7g Fat; 47.5g Carbs; 7.1g Protein; 38.2g Sugars

Ingredients

1 cup dark cocoa candy melts
1 stick butter
2 eggs
4 tablespoons superfine sugar
1 tablespoon honey
4 tablespoons self-rising flour
A pinch of kosher salt
A pinch of ground cloves
1/4 teaspoon grated nutmeg
1/4 teaspoon cinnamon powder

Directions

- Firstly, spray four custard cups with non-stick cooking oil.
- Put the cocoa candy melts and butter into a small microwave-safe bowl; microwave on high for 30 seconds to 1 minute.
- In a mixing bowl, whisk the eggs along with sugar and honey until frothy. Add it to the chocolate mix.
- After that, add the remaining ingredients and mix to combine well. You can whisk the mixture with an electric mixer.
- Spoon the mixture into the prepared custard cups. Air-bake at 350 degrees F for 12 minutes. Take the cups out of the Air Fryer and let them rest for 5 to 6 minutes.
- Lastly, flip each cup upside-down onto a dessert plate and serve with some fruits and chocolate syrup. Bon appétit!

434. Chocolate Banana Cake

Ready in about 30 minutes
Servings 10

This is one of those desserts that taste better the following day. You can omit the frosting; the cake will be great anyway.

Per serving: 263 Calories; 10.6g Fat; 41.0g Carbs; 4.3g Protein; 16.6g Sugars

Ingredients

1 stick softened butter
1/2 cup caster sugar
1 egg
2 bananas, mashed
3 tablespoons maple syrup
2 cups self-rising flour
1/4 teaspoon anise star, ground
1/4 teaspoon ground mace
1/4 teaspoon ground cinnamon
1/4 teaspoon crystallized ginger
1/2 teaspoon vanilla paste
A pinch of kosher salt
1/2 cup cocoa powder

Directions

- Firstly, beat the softened butter and sugar until well combined.
- Then, whisk the egg, mashed banana and maple syrup. Now, add this mixture to the butter mixture; mix until pale and creamy.
- Add in the flour, anise star, mace, cinnamon, crystallized ginger, vanilla paste, and the salt; now, add the cocoa powder and mix to combine.
- Then, treat two cake pans with a non-stick cooking spray. Press the batter into the cake pans.
- Air-bake at 330 degrees F for 30 minutes. To serve, frost with chocolate butter glaze.

435. Butter Sugar Fritters

Ready in about 30 minutes
Servings 16

Fritters cook happily in an Air Fryer with the hot air making them extra crispy. If you are on your "cheat day", this recipe would be perfect for you!

Per serving: 231 Calories; 8.2g Fat; 36.6g Carbs; 3.3g Protein; 12.8g Sugars

Ingredients

For the dough:
4 cups fine cake flour
1 teaspoon kosher salt
1 teaspoon brown sugar
3 tablespoons butter, at room temperature
1 packet instant yeast
1 ¼ cups lukewarm water

For the Cakes:
1 cup caster sugar
A pinch of cardamom
1 teaspoon cinnamon powder
1 stick butter, melted

Directions

- Mix all the dry ingredients in a large-sized bowl; add the butter and yeast and mix to combine well.
- Pour lukewarm water and stir to form soft and elastic dough.
- Lay the dough on a lightly floured surface, loosely cover with greased foil and chill for 5 to 10 minutes.
- Take the dough out of the refrigerator and shape it into two logs; cut them into 20 slices.
- In a shallow bowl, mix caster sugar with cardamom and cinnamon.
- Now, brush with melted butter and coat the entire slice with sugar mix; repeat with the remaining ingredients.
- Treat the Air Fryer basket with a non-stick cooking spray. Air-fry at 360 degrees F for about 10 minutes, flipping once during the baking time. To serve, dust with icing sugar and enjoy!

436. Father's Day Fried Pineapple Rings

Ready in about 10 minutes
Servings 6

Coconut adds rich and sophisticated flavor to this amazing dessert. Also known as beignets, these pineapple rings are crispy and tender at the same time. For a more luscious taste, soak pineapple rings in rum before dipping them in the batter.

Per serving: 180 Calories; 1.8g Fat; 39.4g Carbs; 2.5g Protein; 14.9g Sugars

Ingredients

2/3 cup all-purpose flour
1/3 cup rice flour
1/2 teaspoon baking powder
1/2 teaspoon baking soda
A pinch of kosher salt
1/2 cup water
1 cup rice milk
1/2 teaspoon ground cinnamon
1/4 teaspoon ground anise star
1/2 teaspoon vanilla essence
4 tablespoons caster sugar
1/4 cup unsweetened flaked coconut
1 medium-sized pineapple, peeled and sliced

Directions

- Mix all of the above ingredients, except the pineapple. Then, coat the pineapple slices with the batter mix, covering well.
- Air-fry them at 380 degrees F for 6 to 8 minutes. Drizzle with maple syrup, garnish with a dollop of vanilla ice cream, and serve.

437. Oaty Plum and Apple Crumble

Ready in about 20 minutes
Servings 6

The fruit crumble with a crunchy, oaty topping is a delectable dessert for any occasion. You can make it in bulk because it freezes well, whole or in portions.

Per serving: 190 Calories; 7.9g Fat; 28.7g Carbs; 1.6g Protein; 16.7g Sugars

Ingredients

1/4 pound plums, pitted and chopped
1/4 pound Braeburn apples, cored and chopped
1 tablespoon fresh lemon juice
2 ½ ounces golden caster sugar
1 tablespoon honey
1/2 teaspoon ground mace
1/2 teaspoon vanilla paste
1 cup fresh cranberries
1/3 cup oats
2/3 cup flour
1/2 stick butter, chilled
1 tablespoon cold water

Directions

- Thoroughly combine the plums and apples with lemon juice, sugar, honey, and ground mace.
- Spread the fruit mixture onto the bottom of a cake pan that is previously greased with non-stick cooking oil.
- In a mixing dish, combine the other ingredients until everything is well incorporated. Spread this mixture evenly over the fruit mixture.
- Air-bake at 390 degrees F for 20 minutes or until done.

438. Butter Lemon Pound Cake

Ready in about 2 hours 20 minutes
Servings 8

Lemon is always in season, so you can enjoy this cake all year long. Adding a thick lemon glaze improves the flavor and texture of this pound cake.

Per serving: 227 Calories; 9.2g Fat; 34.3g Carbs; 4.2g Protein; 16.6g Sugars

Ingredients

1 stick softened butter
1/3 cup muscovado sugar
1 medium-sized egg
1 ¼ cups cake flour
1 teaspoon butter flavoring
1 teaspoon vanilla essence
A pinch of salt
3/4 cup milk
Grated zest of 1 medium-sized lemon

For the Glaze:
1 cup powdered sugar
2 tablespoons fresh squeezed lemon juice

Directions

- In a mixing bowl, cream the butter and sugar. Now, fold in the egg and beat again.
- Add the flour, butter flavoring, vanilla essence, and salt; mix to combine well. Afterward, add the milk and lemon zest and mix on low until everything's incorporated.
- Evenly spread a thin layer of melted butter all around the cake pan using a pastry brush. Now, press the batter into the cake pan.
- Bake at 350 degrees F for 15 minutes. After that, take the cake out of the Air Fryer and carefully run a small knife around the edges; invert the cake onto a serving platter. Allow it to cool completely.
- To make the glaze, mix powdered sugar with lemon juice. Drizzle over the top of your cake and allow hardening for about 2 hours.

439. Festive Double-Chocolate Cake

Ready in about 45 minutes
Servings 8

You can't go wrong with a classic chocolate cake for a holiday party! For a flavor-enriched version, don't skip the frosting.

Per serving: 227 Calories; 12.7g Fat; 39.5g Carbs; 3.6g Protein; 24.3g Sugars

Ingredients

1/2 cup caster sugar
1 ¼ cups cake flour
1 teaspoon baking powder
1/3 cup cocoa powder
1/4 teaspoon ground cloves
1/8 teaspoon freshly grated nutmeg
A pinch of table salt
1 egg
1/4 cup soda
1/4 cup milk
1/2 stick butter, melted
2 ounces bittersweet chocolate, melted
1/2 cup hot water

Directions

- Take two mixing bowls. Thoroughly combine the dry ingredients in the first bowl. In the second bowl, mix the egg, soda, milk, butter, and chocolate.
- Add the wet mix to the dry mix; pour in the water and mix well. Butter a cake pan that fits into your Air Fryer. Pour the mixture into the baking pan.
- Loosely cover with foil; bake at 320 degrees F for 35 minutes. Now, remove foil and bake for further 10 minutes. Frost the cake with buttercream if desired. Bon appétit!

440. Apple and Pear Crisp with Walnuts

Ready in about 25 minutes
Servings 6

Muscovado sugar is the surprising but superstar addition to this fruit crisp. It is a kind of brown sugar with a specific molasses flavor.

Per serving: 190 Calories; 5.3g Fat; 33.1g Carbs; 3.6g Protein; 13.7g Sugars

Ingredients

1/2 pound apples, cored and chopped
1/2 pound pears, cored and chopped
1 cup all-purpose flour
1/3 cup muscovado sugar
1/3 cup brown sugar
1 tablespoon butter
1 teaspoon ground cinnamon
1/4 teaspoon ground cloves
1 teaspoon vanilla extract
1/4 cup chopped walnuts
Whipped cream, to serve

Directions

- Arrange the apples and pears on the bottom of a lightly greased baking dish.
- Mix the remaining ingredients, without the walnuts and the whipped cream, until the mixture resembles the coarse crumbs.
- Spread the topping onto the fruits. Scatter chopped walnuts over all.
- Air-bake at 340 degrees F for 20 minutes or until the topping is golden brown. Check for doneness using a toothpick and serve at room temperature topped with whipped cream.

441. Family Coconut Banana Treat

Ready in about 20 minutes
Servings 6

There's nothing more uplifting than an aroma of fried banana with cinnamon and coconut! This is a child-friendly recipe that your family will love.

Per serving: 271 Calories; 6.6g Fat; 51.3g Carbs; 4.8g Protein; 19.3g Sugars

Ingredients

2 tablespoons coconut oil
3/4 cup breadcrumbs
2 tablespoons coconut sugar
1/2 teaspoon cinnamon powder
1/4 teaspoon ground cloves
6 ripe bananas, peeled and halved
1/3 cup rice flour
1 large-sized well-beaten egg

Directions

- Preheat a non-stick skillet over a moderate heat; stir the coconut oil and the breadcrumbs for about 4 minutes. Remove from the heat, add coconut sugar, cinnamon, and cloves; set it aside.
- Coat the banana halves with the rice flour, covering on all sides. Then, dip them in beaten egg. Finally, roll them over the crumb mix.
- Cook in a single layer in the Air Fryer basket at 290 degrees F for 10 minutes. Work in batches as needed.
- Serve warm or at room temperature sprinkled with flaked coconut if desired. Bon appétit!

442. Old-Fashioned Swirled German Cake

Ready in about 25 minutes
Servings 8

An old-fashioned cake makes a wonderful ending to any meal. The type of flour you use determines the texture of this dessert – a country-style with all-purpose flour, a chewy cake with self-rising flour, and light and fluffy batter with cake flour!

Per serving: 278 Calories; 13.1g Fat; 38.7g Carbs; 3.6g Protein; 25.6g Sugars

Ingredients

1 cup flour
1 teaspoon baking powder
1 cup white sugar
1/8 teaspoon kosher salt
1/4 teaspoon ground cinnamon
1/4 teaspoon grated nutmeg
1 teaspoon orange zest
1 stick butter, melted
2 eggs
1 teaspoon pure vanilla extract
1/4 cup milk
2 tablespoons unsweetened cocoa powder

Directions

- Lightly grease a round pan that fits into your Air Fryer.
- Combine the flour, baking powder, sugar, salt, cinnamon, nutmeg, and orange zest using an electric mixer. Then, fold in the butter, eggs, vanilla, and milk.
- Add 1/4 cup of the batter to the baking pan; leave the remaining batter and stir the cocoa into it. Drop by spoonful over the top of white batter. Then, swirl the cocoa batter into the white batter with a knife.
- Bake at 360 degrees F approximately 15 minutes. Let it cool for about 10 minutes.
- Finally, turn the cake out onto a wire rack.

443. Vanilla and Banana Pastry Puffs

Ready in about 15 minutes
Servings 8

In this gorgeous recipe, a good replacement for banana would be fresh strawberries and even blackberries. Dust with confectioner's sugar and enjoy!

Per serving: 308 Calories; 17.1g Fat; 34.6g Carbs; 5.2g Protein; 18.4g Sugars

Ingredients

1 package (8-ounce) crescent dinner rolls, refrigerated
1 cup of milk
4 ounces instant vanilla pudding
4 ounces cream cheese, softened
2 bananas, peeled and sliced
1 egg, lightly beaten

Directions

- Unroll crescent dinner rolls; cut into 8 squares.
- Combine the milk and the pudding; whisk in the cream cheese. Divide the pudding mixture among the pastry squares. Top with the slices of banana.
- Now, fold the dough over the filling, pressing the edges to help them seal well. Brush each pastry puff with the whisked egg.
- Air-bake at 355 degrees F for 10 minutes. Bon appétit!

444. Party Hazelnut Brownie Cups

Ready in about 30 minutes
Servings 12

Take your cocktail parties to a whole new level! This recipe is a proof that brownies come from the chocolate heaven.

Per serving: 246 Calories; 14.5g Fat; 27.5g Carbs; 2.4g Protein; 18.6g Sugars

Ingredients

6 ounces semisweet chocolate chips
1 stick butter, at room temperature
1/2 cup caster sugar
1/4 cup brown sugar
2 large-sized eggs
1/4 cup red wine
1/4 teaspoon hazelnut extract
1 teaspoon pure vanilla extract
3/4 cup all-purpose flour
2 tablespoons cocoa powder
1/2 cup ground hazelnuts
A pinch of kosher salt

Directions

- Microwave the chocolate chips with butter.
- Then, whisk the sugars, eggs, red wine, hazelnut and vanilla extract. Add to the chocolate mix.
- Stir in the flour, cocoa powder, ground hazelnuts, and a pinch of kosher salt. Mix until the batter is creamy and smooth. Divide the batter among muffin cups that are coated with cupcake liners.
- Air-bake at 360 degrees F for 28 to 30 minutes. Bake in batches and serve topped with ganache if desired.

445. Sultana Cupcakes with Buttercream Icing

Ready in about 25 minutes
Servings 6

Sultanas, also known as golden raisins, are made from seed-less white-fleshed grapes and they are similar to raisins and Zante currants. There are zillion cute ideas for cupcakes; for instance, you can make a flat rosette ideal for holidays.

Per serving: 366 Calories; 19.1g Fat; 47.4g Carbs; 2.8g Protein; 38.3g Sugars

Ingredients

For the Cupcakes:
1/2 cup all-purpose flour
1/2 teaspoon baking soda
1 baking powder
1/8 teaspoon salt
1/4 teaspoon ground anise star
1/4 teaspoon grated nutmeg
1 teaspoon cinnamon
3 tablespoons caster sugar
1/2 teaspoon pure vanilla extract
1 egg
1/4 cup plain milk
1/2 stick melted butter
1/2 cup Sultanas

For the Buttercream Icing:
1/3 cup butter, softened
1 ½ cups powdered sugar
1 teaspoon vanilla extract
1/8 teaspoon salt
2 tablespoons milk
A few drop food coloring

Directions

- Take two mixing bowls. Thoroughly combine the dry ingredients for the cupcakes into the first bowl. In another bowl, whisk the vanilla extract, egg, milk, and melted butter.
- To form a batter, add the wet milk mixture to the dry flour mixture. Fold in Sultanas and gently stir to combine. Ladle the batter into the prepared muffin pans.
- Air-bake at 390 degrees F for 15 minutes.
- Meanwhile, to make the Buttercream Icing, beat the butter until creamy and fluffy. Gradually add the sugar and beat well.
- Then, add the vanilla, salt, and milk, and mix until creamy. Afterward, gently stir in food coloring. Frost your cupcakes and enjoy!

446. Last-Minute Cherry and Almond Dessert

Ready in about 35 minutes
Servings 4

Who needs a special occasion to bake a double batch of fruit dessert? Almonds give a different twist to this treat!

Per serving: 124 Calories; 7.6g Fat; 14.3g Carbs; 0.9g Protein; 13.8g Sugars

Ingredients

1/3 cup ground almonds
1 teaspoon pure hazelnut extract
1/3 stick butter
1/3 teaspoon pure vanilla essence
1/3 cup cherries, pitted
1/2 cup caster sugar
Maraschino cherries, for garnish
½ teaspoon ground anise star

Directions

- Lightly coat the inside of a baking dish with a pan spray of choice; arrange the cherries on the bottom of the baking dish.
- In a mixing dish, combine the sugar, ground almonds, vanilla, hazelnut extract, and anise star. Now, spread this mixture over the cherry layer.
- Cut in the butter. Air-fry at 380 degrees F for 38 minutes. Serve warm or cold, it's up to you; garnish with Maraschino cherries.

447. Vegan Croissant Bread Pudding

Ready in about 40 minutes
Servings 8

Vegan bread pudding is brought to a whole new level of indulgence with coconut milk creamer, vegan croissants and coconut milk.

Per serving: 289 Calories; 18g Fat; 27g Carbs; 5.5g Protein; 11.2g Sugars

Ingredients

1/3 teaspoon pure coconut extract
1/3 cup caster sugar
1/3 teaspoon vanilla paste
1 teaspoon ground cinnamon
8 vegan croissants, diced
1 ½ tablespoons bourbon
1 1/3 cups coconut milk
3 tablespoons coconut butter, at room temperature
1/2 cup coconut milk creamer
A pinch of kosher salt
Powdered sugar, for garnish

Directions

- Grab two mixing dishes. Throw the diced croissants into the first mixing dish.
- In another dish, whisk the other ingredients, minus the coconut butter and the powdered sugar.
- Ladle this mixture over the croissants and toss to coat. Let the croissants soak for about 12 minutes.
- Divide the croissant bread pudding among 2 mini loaf pans. Drizzle with the coconut butter.
- Bake in the preheated air fryer at 315 degrees F for approximately 28 minutes. Dust with the powdered sugar just before serving. Bon appétit!

448. Blackberry Chocolate Pound Cake

Ready in about 30 minutes
Servings 8

This pound cake is a great dessert to satisfy chocolate cravings. If you are a fan of pound cakes, you will love this dessert that has fresh blackberries and coconut butter.

Per serving: 193 Calories; 13.9g Fat; 16.7g Carbs; 6.7g Protein; 9.5g Sugars

Ingredients

1/3 cup fresh blackberries
1/3 cup coconut butter, room temperature
1/3 teaspoon baking powder
2 ounces sugar
1 cup cocoa powder, melted
1 teaspoon baking soda
4 whole eggs
1/3 cup cake flour
Zest and juice of 1/2 medium-sized orange

Directions

- In a bowl, beat the coconut butter, sugar and orange zest with an electric mixer. Carefully fold in the eggs, one at a time; beat well with your electric mixer after each addition.
- Next, throw in the cake flour, baking soda, baking powder, cocoa powder, and orange juice.
- Pour the prepared batter into a loaf pan. Top with fresh blackberries. Bake in the preheated air fryer for 22 minutes at 335 degrees F.
- Check the cake for doneness; allow it to cool on a wire rack. Bon appétit!

449. Dad's Orange Custards

Ready in about 35 minutes +
chilling time
Servings 6

Here's a custard lover's dream dessert! A silky caramelized sugar completes the whole thing!

Per serving: 267 Calories; 19.1g Fat; 11.4g Carbs; 11.4g Protein; 10.7g Sugars

Ingredients

6 eggs
7 ounces cream cheese, at room temperature
2 ½ cans condensed milk, sweetened
1/2 cup sugar
1/2 teaspoon orange rind, grated
1 ½ cardamom pods, bruised
2 teaspoons vanilla paste
1/3 cup fresh orange juice

Directions

- In a saucepan, melt caster sugar over a moderate flame; it takes about 10 to 12 minutes. Immediately but carefully pour the melted sugar into six ramekins, tilting to coat their bottoms; allow them to cool slightly.
- In a mixing dish, beat the cheese until smooth; now, fold in the eggs, one at a time, and continue to beat until pale and creamy.
- Add the orange rind, cardamom, vanilla, orange juice, and the milk; mix again. Pour the mixture over the caramelized sugar. Air-fry, covered, at 325 degrees F for 28 minutes or until it has thickened.
- Refrigerate overnight; garnish with berries or other fruits and serve.

450. Chocolate Cake with Pine Nuts

Ready in about 30 minutes
Servings 6

This cake is loaded with pine nuts and strawberry jam and finished with chocolate frosting for the ultimate chocolate dessert.

Per serving: 307 Calories; 22.1g Fat; 2.7g Carbs; 8.9g Protein; 12.8g Sugars

Ingredients

4 ounces cake flour
1 ½ tablespoons strawberry jam
1/2 teaspoon vanilla essence
1/3 cup butter
Chocolate frosting, for garnish
4 eggs, beaten
1/3 cup caster sugar
1/3 cup pine nuts, chopped
1/3 teaspoon cardamom
2 tablespoons cocoa powder

Directions

- Lightly grease a cake pan using a nonstick cooking oil.
- Now, using an electric mixer, cream the butter and caster sugar until pale and uniform. Fold in the eggs, pine nuts, and strawberry jam; beat again until everything's well incorporated.
- Throw in the cake flour, cocoa powder, cardamom, vanilla essence, and ground cinnamon. Bake in the preheated air fryer at 315 degrees F for about 17 minutes.
- After that, use a tester to check for doneness. Frost the cake and enjoy. Bon appétit!

451. Strawberry Cheesecake Roll-Ups

Ready in about 15 minutes
Servings 8

These sweet roll ups are so cheap but better than many expensive desserts you've ever had. And they are ready in 15 minutes!

Per serving: 238 Calories; 13.3g Fat; 27g Carbs; 3.9g Protein; 23.6g Sugars

Ingredients

3 ½ cups strawberries, hulled and chopped
½ package refrigerated crescent rolls
1/3 teaspoon lemon extract
1 teaspoon grated nutmeg
Powdered sugar, for garnish
1/3 cup powdered sugar
1 teaspoon vanilla extract
1 ½ package cream cheese

Directions

- Spritz the inside of a baking pan with a cooking spray of choice.
- Then, whip the cream cheese together with powdered sugar, lemon extract and vanilla.
- Divide the cream cheese mixture among crescent rolls; add the strawberries. Fold up the wrappers and spritz them with a cooking spray. Dust with grated nutmeg.
- Bake at 380 degrees for about 8 minutes or until they're golden brown. Bake in batches, turning over halfway through. Dust with powdered sugar and serve. Bon appétit!

452. Healthy Cinnamon Tortilla Chips

Ready in about 5 minutes
Servings 6

Here's an inexpensive, simple and clever way to bring a dessert to the table. Kids will love this sweet and aromatic tortilla chips.

Per serving: 171 Calories; 2.8g Fat; 33g Carbs; 3.9g Protein; 9.7g Sugars

Ingredients

1/2 cup confectioners' sugar
1/2 teaspoon ground cinnamon
Agave syrup, for drizzling
1/3 teaspoon grated nutmeg
6 flour tortillas, cut into quarters

Directions

- Air-fry the tortilla pieces for about 4 minutes at 345 degrees F.
- In a bag, mix the nutmeg, cinnamon and confectioners' sugar. Add the fried tortillas to the bag and shake to coat well.
- To serve, drizzle with agave syrup.

453. Old-Fashioned Fig Cake

Ready in about 25 minutes
Servings 6

Upgrade your favorite cake by cooking it in the Air fryer. It looks unexpectedly amazing!

Per serving: 257 Calories; 8.6g Fat; 40.9g Carbs; 5.4g Protein; 21.2g Sugars

Ingredients

3 figs, mashed with a fork
2 eggs
1/2 cup cake flour
1/3 teaspoon cardamom
1/3 stick butter
½ teaspoon baking powder
1/2 cup caster sugar
1 teaspoon baking soda
A pinch of fine sea salt
1 ½ tablespoons maple syrup
1 teaspoon ground cinnamon
Nonstick cooking spray

Directions

- Firstly, coat the cake pan with a nonstick cooking spray. In a bowl, whip together the butter and caster sugar until pale and creamy.
- Next step, stir in mashed figs, egg, and maple syrup. Now, whisk in the butter/sugar mix; mix again to combine well.
- Sift in the cake flour, baking soda, baking powder, salt, cardamom, and cinnamon. Carefully scrape the batter into the cake pan.
- Bake for about 28 minutes at 325 degrees F. Finally, transfer to a cooling rack before serving.

454. Mother's Day Peanut Cupcakes

Ready in about 15 minutes
Servings 8

This unconventional combo of unsalted peanuts, caster sugar and cream of tartar will amaze your family and guests! Add a dash of dark rum for more sophisticated flavor.

Per serving: 242 Calories; 6.6g Fat; 41.4g Carbs; 4.9g Protein; 36.9g Sugars

Ingredients

4 egg whites
2 whole egg
1/2 teaspoon pure vanilla extract
1/2 pound powdered sugar
1/3 teaspoon cream of tartar
1/3 stick butter, softened
1/3 cup caster sugar
1/3 teaspoon almond extract
1/3 cup cake flour
1 ½ tablespoons unsalted peanuts, ground

Directions

- First of all, beat the softened butter and caster sugar until it is fluffy.
- After that, fold in the egg and mix again; carefully throw in the cake flour along with ground peanuts; stir in the almond extract and vanilla extract.
- Divide the batter among the muffin cups that are lined with muffin papers; air-fry at 325 degrees F for 10 minutes.
- Meanwhile, prepare the topping; simply whip the egg and cream of tartar until it has an airy texture.
- Now, gradually add the powdered sugar; continue mixing until stiff glossy peaks form. To finish, decorate the cupcakes and serve them on a nice serving platter.

455. Apple Pie Roll-Ups with Walnuts

Ready in about 15 minutes
Servings 6

You can't go wrong with fruit roll-ups. Let's get the party started with these light-as-air, sweet bites.

Per serving: 310 Calories; 6.8g Fat; 56g Carbs; 6.4g Protein; 12.2g Sugars

Ingredients

1/2 tablespoon ground cinnamon
3 tablespoons melted coconut butter
1/3 cup powdered sugar
12 egg roll wrappers
1/3 teaspoon freshly grated nutmeg
½ can apple pie filling
1/2 teaspoon vanilla essence
1/3 cup chopped walnuts

Directions

- Place the wraps on a clean surface. Have each wrap facing out on the diagonal so that it is a diamond shape.
- Then, divide the apple pie filling and the walnuts among the wrappers. Fold up the wrapper like a burrito using wet hands.
- Spritz each wrapper with the canola oil; place in a single layer in the air fryer cooking basket. Bake at 345 degrees approximately 11 minutes; bake in batches.
- Meanwhile, combine the powdered sugar, cinnamon, vanilla, and the freshly grated nutmeg.
- When the roll-ups are done, brush them with the melted coconut butter. Dust with the spice/sugar mixture and serve. Enjoy!

456. Easy Orange Fritters

Ready in about 15 minutes
Servings 6

These simple and totally decadent orange fritters are a must-have for a family gathering! They are so cute, perfect for the Air-fryer.

Per serving: 1 77 Calories; 6.6g Fat; 21.7g Carbs; 7.4g Protein; 12.9g Sugars

Ingredients

1/2 cup cake flour
3 eggs
1/3 cup milk
2 teaspoons grated lemon peel
1/3 teaspoon ground nutmeg, preferably freshly ground
1 ½ teaspoons baking powder
1/2 cup orange juice
A pinch of turmeric

Directions

- Grab two mixing bowls. Combine dry ingredients in the first bowl.
- In the second bowl, combine all wet ingredients. Add wet mixture to the dry mixture and mix until smooth and uniform.
- Air-fry for 4 to 5 minutes at 345 degrees F. Work in batches. Dust with icing sugar. Bon appétit!

457. Super Yummy Blueberry Tartlets

Ready in about 15 minutes
Servings 8

This blueberry dessert is absolutely delicious! In addition, it is extra easy to make using an air-frying technique.

Per serving: 276 Calories; 4.6g Fat; 47.9g Carbs; 9.8g Protein; 9.6g Sugars

Ingredients

1/2 cup blueberries, rinsed and dried
1/2 cup caster sugar, plus more for dipping
16 wonton wrappers
1/3 teaspoon ground cardamom
3 eggs, beaten
½ teaspoon crystallized ginger
1/2 tablespoon cornstarch
1 teaspoon ground anise star
½ tablespoon melted coconut oil
Zest of 1/2 lemon

Directions

- Coat the edges of wonton wrappers with the beaten eggs.
- After that, add blueberries together with cornstarch, lemon zest, anise, ginger, cardamom, and 1/2 cup caster sugar to the saucepan that is preheated over a moderate heat; simmer until blueberries burst and the sauce has thickened.
- Divide the filling among wonton wrappers; fold the wrappers diagonally in half over the filling; seal the edges with your fingertips.
- After that, carefully drizzle each tart with a melted coconut oil; dip them in the caster sugar.
- Air-fry at 375 degrees F for 6 minutes, turning over halfway through. Bon appétit!

458. Creamed Peach and Almond Dessert

Ready in about 35 minutes
Servings 6

Once you taste how good this dessert is, it will become a staple during peach season. You can substitute walnuts for almonds and maple syrup for honey.

Per serving: 96 Calories; 3g Fat; 17.3g Carbs; 2.9g Protein; 15g Sugars

Ingredients

6 peaches, pitted and halved
1/2 teaspoon candied ginger
1/3 cup almonds, chopped
Well-chilled heavy cream, to serve
1 teaspoon pure vanilla extract
Melted coconut oil, for a baking pan
1/3 cup honey

Directions

- Firstly, coat a baking dish with a thin layer of melted coconut oil; lower the peaches onto the bottom of the prepared baking dish.
- In a bowl, combine the almonds, honey, vanilla, and the candied ginger. Scrape this mixture into the baking dish.
- Bake at 380 degrees F for 38 minutes. Allow it to cool completely; serve in dessert bowls garnished with chilled heavy cream.

459. Mini Raspberry Tarts

Ready in about 15 minutes
Servings 8

With their perfect balance of sweet and tart flavors, raspberries work best in desserts like tarts. A few sprinkles of icing sugar give these tarts the look of fine French pastry.

Per serving: 228 Calories; 8.3g Fat; 37.5g Carbs; 2.3g Protein; 17.5g Sugars

Ingredients

16 frozen tart shells, baked
1 1/2 tablespoon melted coconut oil

For the Filling:
3 tablespoons orange juice
1 teaspoon ground cinnamon
1 grated nutmeg
1 ½ tablespoons cornstarch
2 cups fresh raspberries
1/3 cup sugar
1 teaspoon ground anise star

Directions

- To make the filling, simmer all filling ingredients over a moderate flame; simmer until raspberries burst and the juices have thickened.
- Divide the filling among tart shells; drizzle each tart shell with the melted coconut oil.
- Air-fry at 365 degrees F for 10 minutes, turning over halfway through. Bon appétit!

460. Classic Raisin Bread Pudding

Ready in about 45 minutes
Servings 4

Bread pudding is a family all-time favorite dessert! Loaded with an assortment of sweet raisin bread, half-and-half and raisins, this dessert will disappear in no time!

Per serving: 347 Calories; 17.6g Fat; 39g Carbs 9.4g Protein; 32.7g Sugars

Ingredients

3 eggs, lightly beaten
1/3 teaspoon ground ginger
1 teaspoon bergamot extract
3 tablespoons butter, softened
1 tablespoon chocolate flavored liqueur
4 slices sweet raisin bread, torn into pieces
1/3 cup golden raisin
1 cup milk
1/3 cup half-and-half
1 teaspoon cloves, ground
1/3 cup powdered sugar

Directions

- Grab two mixing dishes. Throw bread pieces into the first dish.
- In the second dish, mix the remaining ingredients.
- Scrape this mixture into the first dish with bread pieces. Allow it soak for about 15 minutes; press with a wide spatula. Evenly divide the bread pudding mixture among 2 mini loaf pans.
- Set the timer for 28 minutes. Bake in the preheated air fryer at 305 degrees F. Bon appétit!

461. Apple Pie Bread Pudding with Pecans

Ready in about 45 minutes
Servings 8

Dessert doesn't have to be complicated to impress your guests. This bread pudding is elegant, rustic and delectable at the same time. As a matter of fact, it's hard to have any leftovers!

Per serving: 361 Calories; 14.1g Fat; 51.2g Carbs;7.9g Protein; 21.2g Sugars

Ingredients

4 Granny Smith apples, peeled and chopped
1 ½ tablespoons margarine, softened
1 teaspoons apple pie spice
7 small-sized slices sweet bread, torn into pieces
1 1/3 cups milk
1/3 cup pecans, toasted and roughly chopped
2 large-sized eggs, whisked
1 teaspoon natural butter flavor
2 tablespoons cornstarch
1/3 cup brown sugar

Directions

- Take two mixing bowls. Throw bread pieces into the first bowl.
- In the second bowl, mix the milk, natural butter flavor, egg, and apple pie spice.
- Scrape the milk/egg mixture into the first dish with sweet bread pieces. Allow it to soak for about 10 minutes; press with a wide spatula.
- Meanwhile, combine the apples, brown sugar, and cornstarch. Place over the bread mixture. Drizzle melted margarine over the top; top with chopped pecans.
- Evenly divide the bread pudding mixture among 2 mini loaf pans.
- Set the timer for 28 minutes. Bake in the preheated air fryer at 315 degrees F. Bon appétit!

462. Holiday Plum Clafoutis

Ready in about 25 minutes
Servings 8

Here's an interesting twist on the classic French dessert. With custard-like texture, Clafoutis is easy to make in the Air fryer. Serve with a refreshing glass of dessert wine.

Per serving: 175 Calories; 6.1g Fat; 25.7g Carbs; 4.9g Protein; 20g Sugars

Ingredients

3 eggs
1/3 teaspoon pure hazelnut extract
1/3 cup heavy cream
1 ½ cups plums, pitted and halved
1/2 cup milk
A pinch of kosher salt
Icing sugar, for dusting
1/3 cup cake flour
1/3 cup brown sugar

Directions

- Firstly, butter 2 mini pie pans. Lay the plum halves on the bottom of the pans.
- In a saucepan, over a moderate flame, warm the milk and heavy cream until thoroughly heated.
- Remove the pan from the heat; mix in the flour using a wire whisk.
- In a medium-sized mixing bowl, whisk the eggs, along with sugar, and salt until uniform and creamy. Whisk in the creamy milk mixture; add the hazelnut extract. Pour the mixture over the plums.
- Bake at 335 degrees for about 18 minutes, or until browned. To serve, dust with icing sugar and enjoy!

463. Surprisingly Delicious Banana Beignets

Ready in about 15 minutes
Servings 6

Banana and lemon flavors are welcome in any dessert. They make an excellent balance between the sweetness of the fruit and the acidity of the citrus. Banana beignets offer a feast for the senses!

Per serving: 305 Calories; 7.6g Fat; 51.7g Carbs; 9.2g Protein; 31.4g Sugars

Ingredients

1 cup cake flour
1/3 teaspoon freshly grated nutmeg
1 ½ large-sized overripe bananas, peeled and sliced
1/3 cup milk
1 teaspoon ground cloves
1/3 cup granulated sugar
½ tablespoon baking powder
3 eggs
1/2 teaspoon lemon juice
1/2 teaspoon grated lemon peel
A pinch of turmeric

Directions

- Grab two mixing dishes. Drizzle the bananas with lemon juice.
- Combine the dry ingredients in the first bowl.
- In the second bowl, combine all the wet ingredients. Add the wet mixture to the dry mixture and mix until smooth and uniform. Dip each banana slice into the prepared batter.
- Air-fry for 7 to 8 minutes at 335 degrees F, working in batches. To serve, drizzle with maple syrup. Bon appétit!

464. Chocolate Mini Cheesecakes

Ready in about 30 minutes
Servings 8

These mini cheesecakes are packed with many layers of yumminess – chocolate chips, cheese, graham cracker crumbs, eggs and vanilla. Whip up them in half an hour and delight your kids!

Per serving: 248 Calories; 5.6g Fat; 45.8g Carbs; 3.9g Protein; 35g Sugars

Ingredients

For the Crust:
1/3 teaspoon grated nutmeg
1 ½ tablespoons sugar
1/2 cup graham cracker crumbs
1 ½ tablespoons melted butter
1 teaspoon ground cinnamon
A pinch of kosher salt

For the Cheesecake:
2 eggs
1 1/2 cups chocolate chips
1 ½ tablespoons sour cream
1 package soft cheese
1/2 cup sugar
1/2 teaspoon vanilla essence

Directions

- Firstly, line eight cups of mini muffin pan with paper liners.
- To make the crust, mix the graham cracker crumbs together with 1½ tablespoons sugar, cinnamon, nutmeg, and kosher salt.
- Now, add melted butter and stir well to moisten the crumb mixture.
- Divide the crust mixture among the muffin cups and press gently to make even layers.
- In another bowl, whip together the soft cheese, sour cream and 1/2 cup sugar until uniform and smooth. Fold in the eggs and the vanilla essence.
- Then, divide 1/2 of the chocolate chips among the prepared muffin cups. Then, add the cheese mix to each muffin cup. Place another layer using the remaining 1 cup of the chocolate chips.
- Bake for about 18 minutes at 345 degrees F. Bake in batches if needed. To finish, transfer the mini cheesecakes to a cooling rack; store in the fridge.

465. Apple and Cranberry Dumplings

Ready in about 25 minutes
Servings 4

These dumplings are made from store-bought pastry so anyone can prepare them. Perfectly sweet, Gala apples contrast nicely with tangy cranberries and melt-in-your-mouth fine puff pastry.

Per serving: 137 Calories; 3.6g Fat; 29.7g Carbs; 0.5g Protein; 22.6g Sugars

Ingredients

1 teaspoon ground Ceylon cinnamon
1½ tablespoons dried cranberries
1 tablespoons butter, melted
4 Gala apples, cored and peeled
1 ½ sheets puff pastry
1 teaspoon ground cloves
1½ tablespoons granulated sugar

Directions

- Begin by preheating the air fryer to 365 degrees F. Place each apple on one of the puff pastry sheets. To make the filling, mix the dried cranberries, sugar, cinnamon, and ground cloves.
- Now, fill the apple cores with the cranberry mixture. Fold the puff pastry around the apples.
- Drizzle with the melted butter. Lay the apple dumplings in the lined baking dish; set the timer to 22 minutes. Eat warm. Bon appétit!

466. Aromatic Baked Plum Dessert

Ready in about 45 minutes
Servings 4

Here is one of the easiest desserts to make for you family and it feeds a crowd. Always popular, always delicious!

Per serving: 198 Calories; 9.3g Fat; 29.6g Carbs; 0.8g Protein; 24.7g Sugars

Ingredients

1/3 cup honey
1 teaspoon orange extract
3/4 teaspoon candied ginger, minced
1 teaspoon vanilla essence
3/4 pound purple plums, pitted and halved
2 tablespoons cornstarch
1/3 teaspoon ground cinnamon
1 cup whipped cream, for garnish

Directions

- Spritz a baking dish with a nonstick cooking spray or melted coconut butter; arrange plums on the bottom of the baking dish.
- Then, combine the remaining ingredients, minus whipped cream. Spread this mixture over the plum layer.
- Bake at 380 degrees F for 35 minutes. Serve topped with cream. Enjoy!

467. One-More-Bite Strawberry and Almond Cake

Ready in about 25 minutes
Servings 6

Strawberry jam makes a tasty addition to this cake, but you can use another berry jam you have on hand. Fluffy and luscious, this cake would win your heart.

Per serving: 377 Calories; 20.3g Fat; 43.3g Carbs; 5.8g Protein; 0.5g Sugars

Ingredients

1/3 cup strawberry jam
1/3 cup almonds, slivered
1 stick butter
3 eggs, beaten
1/3 teaspoon baking powder
4 ounces all-purpose flour + 1 tablespoon cornstarch, sifted 5 times
1/2 teaspoon vanilla essence
1/3 teaspoon ground cinnamon
1/3 cup confectioners' sugar
1 teaspoon crystalized ginger
Pan oil

Directions

- Lightly grease a cake pan using a pan oil.
- Now, whip the butter and confectioners' sugar using an electric mixer until pale and uniform. Fold in the eggs, almonds, and jam; beat again until everything's well combined.
- Throw in the flour, baking powder, vanilla essence, ginger, and ground cinnamon. Bake in the preheated air fryer at 310 degrees F for about 17 minutes.
- After that, use a tester to check for doneness. To finish, add frosting and allow it to cool completely. Bon appétit!

468. Ciabatta Chocolate Bread Pudding

Ready in about 1 hour
Servings 6

In this recipe, the bread you choose has a huge effect on the entire pudding, the flavor and texture. Further, the eggs are essential to a delicate and moist custard texture. An extra yolk will add even stronger flavor.

Per serving: 482 Calories; 22.9g Fat; 69.3g Carbs; 10.5g Protein; 32.4g Sugars

Ingredients

3/4 cup chocolate chips morsels
2 teaspoons rum
8 slices ciabatta bread, cubed
1/3 cup coconut milk creamer
1/3 teaspoon ground cloves
3/4 cup turbinado sugar
3 ½ tablespoons coconut oil, room temperature
1 teaspoon candied ginger
2 eggs plus 1 egg yolk, lightly beaten
1 cup soy milk

Directions

- Grab two mixing dishes. Place cubed bread in the first dish.
- In the second mixing dish, thoroughly combine the remaining ingredients; mix until everything is well combined.
- Scrape the chocolate mix into the first dish with bread cubes. Allow it to soak for about 20 minutes. Evenly divide the mixture between 2 mini loaf pans.
- Set the timer for 35 minutes. Bake in the preheated air fryer at 305 degrees F. Serve with whipped cream. Bon appétit!

469. Flavorsome Peach Cake

Ready in about 40 minutes
Servings 6

Love at first bite. So easy to make and very impressive looking fruit cake! The best thing is that you can decorate it with various toppings and come up with a different dessert every time.

Per serving: 317 Calories; 13.1g Fat; 46.8g Carbs; 4.7g Protein; 26.7g Sugars

Ingredients

1/2 pound peaches, pitted and mashed
3 tablespoons honey
1/2 teaspoon baking powder
1 ¼ cups cake flour
1/2 teaspoon orange extract
1 teaspoon pure vanilla extract
1/4 teaspoon ground cinnamon
1/3 cup ghee
1/8 teaspoon salt
1/2 cup caster sugar
2 eggs
1/4 teaspoon freshly grated nutmeg

Directions

- Firstly, preheat the air fryer to 310 degrees F. Spritz the cake pan with a nonstick cooking spray.
- In a mixing bowl, beat the ghee with caster sugar until creamy. Fold in the egg, mashed peaches and honey.
- Then, make the cake batter by mixing the remaining ingredients; now, stir in the peach/honey mixture.
- Now, transfer the prepared batter to the cake pan; level the surface with a spoon.
- Bake for 35 minutes or until a tester inserted in the center of your cake comes out completely dry. Enjoy!

470. Lemon Mini Pies with Coconut

Ready in about 15 minutes +
chilling time
Servings 8

Begin by making the crust for these cute, little pies. Fill them with the creamiest and yummiest lemon filling ever. Garnish with meringue or candied ginger. Ta-da!

Per serving: 360 Calories; 14.8g Fat; 46.2g Carbs; 9.9g Protein; 0.3g Sugars

Ingredients

1 box (4-serving size) lemon instant pudding filling mix
1 teaspoon grated lemon peel
18 wonton wrappers
1/3 cup shredded coconut
1 ¼ cups cream cheese, room temperature
1 teaspoon apple pie spice blend
1 teaspoon pure vanilla extract
1/8 teaspoon salt
1/2 teaspoon ground anise star

Directions

- Prepare a muffin pan by adding a cooking spray. Press the wonton wrappers evenly into the cups.
- Transfer them to your air fryer and bake at 350 degrees F just for 5 minutes. When the edges become golden, they are ready.
- Meanwhile, blend all remaining ingredients using your electric mixer; place the prepared cream in the refrigerator until ready to serve.
- Lastly, divide prepared cream among wrappers. Keep them refrigerated until serving time. Bon appétit!

471. Cheesy Orange Fritters

Ready in about 15 minutes
Servings 8

These fritters are tasty right out of the Air fryer, they are kid-friendly and easy to make. These fritters are also good dipped in jelly.

Per serving: 268 Calories; 15.8g Fat; 25.8g Carbs; 6g Protein; 10g Sugars

Ingredients

1 ½ tablespoons orange juice
3/4 pound cream cheese, at room temperature
1 teaspoon freshly grated orange rind
3/4 cup whole milk
1 teaspoon vanilla extract
1 ¼ cups all-purpose flour
1/3 cup white sugar
1/3 teaspoon ground cinnamon
1/2 teaspoon ground anise star

Directions

- Thoroughly combine all ingredients in a mixing dish.
- Next step, drop a teaspoonful of the mixture into the air fryer cooking basket; air-fry for 4 minutes at 340 degrees F.
- Dust with icing sugar, if desired. Bon appétit!

472. Nana's Special Apricot Jam Dumplings

Ready in about 30 minutes
Servings 4

With buttery crust and a nutty jam filling, these dumplings are incredibly fluffy and amazingly yummy. Thanks to the Air fryer, you can recreate this restaurant favorite at your own kitchen.

Per serving: 499 Calories; 34.3g Fat; 48.1g Carbs; 4.9g Protein; 22.1g Sugars

Ingredients

4 sheets of puff pastry
1/3 cup apricot jam
1/3 cup pine nuts, roughly chopped
1/2 teaspoon grated fresh ginger
1/2 teaspoon ground cinnamon
1/2 teaspoon vanilla extract
1/2 stick butter, melted
3 tablespoons granulated sugar

Directions

- In a mixing dish, thoroughly combine the sugar, cinnamon, vanilla, ginger, pine nuts and apricot jam.
- Divide the mixture among 4 puff pastry sheets. Fold the pastry over the filling and carefully seal the edges.
- Brush each dumpling with the melted butter. Air-fry at 345 degrees F approximately 27 minutes. Bon appétit!

473. Baked Pears with Chocolate

Ready in about 45 minutes
Servings 4

These syrupy pears are spiced with high-quality aromatics and topped with chocolate chips. This dessert proves that simple can be great!

Per serving: 378 Calories; 18g Fat; 54.9g Carbs; 2.5g Protein; 42.2g Sugars

Ingredients

4 firm ripe pears, peeled, cored and sliced
1/3 cup turbinado sugar
1/2 teaspoon ground anise star
1 teaspoon pure vanilla extract
1 teaspoon pure orange extract
1/2 stick butter, cold
1/2 cup chocolate chips, for garnish

Directions

- Grease the baking dish with a pan spray; lay the pear slices on the bottom of the prepared dish.
- In a mixing dish, combine the sugar, anise star, vanilla, and orange extract. Then, sprinkle this mixture over the fruit layer.
- Cut in butter and scatter evenly over the top of the pear layer. Air-fryer at 380 degrees F for 35 minutes. Serve sprinkled with chocolate chips. Enjoy!

474. Festive Baileys Brownie

Ready in about 35 minutes
Servings 8

Fudgy, chewy and delectable, this brownie is holiday-worthy dessert! A cheesecake, booze and brownie in one dessert.

Per serving: 415 Calories; 19.6g Fat; 57.7g Carbs; 3.2g Protein; 22.3g Sugars

Ingredients

Cooking spray
1/2 box brownie mix, plus ingredients called for on box
2 tablespoons Baileys
9 ounces semisweet chocolate chips
1/2 cup sour cream
1/3 cup powdered sugar
3 ounces Ricotta cheese, room temperature

Directions

- In a mixing bowl, prepare brownie batter according to package directions. Add the batter to a lightly-greased baking pan.
- Air-fry for 25 minutes at 355 degrees F. Allow them to cool slightly on a wire rack.
- Microwave the chocolate chips until everything's melted; allow the mixture to cool at room temperature.
- After that, add the cheese, Baileys, sour cream, and powdered sugar; mix until everything is blended. Spread this mixture onto the top of your brownie. Serve well chilled.

475. Coconut Strawberry Fritters

Ready in about 15 minutes
Servings 8

Fruit, coconut and sugar! What more could you want? Feel free to experiment and try adding blueberries or blackberries.

Per serving: 145 Calories; 6g Fat; 20.7g Carbs; 2.8g Protein; 9.5g Sugars

Ingredients

3 tablespoons coconut oil
3/4 pound strawberries
1/3 cup demerara sugar
1/8 teaspoon salt
1 ¼ cups soy milk
1/2 teaspoon coconut extract
1/2 teaspoon baking powder
3/4 cup all-purpose flour

Directions

- Thoroughly combine all ingredients in a mixing dish.
- Next step, drop teaspoon full amounts of the mix into the air fryer cooking basket; air-fry for 4 minutes at 345 degrees F.
- Dust with ginger sugar if desired. Bon appétit!

476. Date and Hazelnut Cookies

Ready in about 1 hour
Servings 10

Try these girls' night cookies. Serve with a ton of hot chocolate.

Per serving: 187 Calories; 10.5g Fat; 23.2g Carbs; 1.5g Protein; 9.6g Sugars

Ingredients

3 tablespoons agave syrup
1/3 cup dried dates, pitted and chopped
1/4 cup hazelnuts, chopped
1 stick butter, room temperature
1/2 cup cake flour
1/3 cup corn flour
2 ounces white sugar
1/3 teaspoon ground cardamom
1/2 teaspoon vanilla extract
1/3 teaspoon ground cinnamon
1/2 teaspoon cardamom

Directions

- Firstly, cream sugar with butter and agave syrup until the mixture becomes fluffy. Sift in both types of flour.
- Now, stir in the remaining ingredients. Now, knead the mixture to form a dough; place in the refrigerator for about 35 minutes.
- To finish, shape the prepared dough into the bite-sized balls; arrange them on a baking dish; flatten the balls using the back of a spoon.
- Bake the cookies for 20 minutes at 310 degrees F. Bon appétit!

477. Air Fried Apricots in Whiskey Sauce

Ready in about 45 minutes
Servings 4

Take the next family gathering to a whole new level. Prepare this easy, healthy dessert and make the most of apricot season.

Per serving: 356 Calories; 17g Fat; 43.3g Carbs; 1.8g Protein; 38.2g Sugars

Ingredients

1 pound apricot, pitted and halved
1/4 cup whiskey
1 teaspoon pure vanilla extract
1/2 stick butter, room temperature
2-4 whole cloves
1 cup cool whip, for serving
1/2 cup maple syrup

Directions

- In a small-sized saucepan that is placed over a moderate flame, heat the maple syrup, vanilla, and butter; simmer until the butter has melted.
- Add the whiskey and stir to combine. Arrange the apricots wedges on the bottom of a lightly greased baking dish.
- Pour the sauce over the apricots; scatter whole cloves over the top. Then, transfer the baking dish to the preheated air fryer.
- Air-fryer at 380 degrees F for 35 minutes. Top with cool whip and serve. Bon appétit!

478. Almond and Orange Cake

Ready in about 20 minutes
Servings 6

Are we already in almond-orange heaven? Thanks to the Air fryer, you can dress up the regular cake and delight your guests!

Per serving: 441 Calories; 22.7g Fat; 48.9g Carbs; 10.6g Protein; 24.4g Sugars

Ingredients

1/3 cup almonds, roughly chopped
3 tablespoons orange marmalade
1 stick butter
2 eggs plus 1 egg yolk, beaten
3/4 cup brown sugar
6 ounces unbleached cake flour
1 teaspoon baking soda
1/2 teaspoon baking powder
1/2 ground anise seed
1/2 teaspoon ground cinnamon
1/2 teaspoon ground allspice
Pan oil

Directions

- Lightly grease a cake pan using a pan oil.
- Now, whip the sugar and butter in a mixing bowl; whip until pale and smooth. Fold in the eggs, almonds and marmalade; beat again until everything's well mixed.
- Throw in the cake flour, baking soda, baking powder, allspice, anise star, and ground cinnamon. Bake in the preheated air fryer at 310 degrees F for about 20 minutes.
- After that, use a tester to check for doneness. To finish, add the frosting. Bon appétit!

479. Delicious Fall Clafoutis

Ready in about 30 minutes
Servings 6

This weeknight-easy dessert is chock-full of cream, fruits and spices, it is simply bursting with fall flavors. Serve at room temperature or cold.

Per serving: 354 Calories; 9.6g Fat; 66.6g Carbs; 6.2g Protein; 48.3g Sugars

Ingredients

3/4 cup extra-fine flour
1 ½ cups plums, pitted and
4 medium-sized pears, cored and sliced
1/2 cup coconut cream
3/4 cup coconut milk
3 eggs, whisked
1/2 cup powdered sugar, for dusting
3/4 cup white sugar
1/2 teaspoon baking soda
1/2 teaspoon baking powder
1/3 teaspoon ground cinnamon
1/2 teaspoon crystalized ginger
1/4 teaspoon grated nutmeg

Directions

- Lightly grease 2 mini pie pans using a nonstick cooking spray. Lay the plums and pears on the bottom of the pie pans.
- In a saucepan that is preheated over a moderate flame, warm the cream along with coconut milk until thoroughly heated.
- Remove the pan from the heat; mix in the flour along with baking soda and baking powder.
- In a medium-sized mixing bowl, whip the eggs, white sugar, and spices; whip until the mixture is creamy.
- Add the creamy milk mixture. Carefully spread this mixture over the fruits.
- Bake at 320 degrees for about 25 minutes. To serve, dust with powdered sugar.

480. Coconut and Prune Cookies

Ready in about 1 hour
Servings 10

Serve up no-fuss homemade cookies in less than 1 hour! Cranberries and white chocolate go well too. Serve with a glass of warm milk or for a little more adult version – Prosecco, Madeira or Moscato D'Asti.

Per serving: 227 Calories; 10.3g Fat; 32.5g Carbs; 2.3g Protein; 16.4g Sugars

Ingredients

1/3 cup coconut, shredded
1/3 cup prunes, roughly chopped
2 ounce white sugar
3 ounces powdered sugar
1 ½ cups white flour
1 stick butter, softened
1/3 teaspoon ground cinnamon
1/3 teaspoon green tea powder
1 teaspoon vanilla paste
1/2 teaspoon orange peel zest
1/2 teaspoon baking powder
1/2 teaspoon baking soda

Directions

- Firstly, whip both types of sugar with softened butter until the mixture becomes fluffy. Sift in the flour; add baking powder and baking soda.
- After that, throw in the remaining ingredients; mix well to combine. Then, knead the dough and transfer it to the refrigerator for about 35 minutes.
- To finish, shape the prepared dough into the bite-sized balls; arrange the balls on a baking dish and gently flatten them to form the cookies. Air-fry the cookies for 20 minutes at 315 degrees F. Bon appétit!

481. Father's Day Cranberry and Whiskey Brownies

Ready in about 50 minutes
Servings 10

Finally, you can forget microwave mug cakes because you can create an amazing white brownie in no time. Serve with a good dessert wine like Rutherglen Muscat.

Per serving: 367 Calories; 21.8g Fat; 36.4g Carbs; 6.1g Protein; 28.9g Sugars

Ingredients

1/3 cup cranberries
3 tablespoons whiskey
8 ounces white chocolate
3/4 cup self-rising flour
3 tablespoons coconut flakes
1/2 cup coconut oil
2 eggs plus an egg yolk, whisked
3/4 cup white sugar
1/4 teaspoon ground cardamom
1 teaspoon pure rum extract

Directions

- Microwave white chocolate and coconut oil until everything's melted; allow the mixture to cool at room temperature.
- After that, thoroughly whisk the eggs, sugar, rum extract, and cardamom.
- Next step, add the rum/egg mixture to the chocolate mixture. Stir in the flour and coconut flakes; mix to combine.
- Mix cranberries with whiskey and let them soak for 15 minutes. Fold them into the batter. Press the batter into a lightly buttered cake pan.
- Air-fry for 35 minutes at 340 degrees F. Allow them to cool slightly on a wire rack before slicing and serving.

482. Air Fried Pineapple in Macadamia Batter

Ready in about 20 minutes
Servings 8

This super-quick, fruity dessert is the perfect choice for busy moms! Kids can help make this tropical-style treat.

Per serving: 206 Calories; 10.3g Fat; 26.6g Carbs; 3.8g Protein; 10.7g Sugars

Ingredients

2 cups pineapple, peeled and sliced
1/2 cup ground macadamia nuts
3/4 cup plain flour
1/4 cup cornstarch flour
1 1/3 cups milk
1/4 cup turbinado sugar
1/2 teaspoon baking soda
1/2 teaspoon baking powder
1/4 teaspoon salt
1 teaspoon orange extract
1/2 teaspoon vanilla extract
1/2 teaspoon grated nutmeg
2 tablespoons coconut oil

Directions

- To make the batter, combine all ingredients, minus pineapple, in a large-sized bowl.
- Then, preheat your air fryer to 380 degrees F. Dip the slices of pineapple into the batter.
- Air-fry for 7 minutes or until golden. Serve garnished with chocolate syrup.

483. Granny's Raisin Muffins

Ready in about 20 minutes
Servings 6

Here's a tea time winner – moist, sweet, and simple-to-make! These muffins freeze well too.

Per serving: 560 Calories; 28.2g Fat; 73.4g Carbs; 7.9g Protein; 36g Sugars

Ingredients

3/4 cup raisins
3/4 cup sugar
1/2 cup coconut oil
1 cup sour cream
1 ¼ teaspoons baking powder
2 cups cake flour
2 eggs
1/3 teaspoon ground allspice
1/3 teaspoon ground anise star
1/2 teaspoon grated lemon zest
1/4 teaspoon salt

Directions

- Grab two mixing bowls. In the first bowl, thoroughly combine the flour, baking powder, sugar, salt, anise, allspice and lemon zest.
- Take the second bowl; whisk coconut oil, sour cream, and eggs; whisk to combine well. Now, add the wet mixture to the dry mixture. Fold in the raisins.
- Press the batter mixture into a lightly greased muffin tin. Bake at 345 degrees for 15 minutes. Use a toothpick to check if your muffins are baked. Bon appétit!

484. Cheap Bread Pudding with Sultanas

Ready in about 50 minutes
Servings 8

Prepare this boozy bread pudding to jazz up your weeknights! Bread pudding is a comforting dessert that can be served warm or cold.

Per serving: 283 Calories; 4.7g Fat; 51.4g Carbs; 8.3g Protein; 25.8g Sugars

Ingredients

1 1/3 cups skim milk
3/4 cup caster sugar
1/4 cup Sultanas
3 eggs, whisked
1/3 cups white chocolate chunks
1 loaf stale Italian bread, torn into pieces
1 ½ tablespoons coffee liqueur
1 teaspoon vanilla extract

Directions

- Prepare two mixing bowls. Dump bread pieces into the first bowl.
- In the second bowl, combine the remaining ingredients, minus white chocolate chunks and Sultanas; whisk until smooth.
- Pour the egg/milk mixture over the bread pieces. Allow it to soak approximately 20 minutes; gently press down using a wide spatula.
- Now, scatter chocolate chunks and Sultanas over the top. Then, divide the bread pudding mixture among two mini loaf pans.
- Set the timer for 25 minutes. Bake in the preheated Air fryer at 320 degrees F. Bon appétit!

485. Easy Chocolate Raspberry Cake

Ready in about 30 minutes
Servings 4

Try this luscious cake and delight your beloved one for their special day. This cake made in the Air fryer has deep fruity and chocolate flavor, thanks to a combo of an amazing, zingy filling and a fluffy cake crust.

Per serving: 331 Calories; 14.9g Fat; 47.6g Carbs; 6.5g Protein; 26.9g Sugars

Ingredients

1/3 cup white sugar
1/4 cup unsalted butter, room temperature
1 egg plus 1 egg white, lightly whisked
3 ounces cake flour
2 tablespoons Dutch-process cocoa powder
1/2 teaspoon ground cinnamon
1 tablespoon candied ginger
1/8 teaspoon table salt
For the Filling:
1 packages (6-ounce) fresh raspberries
1/3 cup powdered sugar
1 teaspoon fresh lime juice

Directions

- Firstly, set your air fryer to cook at 315 degrees F. Then, spritz the inside of two cake pans with the butter-flavored cooking spray.
- In a mixing bowl, beat the sugar and butter until creamy and uniform. Then, stir in the whisked eggs. Stir in the flour, cocoa powder, cinnamon, ginger and salt.
- Press the batter into the cake pans; use a wide spatula to level the surface of the batter. Bake for 20 minutes or until a wooden stick inserted in the center of the cake comes out completely dry.
- While your cake is baking, stir together all of the ingredients for the filling in a medium saucepan. Cook over high heat, stirring frequently and mashing with the back of a spoon; bring to a boil and decrease the temperature.
- Continue to cook, stirring until the mixture thickens, for another 7 minutes. Let the filling cool to room temperature.
- Spread 1/2 of raspberry filling over the first crust. Top with another crust; spread remaining filling over top. Spread frosting over top and sides of your cake.
- Enjoy!

486. Almond Butter Cookies

Ready in about 50 minutes
Servings 8

If you thought cookies could ruin your diet, think again. These cookies are made of healthy nuts and gluten-free almond flour. For that reason, they provide a good balance of protein, carbohydrates, and calcium.

Per serving: 252 Calories; 16.2g Fat; 25.1g Carbs; 3.3g Protein; 14.5g Sugars

Ingredients

1/2 cup slivered almonds
1 stick butter, room temperature
4 ounces white sugar
2/3 cup blanched almond flour
1/3 cup cake flour
1/3 teaspoon ground cloves
1 tablespoon candied ginger
3/4 teaspoon pure vanilla extract

Directions

- In a mixing dish, beat the sugar, butter, vanilla extract, ground cloves, and ginger until light and fluffy. Then, throw in the cake flour, almond flour, and slivered almonds.
- Continue mixing until it forms a soft dough. Cover and place in the refrigerator for 35 minutes. Meanwhile, preheat the air fryer to 315 degrees F.
- Roll dough into small cookies and place them on the air fryer cake pan; gently press each cookie using the back of a spoon.
- Bake these butter cookies for 13 minutes. Bon appétit!

487. Country-Style Coconut and Macadamia Cookies

Ready in about 30 minutes
Servings 10

Stop everything. Wrap up in a blanket with a glass of milk, and allow your inner child to enjoy these cute, yummy cookies.

Per serving: 492 Calories; 36.2g Fat; 34.8g Carbs; 11.1g Protein; 11.8g Sugars

Ingredients

3/4 cup coconut oil, room temperature
1 ½ cups coconut flour
1 ¼ cups macadamia nuts, unsalted and roughly chopped
3 eggs plus an egg yolk, whisked
2 cups extra-fine flour
3/4 cup brown sugar
1/4 teaspoon freshly grated nutmeg
1/3 teaspoon ground cloves
1/2 teaspoon baking powder
1/3 teaspoon baking soda
1/2 teaspoon pure vanilla extract
1/2 teaspoon pure coconut extract
1/8 teaspoon fine sea salt

Directions

- In a bowl, combine both types of flour, baking soda and baking powder. In a separate bowl, beat the eggs with coconut oil. Combine egg mixture with the flour mixture.
- Throw in the other ingredients, mixing well. Shape the mixture into cookies.
- Bake at 370 degrees F for about 25 minutes.

488. Chewy White Chocolate Cookies

Ready in about 40 minutes
Servings 10

If you prefer chewy cookies, eat them fresh and warm from the oven. If you prefer crispier cookies, wait until they've cooled completely. Store at room temperature in a cookie jar.

Per serving: 455 Calories; 25.3g Fat; 52.8g Carbs; 6g Protein; 28.6g Sugars

Ingredients

3/4 cup butter
2 ¼ cups cake flour
1/2 cup quick-cooking oats
2 tablespoons coconut oil
3/4 cup granulated sugar
1/3 teaspoon ground anise star
1/3 teaspoon ground allspice
1/3 teaspoon grated nutmeg
1/4 teaspoon fine sea salt
8 ounces white chocolate, chopped
2 eggs, well beaten

Directions

- Put all of the above ingredients, minus 1 egg, into a mixing dish. Then, knead with hand until a soft dough is formed. Place in the refrigerator for 20 minutes.
- Roll the chilled dough into small balls; flatten your balls and preheat the air fryer to 350 degrees F.
- Make an egg wash by using the remaining egg. Then, glaze the cookies with the egg wash; bake about 11 minutes. Bon appétit!

489. Cranberry Pound Cake

Ready in about 30 minutes
Servings 8

Sink your teeth into this luscious pound cake. No matter the occasion, this dessert is sure to warm your heart and stomach.

Per serving: 346 Calories; 21.6g Fat; 34.5g Carbs; 4.7g Protein; 28.3g Sugars

Ingredients

1 cup super-fine unbleached flour
1/3 teaspoon baking soda
1/3 teaspoon baking powder
3/4 cup turbinado sugar
1/2 teaspoon ground cloves
1/3 teaspoon ground cinnamon
1/2 teaspoon cardamom
1 stick butter
1/2 teaspoon vanilla paste
2 eggs plus 1 egg yolk, beaten
1/2 cup cranberries, fresh or thawed
1 tablespoon browned butter

For Ricotta Frosting:
1/2 stick butter
1/2 cup firm Ricotta cheese
1 cup confectioners' sugar
1/4 teaspoon salt
Zest of 1/2 lemon

Directions

- Start by preheating your air fryer to 355 degrees F.
- In a mixing bowl, combine the flour with baking soda, baking powder, turbinado sugar, ground cloves, cinnamon, and cardamom.
- In a separate bowl, whisk 1 stick butter with vanilla paste; mix in the eggs until light and fluffy. Add the flour/sugar mixture to the butter/egg mixture. Fold in the cranberries and browned butter.
- Scrape the mixture into the greased cake pan. Then, bake in the preheated air fryer for about 20 minutes.
- Meanwhile, in a food processor, whip 1/2 stick of the butter and Ricotta cheese until there are no lumps.
- Slowly add the confectioners' sugar and salt until your mixture has reached a thick consistency. Stir in the lemon zest; mix to combine and chill completely before using.
- Frost the cake and enjoy!

490. Chocolate and Apricot Muffins

Ready in about 20 minutes
Servings 6

The great thing about muffins is their versatility. You can decorate them with chocolate crumbs or rainbow sprinkles. For a more festive occasion, a chocolate-sour cream frosting makes a great and delicious addition to these muffins.

Per serving: 414 Calories; 17.9g Fat; 61.5g Carbs; 5.6g Protein; 34.8g Sugars

Ingredients

3 teaspoons Dutch-process cocoa powder
3/4 cup dried apricots, roughly chopped
1 ¼ cups unbleached all-purpose flour
1 cup rice milk
1/4 cup maple syrup
1 stick butter, room temperature
2 eggs
3/4 cup granulated sugar
1 teaspoon pure rum extract
1/2 teaspoon baking soda
1 teaspoon baking powder
1/4 teaspoon grated nutmeg
1/2 teaspoon ground cinnamon
1/8 teaspoon salt

Directions

- Grab two mixing bowls. In the first bowl, thoroughly combine the sugar, flour, baking soda, baking powder, salt, nutmeg, cinnamon and cocoa powder.
- Take the second bowl and cream the butter, egg, rum extract, rice milk, and maple syrup; whisk to combine well. Now, add the wet mixture to the dry mixture. Fold in dried apricots.
- Press the prepared batter mixture into a lightly greased muffin tin. Bake at 345 degrees for 15 minutes. Use a toothpick to check if your muffins are baked. Bon appétit!

491. Almond Phyllo Dough Turnovers

Ready in about 25 minutes
Servings 8

Flaky phyllo dough wrapped around an apple-almond filling. They are so adorable that kids and adults will love them.

Per serving: 407 Calories; 10.4g Fat; 73.4g Carbs; 6.1g Protein; 33.8g Sugars

Ingredients

3 apples, cored, peeled and diced
1/3 cup almonds, roughly chopped
1 teaspoon orange peel
1/2 stick butter, melted
1/2 pack phyllo pastry sheets
1 tablespoon cornstarch
3/4 cup sugar
1/2 teaspoon ground star anise
1/2 teaspoon vanilla extract
1/2 tablespoon ground cinnamon
1/4 cup powdered sugar

Directions

- In a saucepan, cook the apples, cornstarch, sugar, vanilla, and orange peel. Cook for about 5 minutes or until the apple filling thickens; reserve.
- Brush one piece of phyllo dough with the melted butter; use a pastry brush. Cover with another sheet and brush again. Continue with two more sheets of phyllo dough.
- Then, cut the phyllo dough in half the long way.
- Add 1 tablespoon of the apple filling at the end of the dough; scatter chopped almonds over the top. Fold over to create a triangle. It is important that the apple filling is completely enclosed.
- Continue with remaining phyllo dough. Brush with some extra butter. Now, place them in a single layer in the air fryer cooking basket.
- Bake at 345 degrees approximately 15 minutes; bake in batches. Meanwhile, thoroughly combine the powdered sugar with star anise and cinnamon.
- When your turnovers are done, brush them with some extra butter. Dust with the seasoned sugar and serve. Bon appétit!

492. Butter Walnut and Raisin Cookies

Ready in about 55 minutes
Servings 8

Thanks to the Air fryer, you can have freshly made nutty cookies in 55 minutes or less. They go well with a freshly squeezed orange juice.

Per serving: 251 Calories; 14.7g Fat; 28.4g Carbs; 2.1g Protein; 21.5g Sugars

Ingredients

1/3 cup walnuts, ground
1/4 cup raisins
3/4 cup granulated sugar
1/3 cup corn flour
1 stick butter, room temperature
1/2 cup super-fine unbleached flour
2 tablespoons rum
1/2 teaspoon pure vanilla extract
1/2 teaspoon pure almond extract

Directions

- In a small-sized bowl, place the raisins and rum; let it sit for 15 minutes.
- In a mixing dish, beat the butter with sugar, vanilla, and almond extract until light and fluffy. Then, throw in both types of flour and ground almonds. Fold in the soaked raisins.
- Continue mixing until it forms a soft dough. Cover and place in the refrigerator for 20 minutes. In the meantime, preheat the air fryer to 330 degrees F.
- Roll the dough into small cookies and place them on the air fryer cake pan; gently press each cookie using a spoon.
- Bake butter cookies for 15 minutes in the preheated machine. Bon appétit!

493. Sinfully Delicious Coconut and Orange Cake

Ready in about 30 minutes
Servings 6

Here's one of the simplest and most delicious cakes to make in the Air fryer. When it comes to the frosting, you can use a sour-cream whipped icing, buttercream frosting or coconut icing.

Per serving: 427 Calories; 23.5g Fat; 54.9g Carbs; 5.4g Protein; 29.6g Sugars

Ingredients

3/4 cup shredded coconut
1/3 cup coconut milk
2 tablespoons orange jam
1 stick butter
3/4 cup granulated sugar
2 eggs
1 ¼ cups cake flour
1/2 teaspoon baking powder
1/3 teaspoon grated nutmeg
1/4 teaspoon salt

Directions

- Set the air fryer to cook at 355 degrees F. Spritz the inside of a cake pan with the cooking spray. Then, beat the butter with granulated sugar until fluffy.
- Fold in the eggs; continue mixing until smooth. Throw in the flour, salt, and nutmeg; then, slowly and carefully pour in the coconut milk.
- Finally, add shredded coconut and orange jam; mix thoroughly to create the cake batter.
- Then, press the batter into the cake pan. Bake for 17 minutes and transfer your cake to a cooling rack. Frost the cake and serve chilled. Enjoy!

494. Walnut and Prune Muffins

Ready in about 20 minutes
Servings 6

Here is a delicious, old-fashioned finish to your holiday meal. From now onwards, you can make your favorite muffins without any hassle in the Air fryer.

Per serving: 465 Calories; 23.5g Fat; 57g Carbs; 9g Protein; 39.9g Sugars

Ingredients

1/3 cup walnut meal
1/3 cup walnuts, chopped
1/3 cup prunes, coarsely chopped
3/4 cup cake flour
3/4 cup caster sugar
3/4 stick butter, room temperature
2 eggs
1 cup yogurt
2 teaspoons fresh apple juice
1/2 teaspoon baking soda
1 teaspoon baking powder
1/3 teaspoon ground cinnamon
1/2 teaspoon pure vanilla extract
1/3 teaspoon ground cloves
1/2 teaspoon pure hazelnut extract
1/4 teaspoon table salt

Directions

- Grab two mixing bowls. In the first bowl, combine the walnut meal, cake flour, baking soda, baking powder, sugar, and all spices.
- Take the second bowl and whisk the butter, eggs, yogurt and apple juice; whisk to combine well. Now, add the wet mixture to the dry mixture. Fold in the walnuts and prunes.
- Press the batter mixture into a lightly greased muffin tin. Bake at 355 degrees for 13 minutes. Use a toothpick to check if the muffins are baked. Bon appétit!

495. Rich Chocolate Espresso Brownies

Ready in about 40 minutes
Servings 8

Dark chocolate and instant espresso powder pair with a silky mascarpone cheese and aromatic spices for melt-in-your-mouth dessert that is perfect for any occasion. Ancho chile powder adds a subtle heat that enhances the flavor of your brownies; cinnamon and lime zest further spice up these flavorful brownies.

Per serving: 477 Calories; 22.1g Fat; 65.6g Carbs; 7.6g Protein; 58g Sugars

Ingredients

8 ounces dark chocolate, chopped into chunks
2 tablespoons instant espresso powder
1 tablespoon cocoa powder
1/2 cup almond butter
3/4 cup super-fine unbleached flour
3/4 cup white sugar
1 teaspoon pure coffee extract
1/2 teaspoon lime peel zest
1/4 cup almond meal
2 eggs plus 1 egg yolk
1/2 teaspoon baking soda
1/2 teaspoon baking powder
1/2 teaspoon ground cinnamon
1/3 teaspoon ancho chile powder

For the Chocolate Mascarpone Frosting:
4 ounces mascarpone cheese, at room temperature
1 ½ ounces bittersweet chocolate chips
1 ½ cups confectioner's sugar, sifted
1/4 cup unsalted butter, at room temperature
1 teaspoon vanilla paste
A pinch of fine sea salt

Directions

- First of all, microwave the chocolate and almond butter until completely melted; allow the mixture to cool at room temperature.
- Then, whisk the eggs, white sugar, cinnamon, espresso powder, coffee extract, ancho chile powder, and lime zest.
- Next step, add the vanilla/egg mixture to the chocolate/butter mixture. Stir in the unbleached flour and almond meal along with baking soda, baking powder and cocoa powder.
- Finally, press the batter into a lightly buttered cake pan. Air-fry for 35 minutes at 345 degrees F.
- In the meantime, make the frosting. Beat the butter and mascarpone cheese until creamy. Add in the melted bittersweet chocolate chips and vanilla paste.
- Gradually, stir in the confectioner's sugar and salt; beat until everything's well combined. Lastly, frost the brownies and serve.

OTHER FAVORITES

496. Shallot and Mushroom Frittata 270

497. Tofu and Spinach Scramble 270

498. Spicy Ground Pork Omelet 271

499. Herbed Linguica Frittata 271

500. Linguine with Old Bay Shrimp 272

496. Shallot and Mushroom Frittata

Ready in about 40 minutes
Servings 4

Shallots reduce blood pressure and cholesterol levels. They also provide antibacterial and antiviral protection. Some of the impressive health benefits of Porcini mushrooms include their ability to boost our immune system, lower blood sugar and improve digestion.

Per serving: 256 Calories; 18.0g Fat; 3.2g Carbs; 18.2g Protein; 0.9g Sugars

Ingredients

3 cups Porcini mushrooms, thinly sliced
1 tablespoon melted butter
1 shallot, peeled and slice into thin rounds
1 garlic cloves, peeled and finely minced
1 lemon grass, cut into 1-inch pieces
1/3 teaspoon table salt
7 eggs
1/2 teaspoon ground black pepper, preferably freshly ground
1 teaspoon cumin powder
1/3 teaspoon dried or fresh dill weed
1/3 cup goat cheese, crumbled

Directions

- Melt the butter in a nonstick skillet that is placed over medium heat. Sauté the shallot, garlic, thinly sliced Porcini mushrooms, and lemon grass over a moderate heat until they have softened. Now, reserve the sautéed mixture.
- Preheat your air fryer to 335 degrees F. Then, in a mixing bowl, beat the eggs until frothy. Now, add the seasonings and mix to combine well.
- Coat the sides and bottom of a baking dish with a thin layer of vegetable spray. Pour the egg/seasoning mixture into the baking dish; throw in the onion/mushroom sauté. Top with the crumbled goat cheese.
- Place the baking dish in the air fryer cooking basket. Cook for about 32 minutes or until your frittata is set. Enjoy!

497. Tofu and Spinach Scramble

Ready in about 14 minutes
Servings 2

Sick and tired of regular egg scramble? Try this vegan scramble and enrich your breakfast or brunch menu. Better yet, it is so simple to prepare in the Air fryer!

Per serving: 290 Calories; 19.6g Fat; 8.9g Carbs; 26g Protein; 2.2g Sugars

Ingredients

1/2 teaspoon fresh lemon juice
1 teaspoon coarse salt
1 teaspoon coarse ground black pepper
4 ounces fresh spinach, chopped
1 tablespoon butter, melted
1/3 cup fresh basil, roughly chopped
1/2 teaspoon fresh lemon juice
13 ounces soft silken tofu, drained
13 ounces soft silken tofu, drained

Directions

- Add the tofu and olive oil to a baking dish.
- Cook for 9 minutes at 272 degrees F.
- Add the other ingredients and cook another 5 minutes. Serve warm.

498. Spicy Ground Pork Omelet

Ready in about 10 minutes
Servings 2

Some of the most satisfying traditional meals, such as omelet, consist of meat, eggs and vegetables. The best part is – anyone can prepare it with whatever ingredients are in the kitchen.

Per serving: 338 Calories; 22.2g Fat; 4.7g Carbs; 28.2g Protein; 5.2g Sugars

Ingredients

4 garlic cloves, peeled and minced
1/2 tablespoon fresh basil, chopped
1/3 pound ground pork
1/3 teaspoon ground black pepper
1/2 small-sized onion, peeled and finely chopped
1 1/2 tablespoons olive oil
3 medium-sized eggs, beaten
1/2 jalapeno pepper, seeded and chopped
2 tablespoons soft cheese of choice
1/3 teaspoon salt

Directions

- In a nonstick skillet that is preheated over a moderate flame, heat the oil; then, sweat the onion, garlic and ground pork in the hot oil.
- Spritz an air fryer baking dish with a cooking spray.
- Throw in the sautéed mixture, followed by the remaining ingredients.
- Bake at 325 degrees F approximately 15 minutes. Serve with the salad of choice. Bon appétit!

499. Herbed Linguica Frittata

Ready in about 18 minutes
Servings 2

In this rich and appetizing frittata, cheddar cheese and eggs are paired with just the right amount of spiciness (herbs) and fattiness (pork sausage and olive oil). Make a panini to go with leftovers, if any.

Per serving: 299 Calories; 25.1g Fat; 8.2g Carbs; 10.4g Protein; 5.2g Sugars

Ingredients

1/3 cup Cheddar cheese, shredded
2 eggs
1/3 cup Linguica (Portuguese pork sausage), chopped
1/2 onion, peeled and chopped
2 tablespoons olive oil
1/2 teaspoon rosemary, chopped
½ teaspoon marjoram
1 tablespoon cream
Sea salt and freshly ground black pepper, to taste
½ teaspoon fresh sage, chopped

Directions

- Lightly grease 2 oven safe ramekins with olive oil. Now, divide the sausage and onions among these ramekins.
- Crack an egg into each ramekin; add the remaining items, minus the cheese. Air-fry at 355 degrees F approximately 13 minutes.
- Immediately top with Cheddar cheese, serve, and enjoy.

500. Linguine with Old Bay Shrimp

Ready in about 10 minutes
Servings 2

The flavors of Old Bay seasoning and dry white wine combine in this flavorful seafood recipe. Even a clumsy dinner cook can prepare this 5-ingredient pasta in the Air fryer.

Per serving: 114 Calories; 2.2g Fat; 1g Carbs; 22.9g Protein; 0g Sugars

Ingredients

1/2 package linguine pasta, cooked
1 ½ tablespoons Old Bay seasoning
1 1/2 tablespoons dry white wine
1/2 tablespoon extra-virgin olive oil
1/2 pound shrimp, deveined

Directions

- Start by preheating the air fryer to 385 degrees F.
- In a bowl, toss all ingredients, minus linguine pasta; make sure to coat the shrimp on all sides.
- Dump the shrimp into the cooking basket and air-fry for 6 to 7 minutes. Serve over warm linguine. Bon appétit!

Printed in Great Britain
by Amazon